Everyday Life in Early Soviet Russia

Taking the Revolution Inside

Edited by
Christina Kiaer
and
Eric Naiman

Indiana
University
Press
BLOOMINGTON AND INDIANAPOLIS

This book is a publication of

Indiana University Press
601 North Morton Street
Bloomington, IN 47404-3797 USA

http://iupress.indiana.edu
Telephone orders   800-842-6796
Fax orders   812-855-7931
Orders by e-mail   iuporder@indiana.edu

Library of Congress Cataloging-in-Publication Data

Everyday life in early Soviet Russia : taking the Revolution inside / edited by Christina Kiaer and
Eric Naiman.
p. cm.
Includes index.
ISBN 978-0-253-34639-1 (cloth : alk. paper) — ISBN 978-0-253-21792-9 (pbk. : alk. paper)
1. Soviet Union—Social life and customs—1917–1970. 2. Soviet Union—Social conditions—
1917–1945. 3. Quality of life—Soviet Union. I. Kiaer, Christina. II. Naiman, Eric, date
DK268.3.E92 2005
947.084—dc22
2005010929

2 3 4 5 6 13 12 11 10 09 08

Everyday Life in
Early Soviet Russia

Contents

Acknowledgments

This book would never have been possible without the generous support of the Social Science Research Council, which through the Joint Committee on the Soviet Union and its Successor States Program of Support for Research and Development Initiatives funded the 1994 conference in St. Petersburg on Everyday Life in Soviet Russia that served as our volume's point of departure. We are also grateful to the Institute of Slavic, East European, and Eurasian Studies at the University of California, Berkeley, which supported both that original conference and our work on the volume over the past few years. UC Berkeley's Committee on Research also provided crucial support for the production of this volume. We owe a special debt of gratitude to Natalia Lebina, who worked with us to organize that conference, and to the late Natalia Kozlova, who participated in it; their enthusiasm and pioneering work on various aspects of everyday life in the Soviet Union have been an inspiration to us in many ways. Among the readers of this volume, we wish to thank Stephen Kotkin, Susan Reid, and an anonymous reader for Indiana University Press. Gabriel White has been an invaluable research assistant; Candace McNulty has done a splendid job editing the text. Finally, we want to thank Mikhail Goroshko, Marina Koreneva, Natalia Lebina, and Oleg Godisov for enriching our own experience of the everyday in Russia during the period of our work on this project.

Everyday Life in
Early Soviet Russia

Introduction

Christina Kiaer and Eric Naiman

Writing in the avant-garde journal *Lef* in 1923, Sergei Tret'iakov cautioned that "[Representatives of the party] always remember that they are in the trenches and that the enemy's muzzles are in front of them. Even when they grow potatoes around this trench and stretch out their cots beneath the ramparts, they never allow themselves the illusion that the trench is not a trench but a dacha [. . .] or that their enemies are simply the neighbors in the dacha next door."[1] The fragility of this image of potatoes and cots strewn among the trenches vividly evokes the precariousness of everyday life within Bolshevik ideology. These humble, homey objects, along with the domestic image of the dacha and the seemingly friendly members of the neighboring family, threaten the military metaphors of trenches and muzzles that represent the public face of building revolution. Throughout the early Soviet period, private experiences of everyday life were understood to be in potential conflict with the ideally collective and public nature of Soviet experience. This volume examines how Soviet Russia and its citizens sought to resolve this conflict by taking the Revolution inside. The essays collected here investigate the impact of ideology on the interior spaces of the home, the family, the body, and the self.

Tret'iakov's prose evinces the hard-line certainty of the early revolutionary years that public revolutionary deeds would triumph over the complacency of the everyday and the interiority of private life. As Frances Bernstein shows in her essay on the "panic" surrounding an apparent epidemic of sexual impotence among young male workers in the mid-1920s, the dominant belief was that the ideological language of the state could speedily resolve private pathology: the purported sexual panic was remedied by nothing more than calming reassurance on the part of doctors that the young workers were productive members of Soviet society. This confidence in the ease with which the interior could be brought into step with the revolutionary exterior eventually transformed itself into a pervasive anxiety about interiority. The title of Aleksandr Afinogenov's successful play, *Fear* (*Strakh*) of 1931 testifies to the ideological importance of anxiety; as Boris Wolfson's essay shows, the play kept fear ideologically at work as a topic while denying that it was experienced by reliable Soviet subjects. The essays in this volume corroborate the usual division in Soviet history between the early revolutionary fervor of the 1920s and the Stalinist 1930s, but they also insist on the common structural thread throughout this period of the Soviet preoccupation with internal transformation.

All of the essays in this volume draw on original archival materials, many of which became available only after the opening of new archives in recent years. Most of the contributors to this volume are members of the new generation of scholars who undertook their first research after the fall of the Soviet Union, and in tandem with new theoretical developments in the field, such as the study of everyday life and subjectivity and the understanding of the Soviet Union as forming a part of the history of modernity, rather than its totalitarian "other." Our topic of interiority—of the home and of the individual subject—contributes to these new directions in the field. The scholarship represented in this volume does not seek out moments of resistance to Soviet power, but rather seeks to describe how people "lived" the imperative to internalize Soviet ideology—an imperative that shaped the particular parameters of Soviet modernity.[2]

Like other recent historical studies, this volume emphasizes everyday life over party politics.[3] Our contributors address such everyday experiences of the early Soviet era as talking to family and neighbors, hanging a curtain, having sex, hiring a domestic servant, playing with toys—not in the Annales School tradition of cataloguing daily peasant living, but in the more recent theoretical tradition stemming from Henri Lefebvre, in which lived experience becomes a critical concept for analyzing the formation of the subject in modernity.[4] It is in the repeated, routine practices of everyday life rather than party edicts that the incomprehensible, world-shattering concept of revolution begins to take on meaning for subjects, begins to be lived by them, and begins to transform them. Analyzing these practices and their effects can lead to an understanding of what socialism or revolution meant, for the regime and the people. The objects of study are neither famous historical actors (authors or party leaders), nor the increasingly specialized and determining institutional structures of the modern state (the secret police, the legal profession, party censorship), but the lived contradictions of the encounter between individual subjects and institutions of power—the contradictions through which modern modes of identity are formed. The point is not to recover an authentic everyday life or individual identity repressed by ideology, but to analyze their production within it. This method is exemplified by the essay that opens our volume, Sheila Fitzpatrick's account of the production of one woman's identity through her encounter with the NKVD; it portrays the party member Anastasia Plotnikova as a creation of narrative, of stories about her life told to and by the NKVD.

The opening of previously closed archives has yielded many new sources, such as police reports as well as diaries and letters, that illuminate the lives and language of seemingly ordinary or otherwise representative or even symptomatic individuals. Jochen Hellbeck, whose pioneering work with autobiographical sources has reshaped our understanding of the Stalinist subject, calls attention to how the protagonist of a diary that he analyzes, Stepan Podlubnyi, often refers to his "inside" (*vnutrennost'*). Yet in Hellbeck's analysis, this "inside" formed simply another "realm" to be remade by the state: "as [Podlubnyi] understood it, the soul of a Soviet . . . should form a realm of enthusiasm."[5] This volume's focus on interiority participates in this reconceptualization of the Soviet subject as one produced by power rather than repressed by it.[6] Cynthia Hooper's essay on family politics during the Terror, for example, not only contains many examples of individuals who narrate their identities in relation to their perceptions of the expectations of power, but also makes the highly original claim that the significance of the family for an individual's identity was exacerbated by the Terror; it produced the very familial allegiances that it attempted to repress.

Many of the contributors to this volume, whose education was no longer shaped by the Cold War belief in the radical otherness of the Soviet Union, study the operations of Soviet ideology as an aspect of modernity more broadly. Subjects in modernity, in the East and in the West, are continuously solicited into ideological belief, whether under the bombardment of Soviet propaganda or of the propaganda techniques of advertising and media in the West.[7] The task has been not to identify the shortcomings of the Soviet model but to use the forms taken by everyday life and the modern subject in the Soviet Union as a way to call into question our own certainty about how these phenomena work. Almost all the essays in the collection incorporate a comparison of Soviet practices to Western European or American ones. Catriona Kelly, for example, demonstrates that the seemingly peculiar rituals described in materials on the regulation of Soviet children's lives—such as daily schedules for Pioneer camps—are in fact closely allied with similar prescriptions for childcare at the time in the West. Randi Cox shows that early Soviet advertising agencies self-consciously borrowed and modified practices from Western consumer modernity, with the goal of producing a particular, socialist form of it. Rebecca Spagnolo's research on domestic servants in the 1920s reveals a conflicted, putatively socialist version of a practice that was usually representative of exploitation in capitalist modernity. And in a methodological bridging of the East-West divide, Lilya Kaganovsky makes fully historicized and culturally specific use of Lacanian feminist film theory to analyze the operation of ideology in the 1936 film *The Party Card*.

This interdisciplinary volume includes literary scholarship on works of fiction, such as *The Party Card*, along with historical scholarship on nonfictional documents, in the belief that fiction can both amplify and particularize the meanings of such documents. Recent historians of everyday life and the subject in the Soviet Union have embraced "the linguistic turn," paying attention to the role of language in shaping the mentality of an age. Ultimately, this turn pulls historians into the territory of novelists, as the desire to explain what historical actors believed or felt encourages new historiographic forms of close, imaginative, self-consciously heuristic reading. In addition to Kaganovsky's reading of *The Party Card* and Wolfson's reading of *Fear*, Evgenii Bershtein examines the literary writing of Walter Benjamin in *Moscow Diary*, and Christina Kiaer analyzes Sergei Tret'iakov's eugenic play *I Want a Child!* of 1926 as a self-deconstructing text that continually undercuts its own ideological narrative of a futuristic form of sexuality and reproduction. In Kiaer's reading, the play evinces a nostalgia for the everyday life that, just three years earlier, Tret'iakov had so dismissively rejected in the form of the potatoes and cots scattered on the muddy ground of the trenches of revolutionary action.

Everyday Life and the Old Term "Ideology"

Trotsky, who had been the Bolshevik most prominently identified with the dream of worldwide revolution, was one of the first to set the tone for the turn inward. As early as 1923, he published *Problems of Everyday Life* (*Voprosy byta*), in which he acknowledged—through the example of sexual inequality within marriage—that the State could not simply impose new, socially enlightened ways of thinking on people from above, but that these changes would have to come about through fundamental changes in the practices of everyday life.[8] Trotsky's writing opened a wide debate on the idea that becoming a Soviet subject, living a Soviet life, would involve some kind of a new *everyday* life (*novyi byt*)—whether in terms of living arrangements, family and sexual relationships, friendships, personal appearance, leisure activities, or consumer practices.

In contrast to the wide-ranging public and literary debates on *byt*, the state propaganda campaign for the *novyi byt*, initiated in the early 1920s and stemming primarily from the health and cooperative sectors, was more narrowly and pragmatically focused on the twin goals of modernization and collectivization and was aimed primarily at women. A major component of the *novyi byt* was simply the effort to bring a backward, peasant-based population up to speed by promoting modern personal and domestic hygiene; the more ambitious goals of collectivizing child care, cooking, laundry, and shopping in order to emancipate women remained mostly at the level of representational fantasy in posters during the period of the New Economic Policy (NEP). It was not until 1928, when the First Five-Year Plan with its large-scale projects for communal construction was being formulated, that these aspects of the *novyi byt* began to be implemented in earnest. But by the mid-1930s, as historians have amply documented, the concept of the *novyi byt* had been transformed into the parallel but fundamentally different concept of *kul'turnost'*, or cultured life.[9] Modernization was still a goal, and collective institutions continued to be constructed, but *kul'turnost'* now stressed private life and individual consumption as the routes to a modern, rational, cultured, and Soviet everyday life. Despite their different contents, however, both the *novyi byt* and *kul'turnost'* were ideologies of everyday life explicitly promoted by the Soviet state as a means to produce new Soviet subjects, and it is the very explicitness of this ideological colonization of everyday life that sets the Soviet example apart from other modern nations of the same interwar period.

The essays in this volume approach everyday life from the perspective not of the rational, liberal subject who can accept or reject ideology, but of the subject as an effect of ideology, continuously produced and asked to recognize him or herself as a particular kind of subject. This is the notion of the subject of modernity, elaborated by Michel Foucault as the disciplined and confessing subject of the regulatory discourses of psychiatry, criminality, and sexuality, and by Norbert Elias as the self-regulating "civilized" subject who internalizes the "manners" or modes of everyday behavior appropriate to the citizen of the modern state.[10] There is a theoretical conflict at work here between our introduction of the importance of the notion of ideology in early Soviet culture, on the one hand, and our invocation of Foucault for a kind of shorthand definition of the subject in modernity, because Foucault did not use the term ideology, warning that "it is a notion that cannot be used without circumspection."[11] In his understanding, ideology implies the preexistence of a subject, rather than one who is the effect of discourses. The notion of ideology always stands in implied opposition to a notion of "truth," while he is interested rather in "how effects of truth are produced within discourses."[12] He therefore eliminates the term ideology in favor of the more mobile terms of discourse and power. But we would like to suggest that the term "ideology" is in fact the most useful one for making Foucault's complex understanding of the subject in modernity relevant to an understanding of the rationalist aims of early Soviet cultural production, if the term "ideology" is expanded from its usual, narrow definition.[13]

Ideology has been defined in a number of ways, two of which are particularly relevant to our question of Soviet interiority. The first derives from the early work of Marx, responding to Hegel and Feuerbach: ideology is the set of ideas that renders a given reality natural and therefore impervious to intellectual challenge by the subject under its sway. It functions to delimit language or narrative, offering the subject a fixed path through which to comprehend the

otherwise meaningless surrounding world. T. J. Clark has memorably characterized it as "a fixed pattern of imagery and belief, a syntax which seems
obligatory, a set of permitted modes of seeing and saying; each with its own
structure of closure and disclosure, its own horizons, its way of providing
certain perceptions and rendering others unthinkable, aberrant, or extreme."[14]
As developed by Louis Althusser in response to psychoanalysis, ideology is the
set of largely unconscious beliefs through which the subject recognizes herself
as a subject; in Althusser's terms, "*Yes, it really is me!*"[15] This naturalizing of the
world within a particular historical moment and within a particular mode of
production covers over the contradictions of social relations and naturalizes
inequality and exploitation. It is from this perspective, then, that the study of
everyday life takes on its particular significance as the site both of the naturalizing of power hierarchies and of their potential disruption through the contradictions of lived experience. Yet while ideologies change, ideology itself—as a
category seen in Clark's terms as epistemological code or as the "genre"
through which individuals legitimize their position in the world—can never
be transcended. Without ideology's naturalizing effects, there would be no
such thing as "everyday life"; ideology makes possible the experience of "the
everyday."

The Russian Revolution wrought a fundamental transformation of the
social and psychological function of ideology. Among the changes introduced
into Russian life by the triumph of Bolshevism, one of the most profound—and
historically underappreciated—was the bringing of ideology to consciousness.
Neither governments nor ordinary people in Western democracies talked
about "capitalist ideology" because the ideology was so embedded that it did
its work without being named, while the Soviets explicitly placed ideology at
the center of all their programs. But this was ideology in the sense of the
second, and more common, definition that is relevant for our study. This
version of ideology stems from the later Marx, and second generation Marxists
such as Lenin: ideology as the ideas that express a particular class, or the
political consciousness of classes—bourgeois ideology, proletarian ideology,
and eventually Bolshevik ideology. Here, ideology is consciously held and can
be consciously acquired and imposed.[16] In Soviet Russia, ideology no longer
served as the vehicle that prevented exploited subjects from perceiving the
extent and conditions of their exploitation. Rather than an unconscious mechanism that had to be transcended by the enlightened, ideology became something to be mastered, something that could be acquired by speaking, thinking,
acting, and feeling in a specific, studied way. In linguistic terms, ideology was
transformed from a native to an acquired tongue, a language of which there
were no native speakers.

This explicit entry of ideology into public discourse was defining of Soviet
modernity in both its liberating and its terrifying features. Ideology, in its
traditional, naturalizing, unconscious function, may have been the hand-
maiden of exploitation, but it also allowed subjects to cope with the conditions

of their exploitation. It prevented the alienated worker from perceiving the extent of his alienation. When ideology was wrenched by the Bolsheviks from the unconscious to the conscious, alienation became a much more conscious phenomenon as well. As they sought to master the new Soviet ideology, many Soviet citizens were made aware of the extent to which that mastery was beyond their reach or ever in danger of slipping from their grasp. The result was, especially by the 1930s, a widely shared anxiety over the extent to which the individual was alienated from an ideal community of Soviet subjects. An obsessive concern with verification, with measuring the extent to which the self and others lived up to ideological standards, is a theme that surfaces over and over in the essays of this volume. The coming of ideology to consciousness held powerful potential, seeming to promise individuals a magical and scientific key to mastering their own destiny as they overcame the forces of oppression, yet the very consciousness of ideology made alienation far more palpable. Alienation was no longer a condition with which the unconscious subject could "naturally" cope. In effect, the coming to consciousness of ideology defamiliarized many aspects of everyday life and significantly narrowed the scope of the formerly nonproblematic, everyday sphere.

The full coming to consciousness of ideology was, however, necessarily illusory. Bourgeois class ideology was exposed and criticized, including its constructions of gender and race, but ideology in the sense of the many unexamined assumptions through which subjects organize the world was not fully interrogated. This resulted in the paradoxical situation that despite the development of a new, conscious proletarian ideology, the dominant ideological constructs underpinning a naturalized reality, which were indebted to both Enlightenment ideals and Russian history, continued to function. Instead of bourgeois domination we have domination of the communist elites; patriarchal assumptions about gender and the family continue to support power hierarchies. One could argue that the various, partial Bolshevik attempts at collectivity and democracy and the destruction of the family in the 1920s did attempt to destroy the unconscious ideological supports of the dominant ideology, but mostly they failed. For example, as the essays by Kaganovsky, Bernstein, Kiaer, and Spagnolo explicitly demonstrate, and as other essays also suggest, the ideological underpinnings of patriarchy continued to render sexual identity—and gender-based exploitation—a relatively unquestioned, natural phenomenon.

Despite its incompleteness, the surfacing of ideology into consciousness and its newly acquired status as an essential interpretive tool had a profound impact on the formation of individual identity. The subject's status hinged on an ability to use ideology to pierce the deceptive surface of the natural order of things. Bolshevik Marxism taught that appearances and accepted identities had to be questioned; the result was an obsessive concern with questioning some of the assumptions upon which one had always relied.[17] Even the subject's own sense of identity, which for many people is the most natural element of their worldview, had to be relentlessly interrogated. One result was a compulsion to self-criticize and a sense of insecurity about one's own status as a subject of the new, modern society. In this volume the subject emerges as an always imperfect consumer, one who absorbs ideology in an attempt to become the ideal product always before him.

The insistence that everyday life was ideologically significant carried with it the implicit notion that everyday life had to be watched. Historically, the everyday has escaped scrutiny because its routinized, seemingly constant and ideologically impoverished activities were not deemed important enough to contemplate. The classic formulation of this paradigm can be found in the passage from Tolstoy's diary that Viktor Shklovskii used as the basis for his notion of "defamiliarization" (*ostranenie*)—the idea that the essence of art is its success in making things strange:

> I was cleaning in the room and, circling about, walked up to the couch and could not remember whether I had cleaned it or not. Since such actions are habitual and unconscious, I could not remember and already felt that it was impossible to remember. So that if I had cleaned and forgotten, that is, acted unconsciously, it would be all the same, as if it had never happened. If a conscious person had seen it, then it would be possible to reestablish it. If nobody saw or saw but unconsciously, if the entire complex life of many people passes unconsciously, it is as if that life had never happened.[18]

One can read this passage cynically as a precursor for the lethally rosy cast of Socialist Realist discourse. If nobody sees something it never happened, and so it follows that the negative aspects of Soviet life that never make it into press do not count. But Tolstoy's insight is also prescriptive: if life exists because it is watched, surveillance functions as a basic ontological principle. Although the essays in this volume corroborate the claim that surveillance by others was an essential part of Soviet life, a number of them also make the case that surveillance of the self was equally important. Soviet citizens were expected to monitor themselves and their inner, domestic, or private lives.[19] As the film *The Party Card* illustrates with such urgency, a failure in self-vigilance in even the most private reaches of life could easily lead to the loss of one's public as well as private identity.

"Bolshevism Has Abolished Private Life"

The notion of private life is central to our topic of interiority, but approaches to its study developed in the West are not necessarily translatable to Russia. Private life has been defined in many ways, but the most relevant definition, for our purpose here of pinpointing the specificity of the Soviet model, remains Jürgen Habermas's distinction between the public and the private spheres.[20] For Habermas, the formation of a distinct public sphere—the new civic, legal, and public institutions and new cultural forms such as novels that began to emerge in the late seventeenth and eighteenth centuries—produced a social space in which enlightened, rational individuals developed the bourgeois self-identification that is foundational to modernity. The conception of an equally distinct private sphere of domesticity, family relations, sexuality, consumption, and so on, while largely unexamined by Habermas in the presentation of his model, necessarily arose at the same time, as the dialectical complement to this public one. On a literal level, the overtly feminized, domestic spaces of private life provided a necessary safe haven from the masculine trials of competitive capitalism; Walter Benjamin characterized the overstuffed nineteenth-century bourgeois interior as a protective "etui of the private person."[21] Theoretically, as well, the putatively private sphere provides crucial ideological support for the normative subject of the economic rationalism of the public sphere by upholding essentialist notions of gender and social difference, and by providing a space for alternative, sustaining narratives of the self through, for example, sexuality or spirituality.[22]

Svetlana Boym has argued, however, that this structural opposition between public and private, so constitutive of subjectivity in the West, may be less relevant for Russian cultural history: a private sphere was never as fully cultivated in Russia as it was in the West.[23] This disdain for the public/private distinction is a distinctly non-modern, or pre-modern, aspect of Russian culture—at least according to the definition of modernity developed in Western theory. Rather than a space of rejuvenation and protection, "private" or personal life was considered by the intelligentsia to be negative, inauthentic, and foreign, something to be overcome. The private individual of the West, acting in his own self-interest, was opposed to the "myth of the Russian soul," a soul joined with the Russian people or *narod*. Yet the very ferocity with which private life was attacked by the Russian intelligentsia—which glorified the *narod* and had in fact invented it—indicates that the private sphere and one's inability to escape from it were constitutive of intellectual subjectivity in Russia in the late nineteenth and early twentieth century.

Even when the realm of the private or personal assumed a greater place in the artistic and spiritual movements of early twentieth-century Russian modernism, this place was won at the cost of personal life's autonomy. If in the past the intelligentsia's sense of identity was grounded in an ascetic willingness to sacrifice private concerns for the good of a larger community-in-the-making, and private life had been disdained as merely irrelevant, it now became important precisely because it was deemed to have public significance.[24] The private cultivation of the self by the subject of Russian modernism was seen as having the power to unleash creative forces that would transform the community.[25] This subject was an uncommon, exalted one: a potential prophet whose Dionysian impulses, once liberated, might be shaped into a theurgic work of social importance. Bolshevism did not destroy this focus on the importance of the individual; one of its distinguishing features was its willingness—through the Leninist notion of the party as vanguard—to incorporate the prophetic, emancipatory function of the individual proclaimed by Russian modernism into a Marxist worldview. But now it was no longer just the prophet's every action that was significant; rather, in a drastic democratization, the private lives of all Soviet citizens attained communal importance.

Making private activities into the objects of penetrating, even scientific observation and ideological prescription is a constitutive feature of modernity that was of course not unique to the Bolsheviks, as demonstrated by the extensive critical literature on the history of the body, gender, medicine, and sexuality in Europe and the United States.[26] But the Bolshevik mobilization of private life differs from Western models in two fundamental ways. First, this mobilization was overt and explicit, an aspect of the Bolshevik model of consciously propagated ideology, rather than the other model of unconsciously functioning ideology that serves to naturalize a given reality. Second, in Russia the activities associated with private life in the West were most often collapsed into the broader, and more material, category of everyday life (*byt*). Boym offers the highly significant thesis that "[t]he major cultural opposition in Russia is not between private and public but rather between material and spiritual existence, between *byt* and *bytie*."[27] This leads to a fundamental tension in Bolshevik Marxism, which was caught between Marxist materialism, on the one hand, and on the other, the traditional Russian dualism that pitted the devalued material realm of *byt* against the higher spiritual realm of *bytie*.[28] The *novyi byt* campaign aimed not only to modernize and improve the material conditions of everyday life but to give it transcendent communal or public value.

Byt denotes the material, repetitive, unchanging, and therefore deeply conservative activities associated with the domestic sphere and the body, in opposition to the progressive, inventive, emotional, spiritual, and transcendent activities of *bytie*. The very concept of making *byt* into something *novyi*—a progressive force for cultural change—defies the cultural logic of *byt*. The campaign represents, in a deeper sense, an attempt to abolish *byt* and raise all aspects of everyday life to the level of transcendence of *bytie*.[29] For the Bolsheviks, however, the transcendence would be ideological rather than spiritual, with the goal of collective happiness in a Communist future in this world. It should be clear, then, that many of the culturally valued qualities of self-fashioning encompassed by the notion of "private" in Western culture belong not to the everyday (*byt*) but to *bytie*. In Western culture, the private sphere was in a dialectical relation to the public sphere, but the Bolsheviks did not acknowledge that anything of cultural value for the formation of the Soviet subject could be salvaged from the old *byt*—a remnant not only of capitalism but of primitive, pre-modern Russian life.

In some instances, policies of the *novyi byt* such as sex education or psychological counseling actually intensified aspects of private experience that had previously been barred from discourse, in effect creating a discursive space of "private life" as it existed in Western modernity, in order to make it available to conscious ideology. The *novyi byt*, and Bolshevik cultural policies more generally, led to a colonization and even intensification of private life that explicitly linked it with—even transformed it into a vehicle for—the transcendent values of socialist community. At the same time, a new kind of "public sphere" arose, which purportedly aimed, on the basis of Enlightenment principles, to foster rational debate, but which often tended more to the theology of *bytie*. This was recognized by Benjamin in a letter home from Moscow, where he noted that "the tensions of public life—which for the most part are actually of a theological sort—are so great that they block off all private life to an unimaginable degree."[30]

Benjamin is both a theoretical influence on this volume and an object of its study. Evgenii Bershtein places Benjamin's diary of his two-month journey to Moscow in 1926–1927 in the context of the model of the Western intellectual's idealizing pilgrimage to the land of socialism, but insists on the personal specificity of Benjamin's pilgrimage by emphasizing the significance of his affair with the Latvian communist Asja Lacis. On the basis of new archival and interview documents on Lacis, Bershtein argues that Benjamin's struggle to rework his intellectual and Marxist identity was driven by erotic desire and frustration. Western Marxist intellectuals of the 1920s focused extensively on the notion of alienation in Marx; Benjamin analyzes what he sees as the Soviet abolition of private life as a model of release from alienation. Yet his diary's occasionally utopian account of the possibility of an unalienated existence in Soviet Russia is undercut by the constant textual evidence of his own alienation in his failed love affair and his failure to transcend his personal misery in order to take part in the building of socialism going on around him. His ideological insights are coupled with less than resoundingly successful work on the self, but even as he fails in his love life, Benjamin succeeds in demonstrating the centrality of individual desires to the communal project.

Confiding in his diary, the young transplanted peasant Stepan Podlubnyi—a subject of Natalia Kozlova's essay in this volume—also viewed himself as alienated from the society of successfully integrated Soviet subjects around him in Moscow, and like Benjamin he also studied the practices of those subjects as he attempted to make them his own. The diary compellingly displays both the pain and the exhilaration entailed by the process of becoming a cultured Soviet subject, illustrating Svetlana Boym's claim that clichés are "the necessary incantatory noise of the everyday,"[31] oral documents of safe conduct that appear to provide a guarantee of everyday survival. Kozlova offers a moving discussion of Podlubnyi and other diarists of the time, drawing on the personal documents held in the new "People's Archive" (TsDNA), which virtually defines itself as an entity made possible only by the demise of the Soviet state. An archive of diaries appears to offer the promise of revealing what Soviet subjects really felt beneath the ideological mask, but Kozlova reluctantly demonstrates that the promise is illusory: the diaries suggest, instead, that the mask became the face itself. Ideology and its language formed not a

Christina Kiaer and Eric Naiman

fake reality, but the very experience of everyday life. Kozlova's perspective is that the ideological word has become the subject's flesh.

Although arrived at by means of a very different method, the argument that there is no subject outside of ideology has been made by Jochen Hellbeck in his extensive work on Podlubnyi's diary. Yet the different approach is what constitutes Kozlova's contribution to this discussion. Kozlova's method is more empathetic, underlining the significance of emotion and corporeality in the operation of ideology. In another context, Kozlova and her co-author, Irina Sandomirskaia, have suggested that the study of everyday life, their "mission" or "*sverkhzadacha*," amounts to a kind of humanizing or even repopulating of Soviet history: "Today it is said that we have to make the Soviet period more human (*ochelovechit'*). The question arises—who dehumanized it? And what does humanize mean? To settle people there? . . . The attempt to use the history of the little man and his everyday life to unite the ends of the unraveling social fabric is a process of pulling thread and patching holes. And sewing and darning are women's work."[32] While it is true that, in Western as well as Russian culture, everyday life and the private sphere are concepts deeply associated with the feminine, we would like to resist the essentialism of the view that the study of those concepts is in itself a feminine project. (We do note, however, that all but two of the essays in this volume are written by women.) At the same time, we value Kozlova's contribution to the study of everyday Soviet life and the Soviet self for introducing an empathetic and deeply felt approach to the material that illuminates aspects of its significance that might otherwise be lost.

Both Kozlova, with her "humanizing" approach to what she calls her "protagonists," and Bershtein, with his unusual attention to the unhappy love affair in Benjamin's diary, argue that the personal aspects of the diaries both contribute to and interrupt their ideological agendas. Initially a parallel between the figures of Stepan Podlubnyi and Walter Benjamin seems ludicrous; yet, like Podlubnyi, Benjamin consciously attempts to think and act in accordance with the paradise that he sees others living around him. He is a Western intellectual intoxicated by the prospect of the absorption of the private personality into the public sphere, a process he envisioned as one of "withering." But one senses in his desire to eliminate private life the irreducible core of his own private obsession with the lifestyles of Lacis and her other lover, Bernhard Reich, the other two sides of a typical (bourgeois) romantic triangle. Benjamin's belief in the Soviet abolition of private life was utopian and not fully accurate, based on a small, German-speaking sample of zealous members of the left intelligentsia; on the impenetrability, for him, of the everyday life of Russians in the capital; and on the opacity of ideological discourse to one who does not know the basic language (i.e., Russian) in which that discourse is expressed. The story of his visit's failure, though, can also be read as evidence of the seductive, ever elusive promise of Soviet subjectivity. The combination of the desire to become a Soviet subject, and the knowledge that that desire will always fall short in the face of one's own massive inadequacy, defines Soviet subjectivity.[33] The sexual frustration experienced by Benjamin can be seen as a metaphor for the ideological frustration that was one of Soviet subjectivity's principal effects.

For Benjamin, one of the major philosophers of modernity, Soviet subjectivity represented relief from the expanded and alienating privacy—the retreat into the private sphere—demanded by modernity. But Benjamin's assumption that private life in the Western sense was even there to be abolished, and that Bolshevik ideology was solely responsible, is more open to question. For the lack of a positive concept of privacy and private life was not exclusively a Bolshevik accomplishment, but rather, as Boym has suggested, a feature of Russian social life; many of the phenomena that Benjamin describes in Moscow, such as the chaos of tram car passengers or the Soviet citizen's casual relation to concepts of time, describe Russian rather than Soviet traits. This brings the volume back to the fundamental question of Soviet Russia's place in the project of modernity: while the Soviet colonization of private life bears a certain resemblance to Western practices, it also produces a model of subjectivity that, in its combination of myths of the Russian soul and the Russian disdain for private life with Marxist ideals of transcending alienation, is unique in its construction of an individual self.

Once again, the comparison of Benjamin to Podlubnyi is instructive. It is not surprising that a Western intellectual would experience a certain vertigo when confronted with the disjunctively pre-modern aspects of Soviet modernity. More arresting is the spectacle of the Russian peasant, whose path to this modernity requires him to learn the discourse of alienated privacy which, by all rights, should not have been his. From this point of view, the campaign for *kul'turnost'* in the 1930s can be seen not just as a belated replay in Russia of the European "civilizing process," but as an ideological symptom of the Soviet anxiety about the essentially pre-modern character of Russian Communism, which was supposed to be a harbinger of the future. Before privacy could be colonized or abolished in Russia, it had to be invented. The dilemma of alienation ceased to be part of the aura of the intelligentsia and began to be mass-produced, so that all people could aspire to—and never attain—the abolition of their "private life."

Ideological Homework

The insistence on the conscious ideologization of all aspects of life had the potential to transform all of private life into a form of "homework." Through various topics and methods, the essays in this volume demonstrate that this homework was undertaken with more confidence in the 1920s, when it seemed certain that with enough work, ideological transformation could certainly be mastered, while in the 1930s, when this mastery began to seem forever out of reach, it was undertaken with equal fervor, but more anxiety. We have grouped the essays thematically, rather than chronologically, and open with a group of essays that address the anxiety of identity.

Sheila Fitzpatrick's investigation of the production of one woman's identity through her encounter with the NKVD, "The Two Faces of Anastasia: Narratives and Counter-Narratives of Identity in Stalinist Everyday Life," emphasizes the poignancy of the attempt to retrieve an individual's identity and fate, even though her essay maintains a studied distance between Anastasia Plotnikova's identity on paper and her possible extra-discursive subjectivity. Fitzpatrick's presence at the start of this volume is particularly appropriate, because, as the references in subsequent articles reveal, her work on class identity in general and, in particular, on the way in which a new Soviet managerial class became urbanized and "cultured" in the 1930s has had a fundamental influence on many younger scholars. This essay represents a change in methodology for Fitzpatrick; she changes her primary focus from society to narrative, paying as much attention to rhetorical strategies as to underlying social movements. By ending her story with the lines: "The NKVD's story stops at this point, and so does the author's. It is up to the reader to imagine the rest," Fitzpatrick comes close to establishing an equivalence between fiction and history, as she raises the indeterminacy of imagination to a level where it contends with the determination of fact.

Lilya Kaganovsky's essay, "Visual Pleasure in Stalinist Cinema: Ivan Pyr'ev's *The Party Card*," examines the same process of the questioning of identity by the party and NKVD, but this time as represented in an actual work of fiction. The heroine, Anna Kulikova, is deceived by a villainous husband, who steals her party card and passes it to an enemy, leading to her expulsion from the party for her lack of vigilance in her private life. In Kaganovsky's reading, *The Party Card* is about the dangers of interiority that threaten—and, perhaps, define—all good Bolsheviks; the film is able to acknowledge the uncertainty that beset Bolshevik identity under Stalinism by disavowing its universality and displacing it onto women. Since in Russia, as in the West, "the home" has historically been coded as female, it is not surprising that anxiety about interiority and surveillance of it should have led to ideological worry about women. Kaganovsky argues that the best way to read this film is to understand the heroine as representative of all Soviet citizens who enjoyed even a tenuous proximity to institutional power.

Cynthia Hooper, in "Terror of Intimacy: Family Politics in the 1930s Soviet Union," challenges the claim that Stalinism represented a turn toward social conservatism or a "Great Retreat" from the social radicalism of the early revolutionary years by arguing that the state approach to private life amid the family was far more radical than it had been during the 1920s. Drawing on a wide variety of archival sources, she demonstrates that "intimacy" was not a site of private, individual experience that existed outside the reaches of the state, as in the conservative model, but was instead "both idiom and mechanism of the Great Terror"; the NKVD assessed communist identity through family ties. Private life became a crucial testing ground for political belief, in ways that directly contradicted conservative models of privacy, and which, as she demonstrates, were completely unlike the Nazi approach to family.

Boris Wolfson, in "Fear on Stage: Afinogenov, Stanislavsky, and the Making of Stalinist Theater," examines the role of the theater in binding intimate and public concerns together in the early Stalinist period. He shows the unexpected contiguity between Stanislavsky's views on acting and the type of hermeneutic suspicion that was such a central feature of Soviet political life. Several scholars have recently explored the centrality of "performance" to the Soviet experience,[34] and Wolfson's essay makes the point that a goal of theatrical realism was to use performance to uncover "subtexts"; characters were truly alive when their words were not the whole story but needed to be illuminated by things left unsaid. Participation in this shared interpretive enterprise was an essential part of being "in the power" of a Stalinist spectacle. His essay also provides an illuminating example of the Bolshevik faith in ideology as a talking cure: by staging a play called *Fear* that refrains from showing characters who are afraid, the Moscow Art Theater was protecting its audience from anxiety by holding fear and its consequences within the limits of discourse.

The next grouping of essays addresses various manifestations of the Bolshevik confidence in the 1920s that everyday life and the individual subject could be merged with the public goals of the revolution. In "'NEP Without Nepmen!' Soviet Advertising and the Transition to Socialism," Randi Cox shows that consumption was no longer meant to be the private, individual experience that it was under capitalism; rather, Soviet advertising agencies exhorted the consumer to consume as a Soviet citizen—that is, as a member of a specific community. Through her careful, quantitative cataloging of a large sample of advertising posters from the 1920s, we witness, once again, the way in which the ideological agendas that are implicit and naturalized in the cultural production of Western modernity become explicitly and self-consciously ideological in the Soviet context. Advertisements strove to differentiate state-produced commodities from the pernicious privately produced NEP commodities by placing them in the heroic context of the new, socialist production of Soviet enterprises. The personal connection implied here was specifically one of ideological commitment to the socialist project of the Soviet state; the personalization of the commodity was paradoxically public. This belief in the power of ideology was not without its contradictions, in this instance as in the many others discussed in these essays; we may surmise that these advertisements were not entirely successful at motivating consumer desire.

The ideologization of sex, which was discussed with relative openness in the 1920s, is the topic of Frances L. Bernstein's essay. "Panic, Potency, and the Crisis of Nervousness in the 1920s" traces the ideological uses of nervousness about male impotence through a study of Moscow's Counseling Center for Sexual Hygiene, an institution allied with the campaign for a healthy sexual *byt* in the 1920s. Doctors at the center elicited sexual confessions from patients in ways that differed little from those of the Western model of discursive corporeality analyzed by Foucault. Nor is the fact that male sexual dysfunction became a symbolic stage for the expression of ideological anxieties unique to Soviet Russia; feminist scholars have long argued that sexology and particularly psychoanalysis serve the ideological function of allaying male sexual fears in the service of patriarchy. But Bernstein focuses on the explicit nature of this ideological process and the resulting conflict between medical and party "experts" over the authoritative language used to describe sexual pathologies. Bernstein does not attempt to recover the actual sexual behaviors of individual men, but focuses instead on the urge of Soviet doctors continually to invoke the "authentic" voices of actual male workers. Doctors connected the purportedly widespread dysfunction of young Soviet men to worry about the potency of Bolshevism during the compromise period of NEP. Unexamined in this ideological agenda, but obvious from Bernstein's exposition, is the continued powerful presence of the unconscious ideology of masculine potency in relation to feminine passivity that historically buttressed both medical authority and state power.

In her essay "Delivered from Capitalism: Nostalgia, Alienation, and the Future of Reproduction in Tret'iakov's *I Want a Child!*" Christina Kiaer argues that the play *I Want a Child!* offers a biological fantasy of literally producing a new Soviet subject by rationally and eugenically reproducing a Soviet child as a collective social object. Tret'iakov's vision—buttressed by the avant-garde artist El Lissitzky's transparent stage set—would seem to suggest that the practices of everyday life under socialism, including sex, should become fully visible and rational, subject to the surveillance of the disciplining state. Yet Kiaer argues that in his journalistic style, based on the model of the *literatura fakta*, Tret'iakov exposes, with uncanny, newsreel-like precision, the lived contradictions of everyday Soviet experience in the face of new Soviet ideologies of the subject. Tret'iakov's scripting of a literal, biological solution to the problem of forming a new subject is an implicit admission of the ultimate difficulty, if not impossibility, of the Bolshevik goal of forming an ideal Soviet subject through the conscious use of the tools of ideology such as the structures of narrative, public institutions, repressive surveillance, and practices of self-monitoring that this volume explores.

Evgenii Bershtein's essay "'The Withering of Private Life': Walter Benjamin in Moscow," which we discussed at length in the previous section, is the final contribution to deal explicitly with the problem of sexuality. Benjamin's conviction that "Bolshevism has abolished private life" parallels the Bolshevik belief in the possibility of colonizing private realms of experience.

In the final essay in this grouping, "When Private Home Meets Public Workplace: Service, Space, and the Urban Domestic in 1920s Russia," Rebecca Spagnolo examines the seemingly paradoxical continued existence of the domestic servant in a putatively socialist state. Her research reveals the confidence of the various unions representing domestics, as well as of the propaganda materials addressed to them, that illiterate peasant women working as domestic servants could remake themselves into conscious, activist workers, fighting for equitable working conditions—that they could remake themselves, in other words, into ideal Soviet subjects. Although Spagnolo analyzes accounts of the rare court cases when domestics brought grievances against their employers, these documents do not bring us closer to the "true" feelings and motives of either party; rather, we see the self-conscious presentation of appropriate identities to the State in the interest of achieving the particular goal of winning the case. What does emerge from Spagnolo's sources, however, are vivid glimpses of the lived experience of everyday life in urban Russia at that time: the burdens of laundry; servants sleeping on newspapers in corners of kitchens; the impossibly crowded living conditions of employer and servant alike.

Catriona Kelly's "Shaping the 'Future Race': Regulating the Daily Life of Children in Early Soviet Russia," encompasses both the 1920s and 1930s to explore questions of continuity and specificity in the treatment of childhood. She is also aware, like Spagnolo, of the similarities between the treatment of her topic before and after the revolution. She discusses the importance of regimentation and discipline to the Soviet prioritization of childhood, for example, but she cautions that we should not be too quick to see this as evidence of ideological particularity. Her essay is exemplarily comparative and serves as a reminder that the Soviet experience must be seen as part of the shared project of modernity. Kelly's essay provides a handle on the important topic of Soviet sentimentalism that continues to make the notion of the Soviet Union as "happy childhood" nostalgically potent. In the Soviet Union childhood was both a center of and a refuge from ideological discourse; retrospectively, what seems like the least tainted aspect of the Soviet experience may be the place where the day's ideology has its most powerful hold on the present.

Our collection closes with an analysis of diaries, which would seem to have the potential to offer more of a sense of the real person than the NKVD reports analyzed by Fitzpatrick with which we opened. Yet as Natalia Kozlova demonstrates in "The Diary as Initiation and Rebirth: Reading Everyday Documents of the Early Soviet Era," this is a false hope. Her point is not so much that the implicit distinction between ideological word and individual thought ought to be collapsed as it is that Soviet subjects wanted to collapse it. The extent to which that merger was always imperfect endows her contribution to our volume with a sentimental power rarely found in historical writing. Kozlova's contribution can itself be read as a kind of primary document: her reader is confronted not only with the pain experienced by Podlubnyi in his work upon himself but with Kozlova's own search into her roots and her desire to know who "we" (post-Soviets) really are. We end, therefore, on a note of deep personal investment in these questions of Soviet interiority.

Kozlova's article shows us subjects who attempted to master ideology in all its rhetorical and behavioral glory, not only for the pragmatic reason of advancement and survival, but because they desired to inscribe themselves into an ideological community. A central characteristic of Soviet subjectivity was the desire to be a Soviet subject—a desire that inevitably fell short of its goal and which, in the subject's knowledge of his or her own inadequacy, was a defining feature of this ideological age. All Soviet subjects were would-be Soviet subjects, their identities shaped by the gap which necessarily separated them from mastery of the ideological tongue.

The value of Natalia Kozlova's chapter and of the other essays in this volume is their insistence that an essential part of understanding the Russian Revolution and of valuing its subjects' humanity is studying and appreciating the contradictory, painful and yet still invigorating work of bringing the revolution home. We hope that in its interdisciplinarity, this book's exploration of revolutionary interiority brings us closer to an understanding of early Soviet identity while respecting and rendering more detailed the context in which early Soviet subjects lived.

NOTES

1. S. Tret'iakov, "LEF i NEP," *Lef* 2 (1923), 72.

2. On the problems of the historiographic search for resistance, see Thomas Dodman, "The Fate of Red October," *History Workshop Journal* 50 (2003), 258–267, as well as one of the books he reviews, Lynn Viola, ed., *Contending with Stalinism: Soviet Power and Popular Resistance in the 1930s* (Ithaca: Cornell University Press, 2002). Viola's chapter on "Popular Resistance in the Stalinist 1920s" is a particularly thoughtful consideration of the attractions and dangers of using resistance as a historical lens.

3. Scholars conceptualizing the study of everyday life in early Soviet Russia were first brought together at the international conference that we organized, with Natalia Lebina, in St. Petersburg in 1994: "*Russkaia Povsednevnost'* 1921–1941." Over half of the contributors to this volume participated in that conference; in addition to ourselves, they were Sheila Fitzpatrick, Randi Cox, Frances Bernstein, Evgenii Bershtein, and Natalia Kozlova. Since that time, a number of publications have addressed the problem of everyday life. Stephen Kotkin created a new model for analyzing the operations of Soviet power in everyday life during the 1930s in *Magnetic Mountain: Stalinism as a Civilization* (Berkeley, Los Angeles, and London: University of California Press, 1995). More recent works, covering the 1920s as well as the 1930s, include Natalia Borisovna Lebina, *Povsednevnaia zhizn' sovetskogo goroda: Normy i anomalii. 1920-e–1930-e gody* (St. Petersburg: Zhurnal "Neva" i "Letnii sad," 1999) and Timo Vikhavainen [Vihavainen], ed., *Normy i tsennosti povsednevnoi zhizni: Stanovlenie sotsialisticheskogo obraza zhizni v Rossii, 1920–1930-e gody* (St. Petersburg: Zhurnal "Neva," 2000). On the 1930s, see Sheila Fitzpatrick, *Everyday Stalinism: Ordinary Life in Extraordinary Times: Soviet Russia in the 1930s* (New York and Oxford: Oxford University Press, 1999) and Sheila Fitzpatrick, ed., *Stalinism: New Directions* (London and New York: Routledge, 2000), particularly Vadim Volkov, "The Concept of *Kul'turnost'*: Notes on the Stalinist Civilizing Process," and Julie Hessler, "Cultured Trade: The Stalinist Turn towards Consumerism." (Both Volkov and Hessler presented earlier versions of these

essays at the Russkaia Povsednevnost' conference in St. Petersburg in 1994.) For an overview of the concept of everyday life in Soviet studies and a review of recent literature, see Catriona Kelly, "Ordinary Life in Extraordinary Times: Chronicles of the Quotidian in Russia and the Soviet Union," *Kritika: Explorations in Russian and Eurasian History* 3:4 (Fall 2002), 631–651. Despite the recent publication of so many studies of everyday life, Kelly argues that the history of everyday life is still "oozy in terms of its methodology" (638).

4. Henri Lefebvre, *Everyday Life in the Modern World*, trans. Sacha Rabinovitch, with a new introduction by Philip Wander (New Brunswick and London: Transaction Publishers, 1971; reprint 1994). For a succinct introduction to the critical concept of everyday life, see Alice Kaplan and Kristin Ross, "Introduction," *Yale French Studies* 73, Special Issue on Everyday Life (1987), 1–4.

5. Jochen Hellbeck, "Fashioning the Stalinist Soul: The Diary of Stepan Podlubnyi, 1931–1939," in *Stalinism: New Directions*, ed. Sheila Fitzpatrick (London and New York: Routledge, 2000), 95.

6. The totalitarian model of Soviet history, in which Soviet power was assumed to be repressive of a preexisting, unified subject otherwise free of power, has been superseded in recent scholarship by an understanding of the subject as continuously shaped and transformed by power. A cogent history of Soviet studies, outlining the totalitarian, revisionist, and more recent approaches, is offered in Sheila Fitzpatrick, "Introduction," in *Stalinism: New Directions*; for a different, slightly earlier overview, see Stephen Kotkin, "1991 and the Russian Revolution: Sources, Conceptual Categories, Analytical Frameworks," *Journal of Modern History* 70:2 (June 1998). Kotkin first introduced the approach to Soviet subjects not as victims of ideology, but as participants in it, in *Magnetic Mountain*. On the revision required of the Enlightenment notion of the subject, see Igal Halfin and Jochen Hellbeck, "Rethinking the Stalinist Subject: Stephen Kotkin's 'Magnetic Mountain' and the State of Soviet Historical Studies," *Jahrbücher für Geschichte Osteuropas* 44:3 (1996), 456–463. Like Kotkin's, Halfin's and Hellbeck's approach to the Soviet subject is predicated on a reading of subjectivity elaborated by Foucault; see, for example, "What Is Enlightenment?" in *The Foucault Reader*, ed. Paul Rabinow (New York: Pantheon, 1984), 32–50. See also Halfin's *Terror in My Soul: Communist Autobiographies on Trial* (Cambridge, Mass.: Harvard University Press, 2003), and Hellbeck's "Working, Struggling, Becoming: Stalin-Era Autobiographical Texts," *The Russian Review* 60 (2003), 340–359.

7. See Susan Buck-Morss, *Dreamworld and Catastrophe: The Passing of Mass Utopia in East and West* (Cambridge, Mass., and London: MIT Press, 2000).

8. Lev Trotskii, *Voprosy byta* (Moscow: Krasnaia Nov', 1923), 44–45, translated as Leon Trotsky, *Problems of Everyday Life and Other Writings on Culture and Science* (New York: Monad Press, 1973).

9. See Vadim Volkov, "The Concept of *Kul'turnost'*," in Sheila Fitzpatrick, ed., *Stalinism: New Directions*, 210–230, and Sheila Fitzpatrick, "Becoming Cultured: Socialist Realism and the Representation of Privilege and Taste," in *The Cultural Front: Power and Culture in Revolutionary Russia* (Ithaca: Cornell University Press, 1992), 216–237.

10. The widely read works by Michel Foucault on this topic are *The History of Sexuality, Volume 1: An Introduction*, trans. Robert Hurley (New York: Vintage, 1980), *The Birth of the Clinic*, trans. A.M. Sheridan Smith (New York: Vintage, 1975), and *Discipline and Punish*, trans. Alan Sheridan (New York: Vintage, 1979). See also Nor-

bert Elias, *The History of Manners*, trans. Edmund Jephcott (New York: 1978) and *Power and Civility*, trans. Edmund Jephcott (New York: 1982); and Volkov's use of these models in his discussion of *kul'turnost'* in "The Concept of *Kul'turnost'*."

11. Michel Foucault, "Truth and Power," in *The Foucault Reader*, 60.

12. Ibid.

13. Kaja Silverman has suggested that "the great ideology debate of the 1960s and 1970s was broken off prematurely" by the advent of Foucault; she argues that a complex understanding of ideology, founded on Louis Althusser and Lacanian psychoanalysis, will help to conceptualize how the subject's "belief" is solicited and obtained within various modes of production and their symbolic orders. See Silverman, "The Dominant Fiction," in *Male Subjectivity at the Margins* (New York and London: Routledge, 1992), 15 (15–51).

14. T. J. Clark, *The Painting of Modern Life: Paris in the Art of Manet and His Followers* (Princeton: Princeton University Press, 1984), 8.

15. Louis Althusser, "Ideology and Ideological State Apparatuses," in *Lenin and Philosophy*, trans. Ben Brewster (New York: Monthly Review Press, 1971), 178, emphasis original. See also Terry Eagleton, *Ideology: An Introduction* (London: Verso, 1991).

16. On the different versions of ideology in the early and late Marx, see Jorge Larrain, "Ideology," in *A Dictionary of Marxist Thought*, ed. Tom Bottomore (Cambridge, Mass.: Harvard University Press, 1983), 219–223.

17. This point was made by many of the party's foremost figures. See for example G. Zinov'ev, *Filosofiia epokhi* (Moscow and Leningrad: Moskovskii rabochii, 1925), 5:

> The battles that will decide the fate of the Revolution continue, although they are "bloodless," silent, and without the accompanying roar of cannon fire. These battles differ from those we knew earlier on the fronts of the Civil War precisely in their quietness, in their being drawn out in time and fragmented among a whole series of petty episodes; they differ in that they occur in the quotidian economy and in everyday life, in that their development is hidden and without external effects, in that sometimes they are even invisible to the "unarmed" eye.

18. Viktor Shklovskii, "Iskusstvo kak priem," in *Sborniki po teorii poeticheskogo iazyka*, vol. 3. (Petrograd: Opoiaz, 1917), 12. (For a translation of the article, see Viktor Shklovskii, "Art as Technique," in *Russian Formalist Criticism*, ed. and trans. Lee T. Lemon and Marion J. Reis [Lincoln: University of Nebraska Press, 1965], 3–24.)

19. In his already classic comparative study of surveillance in early Soviet Russia, Peter Holquist notes that while surveillance was a part of the common project of European modernity, Soviet surveillance was distinguished by the Bolsheviks' "broader definition of the political sphere—a definition that ultimately encompassed all others" and "led to a much broader spectrum of surveillance interests" than that of their Civil War opponents or of surveillance systems in France, Germany, or England. Peter Holquist, " 'Information Is the Alpha and Omega of Our Work': Bolshevik Surveillance in Its Pan-European Context," *The Journal of Modern History* 69:3 (Sept. 1997): 447.

20. Jürgen Habermas, *The Structural Transformation of the Public Sphere: An Inquiry into a Category of Bourgeois Society*, trans. Thomas Burger (Cambridge, Mass.: MIT Press, 1989). See also Philippe Ariès and Georges Duby, eds., *History of Private Life*, 5 vols. (Cambridge, Mass.: Harvard University Press, 1987).

21. Walter Benjamin, "Paris, Capital of the Nineteenth Century," in *Reflections*,

ed. Peter Demetz, trans. Edmund Jephcott (New York: Schocken Books, 1978), 155.

22. Habermas's model of the public sphere has been criticized from many perspectives, most prominently for the way in which it can be seen to be dependent upon Enlightenment ideals of transparent communication and of the unified subject, and for its suppression of the importance of cultural and economic activities of alternative subjects excluded from the public sphere. Foucault's analysis of the coercive function of the institutions and discursive structures of modernity, for example, challenges the very notion of public vs. private, demonstrating that such private areas of life as sexuality have in fact been intensified, controlled, and mobilized to produce particular kinds of subjects for the modern state. See Foucault, *The History of Sexuality, Volume 1: An Introduction*.

23. Svetlana Boym, *Common Places: Mythologies of Everyday Life in Russia* (Cambridge, Mass., and London: Harvard University Press, 1994), 73–93. She offers historical and cultural evidence for her thesis that the private sphere was underdeveloped in Russia, pointing, among other things, to the complete subjection of the lives of the nobility to the needs of the state well into the modern period; the lack of a concept of individual rights in Russian legal history; the lack of human rights for the many (large) minority populations; the dominance of the nobility over the middle class in cultural creation of the nineteenth century; and the spiritual and Slavophile traditions of Russia.

24. The disastrous personal consequences for the Russian Symbolists of this new glorification of private life is told in detail by Vladislav Khodasevich in *Nekropol'* (Brussels: Petropolis, 1939). See also the essays collected in *Creating Life: The Aesthetic Utopia of Russian Modernism*, ed. Irina Paperno and Joan Delaney Grossman (Stanford: Stanford University Press, 1994), as well as the interest in sexuality generated by the publication of Mikhail Artsybashev's 1907 novel *Sanin*. The reception of *Sanin* is discussed by Petr Pil'skii in his article "Reaktsiia zamuzhem," *Voprosy pola* 5 (1908), 19–24.

25. See Nikolai Berdiaev, *Smysl tvorchestva* (Paris: YMCA Press, 1983 [1916]). This point is also forcefully made in the programmatic essays on Symbolism by Viacheslav Ivanov. See, for example, "O granitsakh iskusstva," in his *Sobranie sochinenii*, 4 vols. (Brussels: Foyer Oriental Chrétien, 1974), 2: 640.

26. See, for example, Thomas Laqueur, *Making Sex: Body and Gender from the Greeks to Freud* (Cambridge, Mass.: Harvard University Press, 1990); Janet Sayers, *Biological Politics: Feminist and Anti-Feminist Perspectives* (London and New York: Tavistock Publications, 1982); G. J. Barker-Benfield, *The Horrors of the Half-Known Life: Male Attitudes toward Women and Sexuality in Nineteenth-Century America* (Evanston: Harper & Row, 1976); Barbara Maria Stafford, *Body Criticism: Imaging the Unseen in Enlightenment Art and Medicine* (Cambridge, Mass., and London: MIT Press, 1991); and in the Russian context, Jane Costlow, Stephanie Sandler, and Judith Vowles, eds., *Sexuality and the Body in Russian Culture* (Stanford: Stanford University Press, 1993), and Christina Kiaer's essay in this volume.

27. Boym, 83.

28. See Christina Kiaer, *Imagine No Possessions: The Socialist Objects of Russian Constructivism* (Cambridge, Mass.: MIT Press, 2005), chapter 2.

29. In contrast to this Bolshevik campaign to abolish material *byt*, the LEF art historian and critic Boris Arvatov developed a Marxist theory of proletarian culture that would emerge not by transcending the material sphere but by "organically" and "flexibly" working within it in a process of "everyday-life-creation" (*bytotvorchestvo*). See his

"Byt i kul'tura veshchi," in *Al'manakh proletkul'ta* (Moscow: Proletkul't, 1925), 75–82, translated by Christina Kiaer as "Everyday Life and the Culture of the Thing," *October* 81 (Summer 1997), 119–128, citations from p. 121.

30. Walter Benjamin, *Walter Benjamin: Moscow Diary*, trans. Richard Sieburth (Cambridge, Mass., and London: Harvard University Press, 1986), 127. This quote is discussed by Evgenii Bershtein in his essay in this volume.

31. Boym, 14.

32. N. N. Kozlova and I. I. Sandomirskaia, *"Ia tak khochu nazvat' kino"—"Naivnoe pis'mo": opyt lingvo—sotsiologicheskogo chteniia* (Moscow: Gnozis, Russkoe fenomenologicheskoe obshchestvo, 1996), 16. Natalia Kozlova's contribution to the study of everyday life in the Soviet Union includes not only this co-authored experiment in reading "naive writing," but also her simultaneous monograph *Gorizonty povsednevnosti sovetskoi epokhi. Golosa iz khora* (Moscow: Institut filosofii RAN, 1996).

33. On the extent to which corporeality was both suffused with and—by virtue of its inevitable material inadequacy—undermining of ideology, see Eric Naiman, "Discourse Made Flesh: Healing and Terror in the Construction of Soviet Subjectivity," in *Language and Revolution: Making Modern Political Identities*, ed. Igal Halfin (London: Frank Cass, 2002), 287–316.

34. See, for example, Julie A. Cassiday, *The Enemy on Trial: Early Soviet Courts on Stage and Screen* (DeKalb: Northern Illinois University Press, 2000) and Jeffrey Brooks, *Thank You, Comrade Stalin! Soviet Public Culture from Revolution to Cold War* (Princeton: Princeton University Press, 2000).

one

The Two Faces of Anastasia

Narratives and Counter-Narratives of
Identity in Stalinist Everyday Life

Sheila Fitzpatrick

Anastasia Plotnikova was a perfectly ordinary woman, albeit a successful one. That may sound like an oblique authorial assertion of her status as a representative of her times, but in fact the "representative" part of the story I will tell has less to do with the woman herself than with the process whereby her life was constructed and reconstructed (by herself) and deconstructed (by the NKVD). Plotnikova's life was not mysterious or especially dramatic, at least no more so than those of millions of her contemporaries. Born in a village in the St. Petersburg region in 1893, she became a communist in 1920. By the mid-1930s, she had held senior administrative positions in Leningrad for almost a decade. In 1936 she was chairman of a district soviet in Leningrad and a member of the Leningrad city soviet. Her husband, whom she had married just before the First World War, had a party job in a factory in the Vyborg district of the city; they had two sons in their twenties, both members of the Komsomol serving in the Red Army. From the little we know about her, she seems to have been practical, clear-headed, resourceful, unreflective, generous, and liked by her colleagues.

Why, then, did Anastasia Plotnikova have an identity problem? It happened in an ordinary Soviet way, probably through a denunciation that gave a different version of her life from the one in her official curriculum vitae. This led the NKVD to investigate whether she had misrepresented herself.[1] It should be emphasized that, while the affair could have had serious consequences for Plotnikova, it was not a case of gross misrepresentation, scandalous discoveries, or a disreputable double life. The circumstances were mundane. Plotnikova had not hidden anything more about herself than any other Soviet citizen. In Stalin's time, almost everyone had something to hide—relatives abroad, relatives who were priests, the wrong class background, military service in the wrong army, being in the wrong place during the civil war, family members arrested or dekulakized, religious belief, criminal convictions, prerevolutionary membership in another political party, sympathy with the opposition in the 1920s, and so on. Because so many people were hiding something, uncovering secrets was a constant preoccupation of communists. This was called "unmasking" or "revealing the true face [*litso*]" of a person.

In the 1920s and 1930s, unmasking was a frequent occurrence. A person's account of herself might be challenged by a written denunciation, as Plotnikova's evidently was; in the course of a routine personnel review (*chistka*), such as was periodically conducted in government offices and the Communist Party; in connection with a promotion, nomination to elective office, or application for membership in a trade union, the party, the Komsomol, or even the Young Pioneers; or in many other circumstances. In the face of a challenge to the narrative of personal identity, the narrator could either admit fault and engage in self-criticism (*samokritika*), in the hope that the offense would be overlooked, or try to rebuff the challenge and rebuild the original self-representation. Sometimes the rebuilding was successful, sometimes not. It was more difficult to rescue an identity under siege in times of intense witch-hunting like the Great Purges than in ordinary times. But Anastasia Plotnikova was lucky. The challenge to her identity—or at least the challenge we know about from the archives—came in the spring of 1936, before the hysteria of the Great Purges took hold.

While unmasking was an everyday practice in Stalin's Russia, these contestations of identity were not trivial. Even in ordinary times, they could result in expulsion from the party or dismissal from a job—and then those black marks, too, had to be kept out of the official curriculum vitae if possible. The Soviet ritual of "criticism and self-criticism"—in contrast, it seems, to the Chinese communist version, and certainly to analogous confessional rituals in the Christian tradition—did not allow an individual's "sins" to be washed away. The black marks remained on the record, even if on a particular occasion the individual's self-criticism was judged satisfactory.[2] It was because there were in this sense no second chances in Soviet lives that it was so important, on the one hand, to hide things, and on the other hand, to prevent the incipient black mark drying on the page.

Communist discourse about identity in the 1920s and 1930s was Manichean. You were either an ally or an enemy of Soviet power—*soiuznik ili vrag*. This absoluteness applied with special force and particularly bizarre effect to class identity: you were either "proletarian," in which case you were innately an ally, or "bourgeois," hence innately an enemy. These were allegedly objective and scientific categories; your own subjective view of Soviet power or your own class identity was irrelevant.

Of course, this was absurd, for both theoretical and pragmatic reasons. No Marxist intellectual could seriously argue that class identities are absolute, let alone that they are "genealogically" determined. Old Bolshevik intellectuals periodically rebuked the crude assumption, made so often in everyday Soviet life, that heritage was destiny as far as class was concerned ("If your father was a bourgeois, you are bourgeois"). Even Stalin finally repudiated this position.[3] An absolutist approach to class identity was particularly inappropriate to Russia in the first third of the twentieth century because of the enormous social turmoil, flux, and mobility associated with war, revolution, and Stalinist "revolution from above" at the end of the 1920s.

Nevertheless, the world remained divided in Soviet communist discourse into sheep and goats—or, more exactly, into sheep, goats, and the infamous "wolves in sheep's clothing"[4] whom it was a communist's duty to discover and unmask. But the very rigidity and impracticality of this framework meant that there had to be ways of getting round it. One of these ways was *semeistvennost'*, mutually protective "family circles" within the communist bureaucracy in which the distinction between "ours" (*svoi*) and "others'" (*chuzhye*) was made on a more personalistic basis. You did not unmask members of your own *semeistvo*. If somebody else tried to unmask them, you did your best—if only for reasons of self-protection—to prevent this. We can see this impulse, as well as the Manichean zeal to unmask which it partially frustrated, in the unfolding of the story of Anastasia Plotnikova's two faces.

•   •   •

Like all Soviet citizens in the 1930s, at least all who were wage- or salary-earners or belonged to the Communist Party, Plotnikova had a curriculum vitae (*Avtobiografiia*) which she periodically updated. This Autobiography was an official document, kept in her personal file along with the formal questionnaires (*anketa, lichnyi listok*) whose thirty to forty questions covered social origin, education, army service, political involvements, and employment history. By convention, the Autobiography dealt with the same range of issues as the questionnaires, but it was free-form and might include discussion of such topics as formative experiences, personal philosophy, family life, and so on.

Plotnikova's Autobiography[5] was notable for its clarity, precision, and absence of personal-confessional motifs. Relatives and their places of residence were named in full, places of work were clearly identified. Loose ends were neatly tied up, and the narrative often seemed to anticipate the reader's possible queries and provide answers. Technically, it was a model Autobiography. The life story it told was also exemplary in Soviet terms.

The account of herself Plotnikova gave was as follows. She was born

Anastasia Khoreva in 1893 in the village of Ponizov'e in Novgorod province, not far from St. Petersburg. The family was poor: "In the village [my parents] were considered poor folk [*bobyli*], since they had no land; my father shared a hut with his brother. Sometimes he had a cow." The father, Miron Khorev, had worked for wages since he was twelve, and Anastasia identified him as "a worker" (*rabochii*) in her narrative. His trade was carpentry, which he practiced sometimes in the village but usually in various industrial enterprises in the Petersburg area. His wife resided permanently in the village and (as was usual in peasant-worker families like the Khorevs') did not accompany him when he went away to work in the city. She sometimes worked as an agricultural laborer (*batrachka*), probably for prosperous fellow villagers.

Anastasia was one of five children. Her two brothers followed their father's trade and became carpenters, working full-time in St. Petersburg; one of them showed his proletarian-revolutionary mettle by joining the Red Guards in 1917. There were also two half brothers, her mother's sons by another marriage, who were likewise carpenters. Anastasia's two sisters were kolkhoz members at the time of writing, one in her native village, the other, Matrena, in Siberia. Starting from the age of eleven, Anastasia worked for wages. First she worked away from home as a child-minder (*nian'ka*), living at home only in the winter. From age thirteen to nineteen she worked as a *batrachka*.

At the age of twenty Anastasia left the village and went to St. Petersburg, where she married and worked in various shoemakers' workshops. In summers, when there was less work at the workshops, she worked at peat and lumber plants. Her husband, Plotnikov, was a shoemaker by trade; since the age of seventeen, "after the death of his mother," he had lived on his own. In 1915 Plotnikov was arrested. No reason for this is given in the Autobiography (though presumably it would have been, had it been a political offence and thus a biographical asset), but it led to his being drafted into the army and sent to the front. In 1916 Anastasia almost succeeded in getting a job as a worker at the famous "Treugol'nik" plant under the *soldatka* (soldier's wife) quota. But at the last minute she was refused on the grounds that she was not a real *soldatka*, but the wife of a man who had been sent to the front as a criminal. With two young sons (born 1913 and 1915) in tow, Anastasia went home to the village and worked as a field laborer until September 1917.

In September 1917, after Plotnikova's husband was invalided home from the front to a hospital in the city, she returned to Petrograd and went back to work in a shoemaking business. Early in 1918 her husband, still unable to walk, was sent home from the hospital with a bad case of scurvy; and in May 1918, the family—Anastasia and her husband, with their two small children, plus Anastasia's sister Matrena, who had recently lost her job as a worker at the "Treugol'nik" plant—left for Siberia. They headed for the village of Kat'kovo in Tomsk province, where some peasants from their home village had migrated a few years before the war.

The arrival in Siberia is a turning point in Plotnikova's narrative. Up to this point, her life story had contained no references to politics; the February and October revolutions were not even mentioned in her narrative. But politics enters abruptly with the family's arrival in Siberia, although there is no indication of an event or conversion experience that would explain this. "In view of Kolchak's seizure of power, we lived semi-legally," is the Autobiography's first sentence on the Plotnikovs' Siberian life from June 1918, as if the two of them had revolutionary pasts that made this self-evidently necessary. The Autobiography goes on to describe the Plotnikovs' activity in the Bolshevik opposition movement in Siberia. Working as farmhands and laborers on the railroad, Anastasia and her husband "developed contact with workers of Kemerovo mine—Comrade Korenev, a member of the Bolshevik Party, Loskutov and others—on whose instructions we worked among the poor peasants, mobilizing the aktiv to overthrow Kolchak; we searched out and collected weapons . . . My husband and I were members of Shevelev-Lubkov's partisan unit . . ."

In 1920 (after Kolchak's defeat and the establishment of Soviet power in Siberia), both Plotnikovs formally joined the Bolshevik party. At that point, they already held a variety of local offices—she was a women's organizer, her husband was secretary of the local (*volost'*) party committee and chairman of a kolkhoz (*kommuna*) they had organized in Katkovo, the village where the family was based.

In January 1923 the Plotnikovs returned to Petrograd (with the prior agreement of their Siberian party organization, as the Autobiography is careful to note) and found jobs there. At first Plotnikova worked as lathe operator in a factory, but after a year or so she moved into organizational work and became secretary of a factory party organization. By the end of 1928, she had risen to the position of department head in a district soviet in Leningrad. From 1930 to 1935, she was party secretary at a big Leningrad plant, "Krasnoe znamia." Her husband, meanwhile, held various positions in factories of the Vyborg district of Leningrad. In the Autobiography, Plotnikova did not specify her exact current position: "Since 1935," she wrote modestly, "I have been working in the soviet of Petrograd district." In fact, she was chairman of the district[6] soviet, which meant that she was the top official in an important subunit of Leningrad's city government.

The life that was presented in this Autobiography was a typical Soviet success story—a proletarian woman, exploited and underprivileged under the old regime, joins the party soon after the revolution, becomes a *vydvizhenka* (an upwardly mobile former worker or peasant, the beneficiary of Soviet "affirmative action" policies), and rises to high position, still keeping contact with her peasant and proletarian roots. To be sure, there were points in the narrative where a careful reader might have asked questions. Was Anastasia's peasant father really so poor, if he was an *otkhodnik* earning wages as a carpenter? Was she glossing over something in her husband's background, about which little was said, other than the apparently insignificant fact that he left home after his mother died? What lay behind the Plotnikovs' sudden emergence as Bolsheviks in Siberia? Could one read significance into Plotnikova's omission of any mention of education (which might imply that she had more years of schooling than would be normal for a landless peasant's daughter), or fault her for failing to state explicitly, as autobiographical narratives of the period often did, that she had a blameless political record and had never been linked with any party opposition?

The challenge that came to Plotnikova's self-representation, however, was fundamental. It concerned the essence of her sociopolitical identity (*klassovoe litso*), rather than peripheral details. According to this counter-representation, Plotnikova's identity was not proletarian but capitalist (kulak).

The NKVD was the fashioner of a counter-narrative[7] of Plotnikova's life, developed in the course of an investigation of Plotnikova.[8] It is not entirely clear from the archival file what caused the NKVD's interest in Plotnikova. The stimulus in the first instance may have been a denunciation written by an unknown person against Plotnikova's cousin, Lipina-Kazunina, which contained damaging allegations about Plotnikova.[9] Another possibility is that the trigger was the arrest of Ol'ga Drobetskaia, a communist who had been a colleague and probably a friend of Plotnikova's at the "Krasnoe znamia" factory. Drobetskaia, a former oppositionist charged with "wrecking," was interrogated in prison about Plotnikova, and her testimony was one of the NKVD's main sources for the counter-narrative.[10] Another important source was testimony from Grigorii Shchenikov, a peasant from Plotnikova's native village, who was summoned later by the police to give information about her childhood and family origins.[11]

In the counter-narrative, Anastasia Plotnikova was not the daughter of a humble landless peasant but the adopted daughter of a "big kulak." From the age of seven she had lived in the home of her aunt Lipina, whose husband was a prosperous businessman who owned half a dozen barges as well as having a "kulak farm." She was the Lipins' adopted daughter, thus a member of a family of rural capitalists and exploiters.

As might be expected of a kulak daughter, Anastasia made a good marriage. The Plotnikovs had a prosperous capitalist shoemaking business, run by Anastasia's father-in-law with the help of her husband and his brothers and, after her marriage, by Anastasia herself. (Opinions differed slightly on this last point: some accounts suggested that Anastasia worked in the Plotnikov family business, others that she was co-proprietor, and the peasant witness, Shchenikov, claimed that Plotnikova "never worked anywhere, either in Siberia or before [after her marriage]."[12]) The shoemaking business survived right up to the family's departure for Siberia in 1918. Contrary to Anastasia's account in her Autobiography, the family party that went to Siberia included Plotnikov Sr., the biggest capitalist of all. (He also returned with them from Siberia in

1923, but tactfully removed himself to Ponizov'e, which was evidently his native village as well as the Khorevs' and the Lipins', and soon died.)

The NKVD's counter-narrative shook some skeletons out of the Plotnikov and Khorev family closets. These turned out to be essentially irrelevant to the NKVD's story (and mine), but what self-respecting narrator could bear to ignore a crime of passion? It turned out that, in addition to being a capitalist, Plotnikov Sr. had killed his wife and her lover in 1909, and spent a year in prison for the crime. Of course, this old scandal was remembered and reported when the NKVD started asking questions about the family; Shchenikov, for example, recalled that Plotnikov's wife's lover, a journeyman in the Plotnikov shoemaking business, was a good accordionist. Our knowledge of the crime, at any rate, lends a new aspect to Anastasia's passing comment in the Autobiography that her husband had not lived at home "after his mother's death." The other skeleton that the NKVD dug out was that one of Anastasia's brothers had been convicted of attempting to rob the mail in 1929. Disappointingly, we are not told whether this latter-day highwayman was the same brother whose revolutionary service as a Red Guard in 1917 was mentioned in the Autobiography.

The discreditable Lipin connection did not end with Anastasia's marriage and departure from the village. It was made all the more damaging because of the Lipins' dekulakization in 1930. Uncle Lipin had died around this time, but Aunt Lipina and her daughter had taken refuge in Leningrad with Plotnikova. Since they were illegal immigrants to the city, Plotnikova should have turned them in to the police; instead, she gave them shelter and helped them get the necessary documentation and jobs. She even helped her cousin, Lipina-Kazunina, join the Komsomol, which made her an accomplice in the latter's concealment of her kulak origins and dekulakization.

This was not the only time Plotnikova had put family interests above those of the party. Indeed, she had been exceptionally generous to her village relatives—Khorevs and Plotnikovs, as well as Lipins—whenever they decided to migrate to the town, both before and after collectivization. "Living in the city of Leningrad, Anastasia Mironovna turned her apartment into a kind of 'peasants' hotel' [*dom krest'ianina*], to which her relatives came, beginning in about 1925–1926, and lived for the time needed in the first place to find a job and then to find housing." Fifteen to twenty relatives were said to have passed through the Plotnikov apartment in this way over the years.[13]

As might be expected from someone with a capitalist background, hiding her real class identity from the party, Plotnikova had political blots on her record as well. She was an ideological waverer, perhaps even a Zinovievite oppositionist. She had "ties" with a member of the defeated Zinoviev opposition and had tried to protect someone arrested as a "wrecker." (This was presumably her friend Drobetskaia, whose prison interrogation became part of Plotnikova's file.) After the 17th national Party Congress, to which Plotnikova was a delegate, she had spread the rumor that "Stalin and Kirov were not elected unanimously in the voting for the Central Committee." She had also reportedly expressed sympathy for the disgraced Zinoviev after she ran into him at a sanatorium in Kislovodsk in 1933, saying he looked "hunted" and "exhausted."[14]

So which was her real face, the kulak or the proletarian? The NKVD had summarized the evidence against her, but it had not predetermined the outcome. A year later it would have been different, but as of July 1936, the verdict lay with the Leningrad city party committee, in particular the head of its personnel department, S. Luk'ianov—and Luk'ianov certainly looks like a friend of Plotnikova's, whom he would have known personally because of her position. His summing up strongly suggests that in the Plotnikova case, a Leningrad "family circle" was protecting its own.[15]

Luk'ianov found that there was convincing evidence that Plotnikova had misrepresented some aspects of her social background and milieu. In the first place, she had concealed information about her own class position by suppressing the Lipin connection in her Autobiography and representing her work in the Lipin household as that of a hired hand (*batrachka*). In the second place, she had been less than candid about her husband's class background, and had described herself as "working for wages" in Petrograd in the war years when she had actually been working in (one of the owners of?) the Plotnikov family business right up to the time of their departure to Siberia in 1918. In addition, Luk'ianov concluded, she had abused her position as party secretary in a factory to get a job for the Lipins' daughter and then to get her into the Komsomol (which meant concealing the fact that she was the daughter of parents deprived of voting rights).

It was true, Luk'ianov found, that Plotnikova had showed bad judgment in telling the story about voting at the 17th Congress and expressing personal sympathy for Zinoviev. But these, he implied, were rather minor offenses, and other charges (meaning the implicit accusation that Plotnikova was a Zinovievite?) had not been confirmed. His recommendation was that Plotnikova should be removed from her job as chairman of the Petrograd district soviet and transferred to a rank-and-file (nonadministrative) position.[16]

Under the circumstances, this was a mild punishment. It was striking, moreover, that Luk'ianov dismissed the 17th Congress story so lightly. After all, Plotnikova was repeating a rumor that has often been thought to be a matter of extreme sensitivity to Stalin—though admittedly her version of it (that Stalin and Kirov *both* received fewer votes than was officially claimed) was not as potentially damaging to Stalin as the version that surfaced in the Khrushchev era.[17] It is hard to believe that, if Plotnikova's case had been reviewed by the Party Control Commission in Moscow, that body would have regarded Plotnikova's reported political lapses quite as tolerantly as Luk'ianov did.

Further circumstantial evidence that Leningrad *semeistvennost'* was working for Plotnikova came later in the summer, when the Petrograd district committee balked at issuing a new card to Plotnikova in the exchange of party cards (i.e., purge of party membership) that was currently being conducted. The district committee's hesitation was perfectly understandable, indeed proper, in the case of someone who had just been investigated by the NKVD and demoted as a result. But Luk'ianov intervened, ordering the immediate issue of a new party card to Plotnikova, "since the Petrograd district committee has no grounds for holding up her case."[18]

There is one more document in the archival file demonstrating both Plotnikova's resourcefulness and the endless possibilities of contestation about social identity. On 24 August 1936 the Ponizov'e soviet issued a new certificate (*spravka*)[19] which, on internal evidence, was surely drafted by Plotnikova herself with the aim of defusing the Lipin/kulak issue and recovering her "good" class identity. The certificate attested to the fact that citizenness Anastasia Mironovna Plotnikova came from a "poor peasant" (*bedniak*) family, her father being a landless *bobyl'* and seasonal worker (*otkhodnik*). "From an early age," the certificate stated, "[Plotnikova] worked for her living. From November 1906 to February 1913 she lived with her uncle Lipin as a hired hand (child-minder and worker [*rabotnitsa*])." But, it was explicitly stated, she was "not part of the Lipin household" (*nichego obshchego k khoziaistvu Lipinykh ne imela*). Anastasia was no longer the Lipins' adopted daughter; she was once again their *batrachka*. For the time being, at least, her proletarian face was back in place.

$$\bullet \qquad \bullet \qquad \bullet$$

Did the NKVD find out "the truth" about Anastasia Plotnikova? Certainly its counter-narrative supplied biographical information that Plotnikova omitted from her Autobiography, though some of it was clearly biased. (Shchenikov's picture of a woman who never worked in her life, for example, is much less plausible than Plotnikova's self-representation as a woman who worked hard at various jobs from an early age). But the overall message of the counter-narrative that Plotnikova was a class enemy of Soviet power seems less convincing than her own claim to be a supporter whose allegiance was grounded in early experience of poverty and wage labor. Even within the conventions of Soviet Marxist argument, Plotnikova's toeholds in various prerevolutionary "capitalist" milieux seem too precarious and intermittent to have generated true bourgeois class consciousness.

While Luk'ianov may not have been an impartial judge, his common-sense conclusion that the new information on Plotnikova was relatively trivial and did not change her basic status as an ally seems appropriate. The Plotnikova who emerges from both narrative and counter-narrative is not someone who was dispossessed by the revolution. But she was definitely (as of 1936) one of its beneficiaries.

Yet there were multiple ambiguities in Plotnikova's social background (and not hers alone) that meant that even the least biased narrative was likely to oversimplify. One set of ambiguities surrounded the position of a peasant-worker like the carpenter Miron Khorev, who was landless but possessed a marketable craft skill. On the one hand, Khorev was a *bedniak*, supposedly on the bottom of the heap in the village. On the other hand, by virtue of his craft skill he might make a reasonable living as an *otkhodnik*, or even (like his fellow villager, Plotnikov the shoemaker) set up a small business in town. Khorev was one of a whole category of literate, skilled, wage-earning *bedniaks* whose existence confounded the attempts of Marxist sociologists in the 1920s to analyze the Russian village in terms of class exploitation.

Another ambiguity concerns the status of a village child taken into the home of relatives more prosperous than her parents, a not unusual situation in early twentieth-century Russia. Such children invariably worked from an early age, as they would have done in their parents' home, but the work for adoptive peasants tended to be more exhausting and exploitative. No doubt Plotnikova gave a one-sided picture of her relationship to the Lipins by describing herself as their *batrachka*. But it would run counter to everything we know of Russian village life to conclude that the Lipins' relationship with her was based purely on familial love, with no value put on Anastasia's labor. Perhaps, since Plotnikova later helped the Lipins in their hour of need, we should conclude that she felt a special affection and gratitude to them. Since she tended to help any relative, however, the evidence is far from conclusive.

Perhaps the closest we can come to "the truth" about Anastasia Plotnikova is that, like most people, her life could have taken various different courses, and her "identity" (*litso*)—that is, her social position, and her own and others' sense of who she was—would have changed accordingly. If there had been no revolution, the Plotnikovs might have done well with their business after the war and she might conceivably have become solidly urban and middle class. But that solidity was still far away for Anastasia in the war years, when she was in danger of losing her foothold in the better life and finding herself back in the village as a landless widow with two dependent small children.

As it turned out, Plotnikova ended up being upwardly mobile by the Bolshevik path, not the bourgeois one. But that, too, had a certain precariousness. She came close to losing her grip on Soviet bourgeois status in 1936. She must have been at high risk in the terror that was to come, not only because of the NKVD investigation and demotion but also because she evidently belonged to the kind of regional party "family circle" that was particularly targeted in 1937. So she may finally have acquired a third face, that of an "enemy of the people," and, if she survived that abrupt change in her life's course, a new social identity as a convict or exile in a place far from Ponizov'e and Leningrad. But the archival documents on the Plotnikova case take us no further than 1936.[20] The NKVD's story stops at this point, and so does the author's. It is up to the reader to imagine the rest.

NOTES

1. The documents on the Plotnikova case used in this essay come from an NKVD investigation of Plotnikova in 1936, reported in one of the Leningrad NKVD's regular informational submissions (*Spetssoobshcheniia*) to the Leningrad obkom: Tsentral'nyi gosudarstvennyi arkhiv istoriko-politicheskoi dokumentatsii g. Leningrada (TsGA IPD, formerly the Leningrad party archive), f. 24, op. 2v, d. 1833, ll. 45, 74–104. Thus, the NKVD is the first narrator of this story, establishing the frame and chronological limits beyond which all is darkness. Nevertheless, its selection of documents allows us to hear other voices, notably those of Plotnikova and Luk'ianov, the head of the Leningrad obkom's personnel department, who had to adjudicate the Plotnikova case.

2. With regard to criminal convictions, the government tried to overcome this problem in the mid-1930s by legislating that certain categories of conviction be retrospectively cancelled (*sniatie sudimosti*). This only produced argument among jurists about whether the fact that a conviction had been retrospectively cancelled should be entered on the record. But there was no procedure, in any case, for "cancelling" black marks like an émigré relative, noble origins, or a past vote for the opposition.

3. For a more detailed discussion of these issues, see Sheila Fitzpatrick, "Ascribing Class: The Construction of Social Identity in Soviet Russia," *Journal of Modern History* 65 (December 1993), and idem, *Tear off the Masks! Identity and Imposture in Twentieth-Century Russia* (Princeton, N.J.: Princeton University Press, 2005).

4. This metaphor really had wings in the 1930s; it crops up everywhere. For Stalin's use of it in connection with "enemies of the people" in 1937, see I. V. Stalin, *Sochineniia*, ed. Robert H. McNeal, vol. I (XIV) (Stanford: Stanford University Press, 1967), p. 190. For popular usage, see Sheila Fitzpatrick, "Supplicants and Citizens: Public Letter-Writing in Soviet Russia in the 1930s," *Slavic Review* 55:1 (Spring 1996).

5. TsGA IPD, f. 24, op. 2v, d. 1833, ll. 87–88: "Avtobiografiia. Plotnikova, Anastasiia Mironovna" (22 May 1936).

6. Petrogradskii raion. Note that the name of the district remained the same even after the city's name was changed from Petrograd to Leningrad.

7. I have chosen to characterize Plotnikova's Autobiography as the original narrative of her life, and the NKVD's revision of it as a "counter-narrative," despite the fact that the first document of the NKVD's revision is dated almost two months before the copy of the Autobiography in this file. This is essentially an arbitrary decision on my part, probably the result of disinclination to participate in Plotnikova's "expropriation" as proprietor of her life. It could be that Plotnikova's Autobiography of 22 May 1936 was itself a counter to the NKVD's counter-narrative; the archive provides no clues as to whether she was aware of the contents of the NKVD's Spravka (dated 1 March 1936) at the time she wrote (or updated) it. Needless to say, all autobiographical narratives are in some sense counter-narratives, i.e. responses to other possible or actual versions of the life.

8. TsGA IPD, f. 24, op. 2v, d. 1833, ll. 74–75: "Spravka na Plotnikovu Anastasiiu" (1 March 1936).

9. This document is not in the file, but it is mentioned in the report of the head of the raion militia to Luk'ianov, 29 May 1936 (l. 80).

10. "Spravka UGB UNKVD LO—iz pokazaniia arestovannoi za kontrrevoliutsionnoi deiatel'nost' b. chlena VKP(b) b. rabotnitsy fabriki 'Krasnoe Znamia' Drobetskoi

Ol'gi Vasil'cvny, 10.IV.1936" (ll. 76–77).

11. "Protokol doprosa 25.V.1936 g. svidetelia Shchenikova, Grigoriia Petrovicha . . ." (ll. 82–83).

12. l. 84.

13. From the report of the head of the raion militia (l. 81).

14. The main source for the information in this paragraph is the interrogation of Drobetskaia (see above, note 5).

15. Memo of 19 July 1936 (ll. 78–79).

16. This "recommendation"—really an instruction—was presumably followed, but there is no direct evidence on this point.

17. In this version, Stalin's jealousy of Kirov, sparked by events at the Congress, led him to order Kirov's assassination: See Robert C. Tucker, *Stalin in Power: The Revolution from Above, 1929–1941* (New York, 1990), 249–252, 260–261, 288–296, and Robert Conquest, *Stalin and the Kirov Murder* (New York: Oxford University Press, 1989). There is still no conclusive evidence implicating Stalin in Kirov's murder, however, and the events at the Congress also remain murky despite the recent opening of archives. For a survey of the current state of the evidence, see Matt Lenoe, "Did Stalin Kill Kirov and Does It Matter?" *The Journal of Modern History* 74:2 (June 2002).

18. Memo from Luk'ianov to F. Ivanov, 15 August 1936 (l. 89).

19. Ponizovskii sel'sovet, 24 August 1936, "Spravka dana grazhdanke Plotnikovoi Anastasii Mironovnoi" (l. 104).

20. There may, of course, be additional NKVD files on Plotnikova in other archives, including the KGB archive, but I have not tried to trace them. My discovery of Plotnikova's story in the TsGA IPD file was serendipitous, and I offer it to the reader in the same spirit.

two

Visual Pleasure in Stalinist Cinema

Ivan Pyr'ev's The Party Card

Lilya Kaganovsky

Весь мир грабастают рабочие ручищи,
Всю землю щупают—в руках чего-то нет . . .
—Скажи мне, Партия, скажи, чего ты ищешь?
И голос скорбный мне ответил:
—Партбилет . . .

[Giant workers' hands grab at the world,
Feeling the earth—there's something missing . . .
O Party, tell me, tell me what are you looking for?
And a solemn voice answers me:
—The Party Card][1]

   —A. Bezymenskii, "Party Card #224332"

The question whether a woman is "open" or "shut" can naturally not be a matter of indifference.

   It is well known, too, what sort of "key" effects the opening of such a case.

—Sigmund Freud, Dora

Under My Wife's Pillow

In 1994, director Leonid Trauberg opened his tribute to Ivan Pyr'ev with the following story about fellow co-director and friend Fridrikh Ermler. He wrote that when *Partiinyi bilet* (Party Membership Card, *aka* The Party Card, 1936) first appeared in theaters in Moscow, the film caused a stir:

Lilya Kaganovsky

> My friend, the Leningrad director F. Ermler, who, from the very beginning
> of the revolution had worked in the party, in the Cheka, secretly confessed
> to me: "You see, I saw this movie and now, more than anything, I'm afraid
> for my party card, what if someone stole it? You won't believe me, but at
> night I check under my wife's pillow, to see if maybe it's there." [*Ponimaesh',*
> *posmotrel etot fil'm i teper' bol'she vsego boius' za svoi bilet, ne ukrali li.*
> *Poverish' li, noch'iu zagliadyvaiu pod podushku zheny, ne tam li on.*][2]

Trauberg goes on to describe his positive feelings about Pyr'ev as a director and
as a human being, yet his opening story looms over the narrative. Ermler's fears
about his own safety are confirmed a paragraph later by the story of Elena
Sokolovskaia, the deputy director of the Mosfil'm studio who brought *The
Party Card* to Leningrad for its Leningrad premier. She also warned Trauberg
that this was a movie to be watched "seriously" (*ochen' ser'ezno*). Despite
Sokolovskaia's exemplary record as a Bolshevik, Trauberg tells us, "the legend-
ary Elena" was arrested and perished in Siberia only a year later.[3]

Ivan Pyr'ev's *The Party Card* is a sinister melodrama about the dangers of
trusting your spouse. Anna Kulikova (Ada Voitsik), a good communist from
solid proletarian stock, marries Pavel Kuganov (Andrei Abrikosov), a new-
comer from Siberia who seems to have all the credentials of Soviet heroism,
but who turns out instead to be an unreformed kulak, murderer, and traitor.
Because of Anna's blindness and trust, Pavel is able to join the plant where she
works, move into her apartment in Moscow, get himself elected to the Communist Party, and make plans for a work transfer to a high-security military
plant. He is also able to steal Anna's party card—that precious symbol of
communist membership dear to every Bolshevik[4]—and to deliver it into the
hands of Soviet enemies. The theft allows the enemy to move about Moscow
freely, and causes Anna to be expelled from the Communist Party for the
negligent loss of her party card. When Iasha (Igor' Maleev), Anna's true love
and the "positive hero" of this film, comes back to Moscow, he discovers
Anna's dishonor. The film ends with Iasha, Fedor Ivanovich (the head of the
local party cell, played by Anatolii Goruinov) and the NKVD bursting into the
couple's apartment to find the brave Anna holding her villainous husband at
gunpoint.

As Ermler's worries make clear, however, what appears to be a story about
the dangers of trusting your husband is actually a story about the dangers of
trusting your wife—and this reading will aim to show the ways in which *The
Party Card* stages Anna's ideological fall in gendered terms. Sokolovskaia's fate
and Ermler's fears certainly suggest that the message of *The Party Card* contained an implicit threat that was directed at the most devout Bolsheviks (those
who had fought in the revolution, had worked for the government, and even
had ties to the Cheka). This threat stemmed from the thirties' rhetorical construction of the party as a monolith whose "purity" had to be maintained
through thorough investigations of the biographical, political, and sexual behaviors of its members. In *The Party Card*, Anna's political purity is couched in

specifically gendered terms—she is guilty not just as a party member, but as a *female* party member—and the projection of guilt onto woman temporarily relieves the putative masculine spectator's anxiety that he too might be guilty of political adultery. As Ermler's fears of finding his party card under his wife's pillow make clear, no spectator ultimately escapes the threat of (political) castration that Pyr'ev's film stages and then disavows. By projecting the guilt onto Anna, however, *The Party Card* helps to turn this spectacle of political castration into visual pleasure, and locate the "discourse of the purge" specifically in the purging of woman.[5]

Purity and Danger

A prolific director, decorated with two Orders of Lenin and four Orders of the Red Banner (*ordena Trudovogo Krasnogo Znameni*), Ivan Pyr'ev had a forty-year career in cinema that started with his first black comedy *Postoronniaia zhenshchina* (*The Foreign Woman*, 1928) and ended with the screen adaptation of *Brat'ia Karamazovy* (*The Brothers Karamazov*, 1968). Yet, during the Stalin period, Ivan Pyr'ev was known best for his "tractor musicals," which, like those of Grigorii Aleksandrov, captured on celluloid Stalin's mantra *"zhit' stalo luchsche, zhit' stalo veselee"* (life has become better, life has become happier).[6] Pyr'ev's musical comedies—*Bogataia nevesta* (*The Country Bride*, 1938), set on a communal farm in Ukraine; *Traktoristy* (*The Tractor Drivers*, 1939), also set on a communal farm in Ukraine; *Svinarka i pastukh* (*The Pig Farmer and the Shepherd*, 1941), set on communal farms in Belorussia and Georgia; and *Kubanksie kazaki* (*The Cossacks of Kuban*, 1949), set on a communal farm in Kuban'—all starred Pyr'ev's wife, Marina Ladynina, who drove a tractor, danced with pigs, and was always willing to sacrifice her own happiness for the happiness of the collective. These comedies showed the prosperity of the great Soviet state through well-choreographed musical numbers, depicting the joys of backbreaking industrialized farming.

Pyr'ev's 1936 film *The Party Card* predates these musical comedies. A melodrama about a class enemy (*klassovyi vrag*) who worms his way into the heart of a young communist woman and into party ranks, starring Voitsik rather than Ladynina, and set in "new Moscow,"[7] the film is in every way the reverse of Pyr'ev's communal farm musicals. Indeed, *The Party Card* in many ways represents the underlying threat to the great Soviet prosperity promised by the musical comedies. If Pyr'ev's tractor musicals showed the happy and successful life of the countryside, his urban melodrama showed the need for "Bolshevik vigilance" necessary for the preservation of that happy life. As Soviet film reviewers in 1936 were fond of repeating, *The Party Card* showed the enemy's new methods of operation and demonstrated the ease with which a class enemy could pass himself off as a loyal Soviet citizen.[8]

Written in 1935 and released in 1936, *The Party Card* appeared in a moment of political and cinematic uncertainty, in terms both of Communist

Party policies of the mid-thirties and of Pyr'ev's own career. For a period of at least three years, Pyr'ev made one false start after another, including a failed collaboration with Mikhail Bulgakov on a screen adaptation of Gogol's *Dead Souls*.[9] Finally, in 1935, Pyr'ev found "what he had been looking for": a rejected screenplay by Katerina Vinogradskaia, called *Anka*.[10] Vinogradskaia had initially intended her screenplay for director Mikhail Romm, who refused to take it on for reasons that are not given but perhaps could be inferred from Pyr'ev's own subsequent history: at its first internal Mosfil'm screening, the film was rejected and Pyr'ev was nearly expelled from the studio. Even the film's release did not save Pyr'ev's career at Mosfil'm—he left the studio and moved to Kiev, where he proceeded, as Maia Turovskaia has put it, to make nothing but "fairy tales" (*stat' rasskazchikom skazok*).[11]

Written in 1933–1934, Vinogradskaia's screenplay was meant to be, as an early reviewer had put it, "the first serious work of art about love. The heroine's love for Pavel, who turns out to be a very subtle [*tonkii*] class enemy, ends in tragedy, from which Anka, as a communist, emerges grown up, richer in political and life experience."[12] The original narrative was set at a biological institute and the original Anka was a student—in his memoirs Pyr'ev remembers her as a "small, red-haired girl"[13]—seduced by the older Pavel, whose only goal was sabotage. Unmasked as an enemy, Pavel moves on to a different location and presumably a different girl, while Anka is transformed into a mature woman and communist (this is the story of the birth of the New Woman), worthy of our admiration. Indeed, the last line of the screenplay, delivered by Iasha in a state of euphoria, read: "Comrades, these are the kinds of women that live in our country!" (*Vot kakie zhenshchiny u nas v strane, tovarishchi!*).[14]

Despite Vinogradskaia's reputation and talent,[15] however, this "first serious work of art about love" clearly centered too much on love, or perhaps more accurately, on sex. Pyr'ev includes the following passage from the screenplay in his memoirs, to demonstrate everything that was wrong with the original version. One of the key scenes, he writes, was the "night of love" (*liubovnaia noch'*) between Anka and Pavel that took place in the institute's garden, in the company of the various laboratory animals that Pavel had just mistakenly set loose:

> Dogs play in the garden, doing somersaults in the grass . . . Jumping white bundles of rabbits . . . Cats glide by with silky backs [. . .] The trees move quietly. The leaves rustle gently in the night. Shadows chase each other. The jumps of a hunt, the call, the chase . . . Attic night. Paradise . . . Two figures under a tree [. . .]
>
> Pavel stands back, having let go of Anka, but now she presses against him herself. Her neck glistens in the dark. She is no longer trying to get away. She is listening to the other, strange heart, this mute Eve. Her arms have grown heavy.[16]

"The above passage," comments Pyr'ev in his memoirs, "clearly explains both the direction that the author wanted to take the screenplay in, and the reasons why so many directors rejected it" (K. n. I, 70). The above passage does in fact show that the screenplay conceived of Anka's vulnerability and seduction in purely sexual terms. In a "wild" nighttime garden, filled with shadowy movements and mysterious animal noises, the young Anka—this "mute Eve"—commits original sin. Her consequent "maturation" comes about as a result of sexual knowledge, of love and betrayal, and of the realization that she has been seduced by the enemy.

Through this misplaced emphasis on sexual seduction, however, Pyr'ev claimed to be able to see in this story the element of contemporary relevance (*aktual'nost'*) that he had been looking for ever since he had first watched *Chapaev*: the moment when the seduced Anka first recommends Pavel for membership in the Komsomol, but, discovering his true kulak origins, runs to stop the election process.[17] This element—Anka's political commitment taking precedence over her love—convinced Pyr'ev that the screenplay could be rewritten and made into a film. After considerable revision either by Pyr'ev and Vinogradskaia or by the GUKF (State Directorate of the Film and Photo Industry), the screenplay shifted radically from love story to political melodrama.[18] The new version centered on the loss of Anna's party membership card, her subsequent trial, expulsion, and eventual vindication. As Soviet critics and later Soviet viewers repeatedly wrote, the film's central problem was Bolshevik vigilance (*bol'shevistskaia bditel'nost'*), while "the main star of the film [was] the party card."[19] Despite the timeliness of its political message, which coincided with the nationwide campaign of party card exchange and verification, Pyr'ev's film was almost not released to the public, and the history of its eventual appearance on the Soviet screen seems typical of the vicissitudes of the Stalinist film industry.

The years 1935–1937 marked a period of particular uncertainty for both films and filmmakers. In 1935 Sergei Eisenstein delivered his famous apology for cinematic formalism and intellectual montage and then went on to make *Bezhin Lug* (Bezhin Meadow), a film that could never be finished because of its "formalist" tricks.[20] Meanwhile, Boris Shumiatskii, the head of the recently centralized Soviet film industry (Soiuzkino), traveled to the United States to study the Hollywood studio system, proposing, on his return, to build a "Soviet Hollywood" on the Black Sea coast—an idea that initially earned him great fame and later was partially responsible for his arrest.[21] Out of 130 planned films for 1935, only 45 were completed (46 out of 165 in 1936; and 24 out of 62 in 1937).[22] Reorganization and centralization led not only to internal instability but also to the introduction of new bureaucratic administrative units in charge of censorship and review. Screenplays as well as finished films were now vetted by many different organizations, whose authority conflicted and overlapped.

In *Cinema and Soviet Society,* Peter Kenez has detailed the extent of censorship and control exercised by various organizational bodies on Soviet filmmaking, commenting on the fact that "even after all these discussions, censorship, evaluations, additions and deletions, a large number of completed films in the 1930s remained unreleased and were considered 'ideological rejects'" (*ideologicheskii brak*).[23] Pyr'ev's *Party Card* was such a reject. Pyr'ev remembers even the shooting of the film as a series of episodes of wrecking and sabotage. The Mosfil'm newsletter regularly blamed the crew for various short-comings; their sets were struck before they could finish filming; they were not given equipment; on days of the shooting they were suddenly prevented from using the sound stage; someone cut the wires of the sound camera with an axe, making synchronous shooting impossible; and every two to three weeks the studio changed administrative heads. Finally, once the movie was finished, the leadership of the Mosfil'm studio found the film to be "unsuccessful, false, and distorting of Soviet reality" and shelved it (K. n. I, 74).

Suffering the consequences of studio infighting and external pressures, *The Party Card* would not have been released but for the sudden involvement of the Central Committee. According to Pyr'ev's memoirs, the film was picked out by the assistant director of Mosfil'm, A. M. Slivkin, to be shown at a closed screening at the Barvikha sanatorium to "major party officials" (*krupnym partrabotnikam*), where a discussion of the film's merits and drawbacks lasted until two in the morning, "despite the strict rules of the sanatorium." Next, the film was rushed to the Kremlin, where it "was judged to be politically correct, of contemporary relevance, and where instead of *Anka* it was given the title *The Party Card*" (*posle prosmotra v Kremle fil'm nash byl priznan politicheski pravil'nym, aktual'nym, vmesto "Anki" emu bylo prisvoeno nazvanie "Partiinyi bilet"*) (K. n. I, 75). Initially about membership in the Komsomol, the corrected version of *The Party Card* dealt with a theme of truly contemporary resonance—membership in the Communist Party—a theme recognized and approved of by the highest ranking Soviet officials, and by Stalin himself.[24]

In the thirties, Communist Party membership was indeed a topic of contemporary relevance. The ongoing political purges and document verifications of 1933–1936 were aimed at reducing the number of members of the Communist Party, that elite core of citizens proudly possessed of party membership cards. Membership in the Communist Party had reached unprecedented numbers: during the collectivization and industrialization campaigns of the First Five-Year Plan (1929–1932) it had grown by 1.4 million members.[25] Bad record keeping, easy access to blank party cards, and a lack of central control over membership elections meant that thousands of politically illiterate, "alien," "parasitic," "unreliable," and "unsteadfast" persons had entered the party since 1931.[26] The 1933 *chistka* (purge), the 1935 *proverka* (verification), and the 1936 *obmen* (party card exchange) were all meant to rid the party of these undesirable elements.

As J. Arch Getty and others have pointed out, in the thirties a party membership card was an extremely valuable commodity. It entitled the bearer to special privileges, entrance to party buildings, special rations of food and clothing; and, before the mid-thirties, it made the party member immune from arrest by civil authorities.[27] As a symbol of power, however, a party membership card also demonstrated the radical contingency of the Stalinist political system and the arbitrary exercises of discipline deployed by the Central Committee. The initial union-wide party purge, regulated by a central directive sent in April 1933, was one in a series of "cleansings" of incompetents, drunkards, and thieves that had been taking place periodically since 1917. It had, however, a more sinister theme: "An enemy with a party card in his pocket," wrote the editors of *Pravda* (11 December 1932), "is more dangerous than an open counterrevolutionary."[28] In a scene much like the one enacted in *The Party Card*, party members were called in front of ad hoc commissions formed by representatives of local party leaderships. Approaching the front of the room, communists placed their party cards on a red-draped table (this procedure entered colloquial speech via the command, *"Partbilet na stol!"* [Party card on the table!]), and, with portraits of the party's leaders in the background, recited their political biographies and answered questions.[29]

In *The Party Card*, the revelation of Anna's missing party card and the meeting of the party's ad hoc commission both take place under the prominently and centrally placed picture of Politburo member and head of the Leningrad party organization, Sergei Kirov. The choice of this portrait was not, of course, incidental. It showed both the attention to matters of political timeliness (the already mentioned *aktual'nost'* that had so attracted Pyr'ev and Stalin) and the stakes of Anna's expulsion from the party. Kirov's assassination on 1 December 1934, at Leningrad party headquarters in Smol'nyi, by Leonid Nikolaev, a former party member still in possession of his party card, meant that the party was indeed in danger of enemy intrusion.[30] Anna's loss of her party card and its use by a female spy to penetrate into buildings of national security echoed the circumstances of Kirov's murder, visually signaled by his portrait and Pavel's reference to "the traitorous shot at Smol'nyi."[31]

The purges, originally scheduled to end on November 1933, were still not officially complete in May 1935, when the party leadership in Moscow decided to extend the *chistka* to a *proverka* or "party document verification," in order "to restore Bolshevik order in our own party house."[32] This verification appeared to be designed to catch those who had "slipped through" the purge, who remained in the party by means of deception (*obmannym putem*) and may also have been hidden "class aliens."[33] The ascension to power in Germany of Adolf Hitler in 1933, the revelation of a "Leningrad Center" responsible for Kirov's assassination, followed shortly by a notice of discovery of a "Moscow Center" that had ties to White Guard organizations, and the trials and death sentences for the accused brought the rhetoric of "vigilance" (*bditel'nost'*) to a fever pitch. In August 1935 the Central Committee annulled the results of the *proverka* and announced the necessity of repeating the entire process.[34]

The May 1936 release of Pyr'ev's *The Party Card* coincided with a third wave of "cleansing." The 1936 party card exchange served as yet a third verification and was governed by even tighter disciplinary procedures. Only the local first secretary could hand out the new cards, which were to be received directly from the Central Committee by NKVD field courier and to be filled out in special ink provided by Moscow.[35] Moreover, local party organizations were to submit to the Central Committee specimens of all the signatures to appear on the cards. Each party card was to have affixed to it the photograph of the member; otherwise, it was void.[36] Central Committee instructions warned against party cards falling into the hands of enemies, declaring that "never before has the title of a party member been so high." The instructions equally stressed the need for party members' purity in light of the presence of enemies both without and within.[37] In September *Pravda* was still calling on the Soviet people to exercise *bditel'nost'* in order "to guarantee the safety of the party from intrusions into its ranks of foreign [*chuzhikh*], antagonistic [*vrazhdebnykh*], or accidental [*sluchainykh*] elements."[38]

This emphasis on "intrusion" of foreign, antagonistic, and accidental elements recalls Mary Douglas's definition of dirt as "matter out of place" or Judith Butler's definition of the "abject" in *Bodies That Matter*.[39] At stake here is a system guarding itself against pollution through self-cleansing, a system whose goal is the production of "subjects." Approaching dirt as "matter out of place," writes Douglas,

> implies two conditions: a set of ordered relations and a contravention of that order. Dirt, then, is never a unique, isolated event. Where there is dirt, there is a system. Dirt is the by-product of a systematic ordering and classification of matter, in so far as ordering involves rejecting of inappropriate elements. This idea of dirt takes us straight into the field of symbolism and promises a link-up with more obviously symbolic systems of purity.
>
> We can recognize in our own notions of dirt that we are using a kind of omnibus compendium which includes all the rejected elements of ordered systems [. . .] In short, our pollution behavior is the reaction which condemns any object or idea likely to confuse or contradict cherished classifications.[40]

In order to maintain itself as a closed system, the Communist Party under Stalin guarded itself against pollution from without through continuous checkups of the purity of its members.[41] The ritual of party card exchange, during which former party members confessed their wrongdoings and sought rehabilitation, was a prelude to the mass arrests and confessions that would find their fullest expression in the show trials of 1937–1938. The marking off of "foreign, antagonistic, and accidental elements" ensured that loyal Stalinist subjectivity could be constructed through erasing, as that which remained in place after all other elements were stripped away.

However, the word "purge" itself—*chistka*—already spoke to the process of systematic and symbolic elimination. Following the evolution of the word *chistka* from its mundane usage (removal of dirt or impurity) to its political connotations, Oleg Kharkhordin notes that the Bolshevik reinterpretation was not particularly novel and that the term "purging" had been applied to recruiting members of the Orthodox clergy to serve in the fighting army at least since the time of Catherine the Great. Like that of the earlier church historians, the Bolshevik use of the term reconceptualized the mundane word *chistka* to become the central term of their discourse. "The aim of the purge in the political sense of the word," writes Kharkhordin,

> is taken to be a cleansing of the body—the church's or the party's—of malignant elements, so that in the end a tightly united corps, ready to preach or fight, is produced. Stress on the unity of the corporate body is a recurrent theme in early Bolshevik sources.
>
> Thus, in 1921, the resolution on the first general purge of the party stated that the penetration of the party body by bourgeois elements made it necessary to conduct the purge so that "the party would be cast as a monolith [*vylita iz odnogo kuska*]."[42]

Though Kharkhordin points out that the notion of the "body politic" in its Western sense was never developed in Russia, nonetheless, he notes the medical and bodily metaphors that proliferated in party discourse. The 1928 Central Control Commission plenum talked about "ulcers" and issued a call to "uproot the degenerate elements in our organizations"; and in 1933 Iaroslavskii wrote in his brochure on the general purge: "a cadaver of [bourgeois society] . . . is decaying in our environment, this cadaver rots and infects us."[43] Similarly, Stephen Kotkin has pointed out that "discussions of the verification, like the purge, combined the rhetoric of hygiene with that of inquisition"[44]— rhetoric that made explicit the Soviet Union's attempt to constitute the nation and the party via the systematic expulsion of its abjected subjects.

Most importantly, however, the party's activities as a kind of "spiritual guide," as Kotkin has suggested,

> turned out to be a source of strength but also a deadly burden for both the party and the country. Life in the party was characterized alternatively by feelings of omnipotence and utter vulnerability, by smug complacency shattered by periods of unremitting tension, by proclamations of ironclad "truths" amid threatening uncertainties.[45]

Pyr'ev's film turned out to be, perhaps, of even more contemporary relevance than he had at first imagined: it staged precisely this anxiety of the party— perceived immediately by Ermler and Sokolovskaia—that stemmed from the party's desire for what Kotkin refers to as "iron discipline, absolute purity and supreme personal sacrifice" in the light of its own vulnerability and "threatening uncertainties." In other words, *The Party Card* did not simply recycle Stalinist rhetoric, turning its party membership card into a fetish object and punishing its female protagonist for the object's misuse. Rather, the film simultaneously acknowledged and (through displacement onto woman) disavowed the terror and uncertainty of Stalinist subjectivity, of what it meant to be so close to and yet so far from power.

Visual and Other Pleasures

Pyr'ev was not alone, of course, in dealing with contemporary subject matter or even specifically with the question of internal enemies. Kenez notes that in the seven years 1933–1939 Soviet directors made eighty-five films, fifty-two of which dealt with the struggle against saboteurs. The hero, writes Kenez, "could never be too vigilant: In Dovzhenko's *Aerograd* the enemy turned out to be his best friend, in Eisenstein's unfinished *Bezhin Meadow* it was the protagonist's father, and in Pyr'ev's *Party Card*, it was the heroine's husband."[46] In *The Party Card*, the rhetoric of hygiene (of purity and cleanliness, as well as contamination) translated into the rhetoric of virginity and the sins of sexuality.[47] Here the topic of national safety from enemy attack was presented in terms of bodily integrity and sexual penetration. Anna is pure and whole before her card is "taken from her," before she gives the enemy that which is most precious. Through her "loss," Anna not only loses her place in the Communist Party, but she "opens" herself and her country up to the enemy.

Indeed, in *The Party Card*, the integrity of Anna's body as the integrity of the Soviet nation-state is overtly articulated. Holding Anna in his arms, Pavel calls her his "Moscow": "the party, my life, my love, Anna" (*Partiia, zhizn' moia, liubov', Anna*). This linguistic conflation of feminine nouns shows that the party itself is threatened by Anna's loss; after all, enemies use her card to penetrate into buildings of highest national security, into what the film poetically calls "the heart" of the party. In Vinogradskaia's original screenplay, Pavel steals a set of keys from Anka, enabling him to commit acts of sabotage. In the final film version, the "keys" become metaphoric: Pavel claims that by losing her card, Anna has given the enemy the "key" to the heart of the Communist Party.

The Party Card is particularly interesting because of the attention it directs to Anna's position as a betrayed and dishonored wife/communist. At her trial, Anna is humiliated by fellow party members (including her own husband) and expelled from the party for her "loss of vigilance."[48] Clearly this loss is more symbolic than actual: a loss of vigilance that is coded as a loss of virginity. The language used during the trial is charged with sexual innuendo. The Russian verb *dat'/davat'*, meaning "to give," has the connotation in spoken Russian of sexual activity, translated most closely perhaps by the idiom "to put out."[49] Thus, the numerous statements made by the party members about what Anna did with her card, "who she gave it to," where and when she might have lost it, as well as the concern about the enemy "using" her card, all point to Anna's status as a sexually promiscuous woman.

"Who did you give it to? Did you lose it?" (*Ty komu davala? Ty teriala?*), asks Fedor Ivanovich, the head of the local party cell and main prosecutor at Anna's trial. The card, he says, is "a symbol of honor, pride, and the struggle of each Bolshevik" (*simvol chesti, gordosti i bor'by kazhdogo bol'shevika*). By losing the card, Anna "loses her right to be in the ranks of the party" (*poteriala pravo byt' v riadakh nashei partii*). One party member suggests that even if in the place of Anna stood his own daughter or the daughter of any of the other party members, they would still have to tell her "with pain and anguish," that "by losing her party card, she has lost [their] trust" (*raz ty poteriala partbilet, to ty poteriala nashe doverie*). As this speech makes clear, anyone's daughter can be substituted for Anna (this is a "female" problem), and the rhetoric of honor and trust further underscores Anna's loss as a sexual misstep.

Fedor Ivanovich tells Anna that her "negligence" is "that crack in the strong wall of our vigilance through which the enemy can crawl inside" (*nebrezhnost', eto ta shchel' v krepkoi stene nashei bditel'nosti v kotoruiu prolezaet vrag*). Her own husband, turning on her in a moment of over-zealous patriotism, tells Anna that she has "lost vigilance" and "given the enemy the key to the heart of our party" (*Ty dala vragu kliuch k serdtsu nashei partii, ty poteriala bditel'nost'*). And Anna herself, though defending her unmarred status, declares, "I didn't lose my card, I didn't give it to anyone—but I . . . I am . . . guilty" (*Bilet ia ne teriala, bilet ia nikomu ne davala—no ia . . . ia . . . vinovata*). During the trial scene, Anna sits in the corner, with her head down—the picture of a disgraced and fallen woman. Cowering, not willing to look up, she sinks under the insistent investigative eyes of her fellow party members, now turned members of the prosecution. She has been fully invested with guilt (in Laura Mulvey's understanding of the term as applied to narrative cinema) and the camera takes great pleasure in investigating Anna's misbehavior.[50]

As Mulvey has noted, "The magic of Hollywood style at its best (and of all the cinema which fell within its sphere of influence), arose, not exclusively, but in one important aspect, from its skilled and satisfying manipulation of visual pleasure."[51] Visual pleasure—the pleasure in looking, voyeurism, scopophilia—is at the heart of cinema, and the image of woman is the central object of its look. Yet, as Mulvey has argued, the presence of the female figure on screen always poses the problem of sexual difference: though in herself pleasurable to look at, she connotes something that the look continually circles around and disavows, "her lack of a penis, implying a threat of castration and hence unpleasure."[52] The viewer (coded as male irrespective of biological gender) has two avenues of escape from this castration anxiety. In psychoanalytic terms, the heterosexual male response to the sight of female lack is always two-fold: preoccupation, re-enactment, devaluation, punishment on the one hand; and disavowal, substitution, overvaluation and the eventual "saving" of the guilty object on the other. The "I know very well . . . but all the same . . ." of the fetishist works precisely on the logic of a dual belief: in order to deny woman's lack, one must first acknowledge it. In order to save the woman, one must first find her guilty.

Pyr'ev's memoirs make clear that in *The Party Card*, one type of visual pleasure has been replaced by another: the "romantic" plotline has been subsumed by the political one. Yet traces of the former's existence not only peek through the political narrative, they also help to make that narrative pleasurable. Ada Voitsik has not been made to look particularly attractive on screen—she is not dressed, made up, or coiffed to elicit the spectator's erotic attention—but she nonetheless serves as the object of the viewer's look, as the central and almost only female figure of the film.[53] As noted earlier in Pyr'ev's commentary on Vinogradskaia's first screenplay, the original story line depicted Anka's relationship with Pavel in sexualized terms. A description of Anka from Vinogradskaia's screenplay reads as follows: "Wearing only a t-shirt, all sweaty, [Anka] is working, surrounded by blindingly sparkling glass" (*V odnoi maike, vsia vlazhnaia, ona rabotaet sredi oslepitel'nogo bleska stekla*).[54] Her meeting with Pavel in part 2 of the screenplay has undeniably erotic undertones:

> Anka is leaning distractedly against the cool wall, making use of a minute of rest. Pavel looks her up and down quickly. Against the wall the girl and her shadow. Long bronze legs, made even longer by the shadow, a youthfully tight, well-worn t-shirt, eyes heavy from the heat.
> /It looks like we were incorrect regarding the appearance of this girl./
> A small stream of water runs slowly between them. A sign on the container on the wall: Boiling water. Cooled."[55]

The repetition of the tight, well-worn t-shirt, the emphasis on the heat, the description of Anka's long bronze legs and Pavel's interest, as well as the small water stream that runs between them, all point to a highly sexualized vision of Anka. Anka's status as *devushka* or *devchonka* (young woman, girl) again helps to produce her as a sex object. However, the inserted editorial remark regarding a mistake in Anka's appearance suggests that Anka's age is disturbing even to Vinogradskaia herself. Anka begins this screenplay as a young girl, but her maturation into the New Woman takes place not through political education but through sexual experience. In *The Party Card* Anna is older, has short hair, and is dressed appropriately in a conservative smock. Her name, too, changes to show an age difference: no longer called by the diminutive "Anka," she is now "Anna," a name that underscores her mature status.[56] She is already politically wise; nonetheless, the basic elements of the seduction and betrayal of a young, sexually inexperienced girl remain the same. Anna's legitimate marriage to Pavel has all the trappings of an illicit love affair; Anna's loss of her party card is coded explicitly as an unintentional loss of virginity.

We begin the movie with a love triangle: Anna as the amorous object of two men, Iasha and Pavel. Though de-eroticized by the filmmakers from her "original" conception (recall here that the original screenplay was about love, not politics), Anna, the perfect communist, is nevertheless the focus of male fantasy, representing access to some kind of communist plenitude. For Pavel in particular, Anna represents "Moscow"—his way of getting a job (Iasha and Anna recommend him to Fedor Ivanovich), a place to live (he moves in with Anna's family), membership in the Communist Party (in the movie Anna does not reveal his kulak origins), and the ability to move up through the ranks of the Soviet system (Anna's brother can get him work at the military plant). The head of the foreign *razvedka* for whom Pavel secretly works explicitly mentions Pavel's marriage to Anna as an example of his success in making a place for himself in the Soviet system.

Moreover, marriage to Anna would represent wholeness and plenitude, signalling entrance into a "true Bolshevik family." This can be seen most clearly during the wedding dinner, when Anna's father speaks sternly to Pavel about the Kulikov family. After listing off the accomplishments of the two sons, he tells Pavel that "the country already knows us a bit. We are the Kulikov family. An ordinary name. But it's with the Kulikovs now that you are going to live. Live according to our traditions. Traditions that are firm, true, and honest. Hold up high the banner of our name! Don't muck it up!" (*Derzhi-zhe vysoko znamia nashei familii! Smotri, ne podgad'!*) This speech could easily be translated into the language of what Katerina Clark has termed the "Great Family."[57] This marriage, in other words, is more than a union with Anna, or even with the imposing Kulikov family—it is a union with the state itself.

Yet Pavel is ultimately denied true "possession" of Anna, and the moment that should be the consummation of their marriage is displaced onto Pavel's theft of her party card.[58] Having returned from a picnic in the countryside with Anna's family, and having just been assured by Anna's brother that he will get the work transfer to the military plant, Pavel is beside himself with joy. Indeed, the entire scene is structured via the trappings of a wedding night. Anna, dressed in white and holding a bouquet of flowers, runs breathlessly into the dark and empty house, illuminated only by the occasional searchlight. Since the rather somber wedding dinner presided over by Anna's father, this is the first time that Anna and Pavel have found themselves "alone" in an apartment usually occupied by Anna's family. Grabbing hold of her, Pavel begins to threaten someone off-screen, boasting of his accomplishments. He says, "I came to Moscow with a small suitcase, begged under fences, asked for things, bent over backwards before the likes of Iasha—now just try it! Not just anyone, but a Muscovite! Not just anyone, but a party member! I am happy, Anna! I am happy that I have you! I am happy that I am in Moscow! [You are] the party, my life, my love—Anna!"

This speech is punctuated by Anna's repeated requests that Pavel let go of her; and their final struggle on the bed looks very much like attempted rape (fig. 2.1). Even the choice of the verb *imet'*—"*ia raduius', chto ia imeiu tebia*" (I am happy that I have you)—connotes sexual possession.[59] Ironically, Anna's virtue is saved by the ringing telephone, and the film's displacement of sexual purity onto political purity occurs precisely at this instant. The telephone call from the head of the foreign *razvedka* for whom Pavel secretly works ensures

Figure 2.1. Film still from *The Party Card*, 1936. Pavel and Anna after their struggle on the bed. Courtesy of Mosfilm-info.

that the political is put above the personal and channels Pavel's sexual desire into political action. Instead of staying in with Anna, Pavel leaves to receive his assignment. Instead of taking possession of his wife, Pavel steals her party card.

The theft of the party card leads to Anna's investigation, trial, and eventual expulsion from the Communist Party. Since Fedor Ivanovich initially believes that Anna lost her card through negligence, the emphasis during the trial is not on the theft but on the loss—Anna's loss of her party card, coded as an inadvertent loss of virginity. The initial investigation takes place in Fedor Ivanovich's office, under the portrait of Kirov. Indeed, throughout the scene, Fedor Ivanovich and Anna stand respectively to the left and right of the portrait, framing it between them. The portrait again reappears during the trial, reminding the viewer of the real-world consequences of Anna's fictional loss.

The details of Anna's investigation provide an insight into the film's construction of psychic and political plenitude that point back to Mulvey's argument about guilt and visual pleasure. They also help us to understand better the stakes of Pyr'ev's film and, indeed, of Stalinist culture. Unexpectedly called upon by Fedor Ivanovich to produce the card, Anna rushes around the factory, but the card she normally carries on her is neither in her briefcase nor in her desk. When she returns, Fedor Ivanovich holds up her "mutilated" party card: Anna's picture has been removed and replaced by a photograph of another woman, a member of the foreign *razvedka*, who for five days used the card to

Figure 2.2. Film still from *The Party Card*, 1936. The mutilated card. Courtesy of Mosfilm-info.

penetrate into the most secure buildings and organizations in Moscow before being apprehended. Anna first jumps at the chance to claim the card as hers (she thinks she recognizes it from its cover), but seeing the picture inside, steps back in horror (figs. 2.2 and 2.3). In this failure to recognize herself in the picture on the card, Anna reveals her distance from the "plenitude" which, until this point, the film has ascribed to her. Thus, even before she is expelled from the Communist Party, Anna is already barred from its membership.

The initial overvaluation of her as the perfect worker, party member, and comrade should remind us of Freud's supposition that the fetish is a substitute not for "any chance penis, but for a particular and quite special penis that had been extremely important in early childhood but had later to been lost . . . the fetish is the substitute for the woman's (the mother's) penis that the little boy once believed in and—for reasons familiar to us—does not want to give up."[60] The "mutilated" party card not only undoes Anna's identification with her own image, evoking not the "instantaneous aspect of the image . . . appearing above all in a contrasting size (*un relief de stature*)," but the body in bits and pieces;[61] it also displaces the original belief in Anna's completeness onto the party card itself, turning it into a fetish object in the full sense of the term: something that takes the place of the original and "has been appointed as its substitute."[62] The party membership card is the "key" that opens the doors to Soviet power. Anna's loss of this key and her inability to reclaim it upon

Figure 2.3. Film still from *The Party Card*, 1936. The horror of misrecognition. Courtesy of Mosfilm-info.

its return—indeed, her inability to recognize herself as its true owner—marks her as castrated in relation to that power. Her loss shows Anna's transformation from idealized Stalinist subjectivity to the abject.

Yet the discovery of Anna's loss is also a moment of wish fulfillment: the open circulation of the party card, freed from the state-controlled correspondence between the document and its bearer, suggests that the party card, as much as being a tool of power (access to buildings, rations, etc.) is also a tool of discipline (exact record keeping, surveillance). To be power's abject is also to be outside its purview, beyond its attention, and no longer subject to its investigations. This too is a kind of visual pleasure: pleasure in briefly identifying with the abjected subject, the one who has temporarily escaped the operations of power.

In *The Party Card*, Anna's loss and consequent "lack" are perceived as contagious. Anna's loss of her party card has made possible the substitution of one woman for another and, as an elderly party member makes clear in his denunciation, "anyone's daughter" could be guilty of Anna's crime. Anna's loss shows that not only Anna, and not only the female spy, but all women are potentially "guilty": guilty of sexual difference, translated as lack, translated as castration in relation to power—in this case, specifically communist, Stalinist power. Anna does not have the "key"—indeed, she never really did. But in the overvaluation typical of the fetishist, we might argue that Anna herself initially stands in for this "key." Particularly for Pavel, for whom marriage to Anna has made possible his permanent residence in Moscow, his acceptance into the Communist Party, and his work transfer to a privileged military plant, Anna is the key that opens all doors. Only with the discovery of her loss and the evidence of her castration (she will be permanently expelled from the party) does Anna's place in the film's symbolic change from the overvalued object of desire to the guilty object of persecution and punishment. It should not come as a surprise, therefore, that Pavel is Anna's main accuser. In the fetishistic logic of the film, Pavel takes great pleasure in discovering and denouncing Anna's lack, and in separating himself from her. "Maybe it's inappropriate for me, the husband, to speak out," he says, "But nevertheless, I will!" By speaking out against his wife, Pavel ensures that her guilt does not contaminate him. He has taken Mulvey's first "avenue of escape" from castration anxiety: "preoccupation with the re-enactment of the original trauma" (Pavel reminds everyone of the "traitorous shot at Smol'nyi"), counterbalanced by the "devaluation, punishment or saving of the guilty object" (at home he tells Anna not to worry, that it will all work out, "you'll get your membership back, you won't be lost with me around").

Mulvey's argument, however, has repercussions beyond the gender dynamic that she outlines in her essay. The trial scene in *The Party Card* takes Mulvey's model further, making Anna's guilt political as well as psychic. A standard trial scene in Stalinist films is itself an instance of "visual pleasure": the on-screen persecution of a hidden enemy puts the viewer temporarily into a position of power, identifying with the prosecutor against the culprit. As Julie Cassiday points out, the action of *The Party Card* revolves around the ubiquitous triad of "party leader, simple person, and wrecker," which appears in all genres of Soviet film of the time.[63] Yet in *The Party Card*, the trial is "unjust" because it is the product of an inversion—the trial of the good communist Anna and not the traitor Pavel. The knowledge that Anna is being tried for a crime she did not commit puts this film's viewer at risk of "unpleasure." No longer able to identify with the prosecution, we are now forced to identify with its victim. Anna is a good worker, a loyal communist. She did not lose her card, but had it stolen from her. Thus, whereas most Stalinist films disavow the possibility of anxiety and guilt about being a good Bolshevik, *The Party Card* allows that guilt into representation, but struggles to contain it within the bounds of gender. It is clear, however, that anyone—man or woman—could be guilty of Anna's crime.

The characters in *The Party Card* can only recognize their radical contingency in relation to power when they witness Anna's "castration" (her public trial and humiliation), and the meaning of the party card and its loss only acquires its full weight when it becomes lack. That is why, at her trial, Anna says, "I didn't lose my card, I didn't give it to anyone—but I . . . I am . . . guilty." Anna is guilty of both ideological and sexual impropriety—thrown off by Pavel's obvious qualifications for heroism and rugged good looks, she relaxes

Figure 2.4. Film still from *The Party Card*, 1936. Iasha comforts Anna. Courtesy of Mosfilm-info.

her vigilance and allows an enemy into her family and into her marriage bed. But she is also guilty of making visible the mechanisms of castration: in a time when every citizen may suddenly turn out to be a hidden enemy and when anyone's party card could be permanently taken away, Anna's misstep and distress over the loss of her party card makes manifest the anxiety of every Pavel, Iasha, and Fedor Ivanovich living in the Soviet Union, implying that their position vis-à-vis power is as precarious as Anna's. And although it could be argued that on the level of the narrative Anna's innocence is restored to her and that she is free, presumably, at the end of the film to marry the true hero Iasha, on the level of the film's enunciation she remains guilty of creating unpleasure by failing to contain her lack within the bounds of sexual difference.

When Iasha, back from Siberia, learns of Anna's disgrace while holding her in his arms, his first reaction is to let go immediately and push her away, suggesting that her condition is catching.[64] Iasha's initial repulsion of Anna and the investigation he and Fedor Ivanovich undertake into her affairs (ostensibly to prove her innocence) again play out the "heterosexual male response to female lack": "the pleasure that lies in ascertaining guilt, asserting control and subjugating the guilty person through punishment or forgiveness."[65] The investigation further suggests that Anna's lack threatens them as well. Unsurprisingly, therefore, the dénouement comes in the form of documents proving Pavel's true identity as a class enemy and murderer. As Kotkin has pointed out, during periods of party card exchange and verification newspapers frequently employed the preferred party euphemism, "documents came forward," to characterize someone as a "class-alien element."[66] These documents, however, are also echoes of the film's fetish object, the party card, and their discovery temporarily seals the gap opened by Anna's loss.

Is My Party Card Safe?

The 1936 audience clearly understood this message. Theaters in Moscow handed out questionnaires asking viewers for their opinion of the movie and newspapers throughout the Soviet Union ran columns devoted to viewers' reactions to *The Party Card* (columns titled *"Zriteli o fil'me"* [Viewers on the Film]).[67] The nature of Anna's guilt is one topic of discussion. A. Pisarev, picking up on the sexual subtext of Anna's loss as well as on the film's fetish object, writes: "This woman lives through two [*sic*] tragedies: she is betrayed by her husband [*"ee obmanyvaet muzh,"* used to speak about an extramarital affair], she is expelled from the party, she loses what is most precious: the party card."[68] "I cannot forgive Anna for her unnecessary [*izlishnee*] trust," writes I. Ia. Makarov, *partgruporg* (head of the party cell organization) of the Stalin Boiler Plant, "She did not demonstrate vigilance, for which she rightfully paid."[69] Similarly, the students of the Tula Communist Party School feel that though Anna is rehabilitated, her future place in the Communist Party is not assured. They pledge to continue the discussion of the film, concerning specifically Anna's subsequent behavior and "future" in the party.[70]

Some audiences are moved to conduct "spontaneous" party card checks upon exiting the movie theater, only to find that most party members are not in fact in direct possession of their documents: many have left them either at home or at the office, whereas a few clearly have no knowledge of the cards' whereabouts. A column titled "How [Well] Do You Keep Your Party Card?" (*Kak vy khranite partbilet?*), appearing in *Rabochaia Moskva* (9/IV/1936), describes a party card check following the screening of Pyr'ev's film. The article lists by name where each party member kept his or her card—only four members have cards in their possession, while eleven claim to have left them at home. The personal nature of this inquiry (and consequent public humiliation via the publication of names) restages the tension between the political and the personal set up by *The Party Card*. Anna's tragedy is private as well as public, and film viewers understand that their personal choices may not be any better than Anna's.

A. T. Mironova, representing the Communal Farm of the Red Army and Navy, claims that while watching the movie, she involuntarily thought about herself: "It has now become very clear to me that we—women—communists—must be especially careful. We must not lose class vigilance even toward the ones we love, lest we become tools in the hands of a fierce enemy."[71] Comrade

Tolchennikova, Communist Party secretary of the Samoilova Plant, writes, "You cannot watch this picture without emotion [*ravnodushno*]. When before your eyes you see the theft of Anna's party card, you are involuntarily seized by anxiety: is my party card safe [*tsel li moi partbilet*]?"[72] K. Zaitseva notes that watching Pavel testify against his wife at the trial, "makes us, women, think about how our husbands treat us and where we should be keeping our party documents."[73] And one Kolesov, a worker at the Transportation Plant, writes in response to the film: "A wonderful picture . . . I will definitely go see it for the third time, and take my wife."[74]

These responses echo Ermler's secret confession with which this article began. Ermler fears for his party card and wonders if it is hidden under his wife's pillow. Like Kolesov from the Transportation Plant, Ermler understands that his wife's proximity to the party card puts it (and him) in danger.[75] Like the guilt-ridden Anna, members of the audience take the "lack" in the film onto themselves. Pyr'ev's film tries very hard to make this lack a "female problem," to contain Anna's castration within the bounds of sexual difference. Yet, ultimately, what *The Party Card* suggests is that the failure of vigilance, and the resulting "breach" or "penetration," happen because the Soviet citizenry itself is unprepared, unwatchful, and easily seduced. The following year, 1937, besides being the year of the hundredth anniversary of Aleksandr Pushkin's death and the twentieth anniversary of the October Revolution, is also the beginning of the Great Terror—another theatrical spectacle meant to remind its audience that the enemy lurks within and that signs of lack, loss, and betrayal could always already be found inside each Soviet citizen.

NOTES

I am indebted to Eric Naiman and Christina Kiaer for their thoughtful readings of this essay, to Julie Cassiday for her help, and to the faculty of the Columbia and Barnard Slavic departments for their many suggestions.

1. A. Bezymenskii, "Partbilet # 224332" (24 January 1924), on the death of Lenin; all translations from the Russian are mine, unless otherwise noted.

2. Leonid Trauberg, "Kakim on byl . . ." (The Way He Was . . .) in Grigorii Mar'iamov, ed., *Ivan Pyr'ev v zhizni i na ekrane* (Ivan Pyr'ev in Life and on the Screen) (Moskva: Kinotsentr, 1994), 117.

3. Trauberg writes that in Odessa everyone knew Sokolovskaia as "Comrade Elena" and that the main character of Ilia Slavin's short story "Intervention" (*Interventsiia*) was modeled on her (Trauberg, 117).

4. See "Results of the Review of Party Documents, 25 December 1935," in *Resolutions and Decisions of the Communist Party of the Soviet Union*, ed. Robert H. McNeal (Toronto: University of Toronto Press, 1974), 3: 160–167, for language about the value of party documents. As Julie Cassiday notes, "Pyr'ev's film taught that the ordinary paper cards issued to Party members were no less sacred than membership itself." Julie A. Cassiday, *The Enemy on Trial: Early Soviet Courts on Stage and Screen* (DeKalb: Northern Illinois University Press, 2000), 182.

5. For a thorough analysis of the "discourse of the purge," see Oleg Kharkhordin,

The Collective and the Individual in Russia: A Study of Practices (Berkeley: University of California Press, 1999).

6. One film reviewer literally incorporated Stalin's famous phrase into his review of *The Party Card*: "the years go by," he wrote, " 'life has become better, life has become happier.' The Kulikov family lives a happy and prosperous life" (*Vyshka*, Baku, 21/IV/1936).

7. As O. Litovskii notes in "Fil'm o bditel'nosti" *Kino-gazeta* 17 (March 30, 1936): 729, the film's other task is to show "the new joyous life, the touching monolith and Bolshevik fusion (*spaika*) of the Kulikov family, and the new socialist Moscow." Stalin's "New Moscow" is the topic of Aleksandr Medvedkin's 1938 film *Novaia Moskva* (New Moscow) and Iu. Pimenov's 1937 painting of the same name. The rhetoric of "fusion" and "merging" (*sliianie*), as Kharkhordin points out, went along with the discourse of the purges, which were necessary to conduct so that "The party would be cast as a monolith" (*vylita iz odnogo kuska*). Kharkhordin, 136, quoting the 1921 resolution on the first general purge of the party, *K proverke, peresmotru i ochistke partii* (Toward the checking, screening, and purging of the party) (Irbit, 1921), 7. Here the "monolith" is Anka's family, and the purge is conducted at the level of this family.

8. RGALI, f. 3058 (Pyr'ev, Ivan Aleksandrovich), op. 1, ed. kh. 481. Articles on and screenplays for *The Party Card*. Inclusive dates 1936–1950.

9. According to Pyr'ev's own account of the events, this collaboration ended when *Pravda* published its attack on Dmitrii Shostakovich for musical formalism ("Sumbur vmesto muziki" [Chaos Instead of Music], *Pravda*, January 28, 1936). See *Kinematograficheskoe nasledie. I. A. Pyr'ev. Izbrannye proizvedeniia*, vol. 1 (Moskva: Iskusstvo, 1978), 59–75. The materials collected in this edition consist of an editorial preface, Pyr'ev's memoirs written in the fifties and sixties, and archival material (articles, speeches, production stills from his films). Further citations will be marked in the text as K. n. I and II.

10. RGALI, f. 631 (Pravlenie soiuza sovremennykh pisatelei SSSR), op. 3, ed. kh. 159, ll. 1–72 (*Anka*, first screenplay) and ed. kh. 371, ll. 1–72 (*Anna*, second screenplay).

11. Maia Turovskaia, "Fil'my i liudi" (Movies and People) (*Kinovedcheskie zapiski* 57, 251–259). Turovskaia suggests that *The Party Card* is not a film about "Bolshevik vigilance," but a film about "survival." Pavel is a brave worker and communist whose only fault lies in his past—he is the son of a kulak—a crime for which there is no amnesty. She argues that our sympathies very much lie with him—as clearly, did Pyr'ev's—and that this unorthodox message comes through the film. Turovskaia quotes from Vinogradskaia's private comments on the film's negative reception at Mosfil'm: "I think I know what the problem is," writes Vinogradskaia, "Pavel is the only true Bolshevik in the movie. The rest are mediocrities, fools [. . .] The enemy is smarter than they are. This is the love of the director for the prominent individual, this is autobiography [. . .] But I can't say anything to them. I, who know everything about the director's intentions."

12. I. Vaisfel'd, "Chto my gotovim na 1935 g." (What We Are Planning for the Year 1935), *Vecherniaia Moskva*, 15/III/1936. RGALI, f. 3058 (Pyr'ev).

13. K. n. I, 69.

14. RGALI, f. 631, op. 3, ed. kh. 159, l. 72.

15. She had originally won recognition for her screenplay *Oblomok imperii* (Fragment of an Empire, dir. Ermler, 1929).

16. RGALI, f. 631 (Pravlenie soiuza sovremennykh pisatelei SSSR), op. 3, ed. kh. 159, l. 34. Quoted in K. n. I, 69–70.

17. It is not surprising, of course, that Pyr'ev picked *Chapaev* (dir. Sergei Vasiliev and Georgi Vasiliev [Lenfil'm, 1934]) as his model, heeding Stalin's call to make more films "like *Chapaev*"—more films about the party's influence on the everyday lives of the Soviet people. Iosif Stalin, "Congratulations to Soviet Filmmakers on the 15th Anniversary of Soviet Cinema" (January 1935), in Richard Taylor and Ian Christie, eds., *Inside the Film Factory: New Approaches to Russian and Soviet Cinema* (New York: Routledge, 1991), 334–335. Like the later *Party Card*, *Chapaev* also owed its popularity and mass distribution to Stalin's direct involvement. See RGASPI, f. 558 (I. V. Stalin), op. 11, ed. kh. 828 and 829. Boris Shumiatskii's notes on Kremlin screenings, 1934–1937, appeared in print for the first time in *Kinovedcheskie zapiski* 61 (2002): 321. Discussion of *The Party Card* appears in *Kinovedcheskie zapiski* 62 (2003): 163.

18. According to Pyr'ev's memoirs, he and Vinogradskaia rushed off to one of the Writers' Union vacation homes in Abramtsevo to rewrite the screenplay. The portrait of the communist family was based in part on Pyr'ev's own experiences living with a working family in a workers' town in the Simonov (Leningrad) region (K. n. I, 70). Archival documentation and newspaper accounts at the time state that the revisions came from the GUKF. RGALI, f. 631 (Soiuz sovetskikh pisatelei), op. 9, ed kh. 371. Here the film's title appears as *Anna*.

19. O. Litovskii, op. cit. Ia. Aveshin writes, "[T]he star of the film is the party card and all the action takes place around it and because of it" (*Bakinskii rabochii*, Baku, 21/IV/1936).

20. Sergei Eisenstein, "Speeches to the All-Union Creative Conference of Soviet Filmworkers" in S. M. Eisenstein, *Selected Works*, vol. III, ed. Richard Taylor, trans. William Powell (London: British Film Institute, 1988), 16–46. For the Russian text, see Eisenstein, *Izbrannye stat'i* (Moscow, 1956). For Pyr'ev's rivalry with Eisenstein, see Nikita M. Lary, *Dostoevsky and Soviet Film: Visions of Democratic Realism* (Ithaca: Cornell University Press, 1986), 111–129.

21. In 1930, Sovkino was renamed Soiuzkino (the change was not mentioned in the press) and given greater authority over the studios of the national republics. See Peter Kenez, *Cinema and Soviet Society from the Revolution to the Death of Stalin* (New York: I. B. Tauris, 2001), 95. After his return from the United States, Shumiatskii famously suggested that "there is an inescapable need to build a single cinema center in the southern and sunniest part of the Soviet Union, near the sea and the mountains." This idea of a "Soviet Hollywood," coupled with the failure to produce the requisite number of films per year, among other failures, led to Shumiatskii's arrest on 8 January 1938 and his denunciation in *Pravda* the following day as a "captive of the saboteurs," "a Fascist cur" (*Kino*, 11 January 1938), and "a member of the Trotskyite-Bukharinite-Rykovite Fascist band" (*Iskusstvo kino*, February 1938). Quoted in Richard Taylor, "Boris Shumyatsky and the Soviet Cinema in the 1930s: Ideology as Mass Entertainment," *Historical Journal of Film, Radio, and Television* 6:1 (1986), 43–64.

22. Taylor, "Boris Shumyatsky and the Soviet Cinema in the 1930s," 60.

23. For a full account, see Kenez, 129–130.

24. G. Mar'iamov, in his 1994 *Ivan Pyr'ev v zhizni i na ekrane*, attributes both the approval and the change in title directly to Stalin: "The nighttime debates at the sanatorium became known in the TsK (Central Committee of the Communist Party). Stalin asked for the film. After seeing it, he acknowledged the picture as politically

accurate and relevant (*actual'nyi*). Instead of the inert title 'Anka,' he gave it the title 'The Party Card,' clarifying that movies should be titled in relation to their content, and that the main idea of this film was vigilance (*bditel'nost'*) and the safekeeping of party cards" (28). In her personal notes from that period, Vinogradskaia writes, "A couple of days after [the film screening at Barvikha] we were called into Shumiatskii's office. Sokolovskaia said to me, 'Stalin has seen the movie. He said it was a brave movie [*smelaia kartina*]. He made a couple of changes and gave it a new name, "The Party Card."' This was a major victory [*Eto byla pobedishcha*]!" RGALI, f. 2983, op. 1, ed. kh. 44, 5–14. Quoted in Turovskaia, "Fil'my i liudi," 258.

25. J. Arch Getty, *Origins of the Great Purges: The Soviet Communist Party Reconsidered, 1933–1938* (New York: Cambridge University Press, 1985), 48.

26. Getty, 48.

27. Getty, 33.

28. Stephen Kotkin, *Magnetic Mountain: Stalinism as Civilization* (Berkeley: University of California Press, 1995), 299, n. 67. For materials on the purges and the screening of Pyr'ev's *The Party Card* in Magnitogorsk, see "Dizzy with Success," 280–354.

29. Kotkin, 300.

30. Kotkin, 303. In Stalin's "Zakrytoe pis'mo TsK VKP(b): Uroki sobytii, sviazannykh s zlodeiskim ubiistvom tov. Kirova" (Secret Letter of the TsK VKP(b): Lessons learned from the events concerning the criminal murder of comrade Kirov), addressed to all the organs of the party, he wrote that members of the Zinoviev group had been hanging on to their party cards in order to appear faithful to the Bolshevik Party and to the Soviet Union. Kirov's murderer, L. Nikolaev, was apprehended by the Cheka three weeks prior to the murder, but because he was carrying a party card, he was not even searched. "Is it so hard for a Chekist to understand," wrote Stalin, "that a party card could be counterfeited or stolen from its owner, that by itself, without a check of its authenticity or a check of the person carrying it, a party card cannot serve as a guarantee [. . .]? Where has vigilance gone?" (18 January 1935), published in *Izvestiia PK KPSS* 8 (1989). In his address to the plenum of the TsK VKP(b) on 3 March 1937, titled "O nedostatkakh partiinoi raboty i merakh likvidatsii trotskistskikh i inykh dvurushnikov" (Regarding the shortcomings of party work and measures to liquidate Trotskyite and other double dealers), Stalin quoted from the 1935 letter, suggesting that the measures taken in party card exchange and verification had failed to prevent Trotskyite elements from penetrating into the party (*Pravda*, 29 March 1937).

31. Getty writes that the decision to conduct a general verification of party records had been taken more than a year after the first revelations of disorder and several weeks before the assassination of Kirov (Getty, 58). *The Party Card*, however, makes clear that the stakes of the verification were better articulated once the murder had taken place.

32. See Kotkin, 301, and *Istoriia vsesoiuznoi kommunisticheskoi partii (bol'shevikov). Kratkii kurs* (1938) (The History of the All-Union Communist Party [of the Bolsheviks]: Short Course) (OGIZ, 1945), 313. Further citations from this text marked as *Short Course*. The 1938 *Short Course* reprints many of the statements and formulations originally published in Stalin's *Questions of Leninism* (Voprosy Leninizma) (Moscow, 1935).

33. Kotkin, 302.

34. Kotkin, 306.

35. Kotkin, 310.

36. Getty, 88.

37. Kotkin, 310.

38. *Pravda*, 29 September 1936, cited in *Short Course*, 314.

39. Mary Douglas, *Purity and Danger: An Analysis of the Concepts of Pollution and Taboo* (London: Routledge, 1966); Judith Butler, *Bodies That Matter: On the Discursive Limits of "Sex"* (New York: Routledge, 1993). When speaking about the subject's assumption of "sex," Butler writes, "The forming of a subject requires an identification with the normative phantasm of 'sex,' and this identification takes place through a repudiation which produces a domain of abjection, a repudiation without which the subject cannot emerge. This is a repudiation which creates the valence of 'abjection' and its status for the subject as a threatening spectre" (Butler, 3).

40. Douglas, 37.

41. Zbigniew Brzezinski, for example, calls the period between 1933–1939 "the permanent purge." Zbigniew Brzezinski, *The Permanent Purge* (Cambridge, Mass.: Harvard University Press, 1956).

42. Kharkhordin, 136, citing *K proverke, peresmotru i ochistke partii*, 7.

43. See Kharkhordin, 138–139. Kharkhordin also cites Aaron Solts, who lists the seven "party illnesses"—deadly threats to the collective body (139). In his *Sex in Public*, Eric Naiman points out the way the notion of a "collective body" was produced through the discourses of different groups and tendencies, but specifically, the way in which this metaphor pervaded Proletkul't texts. He writes, "[the poetic images] of Proletkul't were taken seriously in a way in which poetic images rarely are—they were hyperbolized and came to dominate other genres of social discourse [. . .] Proletkul't literary critics were also critics of culture, and they nurtured the language of the collective body because they saw its value when projected off the page into 'real' life." Naiman, *Sex in Public: The Incarnation of Early Soviet Ideology* (Princeton: Princeton University Press, 1997), 71. The image of this collective body remained in place after Proletkul't's demise, and found its way into the discourse of purity and contamination that characterized the purges.

44. Kotkin, 307.

45. Kotkin, 298.

46. Kenez, 149.

47. "Our Party organization is young and unquestionably more contaminated (*zasorenno*) than others," quoted in Kotkin, 307, n. 115. Arguably, Pyr'ev and Vinogradskaia are reworking the "old" equation of sexual purity with ideological purity. The discourse of class enemies echoes A. B. Zalkind's claim in his 1926 *Polovoi vopros v usloviiakh sovetskoi obshchestvennosti* (The Sexual Question in Soviet Public Context), that "sexual attraction is a class enemy" (in Naiman, 137).

48. Anna's "trial" takes place during an ad hoc meeting of the factory's cell of the Communist Party, presided over by Fedor Ivanovich, the head of the local party cell. The interrogation is private—it takes place without an audience, a feature that Kotkin notes was typical of the "verification" as opposed to the "purge" (Kotkin, 307). I have followed Cassiday's lead here in referring to the interrogation as Anna's "trial," which links *The Party Card* to other feature films of the thirties whose action culminated in trial sequences, as well as to the decade's reworking of the *agitsud* into trial documentaries (Cassiday, 182).

49. *dat'*; nesov. (sov. *davat'*): 2. komu. Ustupat' muzhchine, soglashat'sia na seksual'nuiu sviaz' (o zhenshchine) (*to give*: 2. to whom. To give way to a man, to agree to sexual relations [about a woman].)

davalka, -i, zh. 1. Prostitutka, zhenshchina s somnitel'noi reputatsiei (*"giver"*: a prostitute, a woman with a questionable reputation.)

In *Slovar' moskovskogo argo* (Dictionary of Moscow Slang), ed. V. S. Elistratov (Moskva: Moskovskii gosudarstvennyi universitet im. Lomonosova, 1994).

50. In "Visual Pleasure and Narrative Cinema," Mulvey writes, "[V]oyeurism, on the contrary, has associations with sadism: pleasure lies in ascertaining guilt (immediately associated with castration), asserting control and subjugating the guilty person through punishment or forgiveness." Laura Mulvey, *Visual and Other Pleasures* (Bloomington: Indiana University Press, 1989), 21–22. We see this in the case of Anna's trial: part of the pleasure of this film comes from first punishing and then forgiving its heroine.

51. Mulvey, 16.

52. Mulvey, 19. Mulvey's argument both stems from and gives rise to psychoanalytic film criticism's concern with "difference." Christian Metz, Jean-Pierre Oudart, Stephen Heath, Mary Ann Doane, and Kaja Silverman, among others, have written on the desire present in all cinema to show us a "hermetically sealed world," with which we are nonetheless invited to identify fully. Suture, voice-over, eye-line matches, a darkened theater, actors who occupy the place of the *"je-idéal"*—all of these are techniques aimed at the erasure of difference. "Plenitude," therefore, is always at stake in cinema—as *The Party Card* and its fetish objects serve to show.

53. Both Pavel's sister-in-law and Pavel's former fiancée, who reveals his real identity to Anna, make brief appearances in the film. The main narrative, however, focuses on the love triangle between Anna, Pavel, and Iasha, with Fedor Ivanovich playing the important role of supervisor/party head/mentor/chief prosecutor.

54. RGALI, f. 631, op. 3, ed. kh. 159, l. 24.

55. RGALI, f. 631, op. 3, ed. kh. 159, l. 25.

56. It also begins to resonate with the other famously fallen woman of Russian literature with the same initials, A.K.

57. On the Great Family see Katerina Clark, *The Soviet Novel: History as Ritual* (Chicago: University of Chicago Press, 1981).

58. I am indebted to Gregory Freidin for the suggestion that Anna's marriage to Pavel is never consummated (screening of *The Party Card*, Slavic Film Group, University of California, Berkeley, April, 2000).

59. *imet'*; nesov. 1. kogo, chto. Vstupat' s kem-to v polovuiu sviaz' (*to have:* to enter into sexual relations);

imelka, -i, zh. Muzhskoi polovoi organ (*"haver"*: the male sexual member). (*Slovar' moskovskogo argo*).

Again, Vinogradskaia's screenplay is explicit where the film is only implicit: "[Pavel is] wild. He is seized by a [feeling of] celebration, a reaction to fear, more powerful than before, in the nighttime garden. He is yelling something incomprehensible, holding Anka by the shoulders like something his own, completely his own. She has closed her eyes for a second, feeling his arms around her. Pavel, laughing, happy, is not leading but practically carrying her down the hall, like a dead woman, lifting her up by her shoulders." RGALI, f. 3058 (Pyr'ev), l. 52.

60. Sigmund Freud, "Fetishism," in *The Standard Edition of the Complete Psychological Works of Sigmund Freud*, vol. 21, trans. and ed. James Strachey (London: The Hogarth Press, 1955), 152–153.

61. Jacques Lacan, *Écrits: A Selection*, trans. Alan Sheridan (New York: W.W. Norton, 1977), 2.

62. Freud, "Fetishism," 154.

63. Cassiday, 183.

64. After his initial discomfort, Iasha takes Anna back into his arms; the set expression on his face, however, suggests that he is now full of Bolshevik determination to right this particular wrong, and does not, I believe, counteract the original moment of repulsion.

65. Mulvey, 21–22.

66. Kotkin, 310.

67. Once the film was approved by the Central Committee for mass distribution, it was shown widely, and became one of the top films of 1936. *Pravda* (8/IV/1936) notes that the opening of the film in Moscow the day before (7 April 1936) generated higher than usual matinee attendance and that the evening shows were completely sold out. Similarly *Rabochaia Moskva* (9/IV/1936) notes that there was not a single theater with unsold tickets. More than 60,000 people had watched the film during the first two days. RGALI f. 3058 (Pyr'ev).

68. *Izhevskaia Pravda*, 22/IV/1936, p. 53.

69. *Sotsialisticheskii Donbass*, Ukraine, 14/IV/1936.

70. *Kommunar*, Tula, 18/IV/1936.

71. *Krestianskaia gazeta*, 8/IV/1936, p. 37.

72. *Leningradskaia Pravda*, 14/IV/1936.

73. *Nasha Pravda*, Moscow, 19/IV/1936.

74. *Elektrozavod*, 22/IV/1936 (p. 53). All quotes in this and the preceding two paragraphs are from RGALI, f. 3058 (Pyr'ev).

75. Ermler's fears of his wife are, of course, the reverse of the movie's literal message. Besides Anna's seemingly irrecuperable guilt, the "protest" suicide of Stalin's wife Nadezhda on the night of 8–9 November 1932 may offer another possibility for interpretation (Kotkin, 299, n 68). As Edvard Radzinskii, among others, has pointed out, following Nadezhda Alliluyeva's suicide the Kremlin became more and more "homo-social," while Stalin took to regularly arresting and executing the wives of Central Committee members (Radzinskii, *Stalin* [Moskva: Izdatel'stvo "Vagrius," 1997]). Wives, therefore, were particularly subject to suspicion—as Ermler's confession suggests.

three
Terror of Intimacy

Family Politics in the 1930s Soviet Union

Cynthia Hooper

In the 1936 Soviet movie *The Party Card*, local officials accuse a communist woman of an unforgivable act of negligence, faulting her for losing her certificate of party membership after they discover it in enemy hands. Viewers, however, understand that Anna Kulikova did not misplace her identification card, but actually had it stolen by her husband, a Bolshevik covertly working for a foreign intelligence agency. Audience members, with their privileged knowledge, must accept that Anna's "true" offense lies in her careless approach not towards objects, but towards people. She is guilty of having let love blind her to her husband's past, of having believed him to be a dedicated communist, and thereby of having allowed him to sully her own moral and political purity. At the end of the film, the genuine villain is unmasked: heroic NKVD officers burst into Anna's apartment just as she, herself, confronts her husband with a gun. Nevertheless, the film contains a somber rather than celebratory message. Anna has been redeemed, but she is still, through the machinations of her conniving spouse, a "fallen" woman.[1]

With its themes of misplaced trust and betrayal, *The Party Card* presents a double-edged vision of Soviet interpersonal relations during the Great Terror years. Prior to her marriage, Anna's perfectly Bolshevik family stands as a microcosm of the state itself. Her father and brothers are in the party; their class origins are proletarian and their household imbued by socialist values. But the film is structured as a type of morality play, in which political and sexual symbolism merge: evil, in the shape of a predatory suitor/husband, succeeds in winning the affections of an insufficiently vigilant virgin bride, drawing her from the path of purity into sin. Emotions of romantic love and tenderness, in such a world, carry the inescapable potential to corrupt, and as a result *The Party Card* presents familial attachments as entities capable not only of preserving socialist values but also of attenuating them. Fittingly, Anna proves her political dedication only by learning to look (albeit belatedly) beyond her unreliable personal inclinations, demonstrating her readiness to investigate her own spouse and ultimately to expose him as a spy.

During the Great Terror, communist leaders came ever more to embrace such double-sided family symbolism. On the one hand, they frequently cast the family as a metaphor for the Soviet party/state, with Stalin as "father" presiding over his Stakhanovite, aviator, or card-carrying Bolshevik "children."[2] On the other hand, however, Moscow officials simultaneously began to emphasize the dangers of a certain kind of more nuclear family, in which members were bound by ties of kinship or sentiment strong enough to undermine all-supreme socialist loyalties. Bolshevik propaganda from the late 1930s, even sagas of military heroism like the 1934 hit film *Chapaev*, extolled the fundamental displacement of biological connections by political ones, and the abandonment of isolated, self-interested "family circles" (*semeistvennost'*) for what Katerina Clark has termed the all-encompassing Soviet "great family."[3] This substitution could be portrayed in terms of glorious transcendence, as in newspaper stories of soldier-heroes who died in action, only to be replaced in the ranks by brothers, clamoring to serve in their siblings' stead.[4] But it could also be presented in a more oppositional way, as an either/or choice between the "good" family of the state and a "bad" set of blood relations, or between uplifting objective pro-socialist patriotism and insidious subjective bourgeois emotion.

Political police files from the era illustrate the extent to which all "private" relations (meaning all affiliations grounded in personal inclination rather than professional necessity) became a primary subject of investigation and incrimination within the Communist Party elite during the Great Terror years. In one typical incident in 1937 Novosibirsk, NKVD officers denounced a colleague for having refused to participate, seven years earlier, in a firing squad to shoot his own uncle—despite the fact that the lieutenant in question had been the first to turn his relative in to police for suspected treason. The officer was saved from immediate party expulsion on grounds of cowardice and disloyalty only when the Novosibirsk regional NKVD chief intervened to argue that his subordinate's request to be dismissed from the execution team should be considered a consequence of strictly physical rather than sentimental weakness. As he explained: "Not every Chekist can carry out a sentence—simply, on occasion by virtue of the condition of his health, therefore to raise that as a motive of direct political accusation would not be completely fair."[5]

Throughout the late 1930s, authority figures at every level exhorted citizens to fight counterrevolution in their everyday lives by casting off any and all offending ties of intimacy or inheritance. Family members of those arrested were forced to participate in public rituals of repudiation in which they acted out their decision to support the Soviet collective through the rejection of their corrupt relations. Adults condemned their spouses at party or trade union gatherings; children denounced parents in student groups or at meetings of their Communist Youth League cells. Far from being secret and shameful activities, such practices were valorized, as the movie *The Party Card* suggests. In the late 1930s, the Young Pioneers adopted as their mascot Pavel Morozov, a fourteen-year-old who had accused his "kulak" father of theft in 1932 and was allegedly murdered by angry relatives in retaliation. A song published in 1938 by the Young Guard press lauded Morozov as an example to all children, proclaiming: "Our comrade—a hero. / For the good of the people / He did not allow his father to steal."[6] Though cited retrospectively by would-be reformers inside the Communist Party as examples of state-induced "perversion," these disavowals of private attachments during the 1930s were ostentatiously celebrated by Bolshevik loyalists at the time as signs of socialist conviction and public health.

This particular shape of political violence, involving the vigilant interrogation of all human interactions not dictated by one's official obligations, raises questions about the relationship between intimacy and terror in the Soviet world. These two terms, when taken together, have generally been employed to encourage historians seeking to understand the dynamic of Stalinist repression to look outside the party/state "machine" for answers and to focus attention instead on individual experience.[7] This essay, in contrast, examines the place of intimacy *inside* the realm of the party/state, as a fundamental condition of Soviet politics, both idiom and mechanism of the Great Terror.

In exploring the highly personalized aspect of 1930s politics, this essay views the Great Terror within a continuum of party-supported efforts after 1917 to inculcate new, specifically non-bourgeois patterns of everyday life among Soviet citizens. During the 1920s, educators took a peasants-into-proletarians focus, aiming to modernize a predominately rural, tradition-bound populace by, for instance, teaching Red Army recruits to brush their teeth, collective farmers to report to work by the clock, and people of all ages to read. But restructuring the private world of intimate relations proved more difficult. Theorists, journalists, and political education officers frequently fought over which standards, exactly, should distinguish a Soviet family from a western European liberal one, or over what position love and sex should hold in a communal world of productive, platonic camaraderie.[8] Despite their disagreements as to the subtleties of content, however, central party leaders and avant-garde intellectuals alike shared in the assumption that appropriately Soviet surroundings could not but succeed in fostering acceptable socialist behaviors.[9] Thus throughout the 1920s they focused on the dissemination of values, aiming to re-form domestic life by sending women into the workforce, building communal apartments and cafeterias, even redesigning furniture to replace the soft and spacious "bourgeois" double bed with more functional sofas and chairs that folded into single-person cots.[10]

Attempts to assess political commitment during the Great Terror, however, took a more suspicious approach to the role of the state in reshaping values. Amid an atmosphere of general alarm about enemies embedded inside the Communist Party, government authorities after 1934 began to interpret socialist lifestyle in a different way than had previously been the case. They no longer accepted it at face value, as simply a direct reflection of individual belief, but rather learned to view it as a possible mask, a seemingly pro-Soviet surface that could be carefully crafted to conceal an internal truth of treachery and disaffection. As a result, rather than placing their energies into the recruiting of new communist converts from among the so-called "non-party masses," officials started to search for new ways of testing the faith of those who already appeared fully devoted to the Bolshevik cause. Simultaneously, they themselves came to be subjected to such scrutiny by their fellow functionaries. State-sponsored projects of social transformation gave way to those of individual verification, as leaders concentrated less on inscribing party/state loyalty, and more on appraising its authenticity.

This fascination with reading belief manifested itself in multiple spheres during the Terror years. In the art world, as Boris Groys has recounted, both painters and critics sought to articulate a set of foolproof rules for analyzing poses and facial expressions to determine character and evaluate a subject's weaknesses and strengths.[11] Related efforts to develop a "science" for deciphering internal political attitudes through a careful study of surface detail—in other words, for discerning a person's genuine identity (*lichnost'*) from his or her official "face" (*litso*)—can be seen inside government personnel departments and party cells around the same time, as those in charge of hiring and firing employees hunted for interpretive techniques that would enable them to "know their cadres" to perfection.

This switch in emphasis from "writing" values to "reading" them was a crucial element of the late 1930s Terror, and a factor which challenges theories that see the years leading up to World War Two as ones of increasing social conservatism. Beginning with an outraged Leon Trotsky, writing in exile in 1937, an array of scholars have described the Stalinist era after the First Five-Year Plan in terms of a retreat away from the revolutionary refashioning of society and a "return," of sorts, to a more convention-oriented form of "cultured life," or *kul'turnost'*, that legitimized "what had once been thought of as 'bourgeois' concerns about possessions and status."[12] These writers have documented a number of fascinating trends in the cultural sphere that support their claims. During the Terror years, confectionary factory workers agitated for triweekly manicures, Stakhanovites competed for such staples of clean and neat domestic life as clocks, tablecloths, and clothing irons, and housewife-activists at national conferences touted their accomplishments in paving sidewalks, planting trees, and providing day care centers with satisfactory linen. Fashions from the mid-1930s favored stockings, dancing skills, and clean shaves over the leather-and-dagger outlaw look that had been popular among militant communists during the mid-1920s.[13]

Nevertheless, in terms of the fusion of politics with private life, the period from 1934–1939 was even more revolutionary than the era which had preceded it, in the extent to which party/state authorities held one another up to public scrutiny, scouring daily behavior for signs of individuals' innermost thoughts and inclinations. Ironically, the fears that fueled such inquiries reproduced the very assumptions of bourgeois society that Bolshevik leaders had so long aimed to transcend, for they posited that individual authenticity was primarily a function of intimacy. The very rhetoric of the Terror implied that a subject was far more likely to reveal his or her "true" self in the sphere of voluntary association, rather than in an official realm more conducive to pretense and lip-service conformity. "Private life" amid the family thus became a crucial testing ground for political belief and a focus of new forms of community surveillance, although this surveillance was consistently portrayed in party meetings and media not in opposition to socialist family values and "cultured" interpersonal relations, but as an essential means of their preservation. Books on child rearing from 1935 to 1937 stressed the importance of filial ties and the obligation of socialist children to respect and obey their parents. However, at the same time, such prescriptions included inevitable caveats, warning, for instance, that rules of deference did not hold in "those cases when parents are people foreign [in spirit] or hostile to socialist society."[14]

As such an example suggests, what distinguished state attitudes towards the private sphere in the late 1930s USSR from those of neighboring dictatorships such as Nazi Germany was, in part, the inclination on the part of Soviet officials to see the family as a key site of potential political corruption, and thus as an entity that must be repeatedly tested. For all that state authorities inside the Third Reich sought to "Nazify" families—by encouraging racially "beneficial" unions, requiring boys to join the Hitler Youth, and paying couples to have more children—they rarely sought to interrogate domestic relations, and even went so far as publicly to decry denunciation within families or among neighbors and friends. Separations between public and private spheres were accepted, even embraced, while in the Soviet case private matters became, in many communities, the very essence of political life.[15]

The consequence of Soviet attempts to expose and exorcise all politically impure interpersonal relations had effects opposite to those intended. As this essay will explore, rather than eradicating any sort of public/private distinction in the minds of communist servitors, the Terror years seem to have brought such divisions into consciousness. Demands of vigilance required party members to assess the relationship between their own "small" and "great" families in ways they had never had to do before. Frantic efforts on the part of many to heal the rift they suddenly perceived to exist between the two paradoxically served not to restore a shattered unity, but only to intensify political and social conflict. The process of the Terror thereby succeeded in turning the Bolshevik family into something of the very force Soviet leaders had initially feared, namely a source of dissension and divided loyalty within the socialist fold.

Control from Below: Instability of Activism

After the Revolution of 1917, communist leaders advertised the USSR as a state whose power was constituted through uniquely socialist means and where the responsibilities for surveillance and enforcement—the practices of party and state control—were consequently vested in the social collective rather than in a set of exclusive institutions staffed by elite cadres of self-interested professionals. While this vision of the Soviet regime cannot be accepted uncritically, contemporary scholars should not underestimate the extent to which the USSR involved so-called amateurs in the monitoring of the government bureaucracy and mobilized rank-and-file workers in evaluating the actions of those in positions of authority. Immediately after 1917 and again during the First Five-Year Plan, forms of popular participation in control work proliferated, with unskilled volunteers serving as judges, public prosecutors, newspaper correspondents, investigators for factory or community complaint bureaus, inspectors, guards, militia patrolmen, and informants. In most regions a handful of state functionaries oversaw a far larger unofficial contingent of self-professed "collaborators."

The Soviet judicial apparatus provides a typical case in point. Court cases at all levels in the USSR during the 1920s and 1930s were always decided by three-person panels, ideally to be made up of one certified "people's judge" and two community-elected "assessors," but frequently composed of only three local volunteers. These amateur assessors held the same voting and witness examination rights as did judges, although they possessed no legal training but served only in their capacity as laborers "from lathe and plow" (*aktiv ot stanka i sokhi*).[16] In 1929, regions such as Vladimir commanded at the county level a mere 55 people's judges, albeit all with party credentials; the vast majority of assignments thus fell to the area's 9,328 assessors, more than 80 percent of whom were not members of either the Communist Party or the Komsomol.[17]

The impact of these grassroots *aktiv* could and did vary. Frequently their signals were manipulated by the very leaders whose power they purported to contain; more often than not, complaints of corruption, petitions to judicial authorities, and letters to *Pravda* were simply thrown away and their authors intimidated into silence. But the Great Terror was a time when the Central Committee actively encouraged all manner of voices "from below" to speak out against official wrongdoing, and in fact their long history of being squelched by self-interested higher-ups became itself an object of investigation.[18] In 1936, for instance, the Politburo instructed community purge commissions across the USSR to provide opportunities for *all* citizens, including those outside the party, to submit any complaints they might have about the conduct of local communists. An open party letter read aloud to all factory workers in the city of Nizhnii Novgorod consequently proclaimed, "We turn to you with the request to send us any material you may possess, regarding the work and personality of our party members, union administrators, and low-level officials. Only material characterizing the *negative* aspects of their work and behavior should be sent . . ."[19]

This new, centrally sanctioned focus on rank-and-file political activity arose as a result of the assassination of Leningrad party secretary Sergei Kirov in 1934. Kirov's shooting was immediately presented to the public as the work of upper-level Bolshevik insiders, and it triggered near-hysterical fears about inca-pacitating numbers of counterrevolutionaries hidden within the most exclu-sive ranks of the Communist Party, including those of the NKVD. Results from a USSR-wide emergency "investigation," conducted by a political police force anxious to avoid further disgrace, "confirmed" the existence of a vast conspir-acy of Trotskyite sympathizers burrowed inside the Soviet regime, one whose leaders allegedly possessed ties to Nazi Germany and other right-wing powers.

Specious as such a proposition undoubtedly was, its successful promulga-tion can be better understood when one considers the increasingly ominous international context in which it was formulated. The years following the death of Kirov featured an international Popular Front alliance against fascist expansionism across Europe, and Soviet newspapers, films, plays, and school-books all exhorted citizens to see themselves as part of a this movement, united in a domestic "popular front" against fascist infiltration from within.[20] The outbreak of the Spanish Civil War in 1936 gave such warnings even greater urgency, for General Franco's coup was taken as proof in the Soviet press of the existence of organized counterrevolutionary forces bent on destroying socialism inside the USSR as well as abroad. Citizens were pushed to volun-teer in community policing initiatives and to "send signals" of suspicious activity to authorities, in order to save their country from becoming a "second Spain." Pressure to participate was such that, even in a garage in Murmansk, a mechanic could be told by the secretary of the repair shop's small party cell: "You still haven't filed a single submission against wreckers, so how can you even ask about being promoted to full party membership?"[21]

Vigilante forms of popular control permeated even the most routine of activities during the late 1930s. Historians such as Sheila Fitzpatrick and Vadim Volkov who argue that this period saw a "great retreat" away from revolutionary zealotry and a turn toward more conservative cultural standards underestimate the fact that while many of the values promulgated during the latter half of the decade were, indeed, seemingly "bourgeois," the means of their promulgation definitely were not.[22] Rather than eliciting conformity indirectly, through an array of institutions and discourses in the typical manner of a liberal state, Bolshevik leaders instead encouraged the imposition of community norms through direct, highly personalized, hands-on acts of surveillance, intervention, and violence. Groups of "civic-minded women" (*obshchestvennitsy*) inspected workers' haircuts in factories and launched unannounced raids of communal apartments at home, frequently posting the names of slovenly housekeepers in building stairwells for all to read.[23] University students denounced peers who refused to return library books promptly, slammed doors, or played "unharmonious" guitar music late at night.[24] Showings of films such as *The Party Card* even inspired teenagers to stage impromptu searches of fellow cinemagoers, to determine which audience members had failed to carry their certificates of party membership with them at all times, as CPSU regulations required.[25]

Not all forms of such activism led to charges of counterrevolution and arrest, but, taken together, they illustrate the extent of mass mobilization in surveillance work, the type of face-to-face interactions that such a micropolitics of control entailed, and the mundanity of most "compromising material" thereby amassed.[26] Across the USSR, workplace newspapers and complaint bureaus collected notices surreptitiously submitted by employees, dissecting the daily activities of workers by name and not only describing the minutiae of dacha visits, drinking habits, and adulterous relationships in garish detail but also casting them as matters of potential political concern. In one typical case of suspected treason, investigators looking into an anonymous allegation regarding two prominent members of the Commission of Soviet Control in Azerbaijan reported a chauffeur's comments that one of them had "made jokes about women in the presence of female colleagues."[27] Even members of the NKVD were not exempt from such peer-on-peer criticism. By 1941, for example, the Soviet Worker-Peasant Militia alone published approximately ten thousand wall newspapers critiquing workplace practices and employee behavior, based on "observations" handed in by amateur officer-correspondents.[28] Sentries in Nizhnii Novgorod reported to party investigators such things as a boss's sudden appearance in a new sheepskin coat; the wife of a low-level militia employee, hired to serve as a housekeeper for the regional chief of police, collected information about his guests and their dinner conversations.[29]

While the Russian Revolution had long been feared in the West for its abolition of private property, it was this aspect of control from below that Nazi leaders referred to with greatest opprobrium during the Great Terror years. In sharp contrast to Soviet agitation of the 1930s, Nazi propaganda, including that put out by ostensibly pro-labor organizations such as Strength through Joy (*Kraft durch Freude*) and Beauty of Work (*Schönheit der Arbeit*), presented both workplace and family hierarchies as organic and consensual.[30] Studies of denunciation show that the German secret police rarely investigated denunciations filed by those lower down on the social scale against their higher-ups or allowed grassroots political activity, however demonstratively pro-Nazi, to impinge on preexisting power relations, except as regarded the removal of Jews from public and professional life.[31] (This was itself an initiative that, while in practice a radical departure from the status quo, came to be presented to the public as a measure of conservation and continuity, one allegedly necessary for the preservation of Aryan values.) Above all, leaders of all major Reich institutions, including the Nazi Party, displayed a tremendous degree of solidarity in resisting periodic efforts by a handful of "hothead idealists" inside the Security Service (SD) to encourage subordinates to inform on the possibly corrupt actions of their superiors. "I forbid once and for all this kind of snooping . . . We are not living in the Soviet Union that we must be shadowed by the NKVD," barked a Nazi regional leader, infuriated by attempts on the part of one investigator to interview a charwoman who mopped up after party meetings.[32]

National Socialist leaders were equally careful not to let even the most ardent pro-Nazi convictions damage kinship ties. To this end, denunciation of family members, even over key political issues, was discouraged in the press, and such cases rarely came to trial. During World War II, the Reich Minister of Justice went so far as to emphasize that "the state does not demand breaches in the marriage trust as a matter of routine" and that the German "National Community" had a "fundamentally greater interest" in preserving filial relations than in investigating any and every suspected crime.[33] Even members of the militarized Schutzstaffel (SS) corps, compelled in theory to adhere to a virulently strict set of racialized marriage laws, experienced a degree of autonomy in their personal lives. For although at least 93 percent of SS marriage applications from 1932–1940 failed to satisfy all race specifications, less than 1 percent were rejected.[34]

These examples highlight certain extraordinary distinctions between Nazi and Soviet domestic politics during the late 1930s. In contrast to the firmly hierarchical, self-professedly "authoritarian" style of National Socialist rule, the Stalinist Terror involved a profoundly destabilizing attempt by Soviet leaders to weed out latent "bourgeois" sympathies and bureaucratic self-interest within their own ranks by overturning established power relations and pitting subordinates against superiors, wives against husbands, children against parents. While German authorities did solicit information from the public regarding activities of Jews and communists, they also deplored what they described as "excessive" informant activity and discarded, by some accounts, more than 90 percent of citizen tips they received; even Hitler urged greater community solidarity, raging in 1933 that "we are living at present in a sea of denunciations and human meanness."[35] Stalin, however, took a far different approach. In 1937 he exhorted citizens to submit any and all allegations of wrongdoing, with the comment: "It would be a bad thing if no one complained. Don't be afraid of quarrelling . . . This is better than friendship at the government's expense."[36]

Friends and Cadres: Behind the Scenes

While communist theorists had always stressed the obligation of party and Komsomol members to intervene in the private life of their peers in order to correct allegedly delinquent or antisocial behavior, after 1934 state and party organizations introduced a number of new measures regarding practices of personnel selection and evaluation, with the intention of scanning even apparently "healthy" conduct for signs of possible hidden decadence. Such an endeavor involved, on the one hand, a series of organizational reforms inside the Soviet bureaucracy, designed to enable officials to keep better track of party members' whereabouts and of the changes in their records over time. Developments in this regard included such things as the repeated verification of party documents (as well as the introduction of identification cards with photographs and Soviet-wide standardized membership cataloguing procedures), and improved communication among party and police personnel departments in different regions (primarily as a result of the evolution of special, NKVD-controlled courier, telephone, and printing services).[37] On the other hand, the aspiration to "know one's cadres" even outside their official capacities inspired new tactics of police surveillance, including the increased solicitation of denunciation, along with the expansion of preexisting informant networks at factories and apartment buildings.[38]

A job search for specialists to work in the Kremlin's secret library of banned Western publications, conducted after a sweeping purge of Kremlin service personnel in 1935, points out the lengths to which those in charge of restaffing even clerical positions went to assess political reliability. Spies were assigned to shadow applicants, collecting details of marital relations, home furnishings, manners, and dress. After describing one candidate as "poorly qualified," her evaluator recommended she nevertheless be hired, based on the fact that "in her home life she has proven to be a woman of reserve, not inclined to close friendships, and is the same at her place of work." Also to her credit was the fact that, although her husband was an alcoholic, she had managed for years to keep him quiet when he was drunk.[39] Another young student was less fortunate. The illegitimate daughter of a woman who worked on a collective farm and whose father was, her handler wrote in seeming sarcasm, "allegedly unknown," the girl was rejected because she appeared too "refined in her dress" and demonstrated "great curiosity" in her Institute classes. In addition, she played a grand piano (which, investigators noted, she "for some reason does not keep in her apartment but with her relatives") and socialized with actors. "Judging from external signs (upbringing, habits, her manner of relating to those around her), it is difficult to believe that Turina is really of proletarian origin," her review read.[40]

This type of obsessive focus by the regime on the private life of its many servitors was accompanied by a tremendous fear of friendship and intimacy, and a desire to find out, in interrogations, even such things as "With whom do you ride home on the metro after work?"[41] For, as much as the Stalinist state aspired to uproot corrupt "family circles," it also to some degree idealized them, in terms of presuming that those who had voluntarily socialized or slept with people later exposed as counterrevolutionaries could not but have known of their "true" identities. Inevitably, perhaps, the practices of the Terror were grounded in the very bourgeois beliefs they were designed to combat, for the premise behind such an assiduous tracing of personal ties was that "private" relationships, however casual, were always more genuine than official ones.

As a result of this paradoxical overvaluation of the personal, while communists were held responsible for the conduct of all those whom they had ever recommended for party membership or promotion, they were sullied even more by the arrests of others with whom they had at any time voluntarily associated. While professional ties could be justified as "obligatory," personal ones could only be explained in terms of individual choice and private sympathy. Thus employees across the Soviet Union, acting in the name of collective security (and undoubtedly anxious to demonstrate their own ability to place political duties over personal attachments), helped investigators trace who among their peers had attended whose birthday celebration or child's christening to a level of specificity almost incomprehensible to outsiders today. As arrests began to spread inside the Commission of Soviet Control in April 1937, employees called upon one Moscow boss to confess how he had, on occasion, hosted people subsequently revealed to be enemies in his home. Stressing his long record of dedicated party service, the speaker explained, amid audience heckling:

> I was not able in all situations and in relation to all people to display such sharp political vigilance that I was able to divine the enemy . . . Wreckers, Trotskyists, Zinovievites, and others in their methods of counterrevolutionary warfare employed the tactics of forming ties of personal acquaintance among a wide circle of party people, in order to . . . create a protected position for themselves. I had a very large group of acquaintances, and I associated in a number of cases with a number of people now exposed as enemies of the party, enemies of the country. With several of them I committed in my acquaintance that degree of slovenliness [*neriashlivost'*], which is unacceptable for us—namely, separate personal meetings.[42]

When the head of the CSC, Nikolai Antipov, was arrested several months later, two employees wrote to his replacement to denounce a third who they claimed had had an affair with their former leader. This accusation appears to have been immediately pursued inside the agency, and after several days the woman in question handed in her own account of her longstanding attachment to Antipov, testifying that she had never been romantically involved with him but had known him since 1915, when the two had engaged in underground revolutionary agitation in the same factory. She concluded simply, "I always considered Antipov to be one of the best Bolsheviks, and I always trusted him. Now, when he turns out to have been in the camp of the enemies, I consider it my obligation to inform you of my acquaintance with him, and ask you to decide the issue of my further work in the CSC."[43]

Inside agencies like the Soviet Control Commission, arrests would be followed by workplace party hearings, which frequently aimed at forcing certain colleagues to admit to having concealed the "true" degree of intimacy they had shared with individuals the NKVD had concluded were traitors. After the Nizhnii Novgorod militia chief was taken into custody in January of 1938, for example, the police party cell conducted a number of inquiries into the precise nature of the chief's ties with his senior officers, aimed at determining whether or not they had all been close friends. "Is it true that you got so drunk at his dacha that you went swimming with your gun on?" members of the militia rank-and-file demanded of the former head of Special Inspection. These accusations of sociability were vehemently denied, down to a level of what scholars today might consider split hairs. "I stopped by his house only in my official capacity," the chief's former deputy insisted. "We drank tea, not vodka, and played chess, not cards." "I never liked him," maintained another. "He . . . always used to laugh at me."[44] Only the former militia party secretary, faced with an overwhelming amount of testimony as to his friendship with the chief, their many years of joint service, and their frequent social contact, dared to argue that "playing cards is not a political crime." Nevertheless, when subsequently asked why he had suffered a seizure at the moment of his boss's arrest, the former secretary insisted that his attack had occurred not as a result of his personal sympathy for the chief (or out of fear for his own future, as the chief's long-standing confidante), but only because he was a "chronically sick" man.[45] In the language of the Terror, displays of physical weakness could be overlooked, while those of emotional susceptibility could not.

As these examples suggest, the more the Terror began to permeate the most exclusive spheres of the party/state, the more it assumed the form of a family drama. This quality was exacerbated by the highly personalized aspect of the upper-level Soviet bureaucracy. Communist Party organizations during the 1920s and 1930s in many ways resembled an ascending, interlocking set of royal courts—in which everybody at one level knew everybody else, and where political careers depended on marriage, patronage, and intrigue. Moscow and most regional capitals were filled with Bolshevik clans and "power couples," in which husband and wife each held top positions in different institutions; more importantly, leading families lived in the same apartment buildings, sent their children to the same schools, attended the same parties, dated and dallied in the same circles. In the words of journalist Simon Sebag Montefiore, members of the Soviet elite "were an incestuous family, a web of long friendships and enduring hatreds, shared love affairs, Siberian exiles and Civil War exploits."[46] Thus one prominent person's exposure as a spy could implicate scores of others, all by virtue of "small family" ties. Even the brief indexes of files collected inside the Commission of Soviet Control attest to both the intimate way the Terror spread and the great personal tragedy that could result:

> 4.5.37—Declaration of controller Cherniak about the arrest of his sister Sagaidak. 5.5.37—Attachment sent to NKVD Agranov with the declaration of E. I. Cherniak. 15.8.37—Second declaration of E. I. Cherniak about the arrest of his second sister—Todorskaia. 22.8.37—Attachment sent to the GUGB NKVD comrade Litvin with the declaration of E. Cherniak. 31.8.3 —Note . . . about relieving Cherniak from work in the Commission of Soviet Control.[47]

During the height of the Terror, workers in the NKVD, procuracy, and various control commissions were required to inform their superiors of a family member's arrest, even those of distant cousins and in-laws. As in the case of friendships, the nature of their family ties to the presumed traitors would subsequently be evaluated in workplace party meetings, and hearing transcripts demonstrate the extent to which many relatives scrambled, at least in public, to disassociate themselves from their tainted kin. In one typical case, at a single meeting of the police party cell in Nizhnii on January 20, 1938, three NKVD officers stood up to condemn brothers jailed for counterrevolutionary activity. One brother had, on his own initiative, turned his sibling in; the other two lived far away from their relatives and had rarely exchanged letters. In one case, an officer claimed that he had had no idea his brother had been taken into custody until his sister-in-law, after borrowing money for a train ticket from the Crimea, had arrived on his doorstep to beg for assistance—at which point, he swore to his fellows, he had shooed her away, proclaiming that he "would offer no aid to wives of enemies of the people." Despite the men's repudiations of their brotherly attachments, all were summarily expelled from the party. The officer with relatives in the Crimea was condemned for a "display of pity" unbefitting a communist, and the one who had denounced his own sibling was accused of a suspicious lack of vigilance, for only in 1937 "suddenly remembering" treasonous comments made almost a decade prior. His explanation, that in general he and his brother "had only talked about family affairs, about our mother who has been bedridden for a year," was itself viewed as an admission of political laxity.[48] Such examples demonstrate the extent to which private life came to be viewed by Bolshevik leaders as the arena in which communists faced the greatest challenges to their political purity; in addition, they show the opportunities for manipulation and difficulties of self-defense that accompanied this official interrogation of intimacy and so fueled the scope of Terror violence.

Kremlin Values: Sentiment as Suspect

At the highest Kremlin and commissariat levels, the subordination of personal interests to state allegiances was embedded in the organization of time, space, and work—elements which were themselves shaped by the priorities of Stalin. The dictator typically rose late but remained at his desk until the early hours of the morning; as a result, armies of bureaucrats labored even longer, routinely working until five or six A.M.[49] The Politburo met after midnight, and according to the recollections of Stalin's daughter, when leaders finally left their Kremlin offices, the general secretary typically invited members of his inner coterie to his dacha, to attend raucous, all-male banquets, filled with vodka drinking, farting contests, and crude practical jokes that lasted through whatever remained of the night.[50] Frequently, too, the dictator employed far more overt means to attenuate his subordinates' ties of family and friendship, playing long-time colleagues against one another and sanctioning the arrest of their closest relatives. These included the wife of his chief private secretary, Aleksandr Poskrebyshev (for her alleged ties to Trotsky, as the sister of his daughter-in-law) and the wife of the chairman of the Central Executive Committee of the USSR, Mikhail Kalinin (for her friendship with a woman who had had a brief affair with Trotsky from 1922 to 1923). In her memoirs, the daughter-in-law of General Voroshilov recounted that all top Bolsheviks felt vulnerable to accusations of lapsed political vigilance in their personal lives, and thus ever more driven to prove their loyalty to the regime:

> Everyone was afraid of everything then, every one of us had some family tragedy. Stalin and the NKVD made everyone feel guilty of something, regardless of their position in society. All of us had someone in prison. With the Voroshilovs it was my parents, with Kaganovich it was his brother, with Budyonny his wife. Everyone bore the stigma of jail—it was policy.[51]

In such a world, any official who appeared overly in love with a spouse or overly fond of time with family risked being viewed as politically "soft." Certainly, the prerogatives of Bolshevik "hardness" made it easier for some wives to rationalize their husbands' abuse or neglect. In her private diary, Iuliia Piatnitskaia, wife of the leader of the Communist International, recalls not only her husband's long nights at the office but also his studied indifference towards her at home as simply the consequence of his political dedication. Her spouse, she maintains, was very literally wedded to his job. Herself a fervent communist who labels numerous people "enemies" in her daily musings and urges her husband to denounce colleagues whose lifestyle she considers suspiciously luxurious, Piatnitskaia writes in an infuriated fashion about the sentimental indulgences of the only neighbor willing to receive her after her husband's arrest, a woman whom she terms the "bourgeois toad," A. G. Zelenskaia. ("She's utter trash, but nonetheless, whether out of curiosity or some other feeling, she's not afraid to speak to me . . . All her life she grabbed whatever she could, was always a bourgeois, and stayed one even inside the party.") According to Piatnitskaia's description, Zelenskaia—whose own husband was thrown into jail before hers—has wallowed in middle-class tastes so long that she mistakenly interprets the Piatnitskiis' relationship as a failed marriage, rather than recognizing it as the embodiment of a committed socialist lifestyle. Piatnitskaia grows especially indignant after one meeting when her neighbor remarks that "things are incomparably better for you, because you didn't have such close relations with [your spouse] . . . It's not so terrible [for you] in comparison to what I have endured and to what those wives endure who lived together well with their husbands."[52] Though Piatnitskaia earlier in her diary confesses to being disappointed by the fact that her husband is "eternally tired," routinely inhospitable, and prone to treating her with such "severity" that it "attracts everyone's attention," after his imprisonment she continually upholds these personal slights as signs of her husband's single-minded love for the Communist Party, traits that make it all the more difficult for her to accept the logic of his arrest.[53]

Documents from the Novosibirsk regional State Security Administration reflect a similar valorization of professional toughness and emotional detachment. The language and symbolism of combat always permeated the NKVD, but the role of the political police as the country's most elite military organization (as well as its historic role as the "unsheathed sword" of revolution) was even more strongly emphasized under the leadership of Nikolai Ezhov, who shaved his head Civil War–style to receive the Order of Lenin in July 1937.[54] Regional NKVD files from this time evoke a shared police culture of weapons-bearing masculinity centered around alcohol consumption, violence, and ostentatious displays of coldness towards prisoners, where police units competed to make the most arrests and officers could be condemned by their peers for such things as allowing a convict a drink of water.[55] The predominantly all-male "brotherhoods" of local police forces and jailhouse staffs professed scorn for any kind of sentimentality, a quality associated with the sphere of personal feeling, and they incorporated this contempt into their secret rituals and jargon. In prisons, for instance, greenhorn recruits would be "invited to a wedding"—NKVD slang for participating in an execution—shortly after being hired, to give them the necessary "hardening."[56] The extent to which many officers accepted these standards can be seen in the case of the former head of the Suzdal penitentiary, assigned a severe reprimand in December of 1937 for suppression of criticism and loss of class vigilance. The warden denied all charges against him but those of familial indulgence, writing:

> My wife Maria Mikhailovna Tantsurina is the daughter of a worker in [a metal factory]; her sister is married there. After the death of their father and mother, the children were taken in by strangers, and my wife was raised by the cab driver Levakin who was dekulakized in 1930 and later reinstated. My wife occasionally answered his letters; I am guilty for that.[57]

The warden went on to justify his innocence with reference to his long record of unflinching severity, even towards his closest colleagues. He claimed that he had always acted as a "Stalinist gendarme," in accordance with his sense of himself as a true revolutionary, unmasking co-workers even in the years before people understood just how widespread counterrevolutionary conspiracies were. He had earned his party card, he concluded, "with my blood and with the weapons in my hands."

A Fractured Universe

Self-presentations such as those above raise the obvious question of belief, prompting outsiders to wonder whether convinced communists embraced the Terror as a glorious, sacred trust, or rather saw the period as a despised event imposed upon them from above. The latter view is the more traditional interpretation of individual agency inside a totalitarian regime and assumes that most Soviet citizens consciously manipulated available political labels in desperate attempts to save their own lives; the former, defended by historians such as Jochen Hellbeck, argues that many citizens displayed a "willing self-mobilization" in government endeavors, even in the exposure of enemies who used to be personal friends. As Hellbeck writes:

> Available diaries from the 1930s suggest . . . that individuals experienced a crisis of sorts when they observed on the pages of their own journals a discrepancy between their actual private thoughts and what they were expected to think as Soviet citizens. This experience of crisis stemmed from the conviction that in the Soviet context one's private and public self ideally were to form a single, integrated whole. And if this could not be achieved, private, personal concerns had to be subordinated to, or be repressed by, the public interest.[58]

As this essay has argued, party meeting transcripts, court cases, letters, and memoirs all highlight the mass participatory aspect of the Terror and point to widespread individual acceptance—whether willing or no—of the pressing need to "cleanse" the private sphere of any and all politically suspect attachments. But the effects of this acceptance were hardly as uniform as Hellbeck assumes, and in fact led many communists to experience tensions and doubts that they had never vocalized before. In the end, Bolsheviks' willingness to reconcile personal concerns with public interest did not restore a collective sense of what "Soviet" family life should mean, but rather triggered a number of tumultuous battles within the party elite over the issue of socialist values.

Ultimately, people displayed tremendous variety in the choices they made and the narratives they constructed to resolve personal-political conflicts. While brothers denounced brothers, as described above, other siblings defended one another, although their fates seem to be less well preserved in archival records.[59] Frequently they are only alluded to with peripheral sadness, as in one rehabilitation file where a petitioner briefly mentions his family's refusal to incriminate him during a show trial, and his brother's consequent arrest and execution.[60] Similarly, while many people expressed, even in relatively private sources such as secret memoirs, what reads as genuine revulsion towards relatives convicted of treason and shock at their disloyalty toward a regime whose judgments the writers themselves continued to embrace, other citizens seem to have responded relatively quickly to the events of the Terror with cynicism and self-interest. Iuliia Piatnitskaia, for instance, noted in her diary how, following her husband's arrest in July of 1937, her relatives immediately tried to move out of the Moscow apartment their extended family had shared, with her own mother allegedly commenting: "If everybody can't be saved, let at least those who can, save themselves."[61]

The shape of Terror violence, particularly the practice of tracing guilt through intimate ties, meant that no individual could feel perfectly aligned with the Soviet "great family" once his or her own "small family" had been touched by suspicion. Even those who had striven to cut themselves off from contaminated, class-alien family members prior to 1934 were frequently sucked back into a nest of biological relations that they had hoped to leave behind. Typical was the case of one communist expelled from the party in 1938 after his brother-in-law's imprisonment for alleged Trotskyite sympathies, despite the fact that the man had urged his sister to get a divorce for many years. "I thought that I had managed to get a long way away from the family," he stated at his expulsion hearing. "I thought I would be clean."[62]

However, by assuming the indelibility of small family loyalties, the Terror paradoxically worked to harden kinship networks, rather than to eliminate them. Unavoidably entangled in others' presumed guilt, relatives often had no choice but to engage, whether out of political conviction or personal self-interest, in frantic processes of counter-denunciation, protest, and appeal, in hopes of reintegrating with the socialist system by peeling the black mark off their family's name and affixing it to someone else's.

Wives and mothers appear to have played a leading role in these struggles to reintegrate the personal and the political spheres. Numerous memoirs recount the crowds of women who gathered around Moscow's prisons and legal offices, championing the causes of loved ones and fashioning informal networks to exchange addresses and information. The former secretary of Sergo Ordzhonikidze wrote to Stalin in 1937 to denounce Ordzhonikidze's widow for her participation in such circles: "She's often telephoned by the wives of traitors to our party. These wives turn to her with requests (to give to Comrade Ezhov). It's not right, and she must be told not to do it."[63] In 1988, Gennadii Terekhov, one of the leading members of the central procuracy under both Stalin and Nikita Khrushchev, remembered the vast numbers of protests that women sent to the USSR Procuracy during the height of the Terror:

> I saw them, read them, these complaints of wives, mothers, sisters of "enemies of the people." Such submissions accumulated by the tons in the basements of the Procuracy . . . The letters made a stunning impression on me of the grandeur of Soviet women, they turned the soul inside out, they are impossible to read without tears . . . There is all the pain, all the pride, all the very best that lies in a Soviet citizen and patriot.[64]

However, such examples should not suggest that women were any less involved in Great Terror "self-mobilization" efforts than were men, or imply that they defended home and hearth in the face of repression while men embraced state-sanctioned violence. On the contrary, together with challenging those accusations they considered unfounded, many women during the Terror period did not hesitate to level charges against other people that they argued were well deserved. In the Nizhnii region, women appear to have played such an energetic role in Terror denunciation drives that in 1939 a party investigator complained of efforts on the part of male party members to retaliate against them for their past actions.[65] For all his romantic praise of Soviet womanhood, an official such as Terekhov did not, even retrospectively, cast women's determination to save their families as strictly a matter of sentiment; instead, he also associated their actions with patriotism and political activism.

Regardless of what individual women petitioners may have really felt, they consistently presented themselves to authorities as wronged true believers, much like Anna Kulikova in the movie *The Party Card*—determined to prove the innocence of one unjustly convicted by exposing the undiscovered guilt of another. As one wife wrote to USSR Procurator Andrei Vyshinskii in December, 1938, in urging him to free her husband and to punish those responsible for his allegedly wrongful incarceration: "I am hereby fulfilling not only a debt of personal interest in saving my husband, but also the obligation of every honest Soviet citizen in preserving the economic power of our native land by combating enemies of the people and exposing them, and in achieving honesty and justice among the leaders at the highest levels of the Soviet state."[66] Such petitions carefully endorsed the processes of popular control and police repression at large, categorizing the problems they noted as exceptional mistakes relating only to their own particular cases.

Thus, far from generating unity, mass mobilization in the micropolitics of terror produced tremendous fragmentation inside the Soviet state and its control apparatus. In attempting to show their solidarity with the Communist Party, petitioners, appellants, whistleblowers, slanderers, informants, prosecutors, and defenders alike (to the extent that their roles and various genres of exposure could, in the Soviet context, even be distinguished from one another) generated numerous alternative, often mutually exclusive "Bolshevik visions," which they all defended in the name of "true socialism" and cast as compatible with Terror priorities rather than in opposition to them. Such fragmentation was further exacerbated by shifts in rhetoric from Moscow. As time went on, central leaders began to warn not only of hidden enemies and those communists who hesitated to denounce them, but also of party members who unfairly slandered colleagues in order to conceal their own crimes and those "silent" and "politically spineless" people who failed to speak out in defense of the innocent.[67] As political vocabulary grew more circular, so, too, did the perceived obligations of party members. They were expected to denounce, but not to denounce incorrectly; they were urged to identify traitors, but also to show "vigilance against false vigilance," by condemning those who wrongly accused others of treason. Without a secure standard of politically correct or personally safe behavior, even the "truest" Bolsheviks were left perpetually unsure of how best to signal their allegiance to the Soviet regime, uncertain whether to accept accusations or reject them, whether to denounce or to defend their peers.

This increasing lack of political and moral clarity in the exercise of violence produced dramatic changes in individual behavior over time. For example, a family Piatnitskaia bitterly condemned in her diary for shunning her following the arrest of her husband ultimately sheltered her younger son one year later, when he escaped from NKVD guards after his mother's own incarceration—prompting him to insert an apologetic footnote of gratitude into her memoir upon its publication.[68] Furthermore, such changes in attitude were not confined to those actions and whispered conversations that took place behind closed apartment doors. On the contrary, they can be traced inside institutions such as the NKVD as well.

While one cannot make assumptions about the innermost thoughts of police employees based on the way they expressed themselves on the job given the fact that they operated in an environment of secrecy and constraint, one can certainly note shifts in collective language and behavior, even over the brief period from 1937 to 1939. In 1937, regional units of the political police displayed elaborate enthusiasm in public for their efforts to uproot counter-revolutionaries. In his recollections, one former NKVD officer from Novosibirsk described his fellow officers as approaching a hysterical "state of ecstasy" upon being informed in 1937 that Ezhov had awarded them second place in the country for their successful routing of the "enemy underground."[69] By 1939, however, such exhibitions of elation had stopped, and in places like Nizhnii Novgorod, state security workers openly characterized the atmosphere inside their organization as one of pervasive apathy, exhaustion, and, above all, mistrust. At several party meetings to discuss "distortions" in police work, local NKVD units raised angry questions about the prevalence of slander, the use of torture in eliciting confession, and the practice of paying outside "witnesses" to testify to fictitious crimes. One militia officer who had been tortured, convicted, then eventually freed and even returned to a job on the force testified in April 1939 to the arbitrariness with which his case had been resolved and the corruption that could underlie the practice of repression in general. He described how he had been initially charged according to articles 58-7, 58-8, and 58-11,

> articles reserved for the most infernal enemy, which means that I was at once a wrecker, a terrorist, and a member of a counterrevolutionary organization. Later I was tried [for negligence] and given five years. I arrived in the [gulag] camp. My wife paid 1300 rubles here to a public defender, and I was released.[70]

In a similar shift, documents show that although in 1937–1938 NKVD officials frequently cited their successful record of unmasking their own colleagues as evidence of their rock-solid political loyalty, by 1939–1940 they generally avoided mention of past denunciation activity, as the cachet associated with dramatic demonstrations of vigilance had faded. In early 1938, the deposed deputy police chief of Nizhnii Novgorod, facing party expulsion, recounted with manifest pride his single-handed exposure of ten traitors on the regional force and concluded, "It is difficult for me, as an honest Bolshevik, to endure, when I am accused of connections [to enemies]—at any moment I would give my life for the Party."[71] But by the spring of 1939, members of the Nizhnii militia began to condemn such examples of peer-on-peer denunciation and to describe them in terms of intrigue and betrayal. They especially excoriated their new chief for having allowed so many of his subordinates to be carted off to special prisons over the past year without having raised a hand to investigate the veracity of the allegations against them. As one officer raged:

> They arrested one of his deputies, you and I know about that. When one of the deputies is arrested, especially someone with whom you have a relationship, in my opinion people must be alarmed and take an interest in the situation . . . If [our chief] had at that time ever approached the matter seriously or felt responsibility for the cases, had ever considered that they dealt with real live people, at his disposal were newspapers, couriers, telegraphs, pencils, papers, railroads, it would have been possible to bring the issue to the attention of the center.[72]

Bolshevik courage—still centered around the idea of those below daring, at personal risk, to speak out against wrongdoing committed by those above—thus came to refer to efforts fully opposite from those that had initially influenced the course of Terror violence. Instead of urging "true communists" to abandon personal ties, officers prompted their colleagues not to forget them and cast their neglect as anti-Bolshevik. It was this lack of attention to "real live people" and small-family loyalties, Nizhnii officers claimed by June 1939, that had led to "the first general fact that is known to everyone . . . that from our organs were repressed the best people of our regional and county police administrations."[73]

Similar shifts in emphasis can be traced at the top party levels. When arrested in October 1938, Ekaterina Kalinina, the wife of the Soviet Central Executive Committee chairman, defended herself from allegations of treason by recounting to her interrogators how she had exposed her own brother as a tsarist police agent in 1924. Another suspected counterrevolutionary, Iurii Piatakov, offered to prove his dedication to Stalin by shooting anybody the dictator ordered, including his own wife.[74] However, by November 1939 standards had changed. Political prisoners sought to have their cases reopened by arguing that Soviet authorities should throw out testimony furnished by individuals who had proven themselves willing to incriminate even their closest relatives. One convict asserted that he had been found guilty of terrorist conspiracy based on the accusations of only one witness, whose account did not deserve to be taken seriously, because "this very same V. V. Keizer," he wrote, "similarly betrayed to the investigative organs his own two blood brothers, despite the fact that he had enjoyed with them, as with me, completely normal relations."[75]

Conclusion

The ending of the Terror coincided with a gradual braking of political violence. The second half of 1939 saw both a marked decrease in numbers of counterrevolutionary cases prosecuted and a reduction in the severity of sentences imposed. But such curbing of repression was accompanied by a number of additional, equally important phenomena. These included the enhanced supervision and standardization of the local press, new emphasis on the importance of "professional" rather than "amateur" control work, limitations on citizens' right of appeal (particularly against verdicts previously rendered by the NKVD), and efforts, supported by Moscow, to reconsolidate the power of local elites, especially by restricting the ability of subordinates to criticize their superiors and the opportunities for denunciations "from below" to be investigated by rival institutions.[76]

It was in this ending of Terror violence, rather than its continuation, that some people saw the greatest betrayal of Soviet values. For in reversing many of the prerogatives of popular control and cutting through what had become self-consuming cycles of accusation and counter-accusation, government leaders also appeared to abandon the idea that past mistakes in the application of repression could or should be corrected. At a discussion of the 18th Party Congress of March 1939 inside the Nizhnii police force, a majority of officers agitated for violence to continue, demanding a resolution condemning "incidences of lack of punishment regarding the slandering of honest and dedicated communists." However, the region's police chief (who was, shortly thereafter, to flee the city secretly, while himself under investigation for alleged Terror abuses) took a different tack, and one that would be adopted wholesale by authorities across the USSR in the months to come. Rather than backing calls for retribution, the chief repeatedly cautioned that "there is not a slanderer behind each [unfounded] expulsion of a communist from the party."[77]

Ultimately, most officials who survived the Terror proved willing, in the words of one, to "put a cross over the past" and embrace the regime's renewed emphasis on loyalty of cadre, professionalism, "cultured work," and the "honor of the uniform."[78] The result was the creation of a hierarchical society far more similar to that of 1930s Nazi Germany than had previously been the case, and one in which conventional liberal distinctions between private and political life grew more accepted. In this world of newly secure officialdom and re-stored top-down chains of command, women were encouraged to minimize their community activism and to return to a nuclear home ever more fre-quently described in apolitical, often patriarchal, terms of stability and com-fort. Their shifting role can be detected in the pages of the journal *Obshchest-vennitsa* (*The Socially Active Woman*), begun in 1936. Discontinued just before World War II, the magazine after 1939 began to urge so-called "house-keepers of socialism" to focus less on neighborhood control, and more on their husbands. The model of active Soviet womanhood became someone who, despite whatever outside responsibilities she might have, never gave her spouse "occasion to complain that his wife neglects the home . . . As before [she began her volunteer activities], she herself does all the housework without help. As before, when her husband comes home he finds a welcoming, atten-tive wife."[79]

This depoliticization of everyday life can be seen, as well, inside organiza-tions of Soviet control such as the NKVD. Explaining the "excesses" of the Terror in terms of an overreliance on volunteer informants and an abandon-ment of trained, science based "agent-informant work," police began to be-moan the fact that they had far too many housewives on their payrolls and far too few "professional" spies.[80] Beginning in 1940 and continuing after World War II, officers mocked the ubiquitous hiring of women whose sole "qualifica-tions" for NKVD collaboration were their excessively inquisitive natures and closeness to the banalities of daily life, and whose applications read only: "I spend a lot of time standing in lines and therefore could help ascertain those who speculate in bread."[81] Similarly, judicial officials in 1940 deplored the tendency of overly zealous citizens to give even the most innocuous of private altercations a political tone, noting:

> The courts continue to see [far too] many cases where accusations of hooli-ganism are leveled against housewives who have quarreled over the kitchen stove and where charges are filed as a result of a cross word, pronounced over the telephone, or a personal insult, or the inflicting of a blow during an argument, and so on.[82]

The willingness of Moscow leaders to accept bureaucratic privilege and to tolerate, even cultivate, a vast, acquisitive, and moderately corrupt cadre of mid-level officials at the expense of low-level community activism accelerated during the post-war years, amid efforts to restore central political authority and rebuild the ravaged state. This phenomenon—what Vera Dunham has de-scribed, in slightly different terms, as the "Big Deal"—stimulated a new set of far more materialistic and conservative social mores, particularly among the layer of bureaucrats Dunham labels a new Soviet "middle class."[83] This trend was not reversed upon Stalin's death; on the contrary, under Khrushchev, Soviet authorities turned, even more, to accepting the nuclear family and its position as a refuge or retreat from the outside world. As Susan Reid has noted, the new subject heading of "family and everyday life" appeared in the USSR's catalogue of books in print in 1954, as the regime initiated a string of projects designed to improve housing, provide workers with single-family, non-communal apartments, and otherwise address long pent-up consumer needs.[84] While the Khrushchev era did see attempts to repoliticize society, revitalize local party cells, and rejuvenate many of the forms of civic activism that had so proliferated during the Great Terror years, the impact of 1950s and '60s control from below remained carefully mediated from above, filtered through closed state institutions and entrenched bureaucratic elites. By the age of Leonid Brezhnev, the types of public involvement in private life so characteristic of the Terror years—so destabilizing at the time, and so capable of toppling established hierarchies of status, gender, and age—had shrunk to little more than a staple of sanctioned Soviet comedy, gently parodied by artists and writers through the 1970s. In the film *Moscow Does Not Believe in Tears* (1979), for example, a volunteer citizens' patrolman stops a teenage couple from holding hands on the street; in *Afoniia* (1975), a plumber is called before a "comrades' court" to be chastised for his drinking habits by his peers; in *Office Romance* (1977), a woman secretly smitten with a married man is confronted by a factory activist who begs her to abandon her dissipated ways or have her love letters "investigated" by the collective; and in *Autumn Marathon* (1979), a professor, assigned an urgent overnight translation, is told by his editor that it will be good for him to stay home one evening and work, rather than running across town between his wife and mistress. When the professor looks at him with astonishment, the editor simply shrugs his shoulders and remarks, "Leningrad—it's a small town."

In many ways, however, the Soviet regime, while it never succeeded in displacing the family, never fully managed to make peace with it, either. As even the comedies above suggest, throughout the post–World War II era, Soviet officials failed to resolve the question of the appropriate relationship between politics and personal life, or the place of an individual's right to happiness apart from state-assigned ambitions and collective endeavors. This ambivalence was poignantly captured in many discussions inside the bureaucracy during periodic efforts to rehabilitate those unjustly convicted of counterrevolutionary crimes. Under Khrushchev, regime authorities criticized certain of the political processes that had led to such massive repression during the Terror years; however, they never proved able to confront the personal tragedy these processes had caused, making no apologies even to those they acknowledged to have been wrongfully condemned. One woman whose husband had been imprisoned for ten years but rehabilitated in 1957 was denied her appeal to the General Procurator to be certified a "victim of repression" as late as 1995. She claimed that her own and her husband's youth "had been wasted in sorrow and persecution," but notes on her file were matter-of-fact. "No basis [for application] . . . [Husband] returned to family after release from place of imprisonment."[85]

Soviet leaders never resolved what value a state should place on a solitary fate sacrificed to politics. At the 22nd Party Congress in 1961, Khrushchev told his audience about feeling awkward one time, when he had been confronted in Kazakhstan by the son of the executed, subsequently rehabilitated, General Ion Iakir, "And what could I tell him?" the General Secretary rhetorically asked.[86] Throughout the course of its existence, the Soviet Communist Party never produced an adequate reply.

NOTES

I would like to thank Laura Engelstein, Christina Kiaer, and Eric Naiman for their thoughtful readings of this chapter. I am also grateful to the American Council for Collaboration in Education and Language Study (ACTR/ACCELS), the International Research and Exchanges Board (IREX), and the Social Science Research Council (SSRC) for supporting the research upon which this essay is based. All translations of original Russian archival materials cited herein are my own.

1. For a further explication of this film and the complications surrounding issues of purity within it, see Lilya Kaganovsky, "Visual Pleasure in Stalinist Cinema: Ivan Pyr'ev's *The Party Card*," in this volume.

2. Robert W. Thurston, "The Soviet Family during the Great Terror, 1935–1941," *Soviet Studies* 43:3 (1991), 557. Thurston argues, very convincingly, that the Terror years should *not* be seen strictly as a time in which Stalin manipulated the use of repression in order to atomize society and destroy all relationships besides that of the individual to the state. He claims instead that the nuclear family played an important role in Soviet propaganda throughout the period, writing that "the drive to bolster the image of the family continued in 1936 by identifying happy, traditional home life with new heroes and other leading figures. Well-known Stakhanovite workers tickled their sturdy children in magazine pictures while the loftiest achievers of the day, the pilots, rode in parades with theirs." However, in his zeal to move away from totalitarian theories of dictatorship, Thurston underemphasizes the dual aspect of the nuclear family during this time—the way that, particularly within the party elite, the family was both celebrated *and* constantly suspected.

3. Katerina Clark, The *Soviet Novel: History as Ritual*, 3rd ed. (Bloomington: Indiana University Press, 2000), 114–135. While Clark emphasizes the compatibility of the Soviet "small" and "great" families, at least on the level of propaganda, this paper argues that the demands of the latter came to displace those of the former during the late 1930s.

4. Clark, 116.

5. A. G. Tepliakov, "Personal i povsednevnost' Novosibirskogo UNKVD v 1936–1946," in *Minuvshee: Istoricheskii al'manakh* (Novosibirsk, 1997), 250.

6. "Pesnia o Pionere-Geroe," in *Pionerskii pesennik*, ed. I. Gorinstein (Moscow:

Molodaia gvardiia, 1938), 185–186. See also E. Smirnov, *Pavlik Morozov: V pomoshch' pionervozhatomu* (Moscow: Molodaia gvardiia, 1938).

7. See *Intimacy and Terror: Soviet Diaries of the 1930s*, ed. Veronique Garros, Natalia Korenevskaya, and Thomas Lahusen, trans. Carol Flath (New York: New Press, 1995).

8. Debates about Soviet morality—of what it should consist and how socialist ethics should differ from bourgeois values—are contained in the collections *Partiinaia etika: Diskussii 20-kh godov*, ed. A. A. Guseinova et al. (Moscow: Politizdat, 1989), and *Bolshevik Visions (Part One)*, ed. William Rosenberg, 2nd ed. (Ann Arbor: University of Michigan Press, 1990). See also N. Krylenko, "Sotsializm i sem'ia," *Bol'shevik* 18 (1936): 65–78. Soviet efforts both to emancipate and to regulate sexual activity are described in Eric Naiman, *Sex in Public: The Incarnation of Early Soviet Ideology* (Princeton: Princeton University Press, 1997). Different kinds of romantic relationships (and the disastrous consequences that accompany allegedly "non-Soviet" ones) are explored in numerous potboiler novels from the 1920s and early 1930s such as Lev Gumilevskii, *Sobachii pereulok* (Moscow, 1927).

9. One of the best discussions of socialist efforts to reshape everyday life (as well as of the tendency of state projects to generate unanticipated outcomes) is to be found in Stephen Kotkin, *Magnetic Mountain: Stalinism as a Civilization* (Berkeley: University of California Press, 1995). Other notable works that focus on questions of socialist *byt* include Frances Bernstein, "Envisioning Health in Revolutionary Russia: The Politics of Gender in Sexual-Enlightenment Posters of the 1920s," *Russian Review* 57 (1998): 191–217; Svetlana Boym, *Common Places: Mythologies of Everyday Life in Russia* (Cambridge, Mass.: Harvard University Press, 1994); Victor Buchli, *An Archaeology of Socialism* (Oxford: Berg Press, 1999); Christina Kiaer, "Delivered from Capitalism: Nostalgia, Alienation, and the Future of Reproduction in Tret'iakov's *I Want a Child*," in this volume.

10. Olga Matich, "Remaking the Bed: Utopia in Daily Life," in John E. Bowlt and Olga Matich, eds., *Laboratory of Dreams: The Russian Avant-garde and Cultural Experiment* (Stanford: Stanford University Press, 1996), 59–80.

11. Boris Groys, "The Birth of Socialist Realism from the Spirit of the Russian Avant-garde," in Bowlt and Matich, *Laboratory of Dreams*, 212.

12. Sheila Fitzpatrick, "Becoming Cultured: Socialist Realism and the Representation of Privilege and Taste," in *The Cultural Front: Power and Culture in Revolutionary Russia* (Ithaca: Cornell University Press, 1992), 218. A variant of this argument was first articulated by exiled Soviet leader Leon Trotsky, in *The Revolution Betrayed* (London: New Park Publications, 1967), first published in 1937. Trotsky in particular castigated what he called the Stalin-era "rehabilitation of the [bourgeois] family" and its hypocritical exaltation as "the sacred nucleus of triumphant socialism" (151). His points regarding the emergence of a self-interested Soviet bureaucracy and accompanying shift in Soviet values were elaborated by Nicholas Timasheff, in *The Great Retreat: The Growth and Decline of Communism in Russia* (New York, 1946).

13. Lewis Siegelbaum, *Stakhanovism and the Politics of Productivity in the USSR, 1935–1941* (Cambridge: Cambridge University Press, 1988), 226, 233, and "The All-Union Conference of the Wives of Managers, Engineers, and Technicians in Heavy Industry: Address by Comrade E. M. Vesnik," in *Changing Attitudes in Soviet Russia: The Family in the USSR*, ed. Rudolf Schlesinger (London: Routledge, 1949), 240.

14. Thurston, "The Soviet Family during the Great Terror," 559.

15. In referring to "public" and "private" life here, I mean essentially "political"

and "nonpolitical." Bolsheviks rejected such a distinction, arguing that the idea of any kind of "nonpolitical" realm was a fiction unique to bourgeois culture. In contrast, the Bolsheviks strove, as Oleg Kharkhordin has noted, to use the "public" to keep "private" life under collective surveillance and to expose "private" behavior to public evaluation. In "Reveal and Dissimulate: A Genealogy of Private Life in Soviet Russia," in *Public and Private in Thought and Practice*, ed. Jeff Weintraub and Krishan Kumar (Chicago: University of Chicago Press, 1994), 343. The Bolshevik proposition that *all* forms of life are inherently political means that historians of the Soviet 1920s and 1930s cannot speak of the "private" sphere, as it exists in liberal society. Nevertheless, after 1917 communist leaders constantly debated the type of relationship that should exist between macro political entities (the "state" or the "body politic" at large) and micro political contexts (the realm of everyday life, and the sphere of intimate, personalized association). In this essay, I refer to the former primarily as "the public" and to the latter as the "personal" or "familial" ("private," in the sense of voluntary, and thus distinct from one's professional/public/state obligations).

16. V. Krylenko, ed., *Sud i prokuratura v bor'be s biurokratizmom i volokitoi* (Moscow, 1929), 28.

17. *Materialy 3-ogo s"ezda sudebnykh, prokurorskikh, administrativnykh i sudebno-meditsinskikh rabotnikov Vladimirskoi gubernii 8–15.2.1929* (Vladimir, 1929), 33–35.

18. See, for example, an investigation by the Commission of Soviet Control into the apparent suppression of low-level employee activism by those in positions of authority in various commissariats in early 1937. Gosudarstvennyi arkhiv Rossiiskoi Federatsii (GARF), f. 7511, op. 10, d. 30, ll. 1–48.

19. Gosudarstvennyi obshchestvenno-politicheskii arkhiv Nizhegorodskoi oblasti (GOPAN), f. 5, op. 1, d. 1009, l. 23. The letter justified its request in terms of a Politburo decree ordering local party cells to stimulate criticism from below.

20. One example was an extraordinarily popular play from 1936 entitled "The Confrontation," which portrayed an encounter between an NKVD official and an undercover Nazi, exposed by the voluntary tips delivered to the police by more than a dozen citizens. In the final scene the Nazi spews racist propaganda, predicting that the Russian people will soon be cleared from their land to make way for "a more competent and more cultured race of men." However, the Chekist counters that the Germans will never succeed in their plans of conquest, owing to the willingness of each and every member of the Soviet population to take part in the hunt for and extermination of fascist spies and saboteurs. In John Scott, *Behind the Urals: An American Worker in Russia's City of Steel*, ed. Stephen Kotkin (Bloomington: Indiana University Press, 1989). See also A. Vyshinskii, "Agenty Gestapo," *Bol'shevik* 18 (1936): 21–38, and M. Erkoli, "God bor'by za antifashistskii narodnyi front," *Bol'shevik* 21 (1936): 17–25.

21. Rossiiskii gosudarstvennyi arkhiv sotsialno-politicheskoi istorii (RGASPI), f. 17, op. 120, d. 323, l. 6. This specific incident was condemned by Moscow as early as March of 1938 and the secretary of the party cell was himself expelled and "exposed as a careerist" in consequence.

22. See Fitzpatrick, "Becoming Cultured," and Vadim Volkov, "The Concept of Kul'turnost': Notes on the Stalinist Civilizing Process," in *Stalinism: New Directions*, ed. Sheila Fitzpatrick (London: Routledge, 2000), 210–230. Volkov's essay on Soviet attempts to "civilize everyday life" includes several intriguing details about the role of social mobilization in this process. For example, when the magazine *Ogonek* began

to publish a weekly "pop quiz" on culture in 1936, readers were encouraged not only to find out the answers themselves but also to test their friends and colleagues (224).

23. My interpretation of the *obshchesvennitsy* movement differs slightly from that of Sheila Fitzpatrick as presented in *The Cultural Front*. Fitzpatrick takes these organizations of "civic-minded women" as indications of the growing importance of "becoming cultured" in Soviet society during the 1930s, reflecting an increasingly conservative shift in socialist values. I believe that while the behavioral standards these groups defended were, indeed, self-professedly "cultured" ones, the extent of their allowed intervention in everyday life and their wide prerogatives in criticizing and judging community affairs, at least until mid-1939, suggest they should be seen not merely as a conservative force, but also as a new form of revolutionary grassroots activism. Some of the more interventionist activities of women's committees during the late 1930s are described in Buchli, *An Archaeology of Socialism* 81–83.

24. Peter Konecny, "Library Hooligans and Others: Law, Order, and Student Culture in Leningrad," *Journal of Social History* 30:1 (1996): 108–109, 123, 125. Like J. Arch Getty, in *Origins of the Great Purges: The Soviet Communist Party Reconsidered, 1933–1938* (Cambridge: Cambridge University Press, 1985), Konecny notes a fascinating combination of both increased activism and increased repression during the 1930s. However, again like Getty, he treats the two phenomena as fundamentally opposite and their combination as paradoxical. In his article, Konecny interprets student activism as inherently heroic and in defiance of standard regime values, writing: "Despite the fearful political environment in the 1930s, students continued to act aggressively in their attempts to motivate sluggish bureaucrats or challenge unjust decisions" (112). I argue, in contrast, that such activism was ubiquitous during the Terror years, contributing to repression rather than standing in courageous opposition to it.

25. Kaganovsky, "Visual Pleasure in Stalinist Cinema," in this volume.

26. For a full discussion of the extensive forms of community policing and popular control encouraged by authorities both during the First Five-Year Plan and the Great Terror years, see Cynthia Hooper, "Terror from Within: Participation and Coercion in Soviet Power, 1924–1964" (Ph.D. diss., Princeton University, 2003).

27. GARF, f. 7511, op. 10, d. 481, l. 1.

28. GARF, f. 9415, op. 3, d. 383, l. 41.

29. GOPAN, f. 817, op. 1, d. 64, l. 53, 82. It is important to note different degrees of voluntarism and coercion in these various types of political control. Some rank-and-file informant activity was spontaneous, while some was carefully organized by higher-ups or by political rivals of those placed under informant scrutiny. While some (such as spying for the political police) could be solicited through either payment or blackmail, a tremendous number of denunciations during the late 1930s appear to have been submitted voluntarily, or as a result of less explicit types of pressures and inducements. In 1937, for instance, the Novosibirsk political police grew so overloaded with incriminating submissions from the public that the regional NKVD chief ordered secretaries and archivists to lead investigations, and chauffeurs fielded from twelve to fifteen denunciations a day. In Tepliakov, "Personal i povsednevnost' Novosibirskogo UNKVD," 256.

30. Anson Rabinbach, "The Aesthetics of Production in the Third Reich," *Journal of Contemporary History* 11:4 (1976): 43–74; Robert Ley, *Deutschland ist schoener geworden* (Berlin, 1936).

31. Robert Gellately, *The Gestapo and German Society: Enforcing Racial Policy 1933–1945* (Oxford: Clarendon Press, 1990), 139, 148–150.

32. Lawrence Stokes, "Otto Ohlendorf, the Sicherheitsdienst and Public Opinion in Nazi Germany," in *Police Forces in History*, ed. George Mosse (London: Sage Publications, 1975), 252.

33. Gellately, *The Gestapo and German Society*, 149.

34. Furthermore, those few SS members whose petitions were rejected but who nevertheless insisted on marrying unsanctioned partners could simply resign, without risking courts-martial or treason charges. In *Nazism 1919–1945: A Documentary Reader*, vol. 2, ed. J. Noakes and G. Pridham (Exeter: University of Exeter Press, 1984), 494.

35. Gellately, *The Gestapo and German Society*, 139, and *Der Prozess gegen die Hauptkriegsverbrecher vor dem internationalen Militaererichtshof*, vol. 20 (1949), 128.

36. Simon Sebag Montefiore, *Stalin: The Court of the Red Tsar* (London: Weidenfeld and Nicolson, 2003), 220.

37. See, for example, E. A. Andreevich, "Structure and Functions of the Soviet Secret Police," in *The Soviet Secret Police*, ed. Simon Wolin and Robert M. Slusser (New York: Published for the Research Program on the U.S.S.R., by F. A. Praeger, 1957), 125, and Mikhail Voslenskii, *Nomenklatura: Gospodstvuiushchii klass Sovetskogo Soiuza* (London: Overseas Publications Interchange, 1984): 310, 312.

38. Instrumental in this regard was the abolition of the Worker-Peasant Inspectorate (Rabkrin) in 1934, and the appropriation of many of its popular control functions in the workplace by so-called Special Departments set up inside factories and administrative offices but under the exclusive jurisdiction of the political police. These departments decoded and stored secret correspondence, oversaw personnel selection and promotion, and cultivated extensive internal networks of spies. By one estimate, as many as 1.7 million workers and bureaucrats were employed in Special Departments by 1940, more than two-thirds of whom were covert operatives holding regular day jobs in their respective enterprises. In Niels Rosenfeldt, *Stalin's Special Departments: A Comparative Analysis of Key Sources* (Copenhagen: C. A. Reitzels Forlag, 1989), 25.

39. RGASPI, f. 17, op. 120, d. 241, l. 102–106.

40. RGASPI, f. 17, op. 120, d. 186, l. 106. This focus on lifestyle did not originate in the late 1930s, but also played a role in previous years. For example, in 1932 the director of a jail in the Nizhnii Novgorod region was indicted for abuse of power after witnesses testified that he had created a "family circle" network of deputies and reliable subordinates composed exclusively of kulaks, people deprived of electoral rights, and class enemies, who "frequently gather for little tea parties at [the director's] apartment, play the piano, and so on." In GOPAN, f. 5, op. 1, d. 1005, l. 241.

41. RGASPI, f. 119, op. 7, d. 13, l. 3.

42. GARF, f. 7511, op. 10, d. 27, l. 14.

43. GARF, f. 7511, op. 10, d. 516, l. 13.

44. GOPAN, f. 817, op. 1, d. 64, l. 18–20, 80–89.

45. GOPAN, f. 817, op. 1, d. 64, l. 89.

46. Montefiore, *Stalin*, 11. As Merle Fainsod first concluded from his study of the Smolensk archives, personalized power networks replicated themselves in each particular local setting, down to the level of individual factories and collective farms. See *Smolensk under Soviet Rule*, rev. ed. (Boston: Unwin Hyman, 1989), 85–86. James Harris offers a similar discussion of local cliques and their collusion in keeping certain

kinds of information from reaching central authorities in *The Great Urals: Regionalism and the Evolution of the Soviet System* (Ithaca: Cornell University Press, 1999). Memoirs suggest that institutions such as the political police and procuracy functioned in a similarly tight-knit, personalized fashion. As described in the writings of NKVD officer Mikhail Shreider, Moscow leaders made a point of rotating upper-level cadres from location to location every few years. As a result, Shreider claimed, intimate ties (both positive and negative) formed between officers scattered at great distances from one another who had over the course of their careers at some point "served together." Mikhail Shreider, *NKVD iznutri: Zapiski chekista* (Moscow: Vozrashchenie, 1995), 38.

47. GARF, f. 7511, op. 10, d. 516, l. 7.

48. GOPAN, f. 617, op. 1, d. 64, l. 10–15.

49. Valentin Berezhkov, *At Stalin's Side: His Interpreter's Memoirs from the October Revolution to the Fall of the Dictator's Empire*, trans. Sergei Mikheyev (New York: Birch Lane Press, 1994), 154.

50. Svetlana Alliluyeva, *Only One Year*, trans. Paul Chavchavadze (New York: Harper and Row, 1965), 383–386.

51. Quotation cited in Larisa Nikolaevna Vasilieva, *Kremlevskie zheny: fakty, vospominaniia, dokumenty, slukhi, legendy i vzgliad avtora* (Moscow: Vagrius, 1992), 157. Viacheslav Molotov's wife was also arrested, but after World War II in 1949.

52. *Golgofa: Po materialam arkhivno-sledstvennogo dela #603 na Sokolova-Piatnitskaia Iu. I.*, ed. V. I. Piatnitskii (St. Petersburg: Palitra, 1993), 37.

53. Piatnitskii, 37, 38, 62.

54. Getty, 119, 183.

55. RGASPI, f. 119, op. 7, d. 108, l. 7. This file contains the case of a supervisor in the Tobol'sk jail who in February 1938 was given a "categorical warning" for thawing snow for a prisoner to drink while standing guard at a punishment isolation cell. An account of the various departments within the NKVD of Kyrgyzia competing over the number of counterrevolutionary arrests can be found in *Izvestiia TsK KPSS* 5 (1989): 74–75. In 1938 in Nizhnii Novgorod, officers inside the NKVD began to accuse one another of having vied to present the most cases to the regional troika, claiming that "in that way many innocent people were condemned." In GOPAN, f. 817, op. 1, d. 65, l. 46. Finally, it is unclear how this ethos of tough masculinity inside the security organs relates to the propaganda of clean-cut *kul'turnost'* common during the late 1930s. Certainly files detailing the daily life of the Nizhnii Novgorod police force also suggest giant differences in the way cultured office life was conceived in theory and the way it manifested itself in practice. Guidelines for administrative office space in 1935 Nizhnii Novgorod sound tremendously sober and disciplined. "On the walls of the rooms may be hung clocks, calendars, portraits in frames and under glass, maps . . . of specifically necessary content, which should be fastened to an oak plank by a string and hung on a single nail" (in GOPAN, f. 284, op. 2, d. 7, l. 108). At the same time, in 1940 police officers were rebuked for such things as catching rats in their office and suffocating them, and for having lost keys to two building entrances so that "we observe every morning how, before bystanders, the commandant takes a hammer or mallet or simply a big stick, and breaks open one or the other door" (in GOPAN, f. 817, op. 1, d. 69, l. 72).

56. Tepliakov, "Personal i povsednevnost' Novosibirskogo UNKVD," 243.

57. RGASPI, f. 119, op. 7, d. 6, l. 3.

58. Jochen Hellbeck, "Speaking Out: Languages of Affirmation and Dissent in

Stalinist Russia," *Kritika: Explorations in Russian and Eurasian History* 1:1 (Winter 2000): 90.

59. O. V. Khlevniuk includes some moving examples of loyalty within families where relatives had been accused of counterrevolution in *1937-i: Stalin, NKVD i sovetskoe obshchestvo* (Moscow, 1992), 184–189. One typical case was that of a woman who was expelled from the party in 1937 for criticizing the work of the NKVD following the arrest of her husband, three sons, sister, and daughter-in-law.

60. GARF, f. 8131, op. 31, d. 18052, l. 1–99.

61. Piatnitskii, 30–31.

62. Sheila Fitzpatrick, *Everyday Stalinism: Ordinary Life in Extraordinary Times—Soviet Russia in the 1930s* (New York: Oxford University Press, 1999), 205.

63. Montefiore, *Stalin*, 220.

64. The comments of Gennadii Afanas'evich Terekhov are reported in Anatolii Golovkov, "Vechnyi isk," *Ogenek* 18 (April 1988), 28.

65. The vociferous participation of women in self-criticism sessions is noted in numerous newspaper articles, such as "Chistka partorganizatsii 1-i fabriki vyzvala ogromnuiu aktivnost' rabochikh," *Stalinets* 211 (12 September 1934), which lauded the "unprecedented activism" of female workers. In several party organizations in the Gor'kii region women had apparently spearheaded criticism of authority figures during the Great Terror years, even traveling to Moscow to file complaints with the Central Committee. In GOPAN, f. 284, op. 6, d. 13, l. 36–37.

66. GARF, f. 8131, op. 31, d. 10, l. 107.

67. In April of 1938, for instance, Stalin approved a circular sent out to all USSR party officials, demanding that every party cell make a special effort to identify both slanderers and the "silent" and "politically spineless" people who had enabled these slanderers to wrongfully condemn loyal Bolsheviks. As Lev Mekhlis, the head of the Political Department of the Red Army, recounted retrospectively at the 18th Party Congress in March of 1939, this pronouncement prompted mass meetings throughout the armed forces condemning arrests from previous years. Mekhlis claimed that half of those who had been expelled from the party in 1936–1937 were reinstated; however, the tumultuous reinstatement process seems to have contributed to a second substantial purge of army military and political leadership that took place in mid-1938. Iu. P. Pctrov, *Partiinoe stroitel'stvo v sovetskoi armii i flote, 1918–1961* (Moscow, 1964), 301.

68. Piatnitskii, 14. In the introduction to his mother's diary, Piatnitskaia's youngest son notes that after his father and brother were arrested, he and his mother were exiled. While in exile, he fell ill and was operated on; during his recovery, his mother was taken into custody and their apartment was sealed. The twelve-year-old boy, unable to walk, was left in a bed in a hallway of the communal apartment and placed under daily NKVD surveillance. Somehow, he managed to escape from the apartment and make his way back to Moscow, where the family in question, whose father was one of Stalin's secretaries, sheltered him as an NKVD fugitive in their apartment for three months.

69. Tepliakov, "Personal i povsednevnost' Novosibirskogo UNKVD," 254. A similar elation was expressed among Nizhnii Novgorod UGB members during 1937, following a visit from NKVD chief Nikolai Ezhov himself—who, as the oblast's elected delegate to the Supreme Soviet, arrived in the city of Gorky to congratulate voters, praise the work of the region's security forces, and call for even greater levels of collective vigilance in a series of triumphalist mass meetings. In *Ocherki istorii Gor'kovskoi organizatsii KPSS*, vol. 2 (Volgo-Viatskoe: Knizhnoe izdatel'stvo Gor'kii, 1966), 390.

70. GOPAN, f. 817, op. 1, d. 67, l. 100.

71. GOPAN, f. 817, op. 1, d. 65, l. 59.

72. GOPAN, f. 817, op. 1, d. 67, l. 68.

73. GOPAN, f. 817, op. 1, d. 67, l. 86.

74. Vasilieva, 77, 121.

75. GARF, f. 8131, op. 31, d. 4, l. 9.

76. This argument takes issue with that of Peter Solomon, who in *Soviet Criminal Justice under Stalin* (Cambridge: Cambridge University Press, 1996) claims that the end of the Great Terror was marked by a "return to legality" denoting the enhanced power of the Soviet procuracy in comparison to the NKVD. My work, in contrast, proposes that protests and appeals to party and judicial organs—particularly high from 1936 through the early months of 1939—were an integral part of the Terror process. Restoring stability and limiting violence coincided with a dramatic rollback in the processing of appeals and discussion of past mistakes. In 1939–1940 the NKVD issued a series of decrees making it increasingly difficult for the procuracy to reverse past decisions made by NKVD troikas and military tribunals; the impotence of the Soviet judiciary in this regard is demonstrated in rehabilitation files such as GARF, f. 8131, op. 31, d. 3209, where procurators in 1939–1940 twice voted to overturn a prisoner's conviction for spying and the NKVD twice refused to allow the convict's release. See Tsentr khraneniia sovremennoi dokumentatsii (TsKhSD), f. 89, op. 73, d. 6, l. 1 for an example of NKVD orders restricting the consideration of appeals.

77. GOPAN, f. 817, op. 1, d. 67, l. 8.

78. GOPAN, f. 817, op. 1, d. 69, l. 22.

79. *Obshchestvennitsa* 6 (1939): 46 and 9 (1939): 25–26. Cited in Fitzpatrick, *The Cultural Front*, 33. Such language contrasts with the political rhetoric of earlier years, when a *Pravda* article from 10 May 1936 urged women to take action outside the home and lauded "the large proportion of women in our country who do not want to be mere housewives if they can be wives of the country." Reprinted in Schlesinger, *Changing Attitudes in Soviet Russia*, 236.

80. "Ob arestakh, prokurorskom nadzore i vedenii sledstviia," RGASPI private collection (17.11.38), 1; Prikaz NKVD "O poriadke osushchestvleniia postanovleniia SNK SSSR i TsK VKP(b) ot 17 noiabria 1938 goda," RGASPI private collection (26.11.38), 1.

81. GARF, f. 9415, op. 5, d. 87, l. 47.

82. GARF, f. 9474, op. 16, d. 175, l. 14.

83. Vera Dunham, *In Stalin's Time: Middleclass Values in Soviet Fiction* (Durham: Duke University Press, 1990). Dunham's work differs significantly from that of Trotsky, Timasheff, and Fitzpatrick by locating its version of the Soviet Union's "great retreat" primarily in the post–World War II period.

84. Susan Reid, "Cold War in the Kitchen: Gender and the De-Stalinization of Consumer Taste in the Soviet Union under Khrushchev," *Slavic Review* 61:2 (Summer 2002): 216, 245. See also her "Introduction" in *Journal of Design History* 10:2 (1997): 112.

85. GARF, f. 8131, op. 31, d. 18121, l. 46–53.

86. "Zakliuchitel'noe slovo Pervogo sekretaria TsK KPSS tovarishcha N. S. Khrushcheva, zasedanie dvadtsatoe (27 oktiabria 1961)," *XXII s"ezd kommunisticheskoi partii sovetskogo soiuza, 17–31 oktiabria 1961 goda*, vol. 2 (1962), 586.

four
Fear on Stage

*Afinogenov, Stanislavsky, and
the Making of Stalinist Theater*

Boris Wolfson

Klavdia Antipina preserved only two messages that arrived from her husband,
Mikhail Rabinovich, in January 1937. One of them, a postcard, pleaded with
Antipina not to send any more food packages until she received explicit confirmation from Rabinovich that the previous package had reached him in Ukht-
pechlag, one of the largest labor camps in the Russian North. The other
message was an eight-page letter that began by asking Antipina whether she
remembered attending Yurii Zavadskii's production of George Bernard Shaw's
The Devil's Disciple. Now, some three years later, the play was on Rabinovich's
mind as he tried to articulate the change he had begun to sense, from afar, in
his relationship with his wife:

> Do you recall the sudden transformation, the rebirth, of the play's two
> principal characters? Our correspondence reminds me of that transforma-
> tion. Yes, we've swapped our roles. You write to me so often, your letters are
> so long and so interesting. And what has happened to me? I write rarely and
> with difficulty; my letters are dull. [. . .] You have to agree, my darling, that
> my analogy with *The Devil's Disciple* is fairly apt. And not only with regard
> to our correspondence, that is, the display of our feelings for one another,
> but also with regard to those feelings themselves.[1]

As Rabinovich struggled to clarify the terms of the analogy, however, the more precise object of his reference emerged. He was writing not about Shaw's text but about the shared experience of witnessing the fictional characters' transformation on stage. The connection, so palpable in the letter, between the tasks of reconstructing the theatrical encounter and attempting to take stock of a relationship defamiliarized by the Terror, is never made explicit. The evening at the Zavadskii Studio is marked as a private moment within a public spectacle. To Rabinovich, it is an event remarkable both for the immediacy of the transformation embodied in performance and for the inherent detachment from the onstage action afforded by the safety of a spectator's position. But how can the counterpoint between Rabinovich's two letters help us comprehend his attempt to write the theatrical as the intimate? How does the Stalinist context illuminate for us the experience of the Soviet spectator and how is it, in turn, illuminated by that experience?

Several scholars have justly drawn upon theater as a fruitful metaphor for understanding Stalinist culture. Yet, as Julie Cassiday has argued, the value of the theatrical metaphor is diminished unless we take into account the particular ways in which theater itself was conceived and practiced in the early Soviet period.[2] I want to suggest that the relationship between the experience of 1930s everyday spectators and the "theatricalized" history in which they took part cannot be understood without considering how Soviet theater reflected and shaped its audience. To that end, my case study examines the specific choices made by the many authors of a theatrical production: the playwright, the directors, the designers, and the actors. I explore the measures taken by them to "legitimate a certain kind of experience for the audience as significant" at various steps in the process of turning a script into a stage spectacle.[3] The interpretive activity of Soviet spectators, as part of their intimate everyday experience, was framed by meanings manufactured in performance. Together, the strategies for producing these meanings can be said to constitute the rhetoric of Stalinist theater—a crucial component of the larger cultural mechanism for embodying the ideological contradictions of the era.

A recent study has persuasively argued that dramatic works of the early 1930s relied heavily on the conventions of classical melodrama, and that this theatrical sensibility was of a piece with the political outlook of Stalinist purges.[4] In that sense, the widely publicized "debates" and "discussions" about the future of Soviet drama among groups of playwrights vying for political and esthetic authority in writers' organizations old and new were largely beside the point. Vsevolod Vishnevskii's quasi-epic *An Optimistic Tragedy* (*Optimisticheskaia tragediia*, 1932–1934) and Vladimir Kirshon's topical, naturalistic *Bread* (*Khleb*, 1931) dramatized a strikingly similar set of concerns about the relationship between the waverer, the false community, and the virtuous community. Those concerns, in turn, would be enacted not only on the Soviet stage but in the courtroom of the show trials.[5] Like many of the most illuminating inquiries into the relationship between theater and society in the 1930s, the argument about the centrality of melodrama approaches Soviet drama as a collection of written texts. It sidesteps the key question of how the plays it analyzes were embodied on stage, how they were made legible to the Soviet spectators. The very effort to unmask Stalinist stage and courtroom spectacles as subspecies of melodrama should, in fact, acknowledge the disparity between the ways in which these narratives were scripted and the manner in which they were produced. The shows of the 1930s were not perceived as melodramas, in part because they were not staged according to the conventions of the melodramatic performance style (such as broad, one-dimensional portrayals of characters and exaggerated emotional coloring of conflicts), which were increasingly viewed as suspect. The ideological ambiguities of the Stalinist spectacle, as it was experienced by the spectators, resided not only in the structure of the script but in the meanings generated by the interplay of text and performance—the stuff of theater proper. The importance of extratextual meanings was vividly illustrated for the theater audiences of the time by the contemporaneous reinterpretations of the classics, from revivals of Gogol's comedies to stage adaptations of Tolstoy's novels. At issue in producing new Soviet plays was the development of a viable method for balancing the ideological import of written lines and staged actions.

To take stock of the ways in which the tension between dramatic (textual) structure and theatrical practice informed the rhetoric of Stalinist spectacle, I examine the making of Aleksandr Afinogenov's *Fear* (*Strakh*, 1931).[6] *Fear* was one of the great theatrical success stories of the early 1930s: by 1934 it had been staged, according to one account, by three hundred ninety theaters all across the Soviet Union.[7] The play's author, Afinogenov (1904–1941), had made a stunning career as a playwright and a literary functionary. At twenty-five he had seen his first major hit, *The Eccentric* (*Chudak*, 1929), produced by the Second Moscow Art Theater. The success of that production made Afinogenov a celebrity overnight. In 1931, when *Fear*, his next play, went into rehearsal, Afinogenov sat on the governing board of virtually every major playwrights' and writers' organization, and edited the most influential Soviet theater magazine.[8] *Fear* built on the success of *The Eccentric* by turning once again to the central issues of the day: the challenges of constructing the new Soviet society, dealing with the legacy of the past, and mobilizing for the next major phase of class struggle. But the choice to explicitly engage the topic of fear, and to structure his dramatic examination of vital social issues around that single emotion, was an important new move on Afinogenov's part. Moreover, the importance of the play was underlined when it was announced that the Moscow premiere of *Fear* would take place at the First Moscow Art Theater (MAT), the company which at the time was rising to its position as the central institution of Soviet theatrical life.

The MAT, the theater of Konstantin Stanislavsky, has been persistently associated with a specific interpretive mode—stage realism.[9] The "system," or "method," of realistic acting, which is often given Stanislavsky's name, has been institutionalized as *the* basic technique of stage and film actor training on both sides of the Atlantic. In part because "realistic" acting is so ubiquitous, its artistic agenda seems transparent: to manufacture lifelike characters who behave in ways that the spectators find believable.[10] A realistic performance does, of course, lay a claim to verisimilitude of setting and authenticity of feeling. Yet in order to achieve those goals, in order to create a convincing scenic illusion of not being blatantly "theatrical," stage realism focuses on creating uniquely theatrical, extratextual ways of making the dialogue and the action seem natural. Stanislavsky theorized and reshaped the distinctive relationship between action and word that is inherently part of any theatrical event. In his vision for realistic theater, intonation, pause, gesture, gait, and other nonverbal means are used to manufacture the illusion of authenticity by working to justify the actions of dramatic characters. In realistic performance, as it was understood by Stanislavsky, the overarching task of creating a coherent and complex character is translated into a series of mini-objectives: to make a character's motivation in a particular scene legible, the actor has to identify and play each line's "subtext."[11] The idea of subtext deftly blends contradictory interpretive impulses. Ostensibly, the point is to reveal the meaning already contained within the text, to make that meaning more palpable. In practice, however, subtext is a tool that allows directors and actors to infuse new meanings into the script and to add entire nonverbal narratives that are lacking in the written text. Subtext usually achieves the effects of realistic performance—actions that appear psychologically complex and authentically low-key—by seeming to violate or contradict the spoken language. Osip Mandelstam was referring to this subversive potential of Stanislavskian stage realism when he famously described the Art Theater's credo as "mistrust for the word."[12]

At the MAT, the fundamentally modernist impetus to cultivate nonverbal meanings, to resist the text even as it was being explicated, was established as a central tenet of realistic performance. Developed and put to the test in the productions of Chekhov and early Gorky, it could be, and was, applied to very different kinds of drama, including melodrama. Repeatedly attacked throughout the 1920s as esthetically conservative and philosophically retrograde, the Stanislavsky system and the Art Theater were rising to state-sanctioned prominence again by the early 1930s. While it was not as patently revolutionary as the avant-garde stage experiments of the first postrevolutionary decade, Stanislavsky's realistic theater was deeply invested in cultivating the tension between the written word and physical action. If one of the key projects of the 1930s spectacles was to homogenize and limit the range of the interpretive responses available to the Soviet audience, realism as championed by MAT was a curious vehicle for accomplishing that goal. With the change in its status, the Art Theater faced the challenge of translating stage realism's techniques of mistrusting the dramatic word into strategies for staging the "new Soviet reality" thematized in the plays of contemporary authors. From that perspective, the choice of Afinogenov's play for the MAT stage was especially significant: as one of the officers of the militant Russian Association of Proletarian Writers (RAPP), Afinogenov had led the attacks on the theater.[13]

Fear was one of the MAT's crucial opportunities to demonstrate its mastery of the realistic stage and its ability to produce a model Soviet spectacle—ideologically sound, esthetically exemplary. And, not unlike the MAT's greatest triumph of the era, the 1937 production of *Anna Karenina*, *Fear* was "an affair of state." Stalin and other Politburo members attended, taking the time to personally compliment the playwright and the directors. Gorky was spotted at one performance of the play weeping.[14] But *Fear* is also an artifact of the everyday experience of those thousands of spectators who saw it throughout the 1930s and whose theatrical experience it defined. Afinogenov's direct acknowledgment of the relevance of fear from the stage came at a time when more and more people in the play's audience were, or were soon to be, afraid. One of the earliest reviews of Afinogenov's play at the MAT opened with a revealing anecdote:

> A conversation overheard in the theater: "So how do you like it?"—"How do I like it? You can say whatever you want about the Art Theater's production before the show and after the show. But during the show you find yourself entirely in the power of a marvelous spectacle."[15]

To be "in the power" of a Stalinist spectacle: how did the rhetoric of Soviet theater make that experience possible? In the case of *Fear*, was part of the "power" derived from overtly pointing to the importance of fear itself? Were the spectators' emotions engaged by placing an emotion center stage, as it were? And how did the use of emotion as a central trope affect the meanings created in performance?

These questions provide the impetus for my reading of *Fear* as play and spectacle. I first consider the tensions in the dramatic structure of Afinogenov's script, which claims to be "about" an emotion but is chiefly concerned with issues of intentions and added meanings. I argue that science, politics, and visual art provide the metaphors for the play's fundamentally meta-theatrical interest in the anxiety of interpretation. I then examine the strategies for embodying *Fear* at the Moscow Art Theater, and the ideological fault lines explored by that production. The MAT staging tackled the conflicting imperatives of fostering and controlling the ambiguities set up in the script and amplified by the techniques of stage realism. What follows, then, is a story about the hazards of manufacturing meaning and harnessing emotion in Stalinist culture.

Afinogenov's Play: Anxieties of Legibility

Fear chronicles a few months in the life of Professor Ivan Il'ich Borodin, an internationally renowned scientist and the leading researcher at the fictional Institute of Physiological Stimuli. Borodin's familiar world is disintegrating right before his eyes. The professor's favorite student, German Kastal'skii, is denied promotion and is not allowed to attend a conference in Berlin; Borodin's friends and colleagues are being purged from their jobs and arrested; the key positions at the institute are being taken over by the boorish *vydvizhentsy* (upwardly mobile former workers or peasants, the beneficiaries of Soviet "affirmative action" policies), represented by Borodin's newly appointed assistant Elena Makarova and graduate student Khusain Kimbaev, a recent arrival from a Central Asian village. The professor is not fundamentally opposed to the Soviet system, and is especially grateful for the financial support his research has received since the revolution. But he prefers to stay away from politics and concentrate his efforts on testing the hypothesis that all behavior is governed by four unconditioned stimuli: love, hunger, anger, and fear. Makarova, on the other hand, believes that politics has the power to remake human beings and insists that Borodin is moving too slowly. Arguing that science can uncover the way to eliminating petty, obsolete feelings such as jealousy, malice, and fear, she demands that the institute open a laboratory that directly studies human behavior instead of merely describing the involuntary reflexes of rabbits. Infuriated by what he perceives as a concerted attack on his scholarly and personal authority, Borodin consents to a plan of action devised by his protégé Kastal'skii, which aims to turn Makarova's proposal against her. On Kastal'skii's advice, the professor pledges his support for a laboratory of human behavior. Secretly, however, Borodin and his student intend to use the resources of the new lab for a large-scale study that would incontrovertibly demonstrate the fundamental flaws of "the Soviet system of people management."

This devious plan immediately hits a snag. Borodin's son-in-law and assistant, the soft-spoken Professor Bobrov, takes exception to Kastal'skii's attempt to undermine the *vydvizhentsy*, and attempts to warn Makarova that Professor Borodin's support for her proposal is a trap. The demands of "family ethics," however, prevent Bobrov from disclosing the details of his father-in-law's plan, and his vague warning fails to convince Makarova. It is only when Makarova's husband, another graduate student at the institute, becomes infatuated with Professor Borodin's daughter Valia (Bobrov's wife) that the earnest Bolshevik Makarova begins to view Borodin's interest in her project as suspect. Valia soon leaves Bobrov for Makarova's husband, and since Bobrov no longer considers himself constrained by a familial allegiance to Borodin, he attempts to expose the old professor's designs together with Makarova and the peasant Kimbaev. At first their efforts backfire. Makarova's ex-husband, now a Borodin ally, ensures that Makarova is transferred to a distant province, and Kastal'skii uses the recent arrest of Bobrov's former mentor to raise questions about Bobrov's own trustworthiness. But Bobrov and Makarova do not give up: Makarova submits an article condemning Borodin's methods to a scholarly journal.

To forestall the attack, Borodin decides to announce the preliminary conclusions of his study before Makarova's article comes out, at a public lecture to which he invites the foreign press. Borodin's findings vindicate his behavioristic theory. Eighty percent of the Soviet population, he announces during the lecture, is animated by the same impulse: fear.

> The milkmaid is afraid that her cow will be confiscated; the peasant is afraid of compulsory collectivization; the Soviet worker is afraid of the endless purges; the Party worker is afraid that he will be accused of deviating from the Party line; the scholar is afraid that he will be accused of idealism; the technical worker is afraid that he will be accused of sabotage. We live in a time of great fear. Fear compels talented members of the intelligentsia to renounce their mothers, to falsify their social origin, to wiggle their way into high positions . . . Oh yes . . . The fear of being exposed is not so great when you're in a high place. Fear stalks everyone. People become suspicious, aloof, dishonest, sloppy and unprincipled . . . The rabbit who has seen a boa constrictor is unable to move from the spot. His muscles petrify. He waits, submissively, until the rings of the boa constrictor squeeze him and crush him. All of us are rabbits (451/229–230).[16]

The other twenty percent of the population, according to Borodin, are the *vydvizhentsy*, people who should ostensibly be afraid of nothing, since the country now belongs to them. Yet they, too, are victims of fear—a debilitating anxiety that they may never "catch up to and overcome" those who are smarter and better educated than they are.

The first and only response to Borodin's speech is delivered by Klara Spasova, an Old Bolshevik who represents the large factory which has offered to take up the ideological supervision (*shefstvo*) over Borodin's institute. Klara uses the story of her own son, brutally put to death by the Tsarist regime, to make the point that true revolutionaries have always been, and remain, fearless. According to Klara, fear is the curse of those who have been defeated and those who continue to bear ill will toward the Soviet authorities. In Klara's world, in other words, there is no such thing as being needlessly afraid: fear, rather than any material marker, becomes a sign of ideological inadequacy (in the play's first published version, Klara went even further, insisting that the current level of fear experienced by the class enemy was insufficient and had to be multiplied tenfold).[17]

Shortly after the lecture Borodin is arrested and taken to the OGPU offices, where he is confronted by his closest colleagues and protégés. One after another they accuse Borodin of harboring virulently anti-Soviet sentiments and actively conspiring to undermine the authorities. The professor tries to plead with them, but to no avail: even Kastal'skii, who has been arrested while trying to leave the country, blames his mentor for seducing him with a dangerous theory designed to justify a counterrevolutionary movement. After Kastal'skii leaves, the female OGPU investigator offers Borodin an opportunity to defend himself and his theory. Visibly shocked by his friends' disloyalty, the professor is at a loss for words.

In the play's final scene Makarova returns from the provinces to assume directorship of the institute, and is welcomed by Bobrov and Kimbaev, who have assumed the leadership of the institute's party cell. We discover that in the aftermath of Borodin's lecture Makarova's ex-husband has been fired from the laboratory for supporting Borodin and has been expelled from the party for concealing his true (bourgeois) social origins. Disillusioned in him, Borodin's daugher Valia now wants out of the relationship. As she laments her situation and blames her father for destroying her life, Borodin enters. It is not clear if he actually spent any time in prison,[18] but he is defeated, aged. He has come to give Makarova the keys to his former office. When she offers him a job at the institute, however, he accepts the position and vows to work together with the Bolshevik scholars—Makarova, Bobrov, and Kimbaev.

Read for its plot, *Fear* can serve as a "brief course" in thematic and generic concerns of Stalinist drama. The story of Borodin's calamities recapitulates key elements of the intelligentsia conversion narrative cultivated in the late 1920s. At the same time, by staging the predicament of a protagonist who has been led to the brink of disaster by treacherous friends but is able to overcome the temptation and ultimately joins the virtuous community, Afinogenov's play justifies the consistently melodramatic structure of the period's landmark plays.[19] That structure could be used to account for what is likely to strike today's reader as the most unexpected aspect of the play: the explicit manner in which it engages the topic of fear itself. Borodin's eloquent portrayal of the Soviet society as a community of the terrorized and the spitefully insecure does not easily agree with common assumptions about the prevailing (cheerfully confident) tenor of official discourse at the time. Throughout the first three acts, and especially in his long monologue during the confrontation with Klara the Old Bolshevik, *Fear*'s protagonist voices grievances that clearly overstep the bounds of acceptable criticism for remarks written to be delivered from the Soviet Union's most prominent stages. Borodin's claim about the pervasiveness of fear seems compelling and therefore particularly volatile, because, unlike his student Kastal'skii, the old professor is not fundamentally opposed to the Soviet regime and so is not an entirely unsympathetic character. By broaching the topic of omnipresent fear so directly and credibly, does the play not risk provoking a kind of generalized panic among its spectators? Not really, the argument would go. Melodrama courts hysteria. The dramatic stakes have to be driven as high as possible for the overall conceit of "spectacular reversal" to work. Borodin's conversion cannot have the desired effect on the audience unless his arguments are taken seriously before he is shown to have erred; in turn, the conversion (theoretically) renders harmless his social critique, no matter how articulate and persuasive it may seem, by showing how profoundly Borodin has erred and implying that his rhetoric itself is hysterical.[20]

One of the reasons the script of *Fear* appears to sustain a melodramatic reading is that, together with Kirshon's *Bread* and Konstantin Trenev's *Liubov' Iarovaia* (1926), to name just two of its most successful forerunners, Afinoge-

nov's play sanctions stock devices like the love triangle and the conflict between familial and social responsibilities (feeling and duty) as the basic building blocks of a well-made Soviet play. Yet even as Afinogenov employs—most
memorably in Klara's rebuttal to Borodin's lecture—the vintage blend of Bolshevik severity and Victorian sentimentality developed by his predecessors, his
dialogue points to a tension between the conventions of (melo)dramatic writing that he appropriates and the theatrical sensibility (stage realism) that he
cultivates in order to sustain the play's central ideological dynamic.

In *Fear*, the preoccupation with the legibility of motivations is articulated
on several levels, and the anxiety of interpretation provoked by the devices of
stage realism helps to foreground the connection between the different forms
taken by that concern with motivations. On its most literal level it unfolds in
what can be described as the political realm. The ideological allegiances and
intentions of virtually every character in the play are constantly being questioned by the other characters. What is Borodin out to prove with his study?
What does Bobrov really have in mind when he offers his support to the old
professor's opponents, Makarova and Kimbaev? Why is Makarova's ex-husband protecting the professor? For a play that overtly claims fear as its central
theme, *Fear* incorporates surprisingly few situations in which its characters are
actually afraid. But when they are, their fear is linked to discovering the horrible truth about the insincerity of someone's motivations. In the most explicit
instance, ten-year-old Natasha, a loyal and vigilant Young Pioneer, overhears
her father admit to forging his documents in order to conceal his bourgeois
social origins from the party authorities. Seconds before the curtain falls to
mark the end of the second act, Natasha is alone on stage, "screaming with fear
[*ot strakha*]" (according to the stage direction): "Papa! Papa! Where are you
going?! You've deceived the working class!" (431/215). The capacity to provoke fear resides in those whose motivations are oblique and whose actions can
therefore be misinterpreted. The play's larger concern with making legible the
characters' motivations is linked repeatedly to a question of theatrical technique. The rhetorical posture of melodramatic performance requires that evil
speak evil, and that when evil lies, its lies should be instantly transparent to the
audience. But to say "no" and mean "maybe" or "yes" or "sometimes"—to
"play a subtext"—that is not really a melodramatic option; it is a trademark
gesture of the realistic stage.

This fear of hidden meaning functions on a more metaphorical level in
the play's portrayal of Professor Borodin's scientific work. The professor's scholarly interests, as the audience is repeatedly reminded, entail uncovering the
fundamental impulses that govern all human behavior. By establishing causal
connections between actions and stimuli, Borodin is essentially proposing a
generalized interpretation of the motivations animating the actions of his
fellow citizens. This interpretive move causes the greatest anxiety among Borodin's opponents. During one of the confrontations the earnest party member
Makarova accuses the professor of trying to fabricate evidence that would

support a theory about the primacy of physiological causes—"subtexts," as it were—of the Bolshevik revolution (anger) and the five-year plan (sexual activity and hunger) (434/217–218). At the same time, Afinogenov's play makes explicit its ambition to instruct the audience about the symbolic connotations of Borodin's scientific search for motivation. The plot of *Fear* literalizes the devices of didactic theater: its characters acquire/renounce new teachers/students with swiftness matched only by the frantic rate at which the play's various love triangles coalesce and collapse. Every plotline in the play hinges upon a student-mentor relationship, which can result in disaster (Borodin's betrayal by Kastal'skii) or a profound transformation, marked by a reversal of roles (by the end of the play, the peasant *vydvizhenets* Kimbaev is teaching the scholar Bobrov the ABCs of Marxist dialectics). The most important lessons given and learned have to do with the wider implications of Borodin's behavioristic theories.

Borodin's daughter Valia, an aspiring artist, attempts to apply her father's teachings in designing an entry for a sculpture competition. Instead of creating a statue of a single proletarian, she tries to capture the idea of collectivism as a sum of fundamental stimuli—rage, love, suffering, and victory. When she reveals the result, described in the stage directions as a "huge impressionistic mound of muscles, bodies, and faces," to a member of the competition jury, Valia is subjected to a stern lecture about the fallacy of trying to embody an abstract idea, and about the cardinal virtue of all great art—simplicity:

> Ever been out in the fields on a summer evening? Grass fresh as ever, clouds looking like they've just been washed, mist rising from the river, the earth still warm, time passing inaudibly. Everything's simple, right?—the birch trees, the meadow, the clearings in the forest, the rye . . . But this simplicity makes the thoughts and the feelings more pure, more profound. And that's exactly how it is here, too. (405/194)

The jury member who reveals the meaning of art to Valia is Klara Spasova, the Old Bolshevik from the factory. In the third act she will be the one to deliver the rebuttal to Borodin's lecture about the omnipresence of fear, bringing together the play's concerns with esthetics, science, and politics. Klara's version of the sublime anticipates some essential critical tenets of socialist realism: the glorification of transparency and a mistrust of formal experimentation. Valia's attempts to represent the underlying meaning (a kind of "subtext") of human behavior are, for Klara, as profoundly suspect as Professor Borodin's theories about the importance of universal stimuli.

At the end of the play Valia destroys the newest version of her sculpture, the version she has been trying to create in accordance with Klara's advice (464/240). Valia's failure to devise a fitting embodiment for a topical, complicated subject symbolically links the contradictions in *Fear*'s treatment of motivation, as an ideological and esthetic problem, to the question of how the play itself should be interpreted in performance. Within the world of the play, the urgency of revealing the true motivation of every character is underscored by the fear of not possessing sufficient information for distinguishing friends from enemies. Stage realism links sufficiency to complexity, to the tension between text and subtext. On the one hand the play insists on the complexity of human motivations; on the other it insists on the transparency of artistic representation. This contradiction—rich in esthetic, ideological and epistemological (even prosecutorial) implications—lies at the core of the theatrical method that manipulates the feelings and thoughts of the spectators by expressly seeking to capture on stage a picture of the world they will find authentic.

Fear's most unambiguously positive characters, Makarova and Klara, are suspicious of any attempts to discover a more general meaning of human behavior by ascribing physiological "subtexts" to it (whether those subtexts are revealed through laboratory research or encoded in a work of art). According to the ideal model of artistic production and reception outlined in Klara's conversation with Valia, good art induces moral clarity in its audience "simply" by creating an authentic representation of the spectators' experience capable of purifying (purging) their feelings. When that happens, a correct, unambiguous meaning becomes transparent on its own, precluding the need for theories or interpretations. At stake in the play is the need to keep the production of extratextual meanings in check while depending upon the invention of subtexts to create the illusion of multidimensionality and authenticity of stage action. Afinogenov's play simultaneously relies upon the rhetorical resources of stage realism and dramatizes a profound anxiety about the ambiguities that are inevitably produced in the practice of realistic theater. The burden of finding an effective theatrical solution for the interpretive problem posed by the script was taken up in *Fear*'s most famous stage version—the production at the Moscow Art Theater.

From Leningrad to Moscow: Devising "A Play of Steel"

By early October 1931 Konstantin Stanislavsky was getting nervous: *Fear*, which had originally been scheduled to premiere at the Moscow Art Theater the previous spring, was not yet ready to open, and the director worried that Afinogenov's play was "losing its edge."[21] The topicality of Afinogenov's work was transparent. The tribulations of fictional professors resonated with the still recent show trial of Professor Ramzin and seven other economists accused of masterminding a counterrevolutionary organization.[22] The figure of the famous physiologist Borodin, at the same time, echoed that other world-renowned authority on conditioned reflexes and unconditioned stimuli, Ivan Pavlov, whose publicly expressed skepticism about the Soviet worldview was well known.[23] Yet Stanislavsky's concerns about the timing of the Moscow production seem misplaced. The Leningrad State Academic Theater of Drama (the former Aleksandrinskii Theater) had already beaten the MAT to the punch when *Fear* opened there 31 May, and the Moscow premiere was not likely to fully reclaim the topical cachet instantly acquired by the Leningrad production. Instead, the stakes of the Art Theater's rivalry with the Aleksandrinskii were raised by a more explicitly theatrical dilemma. Even before the opening night in Leningrad, news of the disaster that very nearly befell the play spread throughout the theater community: one of the final rehearsals almost led to the banning of the production and the script. The fate of both was decided at a final dress rehearsal attended by Leningrad's highest-ranking party official, Sergei Kirov. Now that the Aleksandrinskii production was running, and Afinogenov's associates at RAPP were bombarding Stanislavsky with demands that the Moscow production of *Fear* open without any further delay,[24] the MAT faced the challenge of producing a version that not only avoided the pitfalls of the Leningrad production but offered a more convincing, more successful resolution to the problem of staging the play.[25]

At a public discussion of the Leningrad *Fear* in June 1931 the production's director, Nikolai Petrov (at the time also the artistic director of the Aleksandrinskii Theater), claimed that his ultimate goal in directing Afinogenov's play had been "to organize the audience by artistic means so that [the audience's] intentions were aimed in the direction we needed them to be in."[26] That, Petrov suggested, could be achieved only by "drawing the spectator into the experience of the stage [literally 'the situation of the scene,' *stsenicheskaia situatsiia*]" (OS 21). In the famous Act III scene when Klara the Old Bolshevik responds to Professor Borodin's critique of the Soviet way of life, the crucial argument could not, according to Petrov, be won by words alone. The task of convincing the audience had to be accomplished by specifically theatrical means. Petrov insisted that at the beginning of the play the full range of interpretive possibilities—"which character is right and which is left" (OS 18)—had to be left open for the spectators. Yet the director also sought to structure the production in a way that would ultimately ensure a single, unambiguous response from the audience to the central confrontation scene.

The tension in Petrov's directorial concept was recapitulated in the production's esthetic, which embraced the key precepts of theatrical realism and simultaneously called those principles into question. The performers, especially the venerable Aleksandrinskii actors Ekaterina Korchagina-Aleksandrovskaia (Klara) and Illarion Pevtsov (Borodin), were encouraged to strive for emotional immediacy and complexity of subtexts characteristic of realistic acting. At the same time, the "stage experience" of the Aleksandrinskii production (to use Petrov's term) was dominated by Nikolai Akimov's striking, controversial set design. Most of the action was set on a wide platform that sloped downward toward the audience at a steep angle; a panel suspended from above along the edge of the stage was lowered and raised to drastically alter the dimensions of the principal acting space at various points in the play. In scale and in detail, the set resisted one of the principal propositions advanced by realistic theater—that stage representation ought to have an indisputable claim to verisimilitude with the real experiences of the spectators and performers. The design prompted the actors to view what they had already accomplished with the help of the realistic technique as potentially inadequate.[27] One actress, self-consciously borrowing the play's key trope, even claimed that Akimov's set was the source of an intense creative fear for her (OS 68).

Yet the tension in the "scenic situation" devised by Petrov and Akimov ultimately ensured the production's success. The famously disastrous rehearsal at which the censorship board banned the production (after Korchagina-Aleksandrovskaia's performance as Klara fell flat and Professor Borodin appeared to have had the final word in the Act III debate) took place outside the walls of the Aleksandrinskii. The play was performed in its entirety, the actors were in costume, but Akimov's set was lacking. By contrast, the night Sergei Kirov watched *Fear* and pronounced the production perfectly acceptable, the play was performed on the newly completed set. The scenic design annoyed and exasperated the cast, but Korchagina's theatrical and ideological "victory" in the crucial debate was indisputable only when the stage action was framed and shaped by Akimov's set.[28] Petrov and Akimov's "stage experience" triumphed, remarkably, even as it cultivated the performers' awareness of the physical resistance offered by the set—the tangible resistance to the very techniques of realistic acting which had been so important in staging the play.

The audiences of the Leningrad *Fear* perceived the resulting "scenic situation" as signaling nothing less than a new kind of theatricality:

> It's interesting that it's not just the audience reacting to the performance—
> the performers are also not acting like they usually do. Don't you have a
> sense that *Fear* is being performed in a way no other show is? Are the actors
> just acting? Oh, no! They've performed a ton of different plays since the
> revolution, but try conducting psychological analysis of how they act in
> *Fear*. Words sound like actions. The ideological import of the production is
> so strong that no actor can possibly undermine it. The theater has turned
> this production into a play of steel. This play, like the original theory about
> conditioning reflexes, is something profound yet at the same time simple.
> No, no, we've never seen a play like this one before. Everybody says that—
> the audience, the theater professionals. (OS 46)

In the formulation of this audience member, the cast is credited with "not just acting," that is, not "just" creating a perfect illusion of verisimilitude (an impossible task in this case, considering the look of Akimov's set). A more sweeping transformation is purportedly at stake: the Aleksandrinskii cast is praised for collectively suiting the word to the action in a manner that irrevocably undercuts an individual actor's authority to introduce new meanings in performance. It is tempting to see the vision for a "production of steel [*stal'noi*]" unfolded in this account as a stab at articulating an esthetic ideal that could be sanctioned by the "man of steel" (Stalin) himself. The ostensibly neutral characterization of the production as "profound yet simple," at the same time, marks the presence of a crucial discourse about esthetics developed in Afinogenov's play.[29] Recall Klara's conversation with Valia Borodina about the virtues of simple art: " . . . this simplicity makes thoughts and feelings more pure, more profound." A transcendent understanding of the world order engendered by this art renders interpretation on the part of the audience altogether unnecessary.

The motif of the production's admirable simplicity emerged in the responses of many audience members of the Leningrad production (OS 25, 47–48, 52, 60), each replicating, to varying degrees, the model of critical reception staged in Klara's encounter with Valia. One audience member's account even suggests that, from this perspective, when Klara's rebuttal of Borodin fails to convince an occasional spectator, its very flaws serve to emphasize both the theatrical and the real, "everyday" persuasiveness of the scene that follows—the professor's interrogation at the GPU offices:

> [The interrogation scene] made a much greater impression on me personally than Klara's speech. From a scholarly point of view, Klara did not really prove the professor wrong. Her argument led me to conclude that a revolutionary hero is also ultimately motivated by fear. Our GPU is excellent at finding the right moment and impressing things upon [*vozdeistvovat' na*] all kinds of people in fitting ways. Professor Borodin looks at a glass of water and contemplates the life of the paramecia. Then he makes conclusions about human psychology based upon those observations. And they found an excellent remedy for him at the GPU—transferring him into a laboratory of living, breathing human beings. (OS 73)

Inherent in this description is an understanding of the essential continuity between the projects underlying the theatrical spectacle and the GPU interrogation. Yet the implication is patently not that the secret police is somehow theatrical, in the sense that its actions are disingenuous and therefore suspect. The point of the analogy, instead, is to recast the theatrical performance as a kind of "laboratory of living human beings" that derives its legitimacy from practicing a method not entirely unlike the GPU's. That transformative mechanism is illustrated by the remarks themselves. The dramatic authenticity (the simplicity) of the GPU episode in performance convinces this spectator to discard the politically incorrect conclusion he had drawn from Klara's monologue. The interrogation scene, in effect, provides a retroactive motivation for the Klara-Borodin confrontation—not because it justifies the characters' actions but because it unfolds the production's metatheatrical logic for the audience. What at first had seemed a miscalculation on the part of the playwright and/or the actors is now read as an instance of "simple art" at work.

The stage experience into which the spectators of the Leningrad *Fear* were drawn was shaped by manifestly theatrical means. The physical structure of Nikolai Akimov's set led the actors to redefine their use of crucial conventions of the realistic stage and so more effectively manipulate the audience's emotions. The audience accepted that manipulation as a central element of its theatrical experience, even seeing it as the essence of interpretive activity itself. For the Leningrad audiences of *Fear*, the theatrical production of additional, nonverbal meanings was not seen as potentially subversive, because it was recast by the "scenic situation" as a more effective and powerful way of bringing home the meaning of an already familiar narrative of renewal and conversion—a solution so successful, in fact, that the Aleksandrinskii started exporting its production concept to provincial theaters.[30]

Stanislavsky's Production: "Acceptable Distortions" at the MAT

For the Moscow Art Theater, where Afinogenov's play finally opened on 24 December 1931 (some seven months after its Leningrad premiere), importing the Aleksandrinskii production was simply not an option. The MAT production was eagerly anticipated by the critics, many of whom immediately compared it to the play's Leningrad incarnation.[31] One of the statements that captured the distinctiveness of the MAT's *Fear* most vividly, however, appeared in a review that did not explicitly contrast the two productions and has never been published in full. It belongs to the chairman of the central censorship board (Glavrepertkom), Osaf Litovskii. Through complicated bureaucratic maneuvering, the MAT managed to circumvent the standard procedure for gaining official censorship approval, but Litovskii insisted upon articulating his principal objections in a formal letter to the theater's administration. Most of his complaints concerned interpretations of various characters throughout the play, and only one dealt with the staging of a specific episode:

> The OGPU interrogation scene is done in an entirely unacceptable fashion. A windowless room with dirty walls, with black doors upholstered with black felt and oilcloth, which open without a sound—all this creates an unacceptably distorted representation of the way in which the interrogations actually take place. The dreary, muffled feel of the setting is furthermore emphasized by Kastal'skii's utterly persecuted look [*sovershenno zamuchennyi vid*].[32]

Formulating his grievance in terms of "unacceptably distorted representation" reveals no less about the critic than about the object of his scorn. The rhetorical effectiveness of implying a firsthand experience with OGPU interrogations (presumably not in the capacity of a suspect) is predicated upon an assumption about the MAT's relationship with its spectators. Placed on the Art Theater stage, *Fear* had to bear the responsibility for representing a version of reality that was more than just "acceptably distorted." Walls and windows did not merely frame the "stage experience" in a manifestly theatrical spectacle, as they did in Leningrad. In Moscow they were building blocks of a universe that had to be accepted as genuine, especially in those situations when the audience was expected to have no direct knowledge of the reality being presented/distorted. The set design of the MAT production did not strive for precise photographic verisimilitude: the bookshelves in Borodin's apartment and the institute library—the most prominent element of the stage picture—stretched toward the rafters, hyperbolizing the "scholarly" background. But, in contrast to the Aleksandrinskii, the MAT set created no obstacles, physical or metaphorical, for the cast members developing their characters according to the precepts of realistic acting. According to some accounts, the set seemed, instead, to complement and accentuate the actors' movements, making the essentially mimetic stage picture all the more comfortable both for the actors and for the spectators expecting a traditional "realistic" performance.[33] One of the consequences of this "scenic situation," as Litovskii's response suggests, was that the MAT production was from the very beginning expected by the authorities to have a more tangible, and more hazardous, capacity for affecting the ideas and emotions of its spectators than the Aleksandrinskii version ever could have.

The MAT version was directed by Il'ia Sudakov and personally supervised first by Vladimir Nemirovich-Danchenko, then (after Nemirovich fell ill and went abroad to recuperate) by Stanislavsky himself. By the time Stanislavsky took over the production, *Fear* had been staged almost in its entirety. However, even under pressure from Afinogenov and his associates from RAPP, Stanislavsky insisted upon continuing regular rehearsals for nearly two more months. The problem that appeared to require his attention most urgently recalled the crisis in Leningrad; it was the problem of Klara. In the MAT production the part was being performed by Ol'ga Knipper-Chekhova, one of the troupe's most senior members and the widow of Anton Chekhov. Playing a stern Old Bolshevik presented a different set of challenges for her than for the Aleksandrinsii's Korchagina-Aleksandrovskaia. Korchagina was a character actress cast in what was glossed as a dramatic part; Knipper was a dramatic actress searching for theatrical ways of justifying a role which, as she was constantly reminded by her colleagues, she could base on little firsthand experience. Stanislavsky scheduled a number of additional one-on-one rehearsals with Knipper-Chekhova, but barely more than a week before opening night eyewitness reports from the run-throughs maintained that the role was not coming together for her.[34] Knipper might have seemed an unlikely Klara, but there was theatrical logic in this casting decision: in the crucial confrontation scene she was paired up with Leonid Leonidov as Borodin. Leonidov, one of the MAT's great tragic actors, had appeared opposite Knipper before—most memorably in the original production of *The Cherry Orchard*. The contrast between the dramatic context of the two stage encounters was transparent. In 1904 Knipper, as Ranevskaia, unsuccessfully defended the orchard she owned and the way of life it denoted from the onslaught of modernity represented by Leonidov's passionately ruthless Lopakhin. In 1931, she had to personify the future by convincing the audience that Klara's interpretation of the present was more viable than that of the retrograde intellectual portrayed by Leonidov. But the crucial actorly dynamic seemed to persist: now as then, in the third-act showdown, Leonidov's character was not only more forceful but also more visibly powerful than Knipper's.[35] In the Art Theater's famously somber *Cherry Orchard*, the vulnerability with which Knipper invested her character helped frame her opponent's triumph as an event of near-tragic proportions: Lopakhin's advance was revealed to be inexorable and destructive. In the case of *Fear* a nuanced affective justification of Klara's weakness, even (or, perhaps, especially) when performed by an actress of Knipper's stature, was a risky theatrical strategy.

In one respect at least Leonidov's task seemed inherently less complicated than Knipper's: he was playing an *intelligent*, a paradigmatic Art Theater character. Yet while reports from rehearsals repeatedly pointed to Leonidov's performance as the production's strongest, the actor himself struggled with the role, and even asked Stanislavsky to find a replacement for him as Borodin. During one lengthy conversation at Stanislavsky's apartment, Leonidov complained that his performance did not provoke the interest of the few chance spectators who happened to have observed the early rehearsals because his character was so obviously unsympathetic.

> *Leonidov.* But look, there's just nothing positive about Borodin! He's a reactionary—until he gets kicked in the head. You yourself said that he should be arrested!
>
> *Stanislavsky.* The author has proved to me that I was mistaken, that the Borodins should be re-educated rather than arrested. And I think that I was wrong and Afinogenov is right. [. . .]
>
> *Leonidov.* So how would you play Borodin? You, from your position as Stanislavsky the scholar and master of the theatrical craft?
>
> *Stanislavsky.* I would constantly check myself: am I right or wrong in my views on science, on politics, on people in these new, changed life conditions?
>
> *Leonidov.* Yes, but that would be quite a subtext for the entire role! The author's written text quite literally says something entirely different![36]

Arguing from the perspective of someone who had contemplated playing Borodin himself, Stanislavsky insisted that Afinogenov's inexperience as a playwright sanctioned the actors—himself and Leonidov—to compensate for the apparent lack of an explicit justification for this reading in the text.[37] Stanislavsky used the textual authority of the play's finale (Borodin's conversion) to provide Leonidov with ways of "resisting" the text in the opening scenes: convincing the audience, through intonation shifts and understated movement, that from the very beginning he cannot help admiring Kimbaev's thirst for knowledge, and cannot help suspecting Kastal'skii of overstating the anti-Soviet case.[38]

Stanislavsky's approach was informed above all by the logic of stage realism, according to which any character can provoke and hold the interest of the audience if the performer invests that character with sufficient complexity of motivations. Consequently, Stanislavsky's Borodin would not merely enact motivations "left out" by the script; he had to presume that every character around him was also animated by a motivation which the dialogue alone could not convey. From the theatrical perspective, then, Borodin's "reeducation" is justified only in a fictional world where everybody expects others not to be who they claim to be. The plot of Afinogenov's play is structured around a similar expectation: enemies become allies as quickly as friends turn into traitors. As a performance device, however, the subtext of permanent mutual suspicion both fuels and deflates the melodramatic impulse. If someone's betrayal is always imminent, the histrionic effect of revealing one character's "true" identity or motive is diminished. As staged by Stanislavsky, *Fear* cultivated a kind of interpretive paranoia among its performers but stood little chance of provoking a generalized panic (a fear of fear) among its audiences, because it undermined the more openly provocative, hysterical appeal of the melodramatic stage. The Art Theater production was subtly disinfecting the emotional consequences of fear for its spectators even as it sought to make the emotion itself especially palpable on stage.

Embracing Stanislavsky's strategy had important implications for the production's dramatic structure. The OGPU scene had to represent the final stage in a lengthy process. It could no longer mark the moment of sudden and complete revelation; it could only provide the final confirmation for Borodin's suspicions that he had erred in his views on science and in the choice of friends. The burden of engendering his realization was shifted to the third-act argument with Klara. Stanislavsky did expect Leonidov to treat Borodin's lecture on par with the professor's other scholarly endeavors—with a degree of detachment that signaled slowly growing self-doubts.[39] But the crucial step toward "rebirth" (*pererozhdenie*) had to be enacted during, and palpably motivated by, Klara's response. This meant that even as Leonidov's performance acquired a new subtext, the stakes were raised higher than ever for Knipper-Chekhova while the range of strategies available to her was reduced. She was no longer just Borodin's opponent, and could not merely reclaim moral authority by revealing her character's vulnerability, as she did in her other famous confrontation with Leonidov in *The Cherry Orchard*. Klara had to be played as Borodin's future mentor; she needed to persuade her audience that she had convinced him. This added "objective" (to borrow a Stanislavskian term) provided the actress with an impetus to avoid an overly emotional reading of Klara's monologue, to move away from a theatrical gesture that would have been seen as melodramatic.

At one of the last rehearsals before he finally asked Knipper-Chekhova to give up the role, Stanislavsky attempted an experiment. In the audience that day were members of the special "workers' brigade" that had been appointed to assume ideological supervision (*shefstvo*) of the production. Stanislavsky had already run through the confrontation scene twice, both with Knipper and with her understudy, Sokolovskaia. The director then asked all Art Theater actors and students present at the rehearsal but not taking part in the scene to join the cast on stage. After positioning the members of this improvised chorus throughout the acting area, he asked Leonidov and Knipper to repeat the scene and directed the rest to act out their responses to the two performances as members of Borodin's and Klara's fictional audience. Most of the extras were told to express their active support for Klara's rebuttal, and only a few were instructed to back Borodin. According to the "workers' brigade" report, this had an effect on those present at the rehearsal: Knipper's delivery of the monologue was greeted with enthusiastic applause.[40]

The tenacious ideological and esthetic problem of "defeating" Borodin on stage seemed to have been resolved. And yet Stanislavsky chose not to use this device in production. Olga Knipper was replaced with Nina Sokolovskaia, an actress who was slightly older than Knipper but joined the Art Theater troupe only in 1917. Sokolovskaia did not possess Knipper's fame, but neither did she stand the risk of coloring her performance as Klara with the overtones of Knipper's theatrical prehistory. Struggle though Sokolovskaia might with having to portray an Old Bolshevik "authentically," her performance did not require the onstage presence of a mini-chorus of extras, an ersatz audience, to help her assume a posture of authority during the encounter with Leonidov. Stanislavsky's decision signaled his sensitivity to the spectator-spectacle dynamic cultivated by the MAT's *Fear*. Having to add this chorus to the Klara-Borodin confrontation scene meant explicitly enacting the spectators' expected reaction in front of them. Such a theatrical choice might have been appropriate in a production whose principal, perhaps only, aim was to mobilize its viewers for immediate action—a production that dealt, as had many of the spectacles of the 1920s, in broad strokes meant to astonish and electrify. By contrast, the rhetorical strategy of the Art Theater's production, as we have seen, was to avoid an excess of sentiment, to shun the recognizably melodramatic, and instead to create semantic and emotional tension by adding layers of fairly subtle contradictory meanings. For Stanislavsky to show his spectators how he expected them to behave was to acknowledge indulging in a Borodin-like experiment, to proclaim that he had discovered the unconditional theatrical stimulus of his audience's response and that he was now trying to reproduce that stimulus. Even if this measure prompted the audience to applaud Klara during the confrontation scene, then, it jeopardized the success of the production as a whole.

In contrast with the Leningrad production of *Fear*, Stanislavsky's directorial efforts focused on exploring the limits of "acceptable distortions of reality" (to borrow a formulation from the chief censor Litovskii, whose admonition to the MAT we encountered earlier). Just as he had with Leonidov, Stanislavsky encouraged the entire cast to transform their roles by developing and performing nonverbal subtexts that the script did not seem to call for or even allow altogether. No one secured the playwright's advance permission for these changes, yet Afinogenov, who observed rehearsals regularly, seemed pleased with the result. "I experienced the most joy at those rehearsals," he wrote in a retrospective account of his experiences at the MAT, "during which I witnessed the performers moving farther and farther away from the characters I had originally devised."[41] Significant though these modifications may have been, the playwright delighted in them in part because they were to be presented to the audience as if they were *not* distortions created for their benefit. The theatrical efficacy of additional, mostly nonverbal, meanings devised in rehearsal depended upon not being perceived by the viewers as having been added specifically to influence their understanding of the particular dramatic moment. Stanislavsky's approach went hand in hand with the precepts of "simple" art articulated by Afinogenov in the script of *Fear*: stage action, no matter how complex the motivations of characters taking part in it, had to purify and ennoble the spectators' thoughts and feelings without forcing their awareness of what it was trying to accomplish. In the theatrical rhetoric of Stanislavsky's production, the onstage ersatz audience that forced Knipper's "victory" as Klara was, ultimately, an unacceptable distortion.

Pursuing Stanislavsky's strategy entailed taking certain risks. Over the course of several months of rehearsals, the script was complemented with dozens of details that strove to avoid the banalities of emotional extremes and helped the actors create more interesting characters—but would these additions not lead to a weakening of the play's ideological import? Responses to the MAT production suggested that such concerns had not been unfounded. Leonidov's forceful delivery of Borodin's lecture about the omnipresence of fear was singled out by critics, even those usually hostile to the Art Theater, as one of the production's most remarkable achievements.[42] At the same time, several reviews suggested that Klara's rebuttal, even as it was performed by Nina Sokolovskaia, fell short of "defeating the scholarly argument" put forth by Borodin. In this, and in the proliferation of "fine shades, half-tones and subtleties" observed by the reviewers,[43] the MAT's *Fear* was hardly a match for the "play of steel" being performed in Leningrad. But neither the ambiguity of subtleties nor the questions about the meaning of the crucial confrontation scene (questions that had almost proven fatal at the Aleksandrinskii) put this production's future in jeopardy.

To suggest how the production's theatrical strengths were manufactured out of its potential ideological weaknesses, let me briefly consider the implications of one performance detail that, symptomatically, provoked particular dismay of some eyewitnesses. In Afinogenov's play, virtually every time Professor Borodin receives a piece of bad news, he exclaims: "What's happening to people?" According to several reports, the remark repeatedly provoked laughter from the audience. "What's so funny?" one reviewer wondered in indignation.[44] Following as it did upon accusations of political unreliability, reports of arrests, and revelations about betrayals, Borodin's remark did not easily fit the semantic limitations of a generic absentminded professor's verbal tic; in the context of the time, the question it raised had real meaning for the character and for the audience. That the spectators could, and did, laugh at Leonidov's delivery of the line reveals as much about the theatrical rhetoric of the production as about the viewer it successfully nurtured. "What's happening to people?" played as a line with subtext in an audience prepared by the spectacle itself to read the onstage universe as both hyperreal and inherently theatrical, to perceive the verisimilitude of the setting, the actions and the dialogue as contingent upon the meanings illuminated, or created anew, in performance.

Stanislavsky's direction aimed to avoid blatantly melodramatic manipulation of the audience's emotion and instead create a theatrical situation in which there was a palpable sense of meaning being produced and shifted with every moment, with every line and every choice made on stage. Watching the performance unfold in the glare of stage lights from the safe distance of a darkened house, from behind the sharply defined border with the world of the stage, the spectator was witnessing the creation of a compelling theatrical illusion. The secret lives of fictional characters were unraveling in front of the audience. As instructed by Stanislavsky, Leonidov would indicate, with the help of a few silent gestures, Borodin's frustration with the devious Kastal'skii early on in the play, much earlier than the point at which Kastal'skii was unequivocally identified as a villain. Leonidov's gestures made transparent his motivation—but they were played as if they were visible only to the audience, not to the other characters. Over the course of the evening, the MAT production, which hyperbolized the use of theatrical subtext, made numerous oblique meanings legible to its spectators. At the same time, as we saw, Stanislavsky avoided creating a "scenic situation" in which the audience would be asked to acknowledge that its reactions were being prompted or directed by the onstage action. The two devices combined to produce a striking effect of placing the spectators in a position of interpretive authority: deeply invested in the outcome of stage action, they were privy to the (hidden) motivations of fictional characters while ostensibly preserving the anonymity and inviolability of their own. "What's happening to people?" was not a funny line, but it provoked the laughter of those who felt that they, unlike the old professor portrayed by Leonidov, knew what was happening, and had every (theatrical) reason to believe that *it*—whatever it was—would not happen to them, not without their noticing.

This carefully constructed theatrical illusion of interpretive freedom *cum* invincibility is unlikely to have been as effective if the stakes for the audience and for the actors had not been as high as they were in the early thirties, when the first show trials and massive purges were actively introducing the official discourse of traitors, saboteurs and "two-faced liars" (*dvurushniki*) into the everyday experience of Soviet audiences. True, fear was much more of an everyday reality for some spectators of Afinogenov's play than for others. The Moscow Art Theater (even more than the Aleksandrinskii) had been a vital cultural institution of the intelligentsia before 1917 and continued to function as such throughout the early Soviet period; its audiences were guaranteed to include a large number of patrons whose firsthand experience had given credence to many of the complaints voiced by the fictional Professor Borodin. But

Afinogenov's play was written to appeal to as wide an audience as possible: spectators of different generations, genders, professions, political affiliations, and ethnicities could find a character or a situation with which they could, in theory, identify. Many, perhaps even most, of them had not yet had to deal with fear as an aspect of everyday experience. The theatrical rhetoric of the MAT's production treated all of these spectators as emotional and intellectual equals, transcending the conventional dynamic of recognition and identification. It gave each spectator an opportunity to imagine and experience fear as one in the series of motivations made legible by realistic theater—yet another "stimulus" of onstage actions, which the spectator was uniquely positioned to recognize and dissect from afar. Whether or not to accept the terms of this theatrical offering (to laugh or not to laugh at Leonidov-Borodin's unfunny line, for instance) was to some extent each spectator's choice (some, including the exasperated theater critic, did not laugh). But the choice had to be made from within the audience, a random combination of strangers brought together on an average evening by the collective experience of responding to, and so participating in, the spectacle they witnessed together.

From this perspective, the observation of an audience member in Leningrad about the essential continuity between the projects underlying an interrogation at the GPU (as it is portrayed in Afinogenov's play) and a Soviet theatrical production acquires special importance for the MAT's *Fear*. As we saw, in Stanislavsky's production the scene at the OGPU served as the culmination of the interpretive strategies employed by the actors throughout the play. Rather than forcing Professor Borodin's sudden conversion, the OGPU encounter confirmed what the spectators were meant to have conjectured from the beginning: that his motivations were more complex and contradictory, that there was something hidden underneath his lines all along. A crucial affinity between the operations of the OGPU and the rhetoric of realistic theater comes into view here. The goal of a realistic actor is (in theory) to uncover and (in practice) to invent the meaning behind the text. The actors, then, take on the tasks of the OGPU, sharing its investigatory function. But the same can be said, to some extent, of the spectators who are collectively led to suspect that something always lies beyond the text,[45] that all is not as simple as it seems, and that not even the OGPU can expose everything for them during the performance.[46]

Several weeks after *Fear* opened in Moscow, the newspaper *Vecherniaia Moskva* invited a number of playwrights and theater personalities to share their opinions of the production. Yuri Olesha, from whom the Art Theater was still expecting a new play at the time, drafted several versions of his response, some openly hostile to Afinogenov's script. The statement he submitted to the newspaper in the end was short and impeccably polite. Olesha praised the performances of Leonidov and Boris Livanov (who played Kimbaev) and offered just one specific assessment of the production, a self-consciously understated portrait of the writer as a Soviet spectator:

> While I was watching *Fear* and was observing the spectators' reactions, I came to realize that there indeed exists a Soviet audience [*sovetskaia publika*], and that its tastes, sympathies and traditions are now being established. *Fear* has revealed to us the Soviet audience in a broad sense. And that is an enviable accomplishment.[47]

Olesha evades having to express his personal judgment on the new tastes, sympathies, and traditions that were "revealed" by *Fear*. But by acknowledging and proclaiming the existence of the Soviet audience as a phenomenon, his formulation also forces the question of how that audience, a collective body incorporating viewers of such varied backgrounds, is held together. Recall the conversation of two audience members, reported in a review of the MAT production, that led me to ask what it might have meant for Soviet spectators to have found themselves "in the power" of a Stalinist spectacle. For the audiences of *Fear* in Moscow and Leningrad, at the Aleksandrinskii and at the Art Theater, that experience encompassed more than somehow being overcome by the sights and sounds with which the viewers were bombarded over the course of a four-and-a-half-hour-long performance. To be *in* the power of the spectacle was to have laid claim to possessing that illusory, intangible power, a claim to sharing it with the other members of the audience, and so be linked to them through it. I have argued that the illusion of authority perceived by the audience of a Soviet spectacle was created by infusing a production with a set of purely theatrical meanings—meanings that could not be exhaustively, "objectively" captured in words, could not be quoted, and therefore left room for re- and misinterpretation on the part of both actors and spectators. That palpable sense of additional meanings being wrought on stage, live, was a crucial element of the Soviet self-understanding, which thrived on notions of complexity, of finding or inventing things that were hidden. The GPU may have been the ultimate provider of subtexts, but the production of subtexts (and of Soviet selves with subtexts) was what Soviet theater was about.

NOTES

1. Bibira Akmoldoeva and John Sommer, *Klavdiya Antipina: Ethnographer of the Kyrgyz* (McKinleyville, Calif.: Spring Hill Press, 2002), 20–29.

2. Julie A. Cassiday, *The Enemy on Trial: Early Soviet Courts on Stage and Screen* (DeKalb: Northern Illinois University Press, 2000), 3–7, 10–19. For an example of a study that relies on the exclusively metaphoric meaning of theater and performance to make a larger claim about the functioning of Stalinist culture, see Jeffrey Brooks, *Thank You, Comrade Stalin! Soviet Public Culture from Revolution to Cold War* (Princeton: Princeton University Press, 2000), esp. 66–77. In contrast to the work done on 1930s Soviet cinema, relatively little attention has been paid to the theatrical practices in this period. A case in point is a recent collection of articles by the most prominent scholars in the field, which includes ten articles about film and just one (and a half) about theater: Marina Balina, Evgenii Dobrenko, and Yurii Murashov, eds., *Sovetskoe bogatstvo: stat'i o kul'ture, literature i kino* (St. Petersburg: Akademicheskii proekt, 2002).

3. W. B. Worthen, *Modern Drama and the Rhetoric of Theater* (Berkeley: University of California Press, 1992), 1. My reading of the strategies for constructing the Soviet audience is inspired and influenced by Worthen's classic study.

4. Lars T. Lih, "Melodrama and the Myth of the Soviet Union," in *Imitations of Life: Two Centuries of Melodrama in Russia,* ed. Louise McReynolds and Joan Neuberger (Durham, N.C.: Duke University Press, 2002), 178–207. For melodrama as a theatrical vehicle for exploring crucial social issues, see the introduction to the volume (*Imitations of Life*, 9–10).

5. Ibid., 190 (theater), 194–202 (show trials).

6. This essay is a condensed adaptation of a chapter from a larger project that examines the relationship between literature, theater, and self-understanding in the 1930s. My interest in Afinogenov was stimulated by Jochen Hellbeck's groundbreaking work on Afinogenov's self-writing project. See Jochen Hellbeck, "Writing the Self in the Time of Terror: Alexander Afinogenov's Diary of 1937," in *Self and Story in Russian History,* ed. Laura Engelstein and Stephanie Sandler (Ithaca: Cornell University Press, 2000), 69–93. Elsewhere in my work-in-progress I interpret Afinogenov's attempts to articulate a new identity in his intimate writings, in contrast to Hellbeck, as a fundamentally theatrical problem. My reading emphasizes the connections between the rhetorical strategies employed in the productions of Afinogenov's dramas (especially *Fear*) in the early 1930s and the prominence of metatheatrical reflections in Afinogenov's subsequent attempts to make sense of his personal crisis on the pages of his diary.

7. Eugene Lyons, ed., *Six Soviet Plays* (Boston: Houghton Mifflin, 1934), 392.

8. For details of Afinogenov's biography, see Aleksandr Karaganov, *Zhizn' dramaturga: tvorcheskii put' Aleksandra Afinogenova* (Moscow: Sovetskii pisatel', 1964).

9. A complicated and slippery term, "stage realism" denotes a set of esthetic premises that differ in a number of important respects from the conventional understanding of realism in literature and the visual arts. Throughout my argument, I use the term "realism" in this specific theatrical sense. For a nuanced reading of Stanislavsky's theories, see Sharon Marie Carnicke, *Stanislavsky in Focus* (Amsterdam: Harwood, 1998).

10. On the rhetoric of stage realism, see Worthen, *Modern Drama and the Rhetoric of Theater,* 12–29, 54–62.

11. As with my use of the term *realism,* I always refer to the specifically theatrical meaning of "subtext" in the discussion that follows.

12. Osip Mandel'shtam, "Khudozhestvennyi teatr i slovo," in *Sobranie sochinenii,* vol. 2 (Moscow: Art-Biznes-Tsentr, 1993), 333–335, esp. 334.

13. Just five days before he read a draft of *Fear* to the MAT cast, Afinogenov attacked Stanislavsky at the RAPP theater conference ("V reshitel'noe nastuplenie na teatral'nom fronte," *Vecherniaia Moskva,* 27 January 1931, 3). *Fear* represented the MAT's second peace offering to RAPP: earlier in 1931, the theater had staged *Bread* (*Khleb*), the work of another important RAPP functionary, Vladimir Kirshon.

14. The formula "This is an affair of state [*Eto—gosudarstvennoe sobytie*]" in response to the premiere of *Fear* at MAT was attributed to Iurii Olesha by Vsevolod Vishnevskii in his homage to Afinogenov (Aleksandr Afinogenov, *Stat'i. Dnevniki. Pis'ma. Vospominaniia* [Moscow: Iskusstvo, 1957], 268). Stalin's reaction is reported, among others, by the director of *Fear* at the MAT, Il'ia Sudakov (Afinogenov, *Stat'i,* 300). On Gorky's reaction, see Valerii Kirpotin, "U istokov," *Novyi mir* 8 (August 1984):

205–216, esp. 209. (Gorky was known for his emotional response to the performances he attended.)

15. A. Charnyi, "Pochemu 'Strakh'?" *Izvestiia* 7 (7 January 1932), 3. My translation is deliberately literal; the Russian is *"tselikom popadaesh' vo vlast' izumitel'nogo zrelishcha."*

16. The play's canonical Russian text (Aleksandr Afinogenov, *Izbrannoe*, 2 vols. [Moscow: Iskusstvo, 1977], 1: 185–244) corresponds to the second separate edition (Leningrad: GIKhL, 1932). The English version of quotations from the play is based on the only published translation: Lyons, ed., *Six Soviet Plays*, 393–469. All further citations, parenthetically, are to the Lyons translation (edited for style and content; first reference) and the *Izbrannoe* version (second reference), unless specified otherwise.

17. The text of the play's first separate edition (Moscow-Leningrad: GIKhL, 1931) which includes this passage (69) was used by all productions of *Fear* (in Leningrad and across the country) before Afinogenov revised the playscript for the MAT version in late 1931.

18. The promptbook of the MAT production includes a brief exchange at the end of the interrogation scene, in which the OGPU investigator tells Borodin that he is free to go—"out on the street, back home, wherever you want" (MAT Museum, f. BRCh, ed. kh. 287, l. 131). This ending was not included in either printed versions of the play.

19. Lih, "Melodrama and the Myth of the Soviet Union," 188–189.

20. My reconstruction of the case for melodrama follows Lih's argument (esp. 187), which demonstrates how the melodramatic paradigm can help understand the use of similarly explosive rhetoric in Kirshon's *Bread*, the play the MAT staged only a few months before *Fear*. In this argument, the esthetic notion of purging emotions is unambiguously linked with ideological purging. But can we assume that this equivalence is in fact complete and sufficient? Might the character's conversion not allow the audience to enjoy with impunity the critical comments offered by the character, perhaps even identify with them? For that matter, can such critical impulse ever be completely purged from the minds of the spectators?

21. Ol'ga Bokshanskaia, Letter to Vladimir Nemirovich-Danchenko, 4–5 October 1931, MAT Museum, f. 4, op. 8, ed. kh. 1185 (N-D 11655), l. 2 ob.

22. Julie A. Cassiday has explored *Fear's* political context, especially its connection to the trial of the Industrial Party (Cassiday, *The Enemy on Trial*, 175–181).

23. One of the first major reviews of the play deliberately conflated Borodin's lines with remarks attributed to Pavlov in order to make a point about the play's topicality: Isaak Kruti, "Strakh," *Sovetskii teatr* 2:7 (July 1931): 20–25, esp. 20.

24. For the details of events surrounding the MAT opening, see Ol'ga Radishcheva, *Stanislavskii i Nemirovich-Danchenko: istoriia teatral'nykh otnoshenii, 1917–1938* (Moscow: Artist. Rezhisser. Teatr, 1999), 280–283.

25. In addition to important political considerations, producing a memorable—and more successful—*Fear* in Moscow was a matter of theatrical pride for the troupe that considered itself to be Russia's greatest. On the motivations for staging *Fear* at the Art Theater, see Pavel Markov, *V Khudozhestvennom teatre: kniga zavlita* (Moscow: Vserossiiskoe teatral'noe obshchestvo, 1976), 269–275.

26. O *"Strakhe"*: *obrabotannaia stenogramma vyezdnogo zasedaniia prezidiuma leningradskogo oblastnogo otdela soiuza rabotnikov iskusstv v Gosudarstvennom teatre dramy 15 i 27 iiunia 1931 goda* (Leningrad: Lenoblrabis, 1931), 14–15. All subsequent references to this edition, as OS, are given parenthetically. I undertake a detailed

analysis of the Leningrad production elsewhere; this discussion represents a brief summary of that analysis.

27. Many cast members expressed their discomfort with the set, attributing it to the friction they perceived between the principles of realistic acting followed in rehearsing the play and the physical demands of the setting in which they were now asked to perform it. In order to be able to work on Akimov's set at all, Illarion Pevtsov had to invent a classically "realistic" justification for the ten-degree tilt of the principal acting area, which sloped downward toward the audience. Pevtsov convinced himself that his character, Professor Borodin, happened to have lived in a building that had been designed by an eccentric architect who liked slanted floors (OS 75).

28. The two most detailed and informed accounts of the events surrounding the Leningrad opening of *Fear* are Nikolai Petrov, *50 i 500* (Moscow: Vserossiiskoe teatral'noe obshchestvo, 1960), 316–320, and Vasilii Rafalovich, *Vesna teatral'naia. Vospominaniia* (Leningrad: Iskusstvo, 1971), 157–160.

29. The ease with which these remarks seem to appropriate another prominent set of catchphrases used by Afinogenov in *Fear*—a range of quasi-scientific terms from "reflexes" to "analysis"—may be at least in part a testament to the occupational proclivities of the speaker (a physician).

30. Within several months of the opening, the Aleksandrinskii began sending touring "brigades" to the provinces. Their explicit mission was to convince those local theater companies which had been reluctant to stage *Fear* that the play was not subversive—by using their own performance to demonstrate how the play could be staged "correctly." Most provincial theaters found the brigades' performances compelling.

31. S. Amaglobeli et al., " 'Strakh' v Leningrade i 'Strakh' v Moskve," *Literaturnaia gazeta* (23 December 1931): 4; M. Charnyi, "Miting spektaklei," *Izvestiia* 93 (3 April 1932): 4.

32. Osaf Litovskii, Pis'mo zaveduiushchemu khudozhestvennoi chast'iu MKhT i V. G. Sakhnovskomu 27 dekabria 1931 g., MAT Museum, f. 1, sezon 1931/32, 1–1 ob. For the details of the administrative maneuvering, see Radishcheva, *Stanislavskii i Nemirovich-Danchenko 1917–1938*, 282–283.

33. Inna Solov'eva, "Strakh," in *Moskovskii Khudozhestvennyi teatr: sto let*, vol. 1, ed. A. M. Smelianskii (Moscow: Moskovskii Khudozhestvennyi teatr, 1998), 128–130.

34. These reports have been preserved in letters sent to Nemirovich-Danchenko by his secretary, Ol'ga Bokshanskaia; excerpts concerning *Fear* published in Aleksandr Trabskii, ed., *Russkii sovetskii teatr 1926–1932*, vol. 3 (1), *Sovetskii teatr: dokumenty i materialy* (Moscow: Iskusstvo, 1982), 181–182.

35. For a succinct account of the 1904 production of *The Cherry Orchard*, see Laurence Senelick, *The Chekhov Theatre: A Century of the Plays in Performance* (Cambridge: Cambridge University Press, 1997), 67–79.

36. Nikolai Gorchakov, *Rezhisserskie uroki K. S. Stanislavskogo: besedy i zapisi repetitsii*, 3rd ed. (Moscow: Iskusstvo, 1952), 534.

37. Ibid., 536.

38. This suggestion is all the more remarkable considering that the MAT production actually excised some of the lines (preserved in the play's printed editions) in which Borodin articulated his sympathy for the Soviet way of life: Karaganov, *Zhizn' dramaturga*, 156.

39. Gorchakov, *Rezhisserskie uroki Stanislavskogo*, 535.

40. See Bokshanskaia's letter to Nemirovich, 6 December 1931: Trabskii, ed.,

Sovetskii teatr, 181–182; Marianna Stroeva, *Rezhisserskie iskaniia Stanislavskogo, 1917–1938* (Moscow: Nauka, 1977), 319. The following day, Stanislavsky tried placing a cast member in the audience and asking him to interrupt Leonidov's monologue with indignant exclamations. He was unsatisfied with the result (Solov'eva, "Strakh," 129). Stanislavsky, however, was not the only one who tried this approach. One regional production of *Fear*, in Magnitogorsk, relied on "provocateurs" placed among the spectators to get the entire audience engaged in the debate (see: Stenogramma diskussii po pis'mu tov. Amaglobeli po p'ese "Strakh" 16 fevralia 1932 g. pri Sekretariate [Vseroskomdrama], IMLI, f. 371, op. 1, ed. kh. 2, l. 11).

41. Aleksandr Afinogenov, "Tvorcheskii universitet," *Teatr i dramaturgiia* 2:3 (March 1934): 23–27.

42. Ia. Grinval'd, " 'Strakh.' P'esa A. Afinogenova v MKhT I," *Vecherniaia Moskva* (24 December 1931): 4; Iu. Iuzovskii, " 'Strakh' Afinogenova v MKhT," *Literaturnaia gazeta* (28 December 1931): 3; Litovskii, Pis'mo Sakhnovskomu, 1 ob.

43. On "subtleties" see Amaglobeli et al., " 'Strakh' v Leningrade i 'Strakh' v Moskve," 4; Osaf Litovskii, " 'Strakh' v MKhATe," *Sovetskoe iskusstvo*, 30 December 1931, 4.

44. Amaglobeli et al., " 'Strakh' v Leningrade i 'Strakh' v Moskve," 4; Solov'eva, "Strakh," 130

45. The function of subtexts in the play was to lead the actor playing Borodin to show the redeeming qualities in the character, and to allow the audience to see these "good" qualities. The OGPU, by contrast, was preoccupied with uncovering incriminating facts and displaying the "bad" traits of those whom it chose to investigate. In the ideological operation performed by the play, then, the dominant (unacknowledged) paradigm was reinforced by depicting its inverse as business as usual.

46. *Fear* opened in several provincial theaters before the Moscow premiere. The workers of the Kashira power plant sent Afinogenov the official resolution of their post-show debate: "What's good about your play is that it doesn't show the saboteurs and class enemies already exposed [*obnazhennye*]. The audience has to identify them, uncover [them] and make appropriate conclusions. That is something really innovative in your play" (Maksimov, Pis'mo zavkoma Kashirskoi GES 26 noiabria 1931 g., RGALI, f. 2172, op. 1, ed. kh. 13, l. 3—3 ob.)

47. One version of the draft ("I saw Afinogenov's play *Fear*. It is, in my opinion, a terrible play"): Iurii Olesha, "Zapiski Zanda." Materialy, IMLI f. 161, op. 1, ed. kh. 8, l. 8. Published response: Iurii Olesha, "O 'Strakhe' A. Afinogenova," in *P'esy. Stat'i o teatre i dramaturgii* (Moscow: Iskusstvo, 1968), 265–266.

"NEP Without Nepmen!"

Soviet Advertising and the Transition to Socialism

Randi Cox

In 1925, five hundred copies of a poster extolling the virtues of worker-peasant cooperation (*smychka*) were posted around the city of Saratov. The main image is of a worker and a peasant greeting one another. Their dress and facial features are typical of Soviet iconography of the 1920s; the clean-shaven worker wears a blacksmith's smock and carries a hammer, while the bearded peasant holds a sheaf of wheat. Behind the worker stand factories with smokestacks, and a basket of fruit sits at the feet of the peasant. The text, however, is somewhat unusual: "Here we have everything from the soil and the workbench. Trade between the city and the countryside is strengthened by *smychka*." Below the main image are thirty-nine announcements for various products and commercial enterprises in Saratov, including beer, farm equipment, a private repair shop, and the local outlet of the GUM state department store (fig. 5.1).[1]

In some ways this poster is similar to thousands of others published in the 1920s. The style and content of its images are consistent with the propaganda tropes of the era. Yet there are two key differences between this poster and ordinary propaganda. The first difference is the message. Rather than emphasizing an abstract political idea, the Saratov poster urged viewers to purchase and use specific products; it semiotized consumption. That is, it placed consumer goods in a context which conferred meaning on both specific goods and

Figure 5.1. Unknown artist, "Everything from the soil and the bench," 1925. Courtesy of the Russian State Library.

on consumption more generally. Consumption is redefined as an extension of production through the use of class iconography and agitational motifs which readers normally encountered in a political context.

The second, and more striking, difference is how it was made. The Saratov branch of the Union for Aid to Victims of Tuberculosis published the poster in order to raise money for its charitable activities; local economic enterprises paid to have their advertisements included. State propaganda organs played no role in Soviet advertising. During the 1920s, a complicated network of state and semi-state advertising agencies developed when newspapers were required to implement cost accounting measures under the New Economic Policy. Competition between the NEP agencies shaped both the content of advertising art and discussions of a possible role for advertising in a socialist economy. Leading agency administrators argued that advertising could become a specialized form of propaganda which would promote state-produced goods while redefining consumption as a political act. Unfortunately, tension arose between the need to raise revenues and efforts to use advertising for agitational purposes, which limited advertisers' ability to integrate their work into officially recognized propaganda.

Because the administrative structure of NEP advertising agencies influenced the course of the debate over advertising's potential contributions to Soviet society, this article intertwines two stories: that of pressure on the agencies to generate funds for their parent bodies and that of their efforts to use advertising to alter the meaning of consumption on behalf of the revolution. Evidence comes from two main source bases: the administrative records of advertising agencies (most collected during a government investigation of advertising practices) and 497 NEP-era advertising posters held at the Russian State Library's Department of Graphic Publications. Additional advertisements were taken from central newspapers and magazines.

There are countless scholarly works on the productive lives of Soviet workers and peasants of the 1920s, but we know far less about the consumption of the goods that they produced. The phrase "Soviet consumption" usually brings to mind only images of long lines and empty shelves. Yet the development of mass production in the Soviet Union required a corresponding recognition of mass consumption, just as Western societies wrestled with ways to incorporate consumption into their cultures.[2] Official Soviet attitudes toward consumption grew out of an interaction of Marxism, Russian intellectual culture, and the limits of the NEP economy.

One of the remarkable things about the Russian Revolution is the extent to which the Bolsheviks did not aspire just to political power; they believed that it was possible, and necessary, to inspire radical changes in the identity of individual citizens. The new Soviet self would find its purpose through economic activity and through class cooperation. As Marxists, the Bolsheviks saw the economic self as more progressive than any other sort of identity; all other sources of self-worth, such as religion, gender, family, or ethnicity, served either to support or to mask the condition of the economic self. Therefore modernization required Soviet citizens to embrace economic activity as the basis for identity.

But not all economic activity was created equal. If production elevated individuals, consumption, albeit necessary, held the potential to corrupt them. Consumption posed a challenge to the Bolsheviks, because it touched on two contradictory goals of the revolution: the desire to improve the lives of the lower classes, and the desire to put an end to the selfish indulgences of the upper classes. The confusion over the role of consumption in the new Soviet society sheds light on the difficult task the Bolsheviks faced in the transition from underground conspiracy to ruling administration. Values and activities which were useful in one situation turned out to be detrimental in the other.

Before 1917 asceticism had romantic, heroic overtones in radical subculture, while after the revolution the Bolsheviks took responsibility for the material needs of over one hundred million people.[3] This situation required a new understanding of consumption, but it proved difficult to let go of the fear that consumption would distract the New Soviet Man from his civic responsibilities, especially after the introduction of the New Economic Policy. The fear that NEP, with its private trade and revitalized urban nightlife, created a space for the revival of bourgeois consumerism contributed to a cultural association of even modest consumption with gluttony and political irresponsibility.[4] Indeed, the resentment of NEP by rank and file communists reflected, in part, an accusation that the Bolshevik leadership had betrayed the revolution by allowing decadent consumption to take precedence over heroic production.

Moreover, the shortcomings of the Soviet economy in the 1920s encouraged asceticism in revolutionary culture; self-denial served as a marker of willingness to put social obligations ahead of personal desires. Being a revolutionary meant destroying the old order and building a utopian society. It suggested progressive movement through time, and therefore a true communist must always guard against all kinds of corruption, including the temptations of consumerism.[5] The issue was particularly complicated, because consumption could not simply be done away with. Instead, communists needed to figure out where to draw the line between necessity and luxury, between need and want. At what point did consumption become consumerism?

On the other hand, the state had a genuine economic and political interest in promoting the products of state enterprises, which meant promoting consumption. NEP advertising specialists tried to resolve this contradiction by reimagining commodities as a tool for social transformation; their exchange and consumption would encourage modernization and cooperation between classes. These advertisements often politicized consumption and presented it as part of a heroic cycle along with production and exchange. Consuming state-produced goods became a civic obligation for workers and peasants, a demonstration of their support for one another. While some NEP advertisements did stress the pleasures of consumption, even these used agitational motifs to place that pleasure in a political context. Far from being a threat to political consciousness, this reinvented consumption could intensify revolutionary commitment.

In October 1917 most socialists probably would have assumed that Russian advertising would soon be exorcised along with other capitalist institutions, and in fact within two weeks of the Bolshevik seizure of power, the new government limited paid advertising to state publications in hopes of destroying the financial base of the opposition press.[6] Soviet publications turned to advertising in significant numbers only with the introduction of NEP, which required that they support themselves through their own revenues. Advertising first surfaced in *Izvestiia* in late 1921, and by June 1922 clients could buy

Figure 5.2. Advertising page of *Prozhektor* no. 1 (1923),
inside cover.

advertising space in the first column of the first page at double the cost of space
elsewhere in the paper. Over the next four years, advertising revenue played an
increasingly prominent role in newspaper budgets, and advertisements took
up one-half to one full page of most issues of the central daily papers (fig. 5.2).
Other publishers and state bureaucracies soon followed suit.

Almost immediately questions arose about the appropriateness of advertising in Soviet publications. Wasn't advertising one of the ways that capitalists
propped up their decaying system? Wasn't it by nature deceptive, a remnant of
prerevolutionary decadence? How could advertising possibly have a place in
the communist utopia? The key issues in this conversation are nicely encapsu-
lated in an argument between Lenin and David Riazanov at the Eleventh
Party Congress in 1922, one of the few times political elites discussed advertising. At a session devoted to the problems of the Bolshevik press, Riazanov (a

scholar and notorious party gadfly who frequently spoke out against compromises of Marxist purity for the sake of practical efficacy) proposed a ban on advertising in party publications. Riazanov argued that advertising was inherently bourgeois and counterrevolutionary. Initially the delegates supported Riazanov's proposal, but at the closing session of the congress Lenin railed against this "obvious mistake," asking Riazanov, "Where is *Pravda* going to get its funding if it is deprived of advertising?" The delegates backpedaled in the face of Lenin's vehemence, and party publications continued to sell advertising. For Lenin, ever the pragmatist, the importance of *Pravda* as a Bolshevik agitational publication took precedence over concerns about the propriety of advertising. Not once did he mention anything about the content of advertising; he approached it as a mechanism to generate revenue for a press that could not support itself on subscriptions alone.

Riazanov's concerns about advertising, on the other hand, reflected a concern about the impact of consumerism on revolutionary consciousness. He criticized the NEP press for falling back on the "dirty trick" of advertising when it ought to support itself as it did "in the old times, as the communist press throughout the world does, living by means of enthusiasm and devotion" of loyal comrades. Riazanov romanticized the financial struggles of the prerevolutionary underground press and implied that these struggles had a greater moral validity than the new practice of selling advertising. Not only did advertising convert the Bolshevik press itself into a commodity, it also subverted the agitational messages of the newspaper text by distracting readers from communist goals: "Workers need something else to read beside Mostorg advertisements for the opening of a new restaurant with excellent hors d'oeuvres and a volunteer club open from 10:00 to 4:00 in the morning." When Riazanov looked at a Mostorg advertisement, he didn't see propaganda for a state enterprise. He saw an invitation to socialize until the wee hours of the morning. Advertising, in promoting frivolous, nonpolitical activity, was fundamentally incompatible with the serious goals of the revolution, and the party undermined its own revolutionary efforts by publishing it.[7]

Lenin's victory over Riazanov at the Eleventh Party Congress set the tone for advertising debates through 1925. Financing the press took precedence over concerns about the propriety of advertising; Riazanov's fear of the ideological ramifications of advertising was irrelevant. As a result, Soviet advertising agencies developed out of the commercial departments of newspapers and other state organs, rather than through the Commissariat of Education, the Press Section of the party or some other agitational body.[8] Commissioned agents sold advertising door to door to state enterprises and even to some private entrepreneurs; there was no attempt by the state to coordinate advertising with the rest of its agitational arsenal, and censorship of advertisements was minimal. Nor was advertising included in enterprise budgets—sales depended on the persuasiveness of each agent.

By 1925 over fifty Moscow agencies, employing some seven hundred people, competed against one another for over nine million rubles in advertising sales. Many of these agencies, usually associated with a newspaper, publishing house, or other state organ, doubled as the headquarters for national operations, with national sales reaching twenty-one million rubles in 1924/25. There was no single state or party institution that regulated Soviet agencies. Instead, each agency was subject to bylaws established by its parent body, which usually allotted some monopoly on advertising to the agency. In the case of newspapers, the advertising department was the only authorized dealer of ad space in the newspaper. A parent body could also grant monopolies over physical space that came under its jurisdiction; the Commissariat of Transportation, for example, granted its agency, Transpechat', a monopoly on advertising posted in train stations.

Five large agencies, plus the advertising departments of *Izvestiia* and *Pravda*, emerged with dominant monopolies. Dvigatel' (Engine), founded in November 1922, grew out of the advertising department of *Ekonomicheskaia zhizn'*, the newspaper of the Council of Labor and Defense (STO). Dvigatel' approached advertising as propaganda for Sovietized consumption, and of all the agencies its management was the most dedicated to turning advertising into a branch of Soviet agitation. Indeed the name Dvigatel' was a pun, referring to both the Bolshevik passion for machinery and the commercial axiom, "Advertising is the engine of trade." Aided by an STO resolution which required all enterprises under its jurisdiction to place advertisements regularly in *Ekonomicheskaia zhizn'*, Dvigatel' brought in 1,849,000 rubles in revenues in 1924–1925, or 19.56 percent of all Moscow spending on advertising. The second largest agency was the Central Administration of Industrial Propaganda and the Press (TsUP), under *Torgovo-promyshlennaia gazeta*, the newspaper of the Supreme Economic Council (VSNKh). In addition to advertisements in its newspaper and other VSNKh publications, TsUP held a monopoly on advertising posted in factories, factory clubs, Komsomol cells, and VSNKh offices throughout the country.

Three major "departmental" agencies exploited monopolies over areas controlled by their parent bodies. The Moscow city soviet established Mosreklama (Moscow Advertising) in December 1922. It held a monopoly over all outdoor advertising in Moscow; it both produced advertisements for clients and collected hanging fees for granting other agencies access to its monopoly. Revenues supported the administrative operations of the Soviet, especially its work with homeless children. Transpechat' (Trans-print) and Sviaz' (Connection) held monopolies on advertising posted on the property of the Commissariat of Transportation and the Commissariat of Post and Telegraph, respectively. The proceeds of these two agencies were to go to maintaining the infrastructure of their parent commissariats. Of the big firms, the departmental agencies were the least concerned with advertising's agitational potential, especially before 1925. They had no links to newspapers, and most of their advertisements were posters or special advertising guidebooks.

The definition of Soviet advertising as a source of revenue initially encouraged publishers to accept ads without considering the likely interest of readers in the advertised goods; generating revenue was more important than matching up consumers and producers. Lenin had unwittingly provided Soviet advertising agents with the perfect sales pitch. Independent commissioned agents persuaded managers of all kinds of state enterprises to purchase advertising, not on the grounds that it would influence Soviet consumers, but on the grounds that their purchase would give much-needed financial support to the parent newspaper or office, a practice sarcastically known as "charitable advertising." This practice led to a hodgepodge of ads that often seemed at odds with the surrounding text.[9]

A number of agency administrators, especially at Dvigatel' and TsUP, recognized that competing monopolies and commissioned sales caused strife between Soviet organs and prevented the development of "modern" advertising campaigns which could aggressively promote the products of Soviet industry. Instead, they argued, agencies and clients should approach advertising as a subset of agitation, delivering a single message: buy this product. They should shape advertising content so as to channel consumer behavior in directions beneficial for both the economy and overarching Soviet goals. In an effort to determine the most effective way to do that, advertisers began to publicly debate the relationship of advertising to trade, consumption, and political obligation. How should agitational advertising work? Which goods should be advertised? Which consumers should be the target of Soviet advertising? How could advertising shape consumer attitudes? How should socialist advertising differ from capitalist advertising? From this discussion emerged a systematic agenda for socialist advertising stressing three major goals: competition with Nepmen, building relations between social classes, and consumption as a path to modernization.

One evening in 1924 Ilya Ehrenburg stopped by Osip and Lili Brik's Moscow apartment, only to find Vladimir Mayakovsky working on a design for an advertising poster. By way of explanation, Mayakovsky told Ehrenburg that "one ought to help the government in its struggle against private trading."[10] Such help was necessary indeed. The state trade network was miserably inadequate, unable to distribute even the small quantity of manufactured goods produced by Soviet enterprises. As a result, enterprises often resorted to private middlemen to get their products to consumers, especially in rural areas. State retailers were in a somewhat better position in the cities, but even here private bazaars competed effectively against the state. Advertising administrators argued that their work could come to the state's rescue by giving consumers two solid reasons to shop at state and cooperative stores: good deals and political obligation. On a practical level, state retailers could offer lower prices than private traders, who marked up goods to make a profit, and advertisements might attract consumers by calling attention to this disparity. On a theoretical level, agitational advertisements urged class-conscious citizens to consider the political implications of consumption; every kopek spent in state shops became capital to be reinvested in state industry, rather than profit lining the pockets of speculators. Agency administrators suggested that consumption be viewed as part of a never-ending economic cycle along with production and distribution. Once consumers understood that, they would be more inclined to shop at state and cooperative stores. In this sense, advertising would support the state's effort to use the competitive atmosphere of NEP as motivation to improve state industry and trade.[11]

In March 1925, the Newspaper Association of the Press Section of the party urged agencies not to accept private advertisements in those sectors of the economy where Nepmen were in competition with the state. Such advertisements undermined state retailers, especially in the countryside where "advertising should be a means to fight private capital."[12] That fall, L. Gimmel'farb, a Dvigatel' administrator, described advertising as a way both to discredit private traders and to publicize the achievements of state industry. Whereas competitive advertising in capitalist countries functioned to minimize the damage caused by overproduction, Soviet competitive advertisements would assure the consumer that state goods were superior to private goods:

> Our goal is to show the consumer the best that our state produces, to attract his attention and remind him of goods, to bring state products to the general public, to urge the consumer to spend his money on state products, turning him away from the private producer and merchant toward our state and cooperative traders in every possible way . . . [Even] in our economic system, advertising is an engine of trade.[13]

Such agitational advertisements sometimes explicitly urged consumers to reject private goods out of a combination of political responsibility and self-interest. Shopping at state stores, they suggested, was a practical strategy in the frustratingly complex retail market of the 1920s; consumers could simultaneously take advantage of good deals and strike a blow against private trade. A 1923 ad in *Pravda* for Mossukno, a state clothing store in Moscow, made the point plainly in its headline: "NEP without the Nepman!" (fig. 5.3). The ad reminded consumers that they (theoretically) did not have to resort to the private market, where prices were generally higher. Instead they could turn to Mossukno, which, the ad pointed out, accepted installment payments and offered discounts to workers and state employees. Moreover, the suggestive slogan played on popular hostility toward Nepmen, who were often perceived as dishonest speculators. Workers and others who resented the state's tolerance of private trade might be tempted to shop at Mossukno out of political responsibility or even a sense that doing business in a private shop was just not right. Mossukno gave them the opportunity to avoid contact with the Nepman, a distasteful reminder that the revolution was not complete.

Figure 5.3. Unknown artist, "NEP without the Nepman!" Print ad for Mossukno Store No. 3. *Pravda*, 18 November 1923.

Politicized advertisements were not clumsy or humorless; in fact they often relied on humor to draw the reader's attention. Mossel'prom, a state foods trust, publicized its mail order service as an alternative to costly provincial private retailers. One 1924 ad shows a skinny consumer painfully squeezed between a fat peasant wholesaler and an even fatter Nepman until money falls from his pockets (fig. 5.4). A verse drives the point home:

> Who here is the most unhappy?
> Obviously, the individual consumer.
> Poor thing, squeezed between the wholesaler and the middleman.
> But we are ready to send goods to your home,
> Quickly and at wholesale prices.
> Send us your order by postcard or telegram right away.

On the surface, this consumer suffered because of the high prices charged by middlemen, in contrast to Mossel'prom's more reasonable wholesale prices. The illustration gave a second, more political meaning to the advertisement through the use of well-established archetypal portrayals of the middlemen. One is drawn as a *kulak*, a well-off peasant, while the other wears the pinstriped suit and bowler hat associated with capitalists and Nepmen. These images had

Figure 5.4. Unknown artist, "Who is the most unhappy?" Print ad for Mossel'prom's mail-order service. *Izvestiia*, 4 April 1924.

been used in political propaganda since 1917, and their negative political connotations would have been clear to readers of *Izvestiia*. Thus this advertisement set up shopping at Mossel'prom as an inexpensive, politically reliable alternative to doing business with more disreputable types who would overcharge consumers.

Both of these advertisements highlight the conflicted nature of NEP society. On the one hand, the party elite had restored private trade on the grounds that it would contribute to the post-war recovery of the economy. On the other hand, many communists remained fearful that private traders would take advantage of the policy as an opportunity to enrich themselves and thwart the goals of the revolution. For a loyal revolutionary, buying goods from Nepmen must have seemed like giving assistance to the enemy. By offering alternatives to private traders, the Mossukno and Mossel'prom advertisements implicitly sympathize with popular resentment of the state's policy. Yet the reality of daily life in the 1920s was that the supply and distribution of consumer goods rarely met demands; most people had to buy goods wherever they could find them. Perhaps these ads also functioned to remind people that they were *supposed* to take exception to Nepmen.[14]

Agency administrators' second goal was to use rural advertising to build relations between the city and the countryside. When peasants saw the wonderful goods offered by state enterprises, they would cheerfully sell their grain and support rural soviets. It was here that artists developed their most explicit presentation of the relationship between consumption and production. The exchange of Soviet commodities between classes supported production, which in turn strengthened the revolution itself; the politicized commodity exchange of these advertisements offered workers and peasants a sense of self-worth based on participation in an endless cycle of production and consumption. As Soviet producers, workers and peasants allied as classes to build socialism; the next step, according to rural advertising, was to develop an understanding of consumption as a form of class-based cooperation. Such a consumer alliance would benefit all the members of revolutionary classes, both as a group and as individuals. As a 1925 poster put it, "Getting inexpensive goods to the countryside is the basis of relations with the peasantry. Getting inexpensive bread to the worker is a pledge [*zalog*] to the victory of labor."[15] In these advertisements consumption became an extension of production, and like any other economic activity, it had political overtones. Buying and selling goods at state stores and cooperatives allowed commodities and scarce capital to flow between the city and the countryside, while building political and social relationships across the country.

Smychka often appeared as the theme of joint posters, which collected as many as fifty small advertisements on one poster with a unifying concept, such as industries of a specific type or in a specific area. (The joint poster was common during the 1920s; examples of it make up 38 percent of the NEP era posters at the Russian State Library. Joint posters brought in more revenue than single-product posters, and, by bringing several ads together under one theme, they allowed designers to link enterprises to larger social and political goals.) The most common scenario in these posters, as the Saratov poster in fig. 5.1, was a meeting of goods from the city and the country. Workers, bringing manufactured goods in trucks and train cars, came usually from the left side of the poster to the middle, where they were met by peasants delivering agricultural products. On the workers' side, the background featured cranes, bridges, and factories with billowing smokestacks; the peasant side featured electrified fields, schools, and village soviet buildings. Often the worker and the peasant were shaking hands in front of a rising sun, symbolizing the dawn of a new era of cooperation. The visual suggestion of a cycle of production and consumption was augmented by text advertisements for firms that both sold and bought goods, especially consumer societies and cooperatives.

In advertisements that challenged Nepmen and that promoted urban-rural cooperation, the actual consumption of goods was less important than proper methods of obtaining goods. On the other hand, the third theme of agitational advertising focused specifically on the impact of consumption itself, especially on peasants. Administrators argued that advertising could play a civilizing role by introducing modernizing products, such as pharmaceuticals, watches, and light bulbs. The consumption of these goods would contribute to "peasant uplift" by demonstrating the benefits of urban lifestyles. The March 1925 resolution of the newspaper association of the party's press department noted that advertising created a bridge between urban producers and rural consumers by "visually demonstrating to the peasant the role and meaning of one or another of the products of our industry in his life."[16] Whereas general propaganda efforts would acclimate peasants to modern concepts like mechanized agriculture and medical science, advertising would provide specific, practical information about how to obtain and use factory-produced goods. It would persuade peasants that these goods were not novelties or luxuries, but necessities. In 1925 a Dvigatel' administrator made an explicit connection between advertising, the distribution of manufactured goods to the country-side and grain collection: "Such work . . . can be a powerful means for an increase in the cultural level of the population, a summons from the slumbering state of consumer aspirations of the peasant population (especially in conjunction with harvest time), for increased sales and even, to a certain extent, for the struggle against private rural trade in so far as state industry and cooperatives have still not claimed the rural market."[17]

One of the most articulate expressions of advertising's political agenda came from R. G. Driubin, a member of the VSNKh Advertising Commission. In April 1926 he spoke before a VSNKh meeting of national enterprise managers on the goals of advertising and the contrast between socialist and capitalist advertising. Driubin stressed the deceptive nature of American and German advertising, which he argued was intended to increase "irrational" consumption in the hopes of offsetting the overproduction endemic to capitalist economies. Whereas capitalist advertising deceived consumers for the sake of profit and urged them to buy shoddy or unnecessary goods, socialist advertising provided consumers with important information and familiarized them with genuinely useful goods. Driubin even favored advertising for scarce commodities on the grounds that the agitational messages of such advertising would encourage consumers to look for state stores before turning to Nepmen; he maintained, rather naively, that many provincial consumers went to private traders only because they did not know where to find state and cooperative stores. Furthermore, advertising could accustom people to new financial institutions, such as savings banks and state bond programs.

Although he condemned the deceptive practices of western advertising, Driubin shared American admen's faith in the potential for advertising to shape the psychology of consumers. Driubin's ideal socialist advertising would still be manipulative, but such paternalistic manipulation would be for the benefit of the uneducated consumer, rather than to increase corporate profits. He called for the study of advertising in commercial education courses as a "specific discipline of psychotechnics." (Psychotechnics was a term used by German advertisers and indicates that Driubin, like many other Soviet agency administrators, was aware of German advertising theory.) By studying the psychology of advertising, a new cadre of trade specialists would learn how to

direct consumption for the maximum benefit of consumers and for the fulfillment of general social goals. In this speech Driubin focused on advertising's
civilizing mission, often speaking of peasant consumers with disdain. He spoke
of advertising's ability to correct "undeveloped demand" and the state's need
"to overcome the inertia of the narrow-minded psyche" and "to penetrate the
thickness of people." He also praised poet Vladimir Mayakovsky's advertising
verse, noting that even those people who didn't care for his style could not
deny that his catchy slogans had led to an increase in sales for Mossel'prom.
Driubin clearly understood advertising as a medium for directing consumer
beliefs in such a way as to both build support for the Soviet economy and
modernize consumer habits.[18]

The protocols of the VSNKh meeting listed the second commentator, V.
Iu. Gaus, as a representative of Sel'mashinsindikat, but he also had links with
TsUP. Even more than Driubin, Gaus stressed the role of advertising in modernization. Providing consumers with information about goods was only the
first part of the battle—the next step would be to awaken desire for culturally
important goods. Here the word "culture" really meant the introduction of
urban lifestyles and westernized conceptions of modernity in everything from
hygiene to housing construction. It was this potential to contribute to the
modernization of rural life that set socialist advertising apart from its capitalist
counterpart:

> In capitalist countries the main goal of advertising is to increase trade,
> enliven sales, and serve as a weapon of competition, while here the main
> goal of advertising is to increase the cultural level by arousing desire for
> those goods and products whose consumption will lead to cultural uplift
> [*kulturnyi pod"em*]. Here the task is not [just] to "educate" or "inform," but
> to prompt the consumption of these products.[19]

Such advertising, according to Gaus, benefited not only the producer,
who would see increased sales, but also the government, which would be
better able to achieve its social goals thanks to the acculturation of the population through the consumption of transformative, modernizing goods. Gaus
singled out "agricultural machinery, soap, medicines, insurance, [and] fire
extinguishers" as products which would contribute to uplift, and his comments suggest that he believed that the act of consumption had the ability to
change the consumer, both culturally and politically. No matter what resentment peasants might harbor toward the state, the undeniable benefits of state-
produced goods would ultimately bring them around. Gaus went on to argue
that any reorganization of the advertising agencies must create structures that
would focus maximum attention on this primary goal, and therefore the most
important element of reform should be the introduction of programs to train
designers in the psychology of advertising. Gaus also recommended that, given
the lack of homegrown specialists, American and German admen be invited to
teach advertising techniques to Soviet designers. Once schooled in the psycho-

Figure 5.5. Vladimir Mayakovsky, candy wrapper for Red October caramels. No. 3 in a series entitled "Red Army Star," 1923. Courtesy of the Russian State Library.

logical tactics of western advertising, Soviet designers could adapt those techniques for socialist needs.[20]

The agencies' emphasis on the economic and political ramifications of advertising was bolstered by the interest of a number of revolutionary artists, especially the Constructivists, in advertising and consumer theory. In 1923 Vladimir Mayakovsky and Aleksandr Rodchenko began their association as advertising designers under the name Reklam-Konstruktor (Advertising-Constructor), which became the most prolific and successful advertising project by Soviet artists. Between 1923 and 1925 Reklam-Konstruktor (also called Agit-Reklam) produced some one hundred fifty posters, newspaper ads, and product labels for state enterprises, such as GUM, Mossel'prom, and Rezinotrest (fig. 5.5).[21] Others in their cohort, including Nikolai Aseev and Anton Lavinskii, designed advertisements during the 1920s, and Osip Brik wrote a series of articles for *Zhurnalist* on the theory and technique of advertising.[22]

The Constructivists shared the Bolshevik fear of the corrupting potential of consumption, but rather than shying away from consumption, they attempted to convert it into a revolutionary activity. Worried that domestic comforts and old habits of daily life retarded the development of political consciousness, they sought new ways of thinking about consumption in order to transform objects into revolutionary actors that would encourage collective identity.[23] In other words, the Constructivists tried to redefine commodities in order to limit the possibility that mass consumption could lead to vulgar materialism; the revolutionary valuation of commodities in Soviet advertising would allow consumption to effect social transformations and play a healthy role in identity formation. As Osip Brik put it in 1924, "What kind of advertising do we really need in Soviet Russia? We need advertising that does not stupefy the public but instead clears the consciousness."[24]

Both the Constructivists and agency advertising artists incorporated motifs from political posters in order to increase the emotional power of their work; propaganda art provided a preestablished code which allowed them to pack a great deal of meaning into a single image. The importance of propaganda art as a source for agency advertising design is apparent from the sheer number of posters incorporating agitational motifs, defined here as any visual or textual element with pro-Bolshevik connotations and commonly used in state propaganda. Such elements include but are not limited to standardized images of classes, Soviet symbols such as the hammer and sickle, standardized images of technology, and agitational slogans. Of the 279 illustrated posters in the sample dated from 1922 to 1926, 217 (78 percent) featured at least one agitational motif. Designers were more likely to include agitational motifs in joint posters than in single-product posters; agitational themes often served to unify the unrelated firms advertised in joint posters. For the period 1922–1926 the number of agitational joint posters is 130 (95 percent of illustrated joint posters), while the number of agitational single-product posters is only 87 (62 percent of illustrated single-product posters). The use of Soviet political motifs to prompt readers to think about advertising as a subset of Soviet agitation seems to have been sucessful; in a 1925 survey of 120 urban students and village librarians asked to name two advertisements, 27 percent of the responses were in fact political posters, not commercial advertisements.[25]

Agitational images functioned to place advertising within the context of Bolshevik propaganda. While there is no direct documentary evidence that agency administrators worried about inciting bourgeois consumerism, their broad goal of supporting the state required that they find new ways to imagine consumption. Prerevolutionary advertising styles did not fit in well with Bolshevik ascetic tendencies and so had to be scrapped or restrained. Politicized representations of character, setting, and scenario encouraged consumers to place value on commodities by virtue of their heroic role as state-produced goods building socialism through exchange between the city and the countryside. Whereas American advertising attached emotional worth to an object by its role in private life, after it was no longer a commodity, NEP agitational advertising described commodities as valuable precisely because they *were* commodities. NEP commodities could transcend mere bourgeois consumption, because they modernized the countryside, brought technology to workers and peasants, and even defined revolutionary identity by distinguishing socialist consumption from that of the bourgeoisie. Far from presenting an ideological danger, NEP commodities created revolutionary consciousness and offered consumers a tangible way to demonstrate their commitment to socialism. As Rodchenko put in a 1923 poster, "Anyone who has not bought a share in Dobrolet is not really a citizen of the USSR."[26]

By creating a narrative of consumption intertwined with other aspects of Soviet identity, advertising complemented and expanded on Bolshevik notions of class, gender, and ethnicity. When advertising designers portrayed consumers, they turned to images that revealed the self as an economic actor engaged in an interdependent cycle of production-exchange-consumption. Portrayals of producers expanded to include consumption as part of the obligations to one's class; workers' and peasants' civic responsibilities also entailed correct consumer behavior. The integration of the consumer and producer encouraged the use of textual and visual motifs that underlined the dual role of the economic self. The ambiguous representation of characters in NEP advertising reflected this dual identity; rarely were they only producing or only consuming, instead they did both. Illustrations depicted modernity with trains, factories, tractors, cranes, and electric lines—symbols of production and exchange. Even in ads where production was not actually shown, designers reminded viewers of the consumer's productive role by using political vocabulary and dressing characters in class costumes (fig. 5.6). Designers of agitational advertisements de-emphasized gender, age, income level, and other characteristics that might have informed consumer choice; class loyalty would be the determining factor in the new Soviet consumption.

Artists adopted class iconography from agitational posters in order to evoke an instant emotional response to the characters as revolutionary producers. Workers in NEP advertisements were literate young men. Straight lines created chiseled faces, strong chins, and a youthful, lean look. As in Civil War agitation, advertisements portrayed the worker as a blacksmith carrying a hammer and wearing boots, a smock, and the ubiquitous cap. The worker's eagerness and dedication to labor were often indicated by sleeves which had been rolled up, in contrast to the long sleeves of the more lackadaisical peasant (fig. 5.7). As Victoria Bonnell has demonstrated, the worker-blacksmith was the primary symbol of Bolshevik labor in the 1920s; drawing on a multiplicity of traditional, Western, and socialist associations, the blacksmith had come to represent both the physical prowess and the dignity of the worker-hero.[27]

The transplanting of the worker-blacksmith into NEP advertising reveals a fascinating progression of meaning. On one hand, late imperial advertising art often featured class types, including the worker, and it would be possible to see the reappearance of the worker in 1920s advertising as a Sovietization of an old technique.[28] But contemporary viewers, operating in a continually developing culture, likely would have rejected such an interpretation. The blacksmith

Figure 5.6. Unknown artist, "State Tobacco Factory,
Vladivostok," 1926. Courtesy of the Russian State Library.

had followed a twisting path from prerevolutionary graphics (including advertising) though Bolshevik propaganda to finally arrive in NEP advertising. Because the blacksmith was already well established as an archetypal figure,
viewers could not help but "read" the image of the worker-blacksmith in
advertising as an extension of the worker in other forms of Bolshevik propaganda. This movement of images had certain semiotic ramifications. While
propaganda art created a Marxist narrative focused on the effects of changing
the means of production, advertising was necessarily about consumption,
about action in the present, not the future. When advertising designers portrayed workers as consumers, they changed what it meant to be a worker.
Constructivist designers clearly intended for this transferal of meaning to take
place as part of their effort to define socialist consumption. For staff designers,

Figure 5.7. Unknown artist, "State Syndicate 'Sel'mash,'"
1926. Courtesy of the Russian State Library.

however, the process was likely more unconscious—a response to administrators' instructions that advertising should be consistent with other state propaganda. Both the Constructivists and agency administrators wanted advertising to have emotional power; the adoption of the blacksmith-worker gave designers access to an established set of associations, which allowed the creation of complex messages with a simple image.

Advertising designers also lifted their visual representation of peasants directly from propaganda conventions, and like propaganda, advertising art was more ambivalent about peasants than it was about workers. Designers usually drew peasants as older, bearded men in bast sandals, leg wraps, and Russian shirts. Patched clothing and unkempt hair indicated poverty, and often peasant heads drooped forward, in contrast to the straight posture of the more intelligent worker. Take, for example, the peasant in V. M. Kaabak's 1925 poster for agricultural literature. Standing in front of a tractor, he reads a journal, presumably about mechanized agriculture. His neck strains toward the text, and his face suggests confusion, which is reinforced by text encouraging peasants to educate themselves in order to increase yields.[29] Unlike the heroic representation of the worker-consumer, these images portray peasants in need of assistance, ready to be improved by manufactured goods.

Certain scenarios required slightly more nuanced depictions of peasants. In joint posters where peasants exchanged goods with workers in an act of *smychka*, the image of the peasant rarely indicated poverty or confusion; although the worker remained the dominant figure, the peasant might share in the heroism of the moment (see fig. 5.1). Rural posters often used before-and-after scenarios that illustrated transformations of peasant life brought about by consumption of the advertised product, and contrasting images of peasants reinforced the strength of the social transformation. In the before image, peasants appeared especially grubby. Once a peasant opened a savings account or purchased an electric lamp, insurance, or a tractor, however, his posture improved. He acquired leather boots and a new shirt, the sleeves of which he rolled up. He trimmed and combed his hair. He might even dress in red. In other words, he took on attributes normally associated with workers. Propagandists used similar contrasting visual images to distinguish between peasant characters who had embraced Bolshevism and those who had not, and the convention transferred quite easily to advertising art. As one of the main goals of rural advertising was to encourage the peasant to participate in the market, advertising designers used these images to suggest that consumption of state goods would result in an overall improvement of peasant life, both materially and politically. The more peasants became like workers, the happier, and more advanced, they would be come.

Making that point dramatically, a 1925 poster told the tale of two peasants, one who bought insurance and one who did not (fig. 5.8). The poster is drawn in the cartoon panel style of the agitational ROSTA window posters. "Darkness and backwardness," lead Stepan away from the Gosstrakh (State Insurance) office. Then, in successive panels, his cow dies, and without insurance he has to borrow money from a kulak. Hail destroys his crops, and his house burns down. He appeals to the insurance office, but the bureaucrat turns him away. So he is forced to go to work for the fat kulak and suffer exploitation, all for lack of insurance. On the other side of the poster, "consciousness compelled" the second peasant, Ivan, to buy insurance. When similar fates befall him, a Gosstrakh clerk gives him gold coins, which Ivan uses to buy a new horse and new seed after a storm washes away his first planting. Gosstrakh also pays for Ivan to build a new house with a tin roof after the old house, with its thatched roof, burns down. As Stepan slides into poverty, his boots become bast sandals, and his clothes and hair become increasingly ragged. Ivan, on the other hand, is sharply dressed in a red shirt and black boots. The contrast in their appearance mirrors their contrasting fates. Ivan makes the correct choice to purchase insurance, because he is more aware of his political identity and class interests. Stepan's lack of political consciousness is the both the source and

Figure 5.8. Unknown artist, "Everything for peasants?" 1925. Detail from the section "He Who Did Not Buy Insurance." Courtesy of the Russian State Library.

result of his inappropriate consumer behavior. He doesn't buy insurance, because he is "dark." Without insurance, he is forced to turn back to the prerevolutionary ways and appeal to the kulak, first for a loan and then for a job. Stepan's refusal to buy insurance ultimately made the kulak stronger, and if peasant consumers didn't want that to happen to them, they had better buy insurance from the state.

A few designers allowed for the possibility that the development of a socialist consumption also had the potential to rehabilitate the nonrevolutionary classes. In contrast to most Soviet propaganda, which generally portrayed Nepmen as evil outsiders preying on good socialists, some advertisements featured intellectuals and Nepmen shopping at state stores alongside workers and peasants. Mossukno published several ads with this theme, showing men and women from a variety of classes waiting in line to get into Clothing Store No. 3.[30] In Rostov, the Don State Tobacco Factory's posters for *Nasha Marka* (Our Brand) cigarettes depicted similar scenes (fig. 5.9). One example from 1925 shows a Red Army soldier, a male worker with a hammer, an intellectual, his dowdy wife, a male peasant, and a woman in a fur coat with a Nepman in a tuxedo. (Neither of the women is smoking; they are merely accompanying the men, all of whom have cigarettes.) On the surface, this poster seems to repli cate the playful pre-1917 advertising trope of various classes united by a love of tobacco, but the order of the figures, with the soldier and worker on the left and the intellectual and the Nepman on the right, suggests a Marxist class hierarchy, as does the posture of the figures. The worker and the soldier stand straight, while the intellectual looks backward, and the bodies of the Nepman and his wife bend unnaturally. Yet even this ambivalent portrayal of Nepmen was far less hostile than most. Here proper consumer behavior patterns could rehabilitate even those of questionable social origins; so long as they purchased commodities from the state, even Nepmen and bureaucrats could briefly escape their bourgeois tendencies and join revolutionary classes in their movement forward.

Much to the dismay of agency managers devoted to agitation, the images

Figure 5.9. Unknown artist, "Our Brand Cigarettes," 1925. Courtesy of the Russian State Library.

in advertising were not as consistent as those in other forms of Soviet propaganda. Just under one quarter of the posters held at the Russian State Library do not include any agitational motifs; nearly all of these are single-product posters. Others combine agitational motifs with sentimental styles which would have appalled revolutionary artists (fig. 5.10). The lack of regulation or coordination between the agencies gave designers a lot of leeway; because the party had defined advertising as a financial resource, agitational content was entirely voluntary on the part of agencies. The importance of advertising revenues also subjected managers to the whims of clients, who may or may not have appreciated agitational advertisements; several agency administrators complained that clients sometimes insisted on non-agitational designs, which they felt were more emotionally compelling.[31] In addition, many products, such as wine, tobacco, clothing, and cosmetics, did not fit easily into agitational settings.

Like their agitational counterparts, the non-agitational posters used images that would inspire an irrational response to commodities by placing them in an emotional context. However, these posters took motifs from prerevolutionary and western advertising as their starting point.[32] Designers appealed not to collectivist aspirations, but directly to consumer desire with romantic or sentimental scenarios. The most common non-agitational style was the exotic; a third of the non-agitational posters featured romantic images of non-Russian cultures (fig. 5.11). Exotic advertisements played on Russian stereotypes as seductive Gypsies and dashing Cossacks offered teas, wines, and tobacco to Russian consumers. Other posters recalled the Art Nouveau style of late impe-

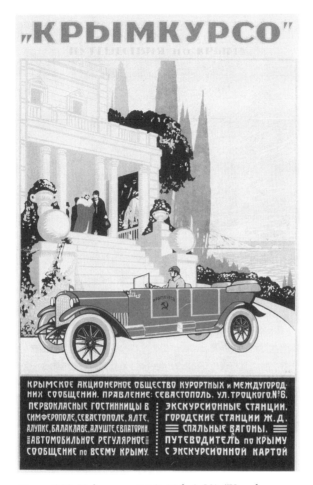

Figure 5.10. Unknown artist (initials A. V.), "Krymkurso.
Travel in the Crimea," circa 1922–1925. Note the hammer
and sickle on the door of the car. Courtesy of the Russian
State Library.

rial advertisements or simply recycled a prerevolutionary design after updating
the name of the client. A few designers made half-hearted attempts to graft
Soviet motifs into sentimental settings, while others placed modernity and
technology in a context that looked more Parisian than Soviet. The headline of
an ad for a tourist airline service, for example, chastised a woman for having
never flown in a plane: "It's a shame for a modern person to admit to having
never experienced the freedom of flight."[33] Rather than a worker's apron or a
peasant scarf, the woman wears fashionable high heels and a skirt, while her
face is hidden behind a swooping hat.

Figure 5.11. Unknown artist, "There are no better wines and cognacs than those of Dagsel'kreditsoiuz," 1926. Courtesy of the Russian State Library.

No matter their style, non-agitational and semi-agitational advertisements tried to make an impression on consumers by appealing to (ostensibly) non-political sensibilities, rather than reinforcing a collective identity. Like Western advertising, they divided consumption from production, rather than emphasizing a continuous cycle of economic activity. It was exactly this division which had so offended revolutionaries before 1917; consumption for the sake of personal pleasure obscured the productive origins of commodities. Yet, it must be emphasized, these were exceptions to the overall propagandistic mood of NEP advertising. The non-agitational posters reveal circumstances that might prompt clients and designers to put aside propaganda conventions. The large number of exotic images reveals the continued dominance of Russian ethnic stereotypes, especially regarding the East. The lack of political images in these posters presented no threat to the development of a class-based collective identity; instead the posters reinforced Russian superiority by emphasizing the otherness of non-Russians. Even in agitational posters, non-Russians were kept separate from the Russian classes. A Russian worker might show goods to a non-Russian "type," but non-Russians rarely appeared in class roles.

Art Nouveau and sentimental posters, on the other hand, were likely more troubling to communists, because they appealed to "feminine" values of luxury, tenderness, and idyllic relations with nature. Some of the most startling images of this type appeared in advertisements for clothing and toiletries. When images of figures dressed in bourgeois urban fashions appeared in agitational advertisements, it was either as a villain or as a Nepman partially rehabilitated by consumption of state products. Yet in advertisements for clothing and cosmetics, such figures frequently appeared ostensibly devoid of any political connotations. Many state clothing and cosmetics firms, including GUM, Mossukno, the All-Union Textile Union, Rezinotrest, and Tezhe, published posters depicting men and women in urban fashions that in any other context would brand them as political enemies (fig. 5.12). Political propagandists might portray workers in smocks and caps, but state clothiers invited them to wear suits and bowties. Images in such posters included women with bobbed hair dressed in high heels, tailored dresses, and smart hats, while the men were portrayed in suits with tailored jackets and slacks with cuffs, although a cap sometimes replaced the more traditional fedora. Such posters no doubt played a large role in the criticism of the Rabkrin investigators and others that advertising was not always sufficiently agitational (see below).[34] However, I would argue that, rather than suggesting a lack of revolutionary zeal on the part of agency artists, these conflicted images reflected the precarious position of the clothing and toiletries industries during NEP. Christina Kiaer, for example, has observed that Constructivist efforts to work with the Leningrad Clothing Trust (*Leningradodezhda*) to mass produce "proletarian" clothing never got past the experimental stage, and advertisements for that firm also suggest that traditional tastes in fashion dominated the clothing trade during the 1920s.[35]

By the end of 1925 it had become apparent that Soviet advertising could not function effectively as both propaganda and financial support for the press. Had advertising been conducted from the start as part of the general Soviet propaganda effort, a state advertising organ might have been able to build stronger relationships with their clients; as it was, the structure of agencies as commercial branches of their parent bodies fostered institutional behavior that discredited advertising. Vicious competition, monopolies, and commissioned sales had led to hostile relationships between agencies and their clients. Because advertising costs were rarely included in enterprise budgets, even agitational advertising was a fiscal burden, and in 1925 industrial directors, especially in the provinces, grumbled that it was not their responsibility to subsidize the press. To make matters worse, many of them began to refuse to buy adver-

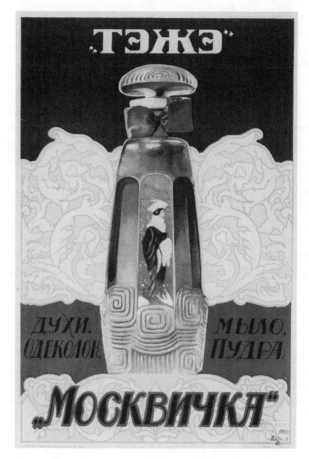

Figure 5.12. Unknown artist, "Tezhe 'Moskvichka,'" 1926.
Courtesy of the Russian State Library.

tisements on the grounds that, while advertising was perhaps agitationally or financially important to the press, it had little real impact on the economic performance of its clients.

Agency managers blamed one another for clients' increasing reluctance to buy advertisements through agents, especially in the provinces, and for a rapid rise in prices and commissions. Conflicts escalated in 1925 and 1926 between those managers who saw advertising's primary goal as agitation for Soviet industry and those who saw agitation as a side effect of advertising's ability to generate revenue for the press. The agitational faction, led by A. F. Gladun at Dvigatel', used its access to the press to publicize the inefficiencies and absurdities of the agency system, which impeded the creation of agitational advertising campaigns. Even the most talented artist could impart only so much meaning into a single advertisement; the agitational effectiveness of advertising would be dramatically increased if advertisements could be linked in an extended campaign that would reinforce their message through repetition, as American advertising campaigns did. Mounting such a campaign required that clients have access to all forms of advertising—newspapers, magazines, posters, flyers, electric billboards, subway and tram postings, even radio and film—but monopolies made that impossible. In addition, the failure to include advertising in budgets meant that most state enterprises, able to afford only a few advertisements at one time, could not commit to an extended campaign, which unfortunately also meant that clients endured repeated visits from agents. The only solution, Gladun argued, was to replace the multitude of agencies with one state organ that would approach advertising as marketing for Soviet goods and propaganda for Soviet economic policies. Such an organ would be able to take advantage of the extensive scientific research on advertising that had been going on in the West and adapt that research to meet Soviet agitational needs.[36] The revenue faction, centered around Mosreklama, Sviaz', and Transpechat', responded, perhaps justifiedly, with counter-accusations that calls for planned advertising were merely disguised bids for power by the largest agencies. They disputed the claim that the agencies could not produce good agitation and argued that a huge bureaucratic agency would destroy designers' creativity.[37]

This debate, conducted in the pages of the central economic newspapers, attracted the attention of Rabkrin, the Workers and Peasants' Inspectorate, which conducted oversight of state institutions. The Rabkrin Committee for Ad-hoc Investigations studied Soviet advertising agencies through the second half of 1925, and in February 1926 the investigators agreed that the agency system should be scrapped in favor of one organ which would conduct advertising as consumer propaganda without regard to generating press revenues. More seriously, the investigators charged that the agencies had abused their power as Soviet organs. The definition of advertising as a source of revenue for the press made it possible to pressure clients into buying advertising that they did not need. Enterprises engaged in heavy industry, in particular, had no need to reach a mass consumer base, but agents in search of commissions often persuaded enterprise directors to buy "charitable advertisements" by insinuating that a refusal to buy advertising in support of the Soviet press revealed a lack of political commitment. Whenever they could, the agencies supplied agents with letters from party figures as high-ranking as Feliks Dzerzhinskii, the chairman of VSNKh, which urged managers to buy advertisements in publications of particular political worth.[38] How could any Soviet administrator turn down an agent armed with such a letter? Charitable advertising tactics, critics charged, amounted to nothing less than emotional and political blackmail of Soviet managers. Rabkrin investigators also discovered that 14 percent of total Moscow advertising revenues came from *private* clients (mostly small workshops), which discredited the claim that the agencies conducted propaganda for the Soviet economy. The proportion was even higher among the departmental agencies, which were motivated largely by the need to generate income; 21.5 percent of the revenues of Mosreklama, the agency of the Moscow city soviet, came from private clients, an obviously unforgivable transgression for a government organ.[39]

The collapse of NEP advertising was as swift as its rise had been. The Rabkrin Collegium forced the liquidation of Dvigatel' and obligated the other agencies to merge into one organ under the Commissariat of Trade's Committee on Press Affairs, but the scandal that erupted when *Pravda* published Rabkrin's findings led to plummeting sales and the bankruptcy of most of the big agencies over the next six months. Newspaper advertising departments saw their revenues fall between 40 percent and 85 percent by the end of 1926, and the Committee on Press Affairs urged newspaper editors to look for new sources of revenue as advertising was no longer reliable.[40] As a result, in November 1926 Rabkrin dropped its demand for unification.[41] Small agencies, especially at newspapers and journals, continued to sell advertising through commissioned agents throughout the First Five-Year Plan, but rapid industrialization meant that few firms had funds to spare for advertising, which was still not included in enterprise budgets. The introduction of rationing of key consumer goods also led to a decline in advertising sales. Advertising posters held currently at the Russian State Library drop from a high of 115 posters from 1925 to 55 in 1927 and to 21 in 1929.

By the end of 1926 it had become clear to agency administrators that no one outside of the advertising community took their work seriously as economic agitation. As they discussed reform plans over the next four years, some administrators became convinced that the key to resurrecting advertising was to let go of their attempts to integrate existing Soviet propaganda models into advertising. American and German research offered "scientific" proof of the effectiveness of certain advertising motifs, especially those which emphasized the pleasure of consumption. The remaining Soviet agencies, still motivated by the desire to increase the sales of state products, began to experiment with advertising design that appealed to the senses rather than the conscience of the consumer. American researchers, in particular, had conducted extensive experiments on the psychological impact of advertising on consumers, and the science that supported American advertising suggested to Soviet observers that its techniques were more successful at directing consumer behavior than agitational ads were. The Association of Advertising Workers (ARR), founded in 1926, called for Western-type market research and education for Soviet designers, although repeated calls for research and training in 1936 suggest that no action was ever taken in this regard. A special section of the ARR under D. I. Reitynbarg, the association's secretary, set up a library of foreign advertising literature at the House of the Press in Moscow.[42]

Reitynbarg championed increased awareness of foreign advertising theory. In 1926 he translated several German articles for *Zhurnalist*, including an article by Hans Han entitled, "The Psychology of Advertising in America." In this piece Han argued that American advertising owed much of its success to its single-minded focus on creating a lasting association between the product and the name of the advertiser. Other information, even about the quality or the price of the product, distracted the reader and should be omitted. Instead, American advertisements encouraged the intended association by placing commodities in a "pleasant" context which attracted the reader's attention and created a memorable impression, prompting the purchase of goods. Han gave examples of American posters with images of blissful consumers intended to provoke the envy of readers, who would then purchase the advertised product to claim that happiness for themselves.[43] Although *Zhurnalist* offered Reityn-barg's translations without making explicit comparisons to Soviet techniques, the German language of advertising as "psychotechnics" and the American emphasis on research found its way into Soviet discussions of advertising during the late 1920s. A. Kuntsin, for example, argued in 1928 that the slowdown of advertising sales provided the perfect opportunity to study and expand on Western "advances" in the science of advertising through experimentation.[44]

The goal of these debates was to make Soviet advertising more relevant to the Soviet economy, but, responding to Western advertising science, advertising administrators began to let go of their conviction that advertising should look like political propaganda. Perhaps, some strategists wondered, advertising could be even more effective in promoting state goods if designers abandoned the politically motivated union of the producer and consumer and focused instead on consumption as a cultural pleasure, as Western ads did. The late 1920s saw the flourishing of a variety of styles, as agitational styles gave way to more "psychological" approaches to consumption. According to the "pleasantness principle" described in Reitynbarg's translations, political motifs and other broad pro-Soviet images only distracted the reader from the immediate message of consumption. Designers replaced the unified economic self with a consumer self, not out of a rejection of advertising's agitational mission, but in an effort to make it more effective at promoting products. While 78 percent of illustrated posters from 1922 to 1926 had incorporated agitational motifs, only 44 percent of illustrated posters from 1927 to 1929 did so. Part of this decline stemmed from a overall reduction in the publication of joint posters, which tended more toward agitation than single-product posters had, but even among single-product posters the proportion of agitational motifs dropped from 57 percent for 1922–1926 to 39 percent for 1927–1929.

The non-agitational motifs that had appeared during NEP got a second wind as designers brought the consumer self to the fore. Commodities appeared more often in non-productive contexts and promised personal happiness, rather than social transformation. The consumer self operated in isolation from the producer self; in these advertisements, the determining factor in consumer choice was the desire for personal pleasure and improvement through Soviet commodities. Consumption became a cultural obligation, not

Figure 5.13. Dmitri Tarkhov, print ad for Tezhe's Camelia Cream. *Prozhektor*, no. 37 (1929), inside cover. Note the French-language label. Courtesy of the Russian State Library.

a sociopolitical one, a tendency that would only increase into the 1930s. For example, in 1927 an ad for Kalodont toothpaste argued, "A healthy body has a healthy spirit, and healthy teeth are a sign of a healthy body. Kalodont is the only sure way to have healthy teeth always."[45] The shirtless man in the illustration has the strong figure that might have been associated with NEP worker-heroes, but here with no clothes to identify him as a producer, his consumption and his healthy spirit are individual. Whereas an American advertisement might have associated attractive teeth with popularity, and a NEP agitational advertisement might have stressed the working class vigor, this advertisement focused on a link between health, masculinity, and personal development. Similarly, in 1930 an ad for Chlorodont, an imported German toothpaste, featured an endorsement from Ol'ga Chekhova, a popular Russian film actress who had emigrated to Paris after the revolution. Tezhe, the main Soviet soap and cosmetics trust, and its Leningrad subsidiary, Lenzhet, used French-language labels on their products and in their advertisements in order to create an atmosphere of glamour (fig. 5.13).[46]

These first attempts at a more Western approach drew criticism from more militant quarters. Alarmed by the disappearance of productivist heroism in advertising, the Association of Artists of the Revolution (AKhR), among others, argued that Westernized ads, product labels, and shop windows threatened to destroy revolutionary consciousness by agitating for the return of *meshchan-stvo*, a complex term denoting the vulgar materialism and self-indulgence assumed to be characteristic of the petty bougeoisie.[47] Although I have not found any published response to such criticisms, the debates within the advertising community suggest that AKhR missed the point. These new advertisements were not intended to elevate consumption above production. Instead designers operated on the assumption that if sentimental or glamorous images increased the sale of state goods, then they supported the Soviet economy and encouraged commitment to socialism, despite their bourgeois appearance. Such a shift could not have come at a worse time. While advertising designers focused their attention on the consumer self, the rest of Soviet culture was moving toward an increase in productive urgency and militant heroism with the advent of the First Five-Year Plan. Experimentation with images of a consumer self clashed with the emerging narrative of revolutionary sacrifice. But this time there was no scandal. The end of NEP rescued the press from the demands of cost accounting, and advertising simply faded away in the early 1930s.[48]

What might have happened if NEP advertising had been more successful? Historians are generally loath to ask "what if" questions, but this one is tempting; it concerns the possibility of a state administration for consumer propaganda. Had a unified organ come about, its main responsibility would have been to create and refine an official state position on the psychological and economic basis of consumption in a socialist society. Given how problematic consumption was throughout the seventy-five-year history of the USSR (an impoverished country whose search for utopia instead resulted in strict hierarchies of access to goods and privileges), it is hard not to see the loss of advertising as a missed opportunity. The history of NEP advertising is the story of a road not taken, but it is also one that underscores the difficulties the Bolsheviks faced in the transition from a revolutionary conspiracy to government administration. As a narrative of consumption, advertising got to the heart of some of the key questions of the 1920s: What will the new life be like? What will be important to people on a day-to-day basis? How will the revolution change the ways in which people interact with one another? Where should one draw the line between consumption for survival and consumption as decadence? These were questions which NEP society had a very difficult time answering.

NOTES

I am indebted to The American Council of Teachers of Russian (ACTR) and Stephen F. Austin State University for financial support for the research of this article. I am also grateful for the comments of Kari Bronaugh, Karen Kettering, Christina Kiaer, Michaela Pohl, and the anonymous readers for Indiana University Press.

1. "Zdes' vse ot zemli i ot stanka," Department of Graphic Publications (Otdel Izoizdaniia, henceforth OI) of the Russian State Library, R2 IV 1/1Z, 1925.

2. The literature on consumption and society is vast. Works especially useful for this study include Arjun Appadurai, ed., *The Social Life of Things: Commodities in Cultural Perspective* (Cambridge: Cambridge University Press, 1986); Victoria de

Randi Cox

Grazia, ed., *The Sex of Things: Gender and Consumption in Historical Perspective* (Berkeley: University of California Press, 1996); Jackson Lears, *Fables of Abundance: A Cultural History of Advertising in America* (New York: Basic Books, 1994); William Leiss, Stephen Kline, and Sut Jhally, *Social Communication in Advertising: Persons, Products and Images of Well-Being* (Scarborough, Ont.: Nelson Canada, 1990); Roland Marchand, *Advertising the American Dream: Making Way for Modernity, 1920–1940* (Berkeley: University of California Press, 1985); and Rosalind Williams, *Dream Worlds: Mass Consumption in Late Nineteenth Century France* (Berkeley: University of California Press, 1982). For an excellent overview, see Don Slater, *Consumer Culture and Modernity* (Cambridge: Polity Press, 1997).

3. The archetypal nineteenth-century revolutionary ascetic was Rakhmetov, a character in Nikolai Chernyshevskii's influential novel *What Is to Be Done?* On revolutionary asceticism in the nineteenth century and the early Soviet period, see Svetlana Boym, *Common Places: Mythologies of Everyday Life in Russia* (Cambridge, Mass.: Harvard University Press, 1994), 29–120; and Marcia A. Morris, *Saints and Revolutionaries: The Ascetic Hero in Russian Literature* (Albany: State University of New York Press, 1993).

4. Eric Naiman, "Revolutionary Anorexia (NEP as Female Complaint)," *Slavic and East European Journal* 37:3 (1993), 305–325, especially 306–309.

5. On the fear of corruption see Igal Halfin, *From Darkness to Light: Class, Consciousness and Salvation in Revolutionary Russia* (Pittsburgh: University of Pittsburgh Press, 2000); Oleg Kharkhordin, *The Collective and the Individual in Russia* (Berkeley: University of California Press, 1999); and Eric Naiman, "The Case of Chubarov Alley: Collective Rape, Utopian Desire and the Mentality of NEP," *Russian History: Histoire Russe* 17 (Spring 1990), 1–30.

6. This summary of the institutional history of NEP advertising agencies is based on Randi Barnes Cox, "The Creation of the Socialist Consumer: Advertising, Citizenship and NEP" (Ph.D. diss., Indiana University, 2000), ch. 1.

7. Kommunisticheskaia partiia Sovetskogo Soiuza, *Odinnadtsatyi s"ezd RKP(b), mart–aprel' 1922 goda: stenograficheskii otchet* (Moscow: Gosudarstvennoe izdatel'stvo politicheskoi literatury, 1961), 516–517, 622–623.

8. In contrast, German advertising agencies in the 1930s had tight links to Nazi propaganda organs. Uwe Westphal, *Werbung im Dritten Reich* (Berlin: Transit Buchverlag, 1989).

9. A. K. Minchenko, chairman of the Advertising Commission of the Committee on Press Affairs under the Commissariat of Trade complained about advertisements for industrial blast furnaces in *Krest'ianka* (Peasant Woman) and *Proletarii u rulia* (Proletariat at the Helm), both of which were aimed at a popular audience. A. Minchenko, "Reklama v tsifrakh," *Biulleten' Komiteta po delam pechati* 7–8 (1926), 24–31.

10. Ilya Ehrenburg, *Memoirs: 1921–1941*, trans. Tatania Shebunina and Yvonne Kapp (Cleveland: World Publishing Company, 1963), 70.

11. The view of NEP competition as a spur to state trade is most closely associated with Aleksei Rykov and Nikolai Bukharin. However, no evidence exists to suggest that either man ever became involved with the advertising controversy or that advertising administrators ever appealed to them for support.

12. RGAE, f. 2139, op. 1, d. 106, ll. 4–5.

13. L. Gimmel'farb, "Ozdorovlenie i sovetizatsiia reklamnogo dela v SSSR," *Ekonomicheskaia zhizn'*, October 4, 1925.

14. Christina Kiaer has explored the paradox of advertising in the work of the avant-garde. In the long run, these utopianists hoped for a marketless economy in which goods were abundant and many activities, such as dining, were performed communally. In their daily lives, however, they hired themselves out to clients for whom they designed advertisements promoting the sale of goods to be used in private homes, not communal living spaces. See Christina Kiaer, *Imagine No Possessions: The Socialist Objects of Russian Constructivism* (Cambridge, Mass.: MIT Press, 2005), especially ch. 4.

15. "Promyshlennost' i kooperatsiia kubani na 1925 god," OI, R2, I/1P, 1925.

16. RGAE, f. 2139, op. 1, d. 106, ll. 4–5.

17. GARF, f. 374, op. 12, d. 326, l. 185.

18. RGAE, f. 2139, op. 1, d. 106, ll. 81–86.

19. Ibid., ll. 86–87.

20. Ibid.

21. Aleksandr Rodchenko, "Rabota s Maiakovskim," in V. A. Rodchenko, *A. M. Rodchenko: Stat'i, vospominaniia, avtobiograficheskie zapiski, pis'ma* (Moscow: Sovetskii khudozhnik, 1982), 64–68.

22. Ironically, Agit-Reklam was considered a private advertising firm, as it was not affiliated with any state or party organ and its revenues went to private citizens, the artists. On the avant-garde and NEP advertising, see Mikhail Anikst, ed., *Soviet Commercial Design of the Twenties* (New York: Abbeville Press, 1987); Cox, "The Creation of the Socialist Consumer," ch. 5; Kiaer; and V. N. Liakhov, ed., *Sovetskii reklamnyi plakat, 1917–1932* (Moscow: Sovetskii khudozhnik, 1972).

23. On the Constructivists and objects, see Kiaer and Paul A. Klanderud, "Maiakovskii's Myth of Man, Things, and the City: From *Poshlost'* to the Promised Land," *Russian Review* 55 (January 1996), 37–54.

24. O. M. Brik, "Kakaia nam nuzhna reklama," *Zhurnalist* 10 (1924), 62.

25. D. I. Reitynberg, "Nigde krome . . ." *Zhurnalist* 10 (1925), 59–60.

26. Dobrolet was the Voluntary Share Society for Assisting in the Development of Soviet Aviation.

27. On class iconography in Bolshevik agitation, see Victoria E. Bonnell, *Iconography of Power: Soviet Political Posters under Lenin and Stalin* (Berkeley: University of California Press, 1997); and Steven White, *The Bolshevik Poster* (New Haven: Yale University Press, 1988). On the worker-blacksmith see Bonnell, 23–34.

28. On class images in prerevolutionary advertising, see Sally West, "Constructing Consumer Culture: Advertising in Imperial Russia to 1914" (Ph.D. diss., University of Illinois, 1995), ch. 4.

29. Reproduced in Anikst, 87.

30. OI, R2 II16/3M, no date; *Izvestiia*, November 28, 1923.

31. For agency complaints about clients' "ignorance," see A. Grober, "Puti gazetnoi reklamy," *Krasnaia pechat'* 16 (1925), 41; and N. Sinitsyn, "Etapy sovetskoi reklamy," *Zhurnalist* 12 (1927), 46–48.

32. For examples of prerevolutionary styles, see Mikhail Anikst and Elena Chernevich, eds., *Russian Graphic Design, 1880–1917* (New York: Abbeville Press, 1990), 86–137; and N. G. Miniailo, *Torgovaia reklama i upakovka v Rossii, XIX–XX vv.* (Moscow: Gosudarstvennyi istoricheskii muzei, 1993).

33. OI, R2 XVII4/2V, no date.

34. For example, in the catalog for a Leningrad exhibition of political and com-

mercial posters, Moisei Brodskii criticized Tezhe's "tasteless" advertisements, which relied on the "dubious traditions" of the past. Rather than looking to the agitational posters of the Civil War for inspiration, Tezhe and other cosmetic firms used product names such as "Flirt," "First Kiss," and "Foxtrot" to appeal to old values and tastes. Moisei Brodskii, "Tseli i zadachi vystavki," in V. K. Okhochinskii, ed., *Plakat i reklama posle oktiabria* (Leningrad: Dom pechati, 1926), 4–9.

35. Kiaer, ch. 2, especially 74–76; "Leningradodezhda," OI, R2 IV 2/3L, 1925.

36. A. F. Gladun, "Reklama v sovetskom khoziastve," *Ekonomicheskaia zhizn'*, June 10, 1925. Also see Gladun, "Kakoi dolzhna byt' sovetskaia reklama," *Ekonomicheskaia zhizn'*, June 20, 1925; V. Iu. Gaus, "Nedostatki sovetskoi reklamy," *Zhurnalist* 2 (1925), 58–60; "Voprosy reklamy," *Zhurnalist* 2 (1925), 48–49; and An. Te, "Reklama—propaganda," *Zhurnalist* 11 (1926), 64–65.

37. N. V. Sinitsyn, "Fantazii v oblasti reklamy," unpublished letter to *Ekonomicheskaia zhizn'* dated July 6, 1925, GARF, f. 374, op. 12, d. 691, ll. 147–151; I. Matveev, "Eshche o tom kakoi dolzhna byt' sovetskaia reklama," *Ekonomicheskaia zhizn'*, July 15, 1925.

38. See, for example, VSNKh Circular #177 of March 22, 1924, in which Dzerzhinskii encouraged all VSNKh enterprises to place advertising in the journal *Predpriiatie* because it had no other means of financial support; see *Torgovo-promyshlennaia gazeta* (March 25, 1924), 6. The publishing house of Pravda/Bednota, which published *Predpriiatie*, sent potential clients two thousand copies of a form letter that quoted this circular, along with statements from other high-ranking figures; see GARF, f. 374, op, 12, d. 325, l. 115.

39. For the Rabkrin reports, see GARF, f. 374, op. 12, d. 693, ll. 1a–43 and GARF, f. 374, op. 12, d. 1125, ll. 1–61. The findings were summarized in two articles: Boris Roizenman, "Ne vsiakii 'Dvigatel'' khorosh," *Pravda* (February 2, 1926), 3; and Roizenman, "Reklamnoe delo," *Pravda* (March 24, 1926), 5.

40. A. Karpovich, "Reklama v biudzhete gazetno-zhurnal'nykh izdatel'stv," *Biulleten' Komiteta po delam pechati* 13–14 (1926), 25–29; A. Minchenko, 30–31.

41. GARF, f. 374, op. 12, d. 1123, ll. 1a–2.

42. "Sredi reklamnykh rabotnikov," *Zhurnalist* 5 (1927), 64.

43. Khans Khan, "Psikhologiia reklamy v Amerike," trans. D. I. Reitynbarg, *Zhurnalist* 8–9 (1926), 63–66. See also Reitynbarg's summary and translation of several short German articles, "Konkurs na gazetnuiu reklamu," *Zhurnalist* 2 (1926), 64–67.

44. Al. Kuntsin, "Pora nachat' izuchenie," *Zhurnalist* 7–8 (1928), 38.

45. *Prozhektor*, July 31, 1927.

46. *Prozhektor* 15, 1930; ibid., no. 37, 1929. See also various issues of *30 dnei* 1927 and 1928, back covers; Anikst, *Soviet Commercial Design*, 130–131.

47. See E. Atsarkin, "Etiketki i obertki pod khudozhestvenno-politicheskii kontrol'!" *Za proletarskoe iskusstvo*, no. 11–12 (1931), 40–41; O. Kuz'ma, "Za novuiu etiketku," *Iskusstvo v massy* 2 (1930), 31; D. Liakhovets, "Krovat' v ideologiei," *Iskusstvo v massy* 2 (1930), 30–31; V. S. "Oformlenie byta, proizvodstvennye organizatsii ne raskachalis'," *Iskusstvo v massy* 4 (1930), 22–23; and B. Zemenkov, "Udarim po agitpunktam meshchanstva!" *Iskusstvo v massy* 2 (1930), 29–30.

48. Advertising reappeared in the second half of the 1930s under different circumstances. See Randi Cox, "'All This Can Be Yours!' Soviet Advertising and the Social Construction of Space, 1928–1956," in *The Landscape of Stalinism: The Art and Ideology of Soviet Space*, ed. Evgenii Dobrenko and Eric Naiman (Seattle: University of Washington Press, 2003).

six

Panic, Potency, and the Crisis of Nervousness in the 1920s

Frances L. Bernstein

Nervousness is becoming the social disease of our time.
  —Dr. L. A. Prozorov[1]

> They arrived together, comrades Kh. and N. Both are workers. One is
> nineteen, the other eighteen years old. First one came in to see me, a pale,
> thin youth. I asked him the usual question—"What is troubling you?" "For
> over a year now I've had nocturnal emissions, it worries me. I did not know
> about the existence of the Counseling Center, for a long time I have wanted
> to see a doctor, but a private one costs a lot of money. I cannot work, I'm
> upset all the time, I have given up my studies at the factory school, I
> constantly think about my illness. My comrade is here with me. He has the
> same problem, and we decided together to come to the clinic for help."[2]

In the mid-1920s, the medical and popular health press began to devote
considerable attention to a phenomenon physicians claimed to be encountering with increasing frequency. Doctors reported that young men from all walks
of life were arriving in alarming numbers at their clinic doors, complaining of a
wide variety of debilitating sexual disorders. Like the two workers in the case
history above, they were described as shaking, insecure, paralyzed with fear,
often threatening to end their lives. According to one venereologist, the number
of these cases had reached such "completely inconceivable proportions [that] if
it were possible to conduct an anonymous survey on the sexual abilities of men
in the USSR, we would be left with extremely discomforting conclusions."[3]

The medical discourse surrounding this "epidemic" of male sexual dysfunction and the reasons it proved so discomforting in NEP Russia are the subject of this article.[4] In particular it focuses upon the representation of this illness—its etiology, diagnosis, and treatment—by the staff of the Moscow Counseling Center for Sexual Hygiene.[5] Originally founded to provide premarital advice and venereal disease screenings, the clinic gradually reinvented itself through the popular press as an authority in the care of impotent men. In this essay, I argue that the purported diagnostic and treatment success with male sexual dysfunction lay in medical writers' ability to exploit the widespread sense of unease and crisis pervasive throughout Soviet society during the 1920s. Yet nervousness was not limited to clinic patients. The medical construction of this illness expressed physicians' own anxieties about the male body and the professions' authority over the realm of sexuality, as well as more generalized fears about the potential impotence of the new state.

Towards a Healthy Lifestyle and the
Counseling Center for Sexual Hygiene

On 1 January 1925, at the height of the New Economic Policy, a new periodical appeared in Moscow. Published by the outpatient clinic of the State Venereological Institute, Towards a Healthy Lifestyle (Za zdorovyi byt) would be "dedicated to questions concerning the fight against venereal diseases and prostitution, the family and marriage, sexual enlightenment and education."[6] The only newspaper in the 1920s devoted exclusively to the sex question, Za zdorovyi byt joined the ranks of the growing numbers of "sanitary enlightenment" publications whose aim was the transformation of daily life through a widespread program of health and hygiene propaganda.[7] According to its writers, popular ignorance was the only obstacle to sexual health; accordingly, once people received the proper information, all sexual problems would disappear. This orientation was reiterated on page three of the first issue, in an announcement publicizing the opening of a "Counseling Center for Sexual Hygiene" (Konsul'tatsiia po polovoi gigiene), which offered free advice on sex to the public: "The fundamental reason for sexual irregularity lies in the fact that wide segments of the population are very poorly informed about the essence of the sexual question, how sexual abnormalities come about, how one should conduct a proper sex life, etc."[8]

Jointly established by the State Venereological Institute and the Institute of Social Hygiene,[9] the "Counseling Center for Sexual Hygiene" (alternatively called the Counseling Center for a Healthy Lifestyle [Konsul'tatsiia po ozdorovleniiu byta]) aimed to provide Muscovites with the opportunity to receive information and advice tailored to their own particular sexual experiences. The clinic would focus on prevention of illness rather than treatment of preexisting conditions, an emphasis underlined by the very names given to the clinic: "making lifestyle healthy" linked the mission of this institution to the widespread revolutionary "fight for a new lifestyle" (*bor'ba za novyi byt*), which was aimed at the radical restructuring of all aspects of a person's life; "sexual hygiene" referred to the rules that were to govern one's sexual life, involving such issues as frequency of sexual intercourse, the use of birth control, and the proper sanitary regime during menstruation.

The center was housed in the Institute of Social Hygiene at number 14 Vozdvizhenka in central Moscow. It opened its doors to the public in November 1925 and received visitors twice weekly, on Monday and Thursday from six to seven in the evening. Soon thereafter the Neuropsychiatric Dispensary joined as a sponsoring institution.[10] The procedure at the clinic was as follows: upon arrival at the office, the person seeking advice was greeted by either a venereologist-urologist or a psychoneurologist.[11] To underline the confidential nature of the visit, the doctors, who rotated staffing responsibilities, worked unassisted. The visitor filled out a questionnaire that solicited biographical information, and then related his or her question. If the doctor was unable to resolve the issue immediately, the subject was directed to an appropriate medical institution for more specialized care.[12] Over the next several years, counseling centers based upon the Moscow model opened in many cities throughout the Soviet Union, including Tashkent, Tbilisi, Iaroslavl', Leningrad, Odessa, and Khar'kov.[13]

By 1927, physicians associated with the center had gathered enough data to permit the first published analyses of the institution's progress. Every account of the clinic written for a medical audience began with a lengthy discussion of its foreign predecessors, tracing its roots from the founding of the first sex counseling center in the United States in 1895 to its continued extension throughout Europe and especially Germany.[14] After this preliminary historical introduction the authors turned to the Moscow Counseling Center, presenting it as the Soviet contribution to the growing international movement. As their comments reveal, they fully expected their data to conform to the statistics provided by their European colleagues. Yet the Russian physicians found themselves faced with a very different portrait of sexual behaviors and concerns.

Whereas, according to the studies cited, the largest segment of those visiting the counseling centers in Berlin, Dresden, and Mannheim sought information on sexual hygiene, or wished to confirm their health before marriage, the vast majority of those who came to the Moscow Counseling Center were men suffering from sexual dysfunction. In fact, 59.6 percent of this institution's first-year visitors were men, predominantly in their twenties, who complained of impotence, premature ejaculation, nocturnal emissions, or masturbation-related sexual failure. Four times as many men frequented the clinic as women, another point of difference between the Russian and the European clinics, where the gender ratio was more even. Only in terms of age and social origin did the Russian statistics resemble those of their European counterparts; white-collar workers predominated in both, with students following in second place and "proletarians" a distant third. This comparatively low attendance of workers was attributed by the Russian doctors to the artificial nature of the sample, since advertisements of the clinic's existence had been intentionally limited to only a few factories and educational institutions.[15]

The authors' interpretation of these data posited a hierarchy of sexual development, in which Russians lagged far behind their European neighbors. Yet this conclusion resulted in part from a flawed comparison: the German clinics to which the Russians referred were the *Eheberatungstellen,* or marriage counseling bureaus, where Germans turned for advice on eugenics and premarital venereal disease testing; in other words, precisely those areas targeted for attention at the Moscow Counseling Center.[16] The Russian doctors compared their clinic to the German marriage counseling bureaus because they envisioned the goals of the two institutions to be the same: prevention of illness rather than treatment of already existing disease.

The Counseling Center for Sexual Hygiene had been established as a place where people could take an active role in ensuring their sexual well-being. In the opinion of its founders, attendance would demonstrate the population's commitment to good health through its prophylactic use of the clinic, by embracing the approach to illness that was the cornerstone of Soviet medicine. But the low numbers of women, the rarity of people using the Center to assess their health before marriage (originally identified as the most important purpose of the clinic), and especially the disproportionately high incidence of dysfunction all purportedly demonstrated the Russian population's sexual immaturity and backwardness vis-à-vis the West. Referring to the fact that not one engaged couple had come to the Moscow Counseling Center to seek prenuptial advice (compared to thirty such reported visits at the Berlin bureau during the same time period), the doctors commented, "we see that the idea of a counseling center as such is apparently completely absent among the masses."[17] In the conclusion to reports written for the medical community, they reiterated their commitment to the principles of prophylaxis, vowing to significantly increase their advertising base and devote particular attention to promoting the idea of premarital medical consultations.[18]

Special efforts were also made to attract women: a female-only counseling center was opened at the editorial offices of *Woman's Journal,* and women's health clinics, which previously handled issues strictly related to gynecology and maternity, were encouraged to broaden their sphere of competence.[19] The Moscow Counseling Center also expanded the list of services it provided; in 1929 it divided these into three categories, each of which would be available on a different day. In addition to sex education and hygiene, the center would also offer advice on issues relating to marriage and the family, and a lawyer would be present to answer legal questions. Yet despite these attempts to reach women and the continued reiteration of the clinic's prophylactic orientation, the new title given to one of the three subsets, "Division for Sexual Hygiene and the Pathology of Adults,"[20] reveals the doctors' recognition that the de facto purpose of the clinic had changed.

The alarmingly high rate of male sexual disorders warranted a special response, one that would explicitly target those in danger of succumbing to these maladies. The clinic physicians accomplished this through a strategy of selective representation and exclusion: to the readers of *Towards a Healthy Lifestyle*, which reported on the clinic in every issue, the counseling center became exclusively devoted to the treatment of sexually dysfunctional men. Other publications presented the client pool rather differently. Whereas the popular *Woman's Journal* and the specialist periodical *Psychohygienic and Neurological Research* stressed the predominance of men and their frequent complaints of impotence, they also listed women's reasons for visiting the clinic.[21] But despite the efforts made by the center to reach women, the message ultimately communicated to the public via *Towards a Healthy Lifestyle* was that female sexuality was relevant only as it concerned men.

In the first report of the center's progress published in *Towards a Healthy Lifestyle*, doctors attributed women's low attendance rate to "false shame" (*lozhnyi styd*). Thereafter, women appeared in discussions strictly as a factor contributing to male dysfunction, whether as the disease-infected prostitute to whom the Red Army man erringly turned to prevent nocturnal emissions,[22] or as the beloved wife whose husband feared his impotence would lead her to abandon him.[23] In analyses written for the medical community, in contrast, the center's doctors were not so much dismissive of as simply baffled by female sexuality. To explain their low level of clinic attendance, doctors pointed to women's supposed embarrassment, their shaking and indecisive voices, and their constant concern that they be seen by a woman doctor. Yet the authors offered no suggestions as to how they might increase the comfort of their female patients.[24] The clinic physicians also appeared at a loss in regard to female sexual dysfunction (i.e., frigidity), acknowledging that "for us, in the sense of giving advice, these were perhaps the most difficult cases."[25]

After the first column on the clinic in *Towards a Healthy Lifestyle*, each subsequent issue's report was devoted exclusively to the problem of male sexual dysfunction. The psychoneurologist Dr. Gurvich, the counseling center's newspaper correspondent, described one such case in the next edition. A young man arrived at the clinic, horrified (*v uzhase*) that he was impotent. The doctors learned that his first unsuccessful attempt at intercourse occurred while he was drunk, a condition which, as Gurvich explained to him and to the paper's readers, frequently resulted in sexual failure. At that moment feelings of doubt appeared, increasing every time the man attempted to have sex with his wife, and resulting in further incidents of impotence. Trying to locate the origins of his problem, the man remembered that at one time he had masturbated. He also remembered reading books about the dangerous ramifications of masturbation, and concluded that he was now being made to pay for his old sins.[26] The doctors explained that previous masturbation does not lead to impotence and pointed out the detrimental influence of alcohol on sexual performance. Gradually the man calmed down, and, no longer so pessimistic about his future, found that his sex life began to return to normal. Gurvich concluded: "We believe that when some sort of sexual complication appears, one shouldn't immediately panic, decide that he is finished, think about suicide; instead he needs to see a doctor for advice as soon as possible."

In a later issue of *Towards a Healthy Lifestyle*, Gurvich described the appearance at the center of another young man. Excited, shaking all over, he could barely speak from agitation.[27] Recently married and deeply in love with his wife, his attempt at sex the day before had ended in premature ejaculation. Gurvich quoted him: "You understand, doctor—he spoke with despair—if I can't be cured, I'll kill myself. After all, my wife won't stay with me, and if she leaves me, it would be better to die." After calming him down, the doctors discovered that he had lost his job the morning before due to work reductions. Having spent the day appealing to different authorities to prevent the layoff, he returned home exhausted, "a bundle of nerves" (*iznervnichavshiisia*). Gurvich commented, "After his story it became clear to us that here apparently was one of those many cases when in circumstances of serious exhaustion or after an extremely unpleasant event the sex act might be unsuccessful. But this after all in no way says that a person had developed sexual impotence!" The doctors explained the reasons for his failure, and certain that there were no serious problems, sent him back to his wife. They advised him to share this information with her should there be any future incidents of sexual failure, stating confidently that she would understand him and not think about leaving. Several days later the man returned to the clinic to report that his previous visit had calmed him down so successfully that, no longer afraid, he was able to resume a completely normal sex life.

Subsequent issues of the newspaper focused on other cases, but aside from the specific sexual complaint they deviated little from this pattern. Indeed, this apparent epidemic of dysfunction seemed to spare no one: among the young men who arrived trembling and terrified at the clinic's doors were Red Army men, workers, students, peasants, and party members.[28] Each seemed ready to end his life rather than continue to suffer. Yet after one visit to the counseling center, all were miraculously cured. The answer, as conceived by the doctors, lay in the fact that the problem was not really located in their sexual organs; rather, the ailments were all in their heads. Gurvich diagnosed their illness as "sexual dysfunction of a psychological origin," explained as meaning "from thoughts [*ot dumki*], not having the slightest basis in reality."[29]

The clinic doctors responded to their discovery of the psychogenic basis of the widespread sexual dysfunction in two ways. In reports written for the scientific community, they recommended that more psychoneurologists become involved in the counseling centers.[30] At the same time that the high incidence of dysfunction warranted a shift from preventive care to the treatment of preexisting conditions, the transfer of attention from the body as the locus of sexual disorder to the head determined which medical specialty would be most needed by the clinic's patients. While the involvement of venereologists in the clinic's work and the advocacy of prevention and hygiene continued, the center's primary orientation became and would remain neuropsychiatric. Moreover, as we will see, the physicians' shift of emphasis from the body to the head also reveals that the medical vision of manhood during this time period was decidedly nongenital. Its basis, according to these sources, lay elsewhere.

The physicians' second tactic was a mass campaign of "calming" (*uspokoenie*), which was conducted on the pages of *Towards a Healthy Lifestyle*. Through the repetition of case histories, the doctors hoped to convince their audience that occasional sexual failure did not indicate a real sexual problem.

> We consider it useful to mention [these cases] to show once again that occasional failures during the sexual act say nothing about the appearance of sexual impotence or about severe dysfunctions of the sexual sphere. Many do not know that such failures may frequently depend on purely external reasons (exhaustion, unexpected misfortune, inconvenient setting for the sex act, alcohol intoxication, etc.).[31]

In fact, Gurvich explained, such incidents were normal. In the column cited at the beginning of this essay that focused upon the problem of nocturnal emissions in two young men, Gurvich wrote:

> Fear and worry were so sincerely expressed on the faces of both youths that I decided to have a detailed conversation with them in which I tried to make them understand that they did not have any sort of illness. Nocturnal emissions, which each experienced, are a *completely normal* substitution of the sex act in young people who are not yet sexually active, but have already reached sexual maturity . . . Let us repeat that if a young man not yet sexually active or a Red Army man forced to temporarily interrupt his sex life sometimes has nocturnal emissions, *this is not bad* [*eto ne plokho*].[32]

This insistence on the "normalcy" of occasional sexual dysfunction was central to the campaign of "calming," and aimed to bolster the self-confidence of those shaken by fear of sexual inadequacy and pathology. "And not knowing all this, they become horrified at the slightest failure and often, thanks to ignorance, lose faith in themselves and their capabilities, out of which may develop 'nervousness' [*nervnost'*]."[33]

Indeed, nervousness was considered to be the real malady afflicting these men. Describing a letter to the counseling center written by a twenty-five-year-old peasant suffering from premature ejaculation, Gurvich concluded "after his first failure there appeared in Comrade A. uncertainty in himself, uncertainty in his sexual strength . . . there formed in Comrade A. an illness, but not a sexual illness (his sexual organs, without any doubt, are completely normal); nervousness developed."[34] As this letter demonstrates, Gurvich was so certain that Comrade A.'s nerves were the real culprit that the genitals no longer even needed to be examined to arrive at this conclusion. This point was reiterated in each column, as the authors confidently concluded that once the subject had been calmed, enlightened, and sent home, there would be no further problems.

> How do we treat [nervousness]? Of course, the greatest victory would be if Comrade A., having read this article, understood that he is not physically ill, believed in his strength, and, not fearing failure, began to live a calm sex life. If in the beginning there is failure, then he needs to relate to it calmly, to remember that it will pass, and that the less he pays attention to it, the sooner it will happen. Cases of such cures following an explanatory conversation in our Counseling Center occur frequently.

The association between nervousness and maleness represented an important shift away from earlier medical notions of nervous illness, and especially hysteria, as the particular domain of women.[35] That the doctors subscribed to and conveyed this notion to their patients was confirmed by the information sheets filled out at the clinic; the question about whether the visitor suffered from nervousness was only included in the section to be completed by men.[36]

Soviet Nervousness

The focus of the Counseling Center for Sexual Hygiene on nervousness was not an isolated one. In the years after the revolution and especially during the NEP, a vast amount of public attention was devoted to nerves, evoking the image of a society seemingly wracked with and obsessed by psychological disorders. Readers sent anxious letters about their nervous state to advice columns in newspapers; popular pamphlets counseled on how to detect the symptoms of nervous illness. In the introduction to one such booklet, the psychiatrist M. Rozenshtein wrote, "One can hardly find another expression that has been so frequently used in such different situations as the word nerves, nervousness. Rarely, rarely do we meet people who are not nervous or who don't sometimes feel their nerves."[37] Writers of fiction also drew upon the wide appeal of the topic, as did Mikhail Zoshchenko in "Nervous People" ("*Nervnye liudi*"), an extremely popular sketch published in the journal *Hippopotamus* in 1925:

> Not long ago, a fight took place in our communal apartment. Not just a fight, but an out-and-out battle. On the corner of Glazova and Borova. Of course, they put their hearts into the fight . . . The main reason is—folks are very nervous (*narod ochen' uzh nervnyi*). They get upset over mere trifles. They get all hot and bothered. And because of that they fight crudely, as if they were in a fog. As for that, of course, they say that after a civil war people's nerves always get shaken up. Maybe so, but from that theory the veteran Gavrilich's noggin won't heal up any faster.[38]

Such awareness and concern regarding this "nervous age" extended far beyond Soviet Russia. In the last decades of the nineteenth century, doctors' offices across Europe and the United States were increasingly filled with patients suffering from a variety of nervous disorders.[39] In 1869 the New York physician George Miller Beard identified these symptoms as manifestations of a new disease, which he labeled neurasthenia, literally nervous exhaustion.[40] Neurasthenia was, according to Beard, a distinctly modern illness, a symbol and product of the progress of civilization. Yet rather than express alarm over the outbreak of "American Nervousness," as he called it, Beard proudly identified it as a sign of the country's superiority.[41] The disease's particular national trait was linked to racial, social, and class determinants as well: it only struck "brain workers" (as opposed to "muscle workers") and only the more "advanced" races (especially Anglo-Saxon) and religious persuasions.

As the neurasthenia diagnosis spread to continental Europe, the disease became more democratic: it lost its social particularism and its positive status. European physicians also considered neurasthenia to be a disease of modernity but challenged the notion that it was a symbol of progress. In the European context, modern civilization represented an ominous threat to stability rather than the lofty promises contained in Beard's vision. In their view it was the adverse characteristics of capitalism and modern life—the heated tempo of industrialization, the chaos and temptations of urbanization and city living, the excessive stimulation of dangerous new ideas, the popular press, and inventions—that induced the growing epidemic. As doctors throughout Europe diagnosed ever-increasing segments of the population as neurasthenics, including members of the working class, the disease was linked to widespread fears about degeneration, heredity, and devolution.[42]

Cases of neurasthenia were recorded in imperial Russia as well, and in the wake of the events of 1905 there was a growing tendency to characterize both the revolutionary movement and repressive governmental policy in terms of psychological illness.[43] By the 1920s, a dramatic increase in nervous and mental disorders appeared to have taken place.

> No matter what group of the population is studied, at the present time everywhere one observes an extreme abundance of nervous and mental illness, deviations, dysfunctions, symptoms. Nervous and psychological illness, neuroses and psychoneuroses surpass even tuberculosis and other social diseases.[44]

Psychiatrists and neurologists found evidence of the disease everywhere. One study conducted by the Neuropsychiatric Dispensary among spinners at the Krasno-Presnenskaia Tri-Mountain Textile Mill found 46.4 percent of all workers to be nervously ill, 19.7 percent of whom presented with pronounced neurotic symptoms.[45] At the Moscow Textile Factory 77.7 percent of all those examined (both blue- and white-collar workers) demonstrated nervousness, breaking down to 17.7 percent seriously nervous, 22 percent moderately nervous, and 38 percent mildly nervous. Similar results were obtained from workers at the "Krasnyi Trud" Factory: only 51.5 percent were considered to have healthy nerves.

Yet according to medical data, nervousness was not restricted to factory workers. A study of teachers diagnosed 50 percent as suffering from mild nervousness, a further 26 percent from severe forms of the illness. The high incidence of nervous illness detected among the young was of even greater concern to researchers. A 1925 study conducted with over nine thousand school-age children found only one third to have healthy nerves. Nor was the Communist Party spared: according to research cited by Aron Zalkind, a whopping 80–90 percent of active members suffered from nervous symptoms.[46] Taken together, these findings suggested to medical writers as well as other social commentators an epidemic of nervous illness and an urgent social problem.

Doctors offered a variety of explanations for this apparent upsurge in nervous illness. Some identified World War I as the main source of the new epidemic and located the Soviet experience in the context of a Europe-wide phenomenon.[47] However, most Russian physicians writing about nervousness posited a fundamental difference between the outbreaks in the West and those in the Soviet Union and stressed those factors that only the latter had endured: the two revolutions, the civil war, the blockades and famine, and the massive epidemics that followed. They attributed primary importance to physical and mental fatigue, an exhaustion that itself was considered specifically Russian.[48]

The result of overtaxing an already shaky nervous system, "exhaustion" (*iznoshennost'*, *utomlenie*), as the extreme form of paralysis-like tiredness was called, occupied a key position in discussions about nervous illness in the 1920s.[49] Just as the fatigue linked to nervousness in America was favorably associated with privileged minds doing the positive work of furthering civilization, and in Europe with the enervating burdens of a deteriorating modern world, in Russia it became emblematic of the Soviet condition and the particular circumstances of the post-1917 experience. According to one specialist, "War, Revolution and the never-before-seen-in-the-world tempo of rebuilding all social forms of labor and lifestyle of the peoples of the USSR demanded from the population a colossal stress on the nervous system, deeply exhausted it and increased the likelihood of it becoming injured."[50] Exhaustion could result from

> unregulated, disorganized work, foul living conditions, disordered and completely insufficient food, the absence of rational rest, qualitatively disrupted and quantitatively restricted sleep, the shift from arduous mental scientific work to active social work, a disordered sex life—more and more new blows unceasingly fall upon the overdriven nervous system.[51]

Additionally, poor hygiene and sanitation, overcrowded and underheated housing and schools, and the dislocations and relocations associated with life in the 1920s were also identified as contributing to the inordinately high incidence of neurasthenia in Soviet Russia.[52] Nervous exhaustion could follow alcoholism, debilitating illnesses such as typhus, malaria, and influenza, or a congenital predisposition to weak nerves.[53] Analyses also linked the emergence of the illness to severe psychological or moral shock, or an extremely unpleasant emotional experience.[54] One psychiatrist developed the concept of "acquired invalidism" (*nazhitaia invalidnost'*)[55] to define the most severe form of the disease. Sufferers of this extreme variety of nervousness were purported to become old before their time: apathetic, unable to work or to relate to one's surroundings, they were completely lost to society.

Like their American counterparts, many Soviet doctors were especially concerned with the pathologies of mental laborers, but with one important difference: of chief interest to them were the young proletarian students and party activists who appeared to be particularly susceptible to exhaustion, and hence nervousness.

> And so to the surprise of medicine, which usually has no clients from the proletarian sphere, proletarian students get for themselves before their Party card and their professional card a "psychocard" [*psikhbilet*] . . . these neuropathic dysfunctions never befell the proletariat before in such a quantity and quality. But since we have before us an entire class generation of the Revolution . . . this statistic becomes extremely alarming.[56]

In the eyes of Soviet doctors, young people were engaging in too much intellectual work without sufficient breaks, or without a proper rest period between their mental pursuits and their extensive social (*obshchestvennye*) responsibilities.[57] Another factor identified by physicians, which would become extremely controversial over the course of the decade, was the mental exhaustion experienced by proletarians and peasants who made the transition from manual to mental labor, including those promoted to party organizational work, and the vast number enrolled in institutions of higher learning. They also singled out Red Army soldiers and party activists who had conducted arduous and prolonged work at the front during the revolution and civil war as especially susceptible to the most severe form of neurasthenia, acquired invalidism.

One of the most widely observed factors identified as contributing to the epidemic of Soviet nervousness (and hence the sexual dysfunction which accompanied it) was masturbation. While some medical writers focused upon the exhaustion of the nervous system that followed excessive self-stimulation, others emphasized the significance of "onanophobia," a masturbation-induced form of hypochondria, in the etiology of nervous illness.[58]

> Former masturbators, under the influence of antiquated notions about the supposed danger of their "secret vice" and their "sin of youth," very frequently develop real obsessive fear of the possibility, or more accurately, the imagined consequences of masturbation . . . linked usually with self-reproach and self-flagellation, [it] controls the life of the onanist and in the opinion of many specialists is more dangerous than masturbation itself.[59]

Such expressions of anxiety about the ramifications of masturbation were prevalent throughout medical advice literature. One such arena was the question and answer column in the popular Leningrad health and sanitary enlightenment journal *Hygiene and Health of the Worker and Peasant Family*, in which queries about onanism and its consequences occupied a disproportionate amount of space. Letter writers attributed all kinds of illnesses and problems to the "solitary vice": blue rings under the eyes, inability to do math, tumors and nosebleeds, tuberculosis, cold hands, hair loss, anemia, and venereal disease.[60] Disputing such claims, the column's doctors repeatedly explained that nerves were the real source of the masturbation-related conditions afflicting correspondents like "poor Orlik" and "Slav-ii":

> You complain that people laugh at you in the factory and on the street, and see this as a result of defects in your sex life. We suggest that you are nervously ill, and strongly recommend that you see a specialist in nervous or mental illnesses. It's possible that, having completely cured your nervous system, you also will become strong in sexual relationships. However, considerably protracted treatment is necessary, so you should have patience and put aside thoughts of suicide.[61]

> You are overworked with an excessive load, your nervous system is shattered, and therefore you don't have the strength to cope with your wicked habit. Turn to one of the clinics for nervous illnesses or one of the provincial health clinics to a specialist for nervous illnesses. Besides that, study carefully the brochures of Assistant Professor Mendel'son, *Masturbation and the Fight Against It* and *The Nervous System and Sex Life*.[62]

Readers were informed on the one hand that prolonged and frequent masturbation could lead to neurasthenia, and on the other, that nervousness deprived one of the willpower to break the so-called "wicked habit."

In addition to such manifestations as weak will, hypochondria, paranoia, and obsessive/compulsive behavior, other indications of the disease included shaking and irritability, excitability, insomnia and troubled sleep, severe headaches, dizziness, eye and ear irritation, back and chest pain, heart palpitations, irregular heart beat, stomach upset, frequent mood swings, memory loss, and the inability to concentrate or work.[63] Diagnosed neurasthenics were predominantly young, and suffered excessively from feelings of insecurity, uncertainty, and low self-confidence; as in Gurvich's column, the phrase used most frequently to describe them in the medical press is "uncertainty in oneself, in one's abilities" (*neuverennost' v sebe, v svoei sile*). Soviet medical writings portrayed neurasthenics as completely dissatisfied with their lives, with no chance for future happiness.

Evidence of such psychological despair was everywhere, and Russian society as a whole seemed to reflect many of the most serious symptoms of the individual neurasthenic, in particular a pervasive sense of insecurity and hopelessness. However exhausted the country had been during the revolutions and civil war, the introduction of the NEP in 1921, with its promise of economic respite for private producers and traders, brought no relief to its "shattered nerves." For some this insecurity appeared to stem primarily from the material difficulties associated with life at this time. For others it manifested itself as a crisis of identity, as varied segments throughout society questioned their own status, purpose, and fate, as well as that of the nation. In the aftermath of the Kronstadt rebellion and the Workers' Opposition, for instance, some party members began to doubt the loyalty of the working class and hence their own role as its leader; others were unable to make the transition from an oppositional to a ruling party or mourned the shift from revolutionary fighter to peacetime bureaucrat. The suppression of Kronstadt and the subsequent "retreat" of NEP proved a similar source of distress to many intellectuals and supporters of the revolution, leading to mass resignations from the party and the Komsomol, and anxious discussions about the country's future among the population as a whole.[64]

For medical authors and other social commentators, one of the most disturbing manifestations of this malaise was the wave of suicides reported to be ravaging the country's youth.[65] Suicidal tendencies played an important role in the symptomology of male sexual disorders as well, and physicians considered sexual dysfunction to be a similarly conclusive indicator of mental instability among Russia's young men. Doctors maintained that the fear of sexual impotence frequently prompted the suicide attempts, a connection corroborated by the following review of a book on male impotence in a popular health journal: "Sexual impotence in men is a source of wretched suffering. How strongly it influences the psyche can be judged by the fact that many kill themselves because of it."[66] This relationship between suicide and sexual dysfunction was also communicated through Gurvich's columns in *Towards a Healthy Lifestyle*: each man who arrived at the clinic was described as shaking and pale, unable to work, completely lacking in self-esteem, and threatening to end his life.

If low self-confidence and a neurasthenic malaise appeared to be particular national traits in Soviet Russia in the 1920s, in the estimation of several medical authors male sexual disorders represented a related badge of Soviet uniqueness. Commenting on the high incidence of male sexual dysfunction throughout Europe and Russia before and especially during World War I, the venereologist L. Ia. Iakobzon concluded:

> [T]hen came the World War with all its horrors, the result of which was the appearance of many tens if not hundreds of thousands of cases of sexual dysfunction among the war's participants, and sometimes also in those who remained in the rear. All of this was in the West, all this was here among us. But in the Union there were also other phenomena which played a role: we endured two revolutions and, importantly, years of famine, years of ruin accompanied by hunger, unemployment, epidemics, etc. All of these are factors which could not but have a great influence on the nervous system

and the psyche. From this, naturally, here in the Union sexual dysfunctions should be widespread and moreover should be encountered at a relatively young age.[67]

According to Iakobzon, who directed two clinics for the treatment of sexual disorders in Leningrad, what made the Soviet situation unique was the diverse social and class composition of the cases, a fact corroborated by the visitors to the Counseling Center for Sexual Hygiene. He contrasted his patient sample of Red Army men, semiliterate young peasants, workers, students, and intellectuals to that of a Berlin doctor who contended that the majority of impotents hailed from the "cultured classes."[68] The first reason for the discrepancy, Iakobzon argued, stemmed from that fact that in Europe people of modest means lacked the resources to visit private clinics. Yet it was not just a question of the greater accessibility of medical care in Russia; the arduous conditions of life in the Soviet Union were responsible for this particular manifestation of nervousness as well:

> [H]ere people become exhausted quicker than in the West. There is much proof for this assertion. Truly people here get exhausted faster, and our intelligentsia rarely lives to an old age. In the West it is not rare for professors to live to seventy or eighty, but here I hardly know of any elderly representatives of science. Therefore the second reason for my disagreement with Professor Fiurbringer is the rapid exhaustion of our men.

Frigidity, Medical Silence, and the Politics of the Female Orgasm

In view of the vast attention focused upon male sexual disorders in the 1920s, the lack of medical and public interest in similar problems among women is conspicuous. Was the fact that frigidity (*kholodnost'*) failed to receive even a fraction of the attention shown to male dysfunction due solely to "false shame," the embarrassment believed to prevent women from seeking out help, as was suggested in *Towards a Healthy Lifestyle?*[69] Or were women actually sexually healthier than men? Doctors themselves admitted that this was not the case. Citing "a majority of specialists," *Hygiene and Health of the Worker and Peasant Family* reported in response to a reader's question that frigidity was extremely widespread among women, affecting 50 percent of the female population.[70]

Yet despite the health journal's apparent acceptance of this extremely high figure and its reference to a group of presumed experts on frigidity, most doctors who wrote on issues of sexuality for the general public simply avoided the subject. The counseling center reports in *Towards a Healthy Lifestyle*, as we have seen, mentioned frigidity only in relation to its effect on the sexual abilities of men. Other publications followed its lead in their discussions of the center's work, as in a progress report that appeared in a 1928 issue of *Hygiene and Health.* After stating how many men and women had visited the clinic, the rest of the chronicle was devoted to the different sexual complaints of the male patients. The article concluded by reiterating the importance of such an institution, since people lacked the most fundamental information about sex, and suggested it advertise its existence more widely so that all those who needed it could receive help. Since it excluded women completely, the paper evidently was aimed at a male audience.[71]

The dearth of attention to female sexual problems in newspapers and journals extended to the specialized pamphlet literature on the sex question as well. One representative example was a brochure on the relationship between the nervous system and sexuality, written by the neuropathologist Mendel'son, an editor of *Hygiene and Health* and one of the most prolific writers on sexuality during this period. Despite the considerable attention shown in the pamphlet to male impotence and its relationship to neurasthenia, frigidity was never mentioned. Mendel'son introduced the topic of female sexuality by stating: "The connection between the female sexual apparatus and the nervous system is especially close and complicated; therefore the sex life of a woman contributes to the origin of many neuropsychological illnesses."[72] Yet he devoted only a scant three pages out of thirty-one to describe those factors of a woman's life which, he argued, most frequently led to nervous illnesses—menstruation, pregnancy, abortion, childbirth, and menopause.

The lack of medical interest in frigidity was so pervasive that Iakobzon, one of the only doctors who wrote about the problem, was prompted to argue for its relevance.

> Doctors frequently hear the question: do we need to fight against frigidity in women? I think that we do. I completely share the point of view of the renowned Viennese psychiatrist and psychologist, Professor Freud, that orgasm is a wonderful reward of nature to living things for the fact that they reproduce. Nature entrusted to women all the difficulties of maternity; woman therefore has no less right to satisfaction in sex than does man.[73]

However even in the writings of those few doctors like Iakobzon who acknowledged and addressed the topic of frigidity, there were still crucial differences in the treatment of male and female sexual disorders. Even in dysfunction, men were accorded a sense of agency that was denied women. To be cured of their impotence men were urged to take the active step of dealing directly with doctors, either personally or through a medium such as the counseling center column in *Towards a Healthy Lifestyle.* Women, on the other hand, were completely dependent upon others to combat their frigidity; the problem was seen as either physical, and thus correctable through a surgical operation, or it was believed to be the fault of the woman's sexual partner. In either case, her sexual happiness was entirely in the hands and control of others.[74]

In those cases not diagnosed as physical, the fault lay, according to these doctors, with the husband, who even here in the realm of the female orgasm became the focal point of medical attention. In their estimation, man's sexual behavior in marriage was crucial to the sexual well-being of his mate, especially during the first days of matrimony.[75] Therefore they cautioned that he should refrain from overeagerness on the honeymoon and be especially careful not to force himself on his bride, at the risk of irrevocably turning her against the sexual act. "Many men don't know that the female sexual appetite is in normal conditions less than in men; they also forget that excitement comes from courting them."[76] A far greater problem was men's lack of sexual skill and especially the tendency to ejaculate prematurely:

> Premature ejaculation of semen influences the man predominantly psychologically. Physical satisfaction usually is received fully. This, however, severely influences the woman, since as a result of the shortness of the act she is usually denied physical satisfaction. A significant quantity of illnesses of the female sexual sphere and a significant quantity of nervous illnesses in women have a close and direct tie to premature ejaculation of men in the sex act.[77]

In Iakobzon's analysis, even masturbation, to which a woman "not rarely" turned "to reach orgasm and prevent the painful feeling of dissatisfaction" after her partner's premature ejaculation, could best be treated by "strengthening the sexual abilities of her husband."[78] There was never a question of addressing women directly regarding strategies for attaining sexual satisfaction.[79] If medical writers like Iakobzon considered a woman's right to orgasm at all, it was as the responsibility and province of her man:

> Sexual frigidity may arise in a woman in marriage in connection with the weak sexual abilities of her husband . . . Therefore I tell a woman that the reason for her sexual dissatisfaction is the sexual dysfunction of her husband and that I need to treat him.[80]

Despite a woman's lack of agency in bringing about her own or her husband's sexual pleasure, her ability to achieve orgasm could still be held responsible for the success of the marriage:

> Frigidity in woman can have a social significance: it can dangerously influence the husband, since there are men who can only accomplish the act under conditions that it brings pleasure to the wife. On this ground there are frequent disagreements and fights between the spouses and even infidelity by the husband; in other words, from the frigidity of the wife the harmony in the marriage can suffer and there can arise threats to the future existence of the marriage union . . . On the other hand, a woman's sexual dissatisfaction in marriage can appear for her the stimulus of her search for new sexual ties in which she would experience orgasm. In this way in a woman can appear a true "pursuit of the orgasm" [*pogonia za orgazmom*].[81]

In several of the dysfunction cases described by the Moscow clinic doctors, the male patient's sense of accountability for (and inadequacy about) his partner's sexual pleasure was seen as the decisive factor in the etiology of his nervousness.[82] In the analyses of both Iakobzon and Fronshtein, the husband's inability to bring his wife to orgasm as a result of his own sexual dysfunction might also become the source of a nervous disorder, most likely hysteria or neurasthenia, in her.[83] Although according to Iakobzon such cases of mental illness among women were rare, he maintained that nonetheless they "need to be cured."[84] Yet as with his support for women's right to have an orgasm (during intercourse), Iakobzon remained silent about how this should be accomplished.

With frigidity and female nervous disorders dependent upon the presence of previous sexual dysfunction in men, doctors could rationalize their neglect of women in the treatment of nervousness (and sexual dysfunction, for that matter); once men were cured of their sexual disorders, women would necessarily also be sexually fulfilled and mentally healthy. A number of other factors explain the lack of medical interest and popular fora devoted to the psychosexual problems of women. Of primary importance was the inherent link between women and reproduction. To be "normal" in terms of sexual behavior for a woman meant to be reproductive, and of course frigidity did not prevent pregnancy.[85]

Because nervous illness did not impinge upon a woman's ability to conceive, there was very little interest, in either the medical or the scientific-popular press, in the mental health of "normal" women as sexual beings. In fact, the mental health of sexually active women received attention only when women ceased to be "normal," by engaging in "abnormal" or "deviant" and nonreproductive sex, as prostitutes or lesbians.[86] Of great significance in this regard is the single contribution focusing on the experience of women in the 1926 collection *Soviet Medicine in the Fight for Healthy Nerves*, which was written by Dr. Gurvich, the columnist in *Towards a Healthy Lifestyle*. The only article to address the problem of female sexuality and its relationship to nervous illness, it examined the psychopathology of prostitutes.[87] Doctors may have blamed "false shame" for women's lack of initiative in seeking out advice on sexual matters, but the impression conveyed to both men and women in newspapers, pamphlets, and journals was that the female experience per se was unimportant, at best dependent upon the actions of men. By neglecting "normal" women's sexuality, doctors contributed to and reinforced the idea of women's experience as particular, nongeneralizable, and therefore not a matter of public concern or interest.

Panic, Production, and the Treatment of Male Impotence

With male sexual dysfunction, it was precisely the "normalcy" of those suffering from the illness, and the universality of this complaint across social groups and classes, which made the apparent epidemic so threatening. This fear was not based on population policy; the question of men's inability to reproduce was raised neither by the patients nor the doctors who wrote about them.[88] Significantly, the danger posed by these men was linked not to reproduction but to production:

> [T]hose suffering from sexual impotence usually become unhappy and lose their joy of life, giving in to the most somber thoughts, even to thoughts of suicide. They consider themselves unfit and unnecessary members of society and withdraw from their transformation into useful workers.[89]

> [I]t is clear that a person suffering from sexual dysfunction is not rarely denied the opportunity to give society and the state all the sum of work and all the qualities of work he might have been able to give, if he didn't have a sexual disorder.[90]

In the estimation of medical specialists, young men in the prime of life, who should have guaranteed the country's future, instead posed a grave danger. The very fate of the revolution seemed in jeopardy as ever increasing numbers of young men became incapacitated, suicidal, and unable to engage in the labor that defined the new state's identity.

This discussion of sexual dysfunction demonstrates how the male body functioned as a site for the expression of social and political anxieties during the 1920s. On the symbolic level, there couldn't have been a greater contrast between the pervasive iconographic image of the strapping young proletarian, hammer raised, triumphantly building socialism and the shaking, exhausted, and suicidal men who crowded doctors' offices.[91] In the context of medical discussions on nervousness and impotence, masculinity was defined as the ability to engage in productive labor. Thus anxiety about male dysfunction reflected far broader concerns with the potency, viability, and destiny of the workers' state.

The pages of the medical press portrayed a generation of men suffering severe psychological distress and desperately in need of assistance, both for their own sake and to serve the needs of their country. Less severe a response than suicide to the despair of the times and the dashed hopes of the revolution, the discourse of sexual dysfunction provided men with an acceptable vehicle to express dissatisfaction with NEP Russia and the demands placed on them by contemporary society. If young men responded to their social and political powerlessness by becoming sexually impotent, the role of the medical profession was to help men to accept, or at the very least to live with, the features of life that they also were powerless to change.[92] In his brochure *Sex and Neurasthenia*, Dr. Khaletskii advised his readers: "Be encouraged! Begin to look people directly in the eye, since there's nothing wrong with you. Your uncertainty in yourself will lead to your becoming truly powerless." Should further advice be necessary, he urged his readers to seek out the help of a doctor.[93] These popular medical texts were unanimous in their appraisal of the role of the physician in treatment.[94] In their evaluation, the doctor's power of suggestion was so forceful that often the act of consultation was enough to initiate the healing process.

> All cases of purely psychological sexual impotence respond to treatment, but demand at times great patience from the sick person and also from the doctor. In a majority of cases success is achieved through the influence of skillful psychological influence on the patient: psychological treatment here consists of calming [*uspokoenie*] the sick person by explaining the incorrectness of his thoughts and feelings in order to return to him a sense of trust in his (never really lost) sexual strength and to train him to divert attention away from his own organ.[95]

Doctors were not concerned with establishing a precise relationship between various symptoms of nervous illness or a fixed sequence of the sexual dysfunction's progression; low self-confidence might lead to nervousness, resulting in impotence, or occasions of sexual failure could induce nervousness and hence feelings of insecurity and thoughts of suicide. The physicians' primary imperative was to calm the sufferers of sexual dysfunction who populated their clinics and comprised their readership. Once placated, the authors maintained, the men would become capable of listening to the medical explanations of their conditions and, already half-cured, be able to resume their labor and other obligations. The most crucial advice given by the doctors of the Counseling Center for Sexual Hygiene was the exhortation to "not give in to panic," a warning that ran like a mantra through its newspaper column in *Towards a Healthy Lifestyle:*

> We consider that the case with comrade A. is one of the many incidents when, as a result of an accidental failure, there appears uncertainty in oneself, hesitation during sexual intercourse. This insecurity is due to the tendency to "panic," to thoughts of incurability, etc. A great portion of these cases have no serious foundation. They are completely curable, and frequently after the first conversation with a doctor such sick people begin to feel completely valid.[96]

Significantly, doctors themselves could have been responsible for contributing to the atmosphere of panic. It is likely that some exploited this panic for financial gain, cashing in on the widespread concern with nerves and impotence by publishing advice literature or advertising disreputable miracle cures. Even such a well-respected publication as *Hygiene and Health of the Worker and Peasant Family* arguably transgressed the blurry line between responsible advice and blatant self-promotion by regularly advertising Mendel'son's numerous publications on its medical advice pages. Leaving aside questions of such journalistic and medical improprieties, the harsh tone taken by the advice column and the frequency with which it diagnosed its letter writers as nervously ill also presumably contributed to the sense of crisis.

Conversely, this might also explain the prevalence in Russia of the term "nervousness," (*nervnost'*) instead of its Latin counterpart (*nevrasteniia*). If in the West there was the tendency to elevate the condition of nervousness into the full-blown disease of neurasthenia, in Russia the instinct appeared to have been the opposite. While many Russian doctors wrote about neurasthenia, the word was rarely used by those dealing specifically with sexual dysfunction, and never in the writings of the Counseling Center for Sexual Hygiene. This should be seen as part of the physicians' method of calming; using "nervousness" as opposed to "neurasthenia" removed from it the stigma of a "real" illness and "normalized" the condition, making it seem less alarming, more temporary, and more curable. A second related motivation for avoiding the term "neurasthenia" might have been its association with degeneration and heredity. By labeling impotent men "nervous" as opposed to "neurasthenic," doctors shielded them from anxiety about their tainted lineage.

The proclivity to panic, to transform a social problem into a full-blown "crisis," was a widely observed feature of life in the 1920s.[97] Discontent over such social ills as mass unemployment and child abandonment (*bezprizornost'*) generated anxious and seemingly endless discussions, in which the word "panic" appeared repeatedly, and which cast the very fate of the revolution in doubt. Young men figured prominently in these debates, which questioned their fitness as the standard-bearers of the future socialist paradise and centered frequently around the problems of suicide and sexual depravity.[98] In a lecture on the sex question delivered in early 1926, Commissar of Public Health N. A. Semashko addressed the topic of panic in relationship to the supposed sexual turpitude of the young:

> We have in this sphere a panic, and even several of our well-known comrades feed this panic . . . We will never allow anyone to declare that every one of our *komsomolki* and *komsomoltsy*, every student in a worker school was the personification of depravity . . . [That sexual activity among the young has declined in recent years] needs to be considered before giving in to panicked shrieks about the wave of depravity that has swept over our youth.[99]

N. Shvarts, a physician writing in *Towards a Healthy Lifestyle* in 1929, echoed Semashko's sentiments:

> Now everywhere is heard censure of our youth, that they are dissolute, rude, depraved . . . the depravity of our youth is a bugaboo, with which social opinion frightens itself and others . . . our youth is far from those horrors that are attributed to it, and it would be a good thing if social opinion got rid of that delusion.[100]

The themes raised in these articles—the branding of young people as sexual libertines, the intentional exploitation of a climate of fear, the condemnation of certain "opinion makers"—had first been elaborated by Semashko in a widely cited editorial published by *Izvestiia* in January of 1925.[101] Entitled "How Not to Write about the Sex Question," Semashko's essay was part commentary on and part warning against the "misfortune" that occurred "when cobblers begin to bake pies."[102] Denouncing the biological ignorance characterizing the "cobblers'" writings on sexuality, Semashko made it clear that the misfortune lay primarily in the fact that the authors in question were fellow party members. "It's much sadder," he wrote, "when the rudest, most unforgivable mistakes come from the pens of comrades, whose opinions people are accustomed to heed." Referring to Martin Nikolaevich Liadov's *Questions of Lifestyle*, Semashko opined that everyone would have been better off if its author had limited his scholarly attention to the history of the party. Aron Borisovich Zalkind, on whose biological theories Liadov's work was based, merited even harsher criticism, since Zalkind himself was a psychiatrist. According to Semashko, if these men truly understood biology they would not have been able to reach their very mistaken conclusions about the status of sexuality in contemporary Soviet society. They argued that sexuality had become unnatural and identified the sexual depravity of Russia's youth as the most alarming evidence of the separation of sex from nature.[103] Semashko dismissed such analyses of the immorality of the young as "complete nonsense and sophistry . . . Without a knowledge of biology in general and especially the role of the endocrine glands, one shouldn't take up one's pen and open one's mouth in order to make condemnations regarding the sexual question."[104]

In the commissar's estimation, it was precisely works like those of Liadov and Zalkind that incited panic among the population. Both he and Shvarts suggested that such condemnations would only increase the level of nervousness in young people and hence the cases of impotence doctors were striving to forestall. At issue was a fundamentally different approach to the idea of sexuality: whereas these other "social thinkers" condemned sexual activity *per se* as a sign of immorality, Semashko and the other physicians cited in this study acknowledged the validity of male sexuality, provided it be contained within the medical conception of normal practice.[105] Moreover, in tracing the source of male sexual dysfunction to the head (nervousness), as opposed to the body (biological/physiological disorder), doctors offered these men a way out of their sexual problems. Young men could be easily cured of sexual disorders by heeding the doctors' advice, whereas in the writings of their party comrades they appeared doomed.

The articles written by Semashko and the doctors of *Towards a Healthy Lifestyle* suggest a conflict with party ideologues over issues of jurisdiction. The domain being contested was not simply the sex question itself, but also authority over the population with which it was most closely associated: in this case young men. In part this was a disagreement over method; the medical approach to sexuality stressed education rather than the flat-out condemnations and prohibitions characteristic of party writings on the subject.[106] Yet the particularly harsh criticism to which Semashko subjected Zalkind, a medical doctor, suggests another crucial point of contention. Also at issue was the overt linking of sexuality with the rhetoric of communism and, more importantly, with party writers' invocation of science.[107] Medical authority over sexuality derived from the assertion of a special and unique relationship to science. When they employed scientific language and theories, party writers (with their own distinct and well-established basis of authority) threatened doctors' control of this particular area of knowledge and hence their jurisdictional claims. This may also explain the infrequency of references to the party in "legitimate" medical publications on sex, although many sexual enlighteners, including Semashko, were Bolsheviks.[108] It may have been a Bolshevik revolution that made it possible to approach life from a scientific viewpoint, but medical legitimacy in the realm of sex hinged upon fluency in the higher language of science. By invoking their medical expertise to legitimize their dominion over the sex question, doctors were also demarcating a space to discuss issues of sexuality separate from the sphere of politics, in effect saying that sex and party politics shouldn't mix.[109] Even in regard to issues with such potentially devastating implications for the young state as the epidemic of male impotence (or the conditions of contemporary life that prompted it), doctors approached the subject indirectly, restricting their analyses to allusions about the importance of men to production.

This is not to suggest, however, that physicians were in any way less concerned with control than the party moralists. Like the medical authors who exploited fears about masturbation, the numerous references to suicide, exhaustion, and nerves in the Counseling Center for Sexual Hygiene's columns demonstrate that even these doctors were not above making use of the widespread interest in these issues and anxieties about the young to increase their own authority, even as they criticized others for doing so.[110] In the same way, their campaign of calming, through continual reference to the epidemic of sexual dysfunction, no doubt contributed to the atmosphere of panic surrounding those it sought to mollify. Doctors sought to combat sexual problems through education rather than coercion. Yet they readily exploited this panic over an illness that would be cured by the very fact of relying on them, and their expertise, for treatment.

NOTES

I am grateful to Eliot Borenstein, Atina Grossmann, Mark von Hagen, Paul Josephson, Christina Kiaer, Eric Naiman, Ken Pinnow, Irina Sirotkina, Roger Smith, Susan Gross Solomon, members of the Russian history *kruzhok* of Columbia University, and especially Mikhail Poddubnyi for their valuable suggestions and comments. Support for the research and writing of this study was provided by the Harriman Institute of Columbia University and the American Council of Teachers of Russian.

1. L. A. Prozorov, "Organizatsiia nevro-psikhiatricheskoi pomoshchi v usloviiakh nastoiashchego vremeni, v chastnosti, psikhpomoshchi sel'skomu naseleniiu," in *Sovetskaia meditsina v bor'be za zdorovye nervy. Trudy 1 Vsesoiuznogo soveshchaniia po psikhiatrii i nevrologii i gosudarstvennogo nevro-psikhiatricheskogo dispansera*, ed. A. I. Miskinov, L. A. Prozorov, and L. M. Rozenshtein (Moscow, 1926), 12.

2. B. Gurvich, "O polliutsiiakh," *Za zdorovyi byt* 6 (1929): 2.

3. L. Ia. Iakobzon, *Polovaia kholodnost' zhenshchin* (Leningrad, 1928), 68. Similar factors are cited to explain the publication of a special textbook to familiarize doctors

and medical students with the widespread problem. See Professor B. N. Khol'stov, *Funktsional'nye rasstroistva muzhskogo polovogo apparata i funktsional'nye rasstroistva mochevykh organov nervnogo proiskhozhdeniia* (Leningrad, 1926), introduction.

4. I have intentionally limited the scope of my analysis to medical writings on the sexual question for both practical and theoretical reasons. Of course, doctors held no monopoly on the subject of sex. Soviet Russia in the 1920s was a society seemingly obsessed with the subject, and in recent years scholars have begun to explore many different expressions of this interest. Yet I would argue that the medical discourse on sexuality was nonetheless distinct from the competing and overlapping voices that discussed, debated, or exploited the subject during this era, if for no other reason than that the physicians themselves claimed this to be the case. Their authority stemmed from their "unique" relationship to science; the revolution may have provided the conditions for sexual health, they suggested, but it would take medical expertise and their personal guidance to achieve it. For other recent analyses of the sex question in the Soviet period, see Eric Naiman, *Sex in Public: The Incarnation of Early Soviet Ideology* (Princeton: Princeton University Press, 1997); and Dan Healey, *Homosexual Desire in Revolutionary Russia* (Chicago: University of Chicago Press, 2001). For prerevolutionary Russia, see Laura Engelstein, *The Keys to Happiness: Sex and the Search for Modernity in Fin-de-Siècle Russia* (Ithaca: Cornell University Press, 1992); and Evgenii Bershtein, *Sexuality in Russian Symbolism* (forthcoming).

5. The available data do not permit a satisfactory answer to the question of whether these were cases of "actual" patients presenting themselves for treatment. Furthermore, rather than address such issues of epidemiology, the purpose of this study is to examine the sociocultural significance of this epidemic in the context of NEP Russia, and the ways in which doctors represented their values and concerns in the literature. Indeed, my focus on the medical discourse corresponds to the physicians' own epistemological approach to treatment.

6. *Za zdorovyi byt* (1925–1931), published by the Dispensary of the State Venereological Institute, Moscow.

7. While a number of professionals and social activists in the late Imperial era had advocated a similar course, sex education as a mass phenomenon, receiving official sanction and support, only began after the Bolshevik Revolution, with the establishment of Narkomzdrav in July 1918. On the origins of Narkomzdrav, see *Health and Society in Revolutionary Russia*, ed. Susan Gross Solomon and John F. Hutchinson (Bloomington: Indiana University Press, 1990). On health education before the revolution, see Nancy Frieden, *Russian Physicians in an Era of Reform and Revolution, 1856–1905* (Princeton: Princeton University Press, 1981), 182–185.

8. "Konsul'tatsiia po polovoi gigiene," *Za zdorovyi byt* 1 (1925): 3.

9. For more information on the State Venereological Institute, see Frances L. Bernstein, *The Dictatorship of Sex: Medical Advice for the Russian Masses, 1918–1931* (forthcoming, Northern Illinois University Press); on the Institute of Social Hygiene, see Susan Gross Solomon, "The Limits of Government Patronage of Science: Social Hygiene and the Soviet State, 1920–1930," *Social History of Medicine* 3:3 (1990): 405–435; and "Social Hygiene and Soviet Public Health, 1921–1930," in *Health and Society in Revolutionary Russia*, 175–199.

10. On the commitment of neuropsychiatry to sexual matters, see Healey, *Homosexual Desire*, 141.

11. GARF (TsGA) f. 579, op. 1, d. 841, l. 50. In 1926, the clinic was staffed by Dr.

Frances L. Bernstein

Shishov, a venereologist and urologist; Dr. Gurvich, a psychoneurologist; and Dr. Brukhanskii, a psychiatrist.

12. Ibid. See also B. R. Gurvich and L. E. Zalutskii, "Opyt konsul'tatsii po polovoi gigiene," in *Psikhogigienicheskie i nevrologicheskie issledovaniia*, ed. L. M. Rozenshtein (Moscow, 1928).

13. See "K otkrytiiu konsul'tatsii po voprosam nervno-psikhicheskogo zdorov'ia i polovoi zhizni" (Leningrad), *Gigiena i zdorov'e rabochei sem'i* 9 (1925): 9; Liberman, "Molodezh' i polovoe zdorov'e (K rabote konsul'tatsii po polovoi gigiene)" (Iaroslavl'), *Za zdorovyi byt* 6 (1929): 2; S. Monikh, "Konsul'tatsiia po polovym i brachnym voprosam" (Tiflis), *Za zdorovyi byt* 9 (1930): 4; N. I. Chuchelov, "Opyt raboty konsul'tatsii po polovoi gigiene v Tashkente," *Sovetskii vrach* 2 (1930): 76–78; M. I. Cherkes, "K voprosu ob organizatsii i metode raboty sanitarno-prosvetitel'nykh kabinetov pri vendispanserakh i konsul'tatsii po voprosam polovoi zhizni i polovoi gigieny pri rabochikh klubakh" (Khar'kov), *Vrachebnoe delo* 3–4 (1931), 170–174.

14. See B. Gurvich and Zalutskii, "Opyt konsul'tatsii," *Venerologiia i dermatologiia* 2 (1928): 574–575; idem, "Opyt postroeniia polovoi konsul'tatsii," *Sotsial'naia gigiena* 7 (1928): 136–137.

15. B. Gurvich and Zalutskii, "Opyt konsul'tatsii," 232. This statement is as close as the doctors ever came to an analysis of the reasons why more workers, the group that was supposed to be targeted, did not utilize the consultation. The doctors never explain why they limited advertisements of the clinic's existence. Presumably it had to do with the fact that as the first Russian sex consultation it was considered to be experimental, and further expansion would depend on its success in handling this initial limited client base. Doctors also may have feared a larger turnout than they were able to accommodate.

16. The low incidence of preexisting conditions in the German statistics can easily be explained by the fact that Germans suffering from sexual dysfunction would have sought treatment at clinics geared specifically toward these problems rather than utilizing the *Eheberatungstellen*, an option unavailable to their Russian counterparts, given the embryonic state of Soviet medicine. In fact in Germany there was a complete separation of functions between these clinics and the birth control and sex counseling clinics staffed by sex reformers. On the *Eheberatungstellen* and these other clinics in Germany, see Atina Grossmann, *Reforming Sex: The German Movement for Birth Control and Abortion Reform, 1920–1950* (New York: Oxford University Press, 1995); and Cornelie Usborne, *The Politics of the Body in Weimar Germany* (London: Macmillan, 1992).

17. B. Gurvich and Zalutskii, "Opyt konsul'tatsii," 236.

18. See n. 11, and also L. S. Gurvich, "O rabote konsul'tatsii po ozdorovleniiu byta," *Vestnik sovremennoi meditsiny* 10 (1929): 584.

19. On the consultation at *Zhenskii zhurnal*, see f. 579, op. 1, d. 417, l. 1; "O rabote konsul'tatsii po ozdorovleniiu byta," *Zhenskii zhurnal* 9 (1929): 22; Zalutskii, "Ozdorovlenie byta," *Zhenskii zhurnal* 11 (1930): 21. On the efforts to combine sexual advice clinics with women's consultations, see A. Rakhmanov, "Konsul'tatsiia dlia zhenshchin," *Biulleten' Narkomzdrava* 9 (1926): 3–9; A. Iu. Lur'e, Z. I. Baisheva, and E. S. Kushnirskaia, "Opyt raboty polovoi konsul'tatsii pri ZAGSE," *Zhurnal po izucheniiu rannego detskogo vozrasta* 3–4 (1930): 295–306; A. Iu. Lur'e, "Polovaia konsul'tatsiia," *Za zdorovyi byt* 10 (1930): 1.

20. F. 579, op. 1., d. 841, l. 48.

21. Zalutskii, "Ozdorovlenie byta," *Zhenskii zhurnal* 11 (1930): 21; B. Gurvich and Zalutskii, "Opyt konsul'tatsii po polovoi gigiene," in *Psikhogigienicheskie i nevrologicheskie issledovaniia.*

22. B. Gurvich, "O polliutsiiakh," 2.

23. B. Gurvich, "Polovaia slabost' muzhchin (Iz konsul'tatsii po polovoi gigiene)," *Za zdorovyi byt* 4 (1928): 2.

24. B. Gurvich and Zalutskii, "Opyt konsul'tatsii," 232–233. This is particularly significant, since Dr. Gurvich was a woman. The implications of a woman doctor treating men for sexual impotence are never addressed in any of the sources.

25. Ibid., 238.

26. B. Gurvich, "K ozdorovleniiu byta (Iz konsul'tatsii po polovoi gigiene) II," *Za zdorovyi byt* 2 (1928): 2.

27. B. Gurvich, "Polovaia slabost' muzhchin," 2.

28. Thus, despite the fact that white-collar workers predominated in the statistical medical accounts cited above (see p. 3), the cases described in *Towards a Healthy Lifestyle* presented a far more diverse composition. See f. 579, op. 1, d. 841, ll. 40–42; B. Gurvich, "O polliutsiiakh," and "Eshche o polovoi slabosti muzhchin (Iz konsul'tatsii po polovoi gigiene)," *Za zdorovyi byt* 6 (1929): 2; idem, "Po povodu pisem o polovykh rasstroistvakh," *Za zdorovyi byt* 9 (1930), 2; B. Gurvich and Zalutskii, "Opyt konsul'tatsii po polovoi gigiene."

29. B. Gurvich, "Polovaia slabost' muzhchin," 2.

30. See for example B. Gurvich and Zalutskii, "Opyt konsul'tatsii," 239.

31. B. Gurvich, "Polovaia slabost' muzhchin," 2.

32. B. Gurvich, "O polliutsiiakh," 2. Emphasis in the original. For a similar comment on normalcy, see also B. Gurvich, "Eshche o polovoi slabosti muzhchin (Iz konsul'tatsii po polovoi gigiene)," 2.

33. B. Gurvich, "Polovaia slabost' muzhchin," 2.

34. B. Gurvich, "Po povodu pisem o polovykh rasstroistvakh," 2.

35. On hysteria as a female illness in England, see Elaine Showalter, *The Female Malady: Women, Madness, and English Culture, 1830–1980* (New York: Pantheon Books, 1985). See also Mark S. Micale, *Approaching Hysteria: Disease and Its Interpretations* (Princeton: Princeton University Press, 1994).

36. F. 579, op. 1, d. 841, l. 48 ob.

37. L. M. Rozenshtein, *Nervnost' i bor'ba s nei* (Moscow, 1928), 3.

38. Mikhail Zoshchenko, "Nervous People," *Nervous People and Other Stories,* trans. Maria Gordon and Hugh McLean (London: Victor Gollancz Ltd., 1963), 124. For the Russian, see "Nervnye liudi," *Sobranie sochinenii,* t. 1 (Leningrad, 1986), 322–324. See also "Nervy," also published in *Begemot* in 1925, *Sobranie sochinenii,* 298–299. Other examples of popular fiction from the 1920s dealing with nerves and nervousness include Mikhail Bulgakov, "Sobach'e serdtse," in *Sobranie sochinenii,* vol. 2 (Moscow, 1989), 45–118; Lev Gumilevskii, *Sobachii pereulok* (Riga, 1928); and the satires of Il'f and Petrov.

39. See George Frederick Drinka, *The Birth of Neurosis: Myth, Malady, and the Victorians* (New York: Simon and Schuster, 1984).

40. George Miller Beard, "Neurasthenia, or Nervous Exhaustion," *Boston Medical and Surgical Journal* 3 (1869): 217; see also his *Nervous Exhaustion* (New York, 1879) and *American Nervousness: Its Causes and Consequences* (New York: G. P. Putnam's Sons, 1881). For a fascinating analysis of "American Nervousness" as cultural

history, see Tom Lutz, *American Nervousness, 1903: An Anecdotal History* (Ithaca: Cornell University Press, 1991).

41. Beard, *American Nervousness*, vii–viii.

42. Drinka, *The Birth of Neurosis*, ch. 9, especially 212–213. On neurasthenia in the European context, see Anson Rabinbach, *The Human Motor: Energy, Fatigue, and the Origins of Modernity* (New York: Basic Books, 1990), especially ch. 6.

43. See discussion in Engelstein, *The Keys to Happiness*, ch. 7; and Julie Brown, "Revolution and Psychosis: the Mixing of Science and Politics in Russian Psychiatric Medicine, 1905–1913," *The Russian Review* 46:3 (1987): 283–302.

44. Prozorov, "Organizatsiia," 12.

45. Professor A. Kapustin, "Nervnost' nashego vremeni i bor'ba s nei," *Meditsina* 5 (1927): 5. Unfortunately, none of these articles explain how the studies were conducted, and what factors determined the different designations of nervousness.

46. A. B. Zalkind, "O zabolevaniiakh partaktiva," *Krasnaia nov'* 4 (1925), 196. For more on nervousness among students, see Sheila Fitzpatrick, "Sex and Revolution: An Examination of Literary and Statistical Data on the Mores of Soviet Students in the 1920s," *Journal of Modern History*, June 1978, 266–267.

47. Kapustin, "Nervnost' nashego vremeni," 11.

48. See Dr. R. Borisov, "Nevrasteniia," *Zhenskii zhurnal* 11 (1927): 26–27; Z. G. Lur'e, "Nevrasteniia," *Meditsina* 17–18 (1929): 6–8; Privat dotsent A. Mendel'son, "Nervrasteniia," *Gigiena i zdorov'e rabochei sem'i* 15 (22) (1924): 2–6; 16 (23) (1924): 2–6.

49. David Joravsky refers to the disease as "Soviet exhaustion." See "The Construction of the Stalinist Psyche," in *Cultural Revolution in Russia, 1928–31*, ed. Sheila Fitzpatrick (Bloomington: Indiana University Press, 1984), 113; idem, *Russian Psychology: A Critical History* (Oxford: Blackwell, 1989), 337.

50. V. V. Dekhterev, "Dispanserizatsiia kak osnova bor'by s istoshcheniem nervnoi sistemy," *Klinicheskaia meditsina* 19–20 (1930): 1095.

51. A. B. Zalkind, "Nervnye bolezni sredi uchashcheisia molodezhi SSSR," *Revoliutsiia i kul'tura* (Moscow, 1925): 21.

52. For factors, see Kapustin, "Nervnost' nashego vremeni," 11; Zalkind, "Nervnye bolezni," 20; Professor P. Gannushkin, "Ob okhrane zdorov'ia partaktiva," *Revoliutsiia i kul'tura* 4 (1930): 44 (this is a reprint of an article that originally appeared in 1926).

53. Mendel'son, "Nevrasteniia," 3; E. N. Kameneva, *Chto kazhdomu nuzhno znat' o nervnosti* (Moscow, 1928), 23–24.

54. Mendel'son, "Nevrasteniia," 3.

55. Gannushkin, "Ob okhrane zdorov'ia partaktiva," 43.

56. Ibid. See similar comments in Dekhterev, "Dispanserizatsiia," 1095.

57. Gannushkin, "Ob okhrane zdorov'ia partaktiva," 44.

58. Dr. A. M. Khaletskii, *Polovaia zhizn' i nevrasteniia* (Odessa, 1927), 8; Dr. L. I. Faingol'd, *Polovoe bessilie: Ego prichiny, preduprezhdenie i lechenie* (Odessa, 1926), 25.

59. Mendel'son, *Nervnaia sistema i polovaia zhizn'*, 2nd ed. (Leningrad, 1929), 16. For other discussions of onanophobia, see Professor R. M. Fronshtein, *Rasstroistvo polovoi deiatel'nosti muzhchiny*, 2nd ed. (Moscow and Leningrad, 1929), 28; and Rozenshtein, "Nervnost' i bor'ba s nei," 12.

60. See for example the following "Otvety na voprosy chitatelei" columns in *Gigiena i zdorov'e rabochei i krest'ianskoi sem'i* (19 October 1927): 17; (1 January 1928): 17; (19 October 1928): 17.

61. "Otvety na voprosy chitatelei," *Gigiena i zdorov'e* (7 April 1927): back cover.

62. "Otvety na voprosy chitatelei," *Gigiena i zdorov'e* (13 July 1928): 17.

63. Kapustin, "Nervnost'," 5; Z. G. Lur'e, "Nevrasteniia," *Meditsina* 17–18 (1929): 7; Mendel'son, "Nevrasteniia," 3.

64. On resignation from the party and Komsomol, see Leonard Schapiro, *The Communist Party of the Soviet Union* (New York: Random House, 1971), 313–314; Merle Fainsod, *How Russia Is Ruled* (Cambridge: Cambridge University Press, 1962), 244; Mark von Hagen, *Soldiers in the Proletarian Dictatorship: the Red Army and the Soviet Socialist State, 1917–1930,* (Ithaca, N.Y.: Cornell University Press, 1990), 150. On the crisis of identity among party leaders, see Sheila Fitzpatrick, "The Bolsheviks' Dilemma: Class, Culture, and Politics in the Early Soviet Years," *Slavic Review* 47 (Winter 1988): 599–613. On the general sense of despondency and despair in the 1920s, especially among young people and students, see Kenneth M. Pinnow, "Crisis, Morality, and Class: Bolshevik Moralists and the Problem of Suicide in Postrevolution- ary Russia, 1921–1930" (M.A. thesis, Columbia University, 1990), and Eric Naiman, *Sex in Public,* ch. 7.

65. On the "epidemic" of suicide among youths in the 1920s and discussions of the problem by "party moralists," see Pinnow, "Crisis, Morality, and Class"; Anne Nesbet, "Suicide as Literary Fact in the 1920s," *Slavic Review* 50:4 (Winter 1991): 827–835; and von Hagen, *Soldiers in the Proletarian Dictatorship,* 306–307.

66. "Bibliografiia–Dr. med. L. Ia. Iakobzon, *Polovaia slabost',*" *Gigiena i zdorov'e,* April 1928, 15.

67. L. Ia. Iakobzon, "Sotsial'noe znachenie polovykh rasstroistv," *Gigiena i zdorov'e* 3 (1930): 5.

68. L. Ia. Iakobzon, "Polovye rasstroistva i vrachebnaia taina," *Voprosy pola* (Mos- cow and Leningrad, 1929): 128–133.

69. In Russian, as in English, the very terms for male and female sexual dysfunc- tion (impotence [*bessilie*] and coldness [*kholodnost'*], respectively) and the functioning dichotomy between the two concepts (power versus passivity) reflect widely held cul- tural assumptions about appropriate male and female sociosexual roles and behaviors.

70. "Otvety na voprosy chitatel'ei," *Gigiena i zdorov'e* 7 (1927), back cover.

71. "Khronika-Polovaia konsul'tatsiia," *Gigiena i zdorov'e* 12 (June 1928), 14.

72. Mendel'son, *Nervnaia sistema,* 9. Several doctors described women as being particularly susceptible to mental illness, yet devoted no attention to this phenomenon.

73. Iakobzon, "Kholodnost' zhenshchiny," *Voprosy pola,* 108.

74. Iakobzon, "Polovye rasstroistva i vrachebnaia taina," *Voprosy pola,* 135.

75. This suggestion is offered to men in British medical advice literature as well. See Lesley A. Hall, "'Somehow very distasteful': Doctors, Men and Sexual Problems between the Wars," *Journal of Contemporary History* 20 (1985), 554.

76. Iakobzon, "Kholodnost' zhenshchiny," *Voprosy pola,* 104.

77. Fronshtein, *Rasstroistvo,* 37–38. See also Iakobzon, *Polovaia kholdnost' zhen- shchiny. Dlia vrachei i studentov* (Leningrad, 1927), 66.

78. Iakobzon, *Polovaia kholdnost' zhenshchiny,* 67.

79. In countries such as Weimar Germany, the sex reform movement did focus attention on a woman's ability to achieve orgasm. Significantly, however, these re- formers likewise emphasized the role of the husband in ensuring that such satisfaction take place. See Atina Grossmann, "'Satisfaction Is Domestic Happiness': Mass Work- ing Class Sex Reform Organizations in the Weimar Republic," in *Towards the Holo-*

caust: The Social and Economic Collapse of the Weimar Republic, ed. Michael N. Dubkowski and Isidor Wallimann (Westport, Conn.: Greenwood Press, 1983); idem, "The New Woman and the Rationalization of Sexuality in Weimar Germany," in *Powers of Desire: The Politics of Sexuality*, ed. Ann Barr Snitow, Christine Stansell, and Sharon Thompson (New York: Monthly Review Press, 1983). On such emphasis elsewhere in Europe, see Angus McLaren, "'Selfish Beasts': Marriage Manuals and the Eroticization of Marriage," ch. 3 of *Twentieth-Century Sexuality: A History* (Oxford: Blackwell, 1999), 46–63; and Roy Porter and Lesley Hall, *The Facts of Life: the Creation of Sexual Knowledge in Britain, 1650–1950* (New Haven, Conn.: Yale University Press, 1995), ch. 9.

80. Iakobzon, "Polovye rasstroistva i vrachebnaia taina," 135.

81. Iakobzon, "Kholodnost' zhenshchiny," 106.

82. See for instance B. Gurvich and Zalutskii, "Opyt konsul'tatsii po polovoi gigiene," 234; and B. Gurvich, "Polovaia slabost' muzhchin," 2. This sense of responsibility and the anxiety it produced was also commented upon in European medical literature. See Lesley Hall, "'Somehow very distasteful,'" and Robert A. Nye, "Honor, Impotence, and Male Sexuality in Nineteenth-Century French Medicine," *French Historical Studies* 16:1 (Spring 1989), 64.

83. Iakobzon, *Polovaia kholodnost' zhenshchiny*, 73.

84. Iakobzon, "Kholodnost' zhenshchiny," 105.

85. "Otvety na voprosy chitatelei," *Gigiena i zdorov'e* 7 (1927), back cover. While sex education literature posited maternity as an inevitable, natural, and desirable development in every woman's life, an aggressively pronatalist stance only emerged in the late 1920s. At that time fears about a demographic decline arose, partly as a result of the war scare with Britain, and were expressed most frequently in connection with the debate around abortion. See Susan Gross Solomon, "The Demographic Argument in Soviet Debates Over the Legalization of Abortion in the 1920s," *Cahiers du monde russe et sovietique* 2 (1992).

86. On women as prostitutes, see Frances Bernstein,"Prostitutes and Proletarians: The Labor Clinic as Revolutionary Laboratory in the 1920s," in *The Human Tradition in Modern Russia*, ed. William Husband (Wilmington, Del.: SR Books, 2000), 113–128; and "Envisioning Health in Revolutionary Russia: The Politics of Gender in Sexual Enlightenment Posters of the 1920s," *Russian Review* 57 (April 1998), 191–217. On lesbians, see for example, A. O. Edel'shtein, "K klinike transvestitizma," in *Prestupnik i prestupnost'*, ed. E. K. Krasnushkin, G. M. Segal, and Ts. M. Feinberg (Moscow, 1927), 273–282; N. P. Brukhanskii, "Razvratnye deistviia. St. 168 U.k. Gomoseksualizm," in *Materialy po sekskual'noi psikhopatologii: Psikhiatricheskie ekspertizy* (Moscow, 1927), 62–65. See also Dan Healey's analysis of the medical approach to lesbianism during this time period in *Homosexual Desire*, especially ch. 5.

87. B. Gurvich, "Prostitutsiia, kak sotsial'no-psikhopatlogicheskoe iavlenie," in *Sovetskaia meditsina v bor'be za zdorovye nervy*, 60–68.

88. The only reference to the demographic implications of male impotence I have seen comes from one of the sex survey respondents cited by Sheila Fitzpatrick in her article on sexual mores among students: "The half-starved and restless" condition of student life "threatens complete sexual impotence, so that there is very little chance that we Communists will leave descendants." See Fitzpatrick, "Sex and Revolution," 265. This is a major point of difference between the Russian case and that of France in the nineteenth century, for instance. According to Robert Nye, in that context re-

productive concerns, and especially the ability to bear male progeny, were of paramount importance in medical discussions of male impotence. See Nye, "Honor, Impotence, and Male Sexuality," 53, 55.

89. Faingol'd, *Polovoe bessilie: Ego prichiny preduprezhdenie i lechenie*, 29.

90. Iakobzon, "Sotsial'noe znachenie polovykh rasstroistv," *Gigiena i zdorov'e* 3 (February 1930), 5–6.

91. For examples of these images in political posters, see Stephen White, *The Bolshevik Poster* (New Haven, Conn., and London: Yale University Press, 1988). The contrast between the nervous, impotent youth and his self-assured, productive counterpart had its parallel, as described by Eric Naiman, in the threat posed by a healthy (menstruating) female and the reassurance of an anorexic woman who has stopped bleeding. Arguing that the most powerful marker of female sexuality during the NEP was a woman's ability to menstruate (considered a sign of the disruption of capitalism), Naiman contrasts this with the idealized, ideologically pure female body of the hungry Civil War era, a body which had become anorexic, incapable of menstruating, and hence completely desexualized. See his *Sex in Public*, ch. 6.

92. In her analysis of 1920s sex surveys, Sheila Fitzpatrick interprets the high level of anxiety over impotence among men as owing to the "unusual burden of responsibility and obligation felt by the first postrevolutionary generation of university students" and the lack of clear direction regarding their sexual behavior. See Fitzpatrick, "Sex and Revolution," 265–266. According to Anson Rabinbach, the physician's role as expert was crucial in the treatment of neurasthenics in Europe as well. See Rabinbach, *The Human Motor*, 162.

93. Khaletskii, *Polovaia zhizn' i nevrasteniia*, 27.

94. For similar discussions of the role of the doctor's consultation and the power of medical suggestion as forms of treatment, see Kameneva, *Chto kazhdomu nuzhno znat' o nervnosti*, 28; Z. G. Lur'e, *Nevrasteniia*, 8. Lesley A. Hall reaches similar conclusions in her analysis of British doctors and their treatment of male sexual impotency. See her "'Somehow very distasteful,'" 559.

95. Mendel'son, "Polovoe bessilie," in *Gigiena i zdorov'e* 1(8) (January 1924), 6.

96. B. Gurvich, "Po povodu pisem o polovykh rasstroistvakh," 2.

97. Eric Naiman has described this atmosphere of anxiety and panic as "NEP Gothic." See *Sex in Public*, ch. 4.

98. Aron Sol'ts, in a 1924 speech to students of Sverdlov University, inveighs against suicide-related panic: "We have at present a rather great number of suicides. Comrades, that need not cause us any panic. It is natural and understandable. We are going through an era where the nerves of a very great number of people have been so tested, have endured so much, that they no longer have the strength to do further that which is demanded of them by the party." See Aron Sol'ts, "Communist Ethics," in *Bolshevik Visions: First Phase of the Cultural Revolution in Soviet Russia*, ed. William G. Rosenberg (Ann Arbor, Mich.: Ardis, 1984), 46. On the "problem of youth" in the 1920s, see S. I. Gusev, *Kakova zhe nasha molodezh'? Sbornik statei* (Moscow and Leningrad, 1927). Sexual immorality and suicide are explicitly linked in discussions of the Eseninshchina. On this, see Pinnow, "Crisis, Morality, and Class," 28; and *Upadochnoe nastroenie sredi molodezhi. Eseninshchina* (Moscow, 1927).

99. N. A. Semashko, *Novyi byt i polovoi vopros* (Moscow, 1926), 25–27. Sheila Fitzpatrick has challenged this perception of extreme sexual promiscuity in "Sex and Revolution," 252–278.

100. N. Shvarts, "Razvrashchena li nasha molodezh'," *Za zdorovyi byt* 5 (1929), 2.

101. Coincidentally, this is the same publication date as the first edition of *Za zdorovyi byt*.

102. N A Semashko, "Kak ne nado pisat' o polovom voprose," *Izvestiia* (January 1, 1925): 5.

103. For a more detailed discussion of Zalkind and Liadov's analyses of sexuality, see Naiman, *Sex in Public*, ch. 6.

104. The endocrine glands figure prominently in popular science writing and medical sex advice during the 1920s. See my "Science, Glands, and the Medical Construction of Gender Difference in Revolutionary Russia," in *Russian Modernity: Politics, Knowledge, Practices*, ed. David L. Hoffmann and Yanni Kotsonis (New York: Macmillan, 2000), 138–160; and *The Dictatorship of Sex*, ch. 2.

105. I.e., heterosexual, monogamous sex, excluding sex with prostitutes.

106. Eric Naiman explores the Komsomol's approach to male sexuality in this period, which "endeavored to tease and excite so that they could later condemn and, eventually, control." See *Sex in Public*, especially ch. 7.

107. The specific article Semashko has in mind is "Polovoi vopros s kommunisticheskoi tochki zreniia," first published in *Na putiakh k novoi shkole* 6 (1924), 6.

108. This contrast is made particularly striking in the chapter of Eric Naiman's work cited above (n. 106), which examines party debates on the depravity of the young in relation to a sensationalized gang-rape incident in Leningrad. No medical personnel participate in the discussions.

109. This represents a radical departure from the situation before the revolution, when medical discussions of sexuality were overtly politicized. See Julie V. Brown, op. cit., and Laura Engelstein, op. cit.

110. Similarly, Sheila Fitzpatrick argues that student insecurity resulted in part from confusion over the conflicting messages of authority figures about sexual liberty and sexual irresponsibility. See her "Sex and Revolution," 276.

seven
Delivered from Capitalism

Nostalgia, Alienation, and the Future of
Reproduction in Tret'iakov's I Want a Child!

Christina Kiaer

In Sergei Tret'iakov's controversial and ultimately censored eugenic play *I Want a Child!* (*Khochu rebenka!*) of 1926, an unmarried party member named Milda, whose extensive public organizing work to benefit the collective leaves no time for marriage or children, suddenly discovers that she wants to have a child. As an agronomist well versed in eugenics as well as Leninism, Milda decides that the prospective father must be of 100 percent healthy proletarian stock. Rationalist and antiromantic, she searches out an appropriate specimen. Fixing her sights on the brawny young worker Iakov from the local construction site, she propositions him to father her child. She offers him a contract stating that after conception she will make no claims for his support of her or the child, nor will she ask him to play the roles of husband or father in any way. After considerable discussion he agrees to her terms, and they begin to have sex. As soon as she conceives, she severs all ties with him. Their son is raised communally in collective Soviet children's institutions. She allows Iakov no fatherly access, despite his pleas. In the play's conclusion, set four years later in 1930, Iakov catches a glimpse of his son when the child wins first prize in a "Healthy Baby" contest—displayed as an object of collective consumption, rather than of traditional, individual parental pride.[1]

As this plot summary suggests, Tret'iakov's play scripts a literal, biological

solution to the problem of forming a new Soviet subject. The complex economic and social processes of production and consumption are simplified
here through recourse to the metaphor of biological reproduction. In the "new
everyday life" (*novyi byt*) after the revolution, the dense web of human desires
surrounding sexuality will be rationalized by eugenic choice as simply as the
material clutter of domestic family life will be eliminated from the new collective spaces of everyday life. Developed in the West, eugenics was a science that
imposed the industrial disciplines of scientific quality control and rational
planning onto the sexed body of the individual citizen. In the context of this
play by a left avant-garde writer, eugenics becomes a means to produce a
specifically socialist Soviet subject who will be, from his or her very conception, collectively owned and communally oriented.

The bourgeois sexuality inherited from the old world, with its ideology of
possession, will be penetrated by the rational eye of science: "In *I Want a
Child!*" Tret'iakov said, "love is placed on an operating table."[2] The play
rejects traditional dramatic formulas for building emotion around its potboiler
plot, and instead presents the actions of all the characters as questions for
discussion. The inner reaches of private dramas will be laid out for vivisection
on the operating table, or better yet, placed under a microscope. This is
Tret'iakov's description of the opening shot of the film script that he wrote in
1928 on the basis of the play:

> In the shot a million fibers are moving, and this movement looks like a
> ripened field, swayed by the wind in one direction. On this swaying there
> appears a huge, semitransparent sphere, glimmering with radiating fila-
> ments from the luminous nucleus at its center. This sphere rolls on the
> swaying field. The delicate flagella with their fat little heads, wriggling
> swiftly, move toward the sphere. They surround the sphere with twitching
> rays on all sides. One of them pierces the membrane of the sphere. This
> membrane becomes glassy as soon as it is pierced, grows turbid, and
> through the murk one can see how the head of the flagellum moves toward
> the nucleus and joins with it. With a sharp movement this entire picture is
> jerked out of the shot. This is Milda the agronomist-cattle-breeder working
> with the microscope.[3]

The round glass eye of the inquisitive microscope, rendering visible this heroic
narrative of fertilization, offers a dramatic visual metaphor for the script's
narrative of the penetration of Bolshevik ideology into every aspect of Soviet
everyday life (*byt*). The Constructivist artist El Lissitzky designed a stage set for
the play in 1929 that similarly literalized this vision of an all-seeing Bolshevik
state by making the stage into a transparent glass circle, lit from below and
open to the audience on all sides (fig. 7.1). Devoid of traditional props—or, to
use the unabridged theatrical term, "properties"—Lissitzky's bare stage emphasized the rationalizing and antimaterialist aspects of Tret'iakov's play,
clearing a space for social practice unencumbered by possessions. Their use of
these metaphors of visibility leave Tret'iakov and Lissitzky open to the charge

Figure 7.1. El Lissitzky, model of stage design for *I Want a Child!* 1929. © 2004 Artists Rights Society (ARS), New York / VG Bild-Kunst, Bonn.

that their work imagined Soviet subjects as fully rationalized objects of sur-veillance by the disciplining Soviet state. This would confirm the horror story told by Boris Groys in his influential account of Soviet art: the totalizing impetus in the Russian avant-garde paved the way for the repression and totalitarianism of Soviet society under Stalin.[4]

Tret'iakov wrote for the literary and artistic journal *Lef*, which propagated Constructivism in the arts and a documentary style of literary writing that would become known as "the literature of fact." The original Constructivist program of 1921 had famously called for visual artists to give up painting and sculpture in favor of entering industry to produce objects for use in the every-day life of the new Soviet collective. *Lef* writers and Constructivist artists wanted to transform the primitive and *meshchanskii* (petty bourgeois) *byt* that existed during the New Economic Policy into a modern, rationalized, and collective *novyi byt*. This goal provides fuel for Groys's sweeping argument that the avant-garde, like the Bolsheviks themselves, wanted to obliterate all remainders of past culture in order to remake society in its own totalizing image. Tret'iakov's interest in eugenics in *I Want a Child!* only exacerbates this critique, because eugenics attempts to master the very raw materials of the subject, neutralizing all negative physical and psychological aspects inherited from the capitalist past at the level of the germ plasm. Tret'iakov's play would then offer additional evidence that the Constructivist dream of fostering a new Soviet subject through the Constructivist object—a kind of gentle metaphor, in which it is understood that if you change people's material surroundings for the better, you will also eventually change the people themselves in salutary ways—was instead a totalitarian nightmare of a future in which appropriate Soviet subjects would be produced by any means necessary.

The aim of this essay is to demonstrate, precisely on the unpromising ground of an analysis of Tret'iakov's *I Want a Child!*, that the Russian avant-garde offered a more sympathetic model for imagining the passage of the Soviet subject into the *novyi byt* than is usually understood. The desire for a total break between the capitalist past and the socialist future lies close to Tret'iakov's avant-garde heart, but it is a desire that his text continuously under-mines. Tret'iakov the avant-gardist is also a Marxist dialectician, denaturalizing ideology by pointing out its contradictions. He invokes the potentially socialist aspects of eugenics, such as the destruction of the bourgeois property relations of marriage and family, but he also deconstructs his own eugenic narrative, interrupting it with almost journalistic scenes depicting topical and heated discussions of sexuality, the family, and the material problems of contemporary *byt*, and refusing traditional dramatic formulas for building emotions or deliv-ering character identifications. Tret'iakov also challenges eugenics theoret-ically, through a Marxist critique of its potential alienation of the labor of the male (re)producer and, unusually at this time, through a critique of the tradi-tional gender roles that were reinforced by the contemporary Soviet manifesta-tion of eugenics. The opening image in his film script of the passive ovum and victorious active sperm has by now become a clichéd biological metaphor for male dominance, but Tret'iakov keeps the image firmly in the petri dish; the play scrambles assumptions about traditional gender roles, refusing the sup-posedly natural link between biology and lived gender.

As futuristic as Tret'iakov's play appears to be, with its evocation of a brave new world of eugenic mastery, his text in fact exposes, with uncanny, newsreel-like precision, the lived contradictions of everyday Soviet experience during NEP in the face of new Soviet ideologies of the subject. A small notice an-nouncing the play in the newspaper *Vecherniaia Moskva* in 1926 emphasizes this temporal disjunction, describing its subject as "the problem of sex and marriage in the conditions of the *novyi byt*, and this *novyi byt* is treated by the author as a prognosis for the future."[5] Tret'iakov had finished the first version of the play by late September 1926, because on 28 September he assigned the performance rights to the avant-garde theater director Vsevolod Meyerhold. The signing of this contract was announced in all the newspapers and theater journals in November of 1926, and it was expected that the play would be performed in the 1927–1928 season at Meyerhold's theater.[6] Rehearsals for the production began in February 1927 and were well under way when per-mission to produce the play was denied by Glavrepertkom (*Glavnyi repertuar-nyi komitet*, the censorship arm of Glaviskusstvo). Meyerhold was eventually given permission by Glavrepertkom, in December 1928, to mount it in his theater exclusively as a "discussion piece," rather than a traditional theatrical performance, and only if certain of the most problematic parts were rewritten. The planning of Lissitzky's stage sets, which involved a total rebuilding of the theater interior, was begun in early 1929. But the sets were never completed, and the play was never performed.[7] Tret'iakov's film script was also censored by Glavrepertkom in 1929.[8]

The problem of the play's temporal dissonance dominated the Glavrepertkom discussion of it in 1928. As the remarks of the various censors demonstrate, the play uncomfortably signaled the gap between propaganda visions of the future and present social reality, and laid bare the deep conflicts in Soviet visions of what the utopian future would be like. The Proletkul't theorist Valerii Pletnev claimed the play had not fully developed the eugenic problem sociologically, but then admitted that the real problem was that "perhaps the play has appeared sooner than necessary."[9] Another member of the committee, a "representative" worker named Petrov, similarly proposed that the play was simply ahead of its time, and not yet relevant to Soviet life: "the problem must be posed, but not now (we have not attained that level yet [literally, we have not grown up enough])" (*problemu nado postavit', no ne seichas [ne dorosli]*).[10] The censors, it seems, took one look at the eugenic theme, the frank discussion of sexuality, the nontraditional gender roles—and panicked. This essay will suggest that the censors did not read the play carefully enough, because the process through which the Soviet Union will "grow up" into a more rationalized future is in fact its subject.

In *I Want a Child!* the lived experience of *byt* continually interrupts grand Bolshevik plans for a *novyi byt*. Tret'iakov investigates the human effects of the transition to the new world of socialism, rather than offering a blithe narration of its achievement. Despite their seemingly uncompromising, futuristic vision, Tret'iakov's play, and Constructivism more broadly, share the insight of Walter Benjamin, in his unfinished *Arcades Project*, that a future socialist culture will succeed only if it can redeem the human desires lodged in the everyday practices and material objects of the past. The *Arcades Project* attempted to imagine not just a Marxist revolution but the transition to socialism that would follow it, to imagine a form of socialist culture that would reactivate the original promise of the creativity of industrialism while delivering it from the commodity phantasmagoria of capitalism that prevented its realization.[11] The Constructivist program of designing expedient new objects for mass production in Soviet industry was meant not just to replace the commodity form, but to provide a socialist rejoinder to the commodity's emotional power, because the "socialist objects" of Constructivism would function as active "comrades" in social life.[12] Tret'iakov's play provocatively extends this Constructivist reinvention of the creativity of industrialism onto the territory of the human body itself, using the device of eugenics to imagine a parallel reinvention of procreativity through industrial technology. Like Constructivist socialist objects freed from the pernicious effects of the commodity form, Tret'iakov's socialist form of reproduction would be delivered from the consequences of capitalism:

possessiveness, the alienation of labor, and patriarchal social forms of male dominance and female passivity.

The goal of Benjamin's project was to awaken people from the "dream sleep" of the commodity phantasmagoria into socialist culture through his "materialist history" of the revolutionary potential of mass culture. The moments of potential awakening took the form of a dialectical image: "that wherein what has been comes together in a flash with the now to form a constellation."[13] The transitional nature of Tret'iakov's play, set within the socially chaotic context of NEP but looking toward the socialist future, was meant to provide the contemporary Soviet audience with such an awakening "constellation." Holding the past, present, and future in a fragile solution, this constellation offers counter-evidence to Groys' indictment of the avant-garde for its attempt to obliterate the past to create a totalized future.

A Socialist Eugenics?

The play treads a fine line between describing the actual problems of Soviet *byt* during NEP in 1926, and imagining a futuristic *novyi byt* which is far more radical sexually—both in its incorporation of the highly topical issue of eugenics and in its emphasis on a woman making her own choices about sex and reproduction—than the official propaganda version of the *novyi byt*. The question of *byt* in relation to Bolshevism first entered seriously into public discussion in 1923 with the publication of Leon Trotsky's essays on the subject in the party newspaper *Pravda*, collected that same year in his book *Voprosy byta*, which inaugurated an explosion of public debate about the prospect of a new everyday life under socialism.[14] The phrase *novyi byt* had cropped up regularly in the utopian atmosphere of the civil war years, loosely signifying a range of ideas from simple strategies for the modernization of backward peasant life to radical collective living arrangements, but these ideas had not occupied official party attention. The party's sudden interest in *byt* in 1923 represented, most broadly, a sense that the New Economic Policy had brought about a breathing spell after the upheaval of the civil war, allowing the new government to turn its attention from seizing power to questions of culture and social life. It also signaled a worry that the return to a semblance of normality under NEP would result in a bourgeois influence on morality, sexuality, and domestic life. The party responded by engaging more directly in formulating ideas of appropriate habits of daily life under communism.[15] In the mid-1920s, mass propaganda for the *novyi byt* stemmed primarily from the health sector and consumer cooperatives, and promoted modern hygiene, health, and the collectivization of child care, cooking, laundry, and shopping.

Throughout the 1920s, however, the *novyi byt* was popularly understood to refer to the incendiary questions of the new sexual and family relations promoted by the Bolsheviks. Tret'iakov's choice to take up the theme of eugenics is an instance of his response to current debates on the topic of sexual *byt.* The rationalistic and scientistic veneer of eugenics resonated well enough with other Bolshevik organizational goals that it received a certain amount of attention in the mass press. An unfortunate manifestation of the modernist faith in progress, science, and the eventual control of nature, the theory of eugenics was popular in most Western countries in the 1920s, with varying degrees of racism and coerciveness. In Russia, interest in eugenics first arose around the time of the revolution. The Russian Eugenics Society was founded by the biologist Nikolai Konstantinovich Kol'tsov in 1920, under the auspices of the National Commissariat of Health (Narkomzdrav).[16] The young science was deemed worthy of state support because of its status as a kind of "civic religion," as its founder Francis Galton had called it. It undermined Christianity and shared the Marxist, materialist belief that human beings had the power to shape the future and improve the human condition. But the question of the practical implementation of eugenics was always the problem, in Russia as elsewhere. In the "negative" model of eugenics, unfit men would be forcibly sterilized; this was practiced in several states in the U.S., originally in Indiana. In the "positive" model, people with desirable traits would be encouraged to reproduce with each other, but there was as yet no practical application of this model anywhere, other than the practice of requiring certificates of freedom from hereditary disease in order to obtain a marriage license. The third, "Lamarckian" model of eugenics was based on the idea that genetic material was not immutable, but could be influenced by social conditions, and that this changed genetic material could then be passed on to the next generation. This model appealed to Marxist supporters of eugenics, because it implied that human action could directly change the germ plasm. Anatolii Lunacharskii, the Commissar of Enlightenment, wrote a film script celebrating the Lamarckian idea that eugenics could make people into "captains of the future" rather than "slaves of the past."[17] In this example of a totalizing Bolshevik vision, the transition to the socialist future would be accomplished by the destruction of all the unacceptable elements that humanity had inherited from the capitalist past.

Scientists involved in eugenics in Moscow and Leningrad differed among themselves on the best model of practical implementation to follow, and, in the absence of any officially sanctioned view on the matter, the mass press expressed a range of opinions on eugenics.[18] The significant point for understanding Tret'iakov's play is that there was a widespread popular interest in eugenics in the Soviet Union in the 1920s. It was most often mentioned in relation to the prevention of syphilis and other venereal diseases. Due to its infectiousness and seriousness, syphilis was one of the most pressing public health problems in both the countryside and the cities. Since it was often passed on to children, it provided a convenient starting point for the promotion of eugenics, as did the prevalent belief that alcoholism was hereditary. This could be described as a relatively benign and partial form of the eugenic argument: women should avoid marrying men with venereal disease or alcoholism, because their lives would be easier and happier if they had healthy children. An article about the treatment and prevention of syphilis in the *Magazine for Women* (*Zhurnal dlia zhenshchin*) in 1924, for example, encouraged the reader to participate in public work to combat syphilis, including taking part in "the so-called 'eugenic movement.'"[19] A footnote explained that eugenics is a growing science that aims "to organize . . . all aspects and forms of the battle for rendering humanity healthy, for improving the human race, including the battle against venereal disease."

A year later in the same journal, on the other hand, one of the editors pokes fun at the eugenic movement. "There are many conversations about this fashionable science—eugenics," the piece begins. "How should men marry, how should women marry, in order to fulfill through this act their duty to humanity, to provide the country with a healthy growth, a healthy, strong, and talented generation."[20] The author offers no substantive critique of eugenics, but simply notes ironically that people will always take chances in choosing their partners, and no amount of eugenic propaganda will change that. As a result, the author concludes tauntingly, the poor little science of eugenics will be left all alone like a lonely woman, spilling many tears over all the lost possibilities of giving birth to talented people and unable to stop the births of all the little ordinary individuals, about whom "no stories will be told, no songs will be sung." Negative as these few paragraphs are, they indicate the popularity of eugenics, as well as the content of popular perceptions of it. In most people's minds, eugenics seemed to be associated with the idea of choosing healthy partners, rather than the possibility of state coercion; it involved choices made within marriage and traditional family structures; and it could just as easily be derided within the popular-Bolshevik discourse of materialism —eugenics is idealistic fantasizing about creating "talented" people, not truly materialist in everyday, practical terms—as it could be celebrated as precisely a materialist, down-to-earth science—making humanity healthier by combating the consequences of venereal disease.

Advocacy of the more coercive model of eugenics in the mass press was rare. An article from 1926 in *Smena*, the illustrated magazine for communist youth, gives a fairly garbled account of genetic science, concluding with blithe assurances of the quick and painless nature of the operation for male sterilization, as well as of the great possibilities for artificially promoting good hereditary traits in human beings, along the lines learned from agricultural experiments and animal husbandry.[21] The author seems to have gotten his or her information from the Russian Eugenics Society, which accounts for the article's extreme, partisan viewpoint. The secretary of the society, a young scientist named M. V. Volotskoi, who was a student of its founder, Kol'tsov, was a strong advocate of negative eugenics in the form of enforced sterilization and had published a book advocating it in 1923, which he revised and published again in a second edition in 1926.[22] The *Smena* article was illustrated with the saccharine logo of the society, an etching of three generations of shapely, nude

Figure 7.2. Logo of the Russian Eugenics Society,
reproduced in *Smena*, no. 5 (1926).

Aryan types posed under a classical bower of trees (fig. 7.2), as well as with
photographs—of twins, an "idiot" and a peasant with six fingers and toes—from
the collection of the Museum of Social Hygiene, which had strong ties to the
Russian Eugenics Society. In 1929, another protégé of Kol'tsov, Aleksandr Serebrovskii, claimed that eugenics could contribute to the five-year plan by improving the production of human beings through "the widespread induction of
conception by means of artificial insemination using recommended sperm,
and not at all necessarily from a beloved spouse . . . with the current state of
artificial insemination technology (now widely used in horse and cattle breeding), one talented and valuable producer could have up to 1,000 children."[23]
Serebrovskii would soon have to recant his wild plan and apologize for implying
that the five-year plan had been deficient without it. Although ideas for such
radical and antifamilial models of eugenics could be published freely in the
1920s, they appeared primarily in purely eugenicist publications, rather than in
the popular press; in this regard the *Smena* article is an exception. Eugenics fit
into the officially sanctioned versions of the *novyi byt* only as a component of
organized sexuality and reproduction on the traditional familial model.

As long as eugenics was advocated merely as education and propaganda, it was insistently individual and family oriented: what can the individual man or woman do to ensure that his or her spouse will be an appropriate parent? While the idea of choosing a mate eugenically was ridiculed in the *Magazine for Women* editorial, it was earnestly advocated by one Dr. Bernatskii in an article in the mass-oriented magazine *Hygiene and Health of the Worker and Peasant Family* in 1928, entitled "What You Need to Know in Choosing a Husband or a Wife."[24] According to Bernatskii, four conditions must be met for a marriage to be successful, the foremost of which is the good health of both partners. Although he does not use the term, Bernatskii is clearly a believer in eugenics. He urges young prospective marriage partners to take responsibility for the health of the future generation of the nation, cautioning them with scary statistics about the hereditary nature of "horrible and fatal" diseases such as syphilis, tuberculosis, nervous disorders, and alcoholism. He even cites with approval the advice of a German researcher named Bunge, who recommends that young people should avoid marrying not only anyone with a history of disease, but anyone who has bad teeth. This urgency around the question of hereditary health can only be entertained, however, in the context of the most traditional forms of marriage and family relations. The second condition that must be met in a marriage partner is "the necessity of definite and sharply expressed sexual characteristics, physical as well as spiritual (the male principle and the female principle)."[25] A woman is "more caressing than a man, her movements are light, her voice is softer, she is tidier and neater, she is more observant of details, she loves coziness and cleanliness. In a word, she is 'feminine.' "[26] This union of healthy, appropriately gendered partners will only be strengthened by the third and fourth conditions for successful marriage: mutual interests and, finally, love.

Dr. Bernatskii's emphasis on traditional marriage and gender roles is symptomatic of the conservatism of the intense campaign of the later 1920s for improving the health of sexual *byt* (*ozdorovlenie polovogo byta*). Earnest debates about *byt* within the Komsomol in 1925 and 1926 had centered on the caddish sexual behavior of young male communists, who took advantage of Marx and Engels' critique of bourgeois marriage to get women to have sex outside the bonds of marriage. In a brief scene of a gang rape in *I Want a Child!* entitled "Hooligans," Tret'iakov refers to a contemporary manifestation of worries about the new Bolshevik sexuality: the gang rape by a group of twenty-six young men, some of them Komsomol members, of a young peasant woman in Chubarov Alley in Leningrad in August 1926. Beginning on 12 September 1926, this disturbing rape received extensive press attention as an outrageous example of hooliganism among Soviet youth, against which the press had already been campaigning for several months.[27] Although it may seem unlikely that Tret'iakov would have added a whole new scene to his play within two weeks of its completion just to respond to this media event—the rape was first reported on 12 September, and he signed a contract with Meyerhold to produce the play on 28 September—this is precisely the kind of documentary attention to current events to which Tret'iakov was committed as a writer. The scene of the gang rape does not involve any of the main characters, nor is it organically connected to other scenes, so it could easily have been inserted at the last minute to respond to the press on the Chubarov rape.

According to some of the many condemnations of the Chubarov rapists that appeared in the press, their villainy in relation to Soviet society lay not only in their brutal criminality toward the rape victim herself, but also in the hazard they posed to public health: some of the young men who were first in line in the rape infected not only the woman with venereal disease, but also, necessarily, some of their comrades who followed, in effect homosexually infecting each other with disease through the body of the woman. Tret'iakov chose to emphasize this aspect of the Chubarov case, by having one young man in the gang of hooligans direct another that he must go last, because he is "sick" (Kh.R. 218). Tret'iakov's inclusion of this violent scene intensified the urgency of the questions of sexuality that his "discussion play" raised. Although the scene effectively evokes the horror experienced by the woman, and therefore obviously condemns the rape, it comes across less as a moral condemnation of the individual young men involved than as a highly critical analysis of the irrational and disorganized male proletarian sexuality of the time.

A Feminist Eugenics?

The model of eugenics that Tret'iakov deploys in *I Want a Child!* challenges Dr. Bernatskii's insistence on clearly defined gender roles, as well the traditional sexual morality espoused in the party debates on the sexual question and bourgeois models of domesticity and the family. The central character of Milda is defined by her conscious refusal of traditional femininity. She embodies the figure of the androgynous and asexual Bolshevik woman who emerged in the popular imagination in the civil war years.[28] In her first appearance in the play, she is dressed in a man's suit, standing with her back to the audience in the worker's club attached to the construction site (*stroika*) that is the play's setting. She has dedicated herself to public organizing work at the site, giving lectures at public meetings and fighting to establish a children's day care center at the workers' club. When the workers Iakov and Grin'ko enter the club, Grin'ko mistakes Milda for his male pal "Frolka," whom he grabs from behind and turns around. Upon seeing his mistake, he pushes Milda away, exclaiming, "That's not a person, that's a woman" (*ta tse zh ne chelovek, ta tse zh baba*) (Kh.R. 210)—a slang reworking of the traditional Russian proverb "A chicken is not a bird, a woman is not a person" (*Kuritsa ne ptitsa, zhenshchina ne chelovek*). Grin'ko's scornful misogyny is applied with special venom to the androgynous and authoritative Bolshevik woman.

The rest of the play makes a point of contesting the traditional construction of femininity that supposedly justified this misogyny. A key scene in this contestation unfolds when Milda has invited Grin'ko's comrade Iakov to her room for an "interview" and propositions him to sire a child with her. She seduces him into sleeping with her through the traditionally feminine ruse of physical transformation, aided by the commodity objects associated with bourgeois femininity. Iakov responds negatively to her proposition at first, but Milda disappears behind a screen, emerging a few minutes later transformed: hair waved, face made up and powdered, dressed in a tight, low-cut dress. The "soldier-woman" (*soldat baba*), as Grin'ko calls her (Kh.R. 224), achieves her goal of conceiving a child without a husband or a traditional family—a goal directly contradicting conventions of femininity—by taking on the masquerade of store-bought femininity. When Iakov asks her wonderingly how she managed to transform herself, she answers with customary frankness, "The way all such things are done. From the parfumerie. From the hair dresser" (Kh.R. 227). Yet after this initial scene of seduction, Milda returns to her normal, unfeminine self; there are no more mentions of makeup or dresses. Tret'iakov invokes the familiar dramatic ploy of the Cinderella figure—the transformation of the ugly duckling into the swan—only to defuse its power by refusing to maintain the transformation. The feminine beauty revealed by the transformation is no more natural than the masculine plainness that preceded it; both are constructed, with the help of everyday objects like powder, perfume, curling irons, and dresses—or soldier's trousers and sturdy boots.

In addition to her lack of an appropriately feminine appearance, Milda's clinical and unembarrassed relation to sexuality is the antithesis of traditional cultural expectations of femininity. As Frances Bernstein has demonstrated, among 1920s sexologists, women were assumed to be more prone than men to shyness or "false shame" (*lozhnyi styd*) when it came to sexual matters.[29] In contrast to this ignorant form of feminine shame, Milda demonstrates a rational and informed approach to sex when she is propositioned by a man from her building who pleads his "physical need for a woman" because his wife is out of town. She refuses, suggesting that he can resolve his problem alone in his room: "Onanism at your age and in your position can, in my opinion, only be useful" (Kh.R. 220). Graphic, clinical words such as "onanism" were rarely heard on the Soviet stage; Tret'iakov's language is deliberately factual and informative, to underscore that the play is meant to foster discussion about sex, rather than to eroticize it or moralize against it. Milda's suggestion that masturbation would not be harmful in this man's case in fact conveys to the audience the latest results of Soviet sexological research, which revealed that masturbation was harmful for adults only when it interfered with "normal" sexual life with a partner. The man responds to her frank suggestion by accusing her of a *meshchanskii* prudishness. He, not Milda, is the overt object of parody in this scene, providing a caricature of the kind of opportunistic male attitude toward sex that emerged with the Marxist critique of bourgeois morality, and that was so vehemently criticized at the time in the Komsomol press. Milda's unemotional rationalism is also meant to be parodic; Tret'iakov stated that "[i]t is not true that I want to foist Milda upon the public. I myself included a number of moments that discredit her."[30] Yet while the audience is not meant to heroize or fully identify with Milda, it is asked to take her knowledge and actions seriously.

In solving the narrative problem of how to get this unfeminine rationalist interested in having a child at all, Tret'iakov does not resort to traditional gendered assumptions about women's natural longing for motherhood, but rather invokes the powerful rhetoric of production. In an elaborately staged scene, reproduction is linked to production when Milda encounters a procession of twenty fathers holding infants marching along the street. She starts a conversation with the fathers which quickly degenerates into a eugenics lesson for the audience, as different fathers explain the reasons for the sickliness of their children. One man married a tubercular woman, another married his cousin—explanations indicating that Tret'iakov's brand of eugenics is more aligned with the model of individual, informed choice than with coercive, interventionist models. The crucial moment for sparking Milda's desire, however, comes when "Father no. 1" asks her if she has a child herself. When she says no, he responds: "But a good product would come from you. Your pelvis is one hundred twenty centimeters and you would produce a lot of milk" (A produkt by u vas khoroshii vyshel. Taz santimetrov sto dvadtsat i moloka by mnogo dali) (Kh.R. 214). The proposal that reproduction could be understood within the structures of organized production—her body a well-equipped factory, her breasts providing adequate raw materials, her good health ensuring flawless products—provides the impetus for her sudden desire to have a child. The Constructivists took rational industrial production as their model for artmaking after the revolution; in I Want a Child! it also becomes the model for human decisions about sex and reproduction.

Yet more traditional models of sexual desire also crop up in the play, both by design—in order to signal to the audience the tenacity of the old byt—and in certain cases seemingly unconsciously, suggesting the limits of Tret'iakov's own ability to think beyond the contemporary ideology of sex and gender. Tret'iakov seems to recognize, for example, that the rational, production-based explanation for Milda's sudden desire to have a child will not in itself seem fully convincing as the basis for such a traditionally personal decision. He therefore inserts a few clues for her decision that deliberately summon more conventional assumptions about gender roles. In the film script she is described as caring for the animals in her charge with maternal tenderness (Kh.R.-S 35). In the scene with the "Fathers," Milda hears the cries of the babies and announces to her friend that the sounds of the cries seem to her "like a man was kissing me on the lips" (Kh.R. 213). This is her only expression of sexual desire in the entire play, and it is effectively sublimated into maternal desire. Tret'iakov never offers an explanation for her lack of sexual desire, except for the rational Bolshevik sublimation of her sexual desires into the tasks of production. Yet here, where her sexual desire for once finds expression,

Tret'iakov gives it the form prescribed by Freud himself as properly feminine: the sublimation of feminine phallic desire into the desire to have a child.

In a scene that seems to involve a less conscious deployment of gender stereotypes, Milda's selection of Iakov as the father of her child is explained not only by his proletarian pedigree, but by his possession of the masculine gender characteristics deemed desirable by Soviet proponents of eugenics. Once Milda realizes that she wants a child, her friend, a doctor, offers to introduce her to a eugenically appropriate candidate for fatherhood: a handsome doctor who stems from an old family of the intelligentsia. She meets her friend at his office at the *stroika* to arrange the introduction to this doctor, but from his window she catches sight of the rugged figure of Iakov, at work on the actual construction project itself. Tret'iakov accentuates the contrast between *intelligent* and proletarian by once again invoking the recent Chubarov gang rape, which he had already incorporated into the play in the form of the inserted scene of a gang rape. The reason that Milda notices Iakov outside the window of her friend's office is that they are interrupted in their conversation by a commotion outside: the police have come to the construction site to arrest the leader of the hooligans who committed the gang rape. Iakov, also at work there, vocally defends the rapists: women themselves provoke rape, he says, by wearing perfumes and powder and wiggling their buttocks (Kh.R. 223). Hearing this speech, Milda exclaims "Hooligans!" but her doctor friend replies that Iakov and his comrades are not hooligans at all, but merely strong, healthy young men: "No consumption, no neurasthenia, no venereal disease—exhibition pieces" (Kh.R. 223). Seemingly in response to this affirmation of Iakov's health, Milda starts a conversation with him. Yet the scene suggests that not only his health attracted Milda, but also his display of rough masculine sentiment in his defense of the vicious rape. Tret'iakov uses the instance of Chubarov, the best-known public breakdown of Soviet sexuality, as an additional plot premise to facilitate the meeting of Milda and Iakov, endowing the rape's violence and misogyny with the status of an irrepressible origin of the new model of organized, eugenic sexuality of the future.

Milda's choice of the manly Iakov over the proposed *intelligent*, who is described as delicate and polite, is made more immediate and visual in the film script version. Milda is in her friend the doctor's office when the second doctor enters briefly. In this man, her friend assures her, flows the blue blood of the intelligentsia; he will produce excellent offspring. Tret'iakov then describes a montage of changing, successive portraits of pedigreed people over the course of three hundred years, ending with the portrait of the handsome doctor (Kh.R.-S 40). This montage provides a literal image of eugenics: the positive traits of past generations are passed down through time, creating a link between the past and the future. Yet the almost *mise-en-abîme* effect of the infinite progression of similar portraits through time is stopped at the present moment. There is no montage of the doctor's future offspring coming forward, as it were. The reason for this becomes apparent later, when Milda sees this same blueblooded doctor bandaging the hand of an injured worker: "During the bandaging the contrast was striking between the pale, refined face of the doctor and his narrow, aristocratic hands and the bronze, cast-iron, snub-nosed workers" (Kh.R.-S 40). Through eugenics, class politics will be imposed onto the very germ plasm, protecting the future from the unwanted class characteristics of the presocialist past. Hard-muscled, bronzed masculinity wins out over the pampered, feminized upperclass male body. The favorite Bolshevik symbol of the rough, handsome worker is here presented alongside the teachings of contemporary medical discourse, such as those of Dr. Bernatskii, that the combination of masculine men and feminine women created the healthiest families and offspring.

This scene on the *stroika* celebrating stereotypical proletarian masculinity is in line with the relatively benign understanding of popular eugenics that existed then in the Soviet Union, but it is at odds with the critique of gender stereotypes that dominates the rest of the play. This discordance is another instance of Tret'iakov's "discussion piece" style, in which visions of the rational, gender-egalitarian reproduction of the future are continuously intertwined with the eruption of desires from the past that complicate their realization. Or it may signal that his radical vision of a future socialist sexuality—in which a woman could be as swayed by the ideology of production as by traditionally gendered desire—could not be imagined unconditionally from the perspective of the present.

Industrial Production: An Imperfect Model for the Future of Sex

Tret'iakov stages his most powerful criticism of eugenics by framing it as a problem of productive labor: by projecting industrial models of rational production onto the body, the play proposes, eugenics also risks carrying the exploitative labor practices of the capitalist past into the future. Milda's search for a proletarian specimen to father her child is portrayed as double edged. In her first interview with Iakov, Milda presses him for information about his parents and grandparents. He complies, assuming that she is yet another of the many writers gathering information on the everyday life of workers (*rabochii byt*) at that time. His friend Grin'ko interrupts, boasting that Iakov's father and grandfather were both metal workers from the Putilov metalworking factory, making him nothing less than a "count" of the working class. The Bolsheviks consistently singled out metal workers as the most authentic proletarians; they were provided with better housing and workers' clubs than other worker groups, and generally consulted and quoted and photographed more in the popular press. In the context of this farcical scene, in which Milda has made up her mind that she wants a proletarian father for her baby, the *Putilovskii* metal worker pedigree offers a distinctly comic touch. Yet Iakov is clearly being manipulated, unaware that he is being looked over like a potential stud on a stud farm.

This is made explicit in the pivotal scene, set later that night, in which Milda propositions him. Tret'iakov emphasizes the outlandish nature of her proposition by staging the scene so that the real-life conditions of present, overcrowded Soviet *byt* intrude on her utopian attempt to form a new one. When Iakov visits Milda's room under the mistaken impression that there will be another interview, he encounters the typical, squalid *byt* of a communal building: hooligans congregating outside and neighbors singing loudly or yelling to each other from windows and in the hallways. While Milda begins to formulate her proposition to Iakov, a "Voice" from outside the room calls to her that she has a visitor. She asks to say that she is not at home, and then begins her awkward speech to Iakov: "You, of course, understand that what we have going here is an all-purpose construction project. A cooperative, hospitals, schools. In a word, in order to make things better for people" (Kh.R. 226). She is interrupted by the Voice again, this time crying "They don't believe you"—referring both to the caller that was sent away, and, dramatically, to her speech. Milda locks her door, and continues pedantically, "You know that there is production. This is when products are made in factories or from the earth, and there is reproduction—this is when human stock itself is renewed, or more simply—people are born." Iakov answers patiently that he understands. She continues on in a eugenic vein, explaining that bad conditions of production lead to a low-quality product, just as incorrect conditions of reproduction—disease, alcoholism, idiotism—lead to bad people. Just as she is getting to the point, another Voice interrupts, this time to ask her if she by chance received a letter addressed to another room. When Milda finally manages to tell Iakov that she wants to conceive a child with a healthy worker, and that she has chosen him, he immediately objects that he already has a fiancé. Milda offers him the crucial explanation: "I don't want a husband. I want a child. You yourself aren't necessary to me. I need your spermatozoa." She then presents him with a contract stating that after conception, he will be relieved of any responsibility for supporting her or the child.

This dry business proposition aims for farce, playing the mismatch between the humorless Milda and the "regular guy" Iakov for laughs. Milda's firm belief that the complexities of human emotion can be solved by planning in advance and drawing up contracts parodies the figure of the earnest Bolshevik activist and organizer. It also challenges conventional wisdom about the passivity of feminine sexuality, for Milda knows what she wants, explains it frankly, and is not embarrassed to ask for sex. But the scene also presents eugenics in a critical light, because it enacts the central problem of Marxism itself: the alienated relation of the producer to the product of his labor. Milda has selected Iakov because of his *Putilovskii* proletarian pedigree, and yet she demands of him what has always been demanded of the proletarian: that he produce a product and then give it up, to be alienated from it forever. The body's natural production of sperm and the production of metal machine parts through physical labor in a factory are not comparable forms of production, yet the metaphor of alienated labor is made fully intentional: Iakov responds angrily to Milda's proposition by asking "What am I, a stallion?" (*Zherebets ia zavodskoi, chto li?*) (Kh.R. 227). Tret'iakov puns here on the standard term for "stallion," *zavodskoi zherebets*, which literally means "factory stallion."

In the Constructivist vision of a socialist future, the alienation of the worker from the object of his labor will be eliminated not only through the communist transformation of the means of production, but through the very form of the objects produced: socialist objects will be comrades of the worker, rather than alienating commodities to be possessed by someone richer than himself. This Constructivist dream of a *novyi byt* without possessions provides the context for the powerful justification that Milda offers Iakov for her exploitative demand on his reproductive labor: the product in question, the healthy part-proletarian child, will belong to the collective rather than to Milda herself. Later she will state explicitly that the child will be raised primarily in the children's house (*detdom*) and the kindergarten (*detskii sad*) (Kh.R. 233), and in the film script, she even teaches her child to call her "nana" rather than "mama," so that it will not miss her when she dies. She wants Iakov to give up his sperm to her, not just to fulfill her personal wishes for a child, but to benefit the Soviet collective. This is a private, bodily counterpart to the public, economic demand made by the Bolshevik Party of the Soviet proletariat: accept a continuing alienated relation to your labor, just as under capitalism, because the product of that labor is now expropriated by the state, which "represents" you.

Already in 1923, writing in *Lef*, Tret'iakov had imagined that in the socialist future, the human subject—personified in a character he called the "Futurist inventor"—would no longer latch onto fetishized objects, but would willingly part with the products of his creative labor, offering them to the collective. This subject would be able to flower as a true creator because he floated free of material things: "the Futurist must be least of all the owner of his own production."[31] Three years later, in *I Want a Child!* Tret'iakov has Milda's friend Distsipliner speak lines that carry this battle against possession from production into reproduction:

> To hell with husbands . . . What do you say to a syringe? The government will give the best spermatozoa to the best women producers. The government will encourage such a choice. It will take these children at its own expense and develop a breed of new people . . . In this way there will be scientific control over the person not only during upbringing, not only during birth, but even at the moment of conception. (Kh.R. 221)

The tone of the scene suggests that this outburst is to be viewed as eccentric and dystopian—much as the same real-life suggestion published by the eugenicist Serebrovskii in 1929 would be viewed—but other aspects of the play suggest that these ideas do not lie so far from Tret'iakov's own.

Tret'iakov makes Distsipliner's state institutions with their sperm banks and syringes seem rational and even benign by dramatically emphasizing the pathos of the seduction scene, in which Milda's ideal of collective reproduction is bogged down by the trappings of traditional, bourgeois sexuality. Amidst the farce and didacticism, the scene also invokes sympathy for Milda, who must compromise her own, unfeminine identity with a curling iron and lipstick in order to spark Iakov's desire, just as the audience would be expected to cringe at Iakov, the frank and healthy proletarian, being tricked by bourgeois feminine wiles into betraying his girlfriend and alienating himself from the product of his sperm. Distsipliner's proposal makes some sense: if Milda wants to have a child for the collective, outside the traditional gender constructs of the family, why should she not be able to access proletarian sperm without sinking to a form of feminine deception? If Iakov wants to contribute his healthy proletarian sperm to the collective, why should there not be collective structures that allow him to do so of his own free will, allowing him to release his product into the collective as a non-alienating political choice?

The simple fact that Distsipliner is identified as an inventor suggests that he is a figure for Tret'iakov's heroic "Futurist inventor," who speaks Tret'iakov's own disciplining desire for a socialist future in which both the products of creative invention—socialist objects—and the products of Soviet reproductive bodies under "scientific control"—eugenic children—will belong to the collective. No human characters in Tret'iakov's story experience artificial insemination with a syringe or a "scientifically controlled" conception. But by making Milda's character an agricultural expert involved in animal breeding, Tret'iakov alludes to this more futuristic, and potentially coercive, model of eugenics. The opening shot of the film script shows the fertilization of an egg through a microscope, and the following shot shows Milda turning from the microscope to assist a young peasant man who has brought in a suckling pig. Later she has a daydream that explicitly collapses the distinction between agricultural and human engineering. It takes the form of a montage sequence in which the lines in a book she is reading "transform themselves into a suckling pig, a donkey, a little cucumber, a hothouse seedling, a baby tiger in a zoo, a baby camel and, finally, a child" (Kh.R.-S 7). In the context of these allusions, Distsipliner's outburst about a future of syringes seems less remote from the present-day action of the play, even if the play's narrative does stay within the model of "positive" eugenics, emphasizing individual choice.

The possibility that the character of Distsipliner expresses aspects of Tret'iakov's own extreme views, camouflaged by the "discussion play" format, is suggested by the similarities between Distsipliner's scripted outbursts and a brief, two-page introduction to the film script of *I Want a Child!* that Tret'iakov wrote in late 1928 or early 1929. In this text, he expresses his exasperation with people who irresponsibly pass on their venereal diseases, tuberculosis, malaria, and neuroses to their children, rivaling his crotchety tone in *Lef* in 1923, where he denounced the material clutter and inefficiency of contemporary Russian *byt*, and even the backward Russian people themselves, citing their "inability to walk intelligently down the street, to get on to a streetcar, to exit a lecture hall without shoving each other."[32] He calls for sexual practices to become organized in the same way that other everyday practices have become organized under the *novyi byt*. People have learned to spit in spittoons, wash their hands before eating, and warn others to stay away if they are sick with a cold, he notes, but no one has learned to say "Don't touch me, I have gonorrhea" (Kh.R.-S 33). If the directives of science can penetrate most aspects of *byt*, Tret'iakov complains that where human sexuality is concerned, the penetrating gaze of science is blocked by the "swampy fumes of shame and convention" (Kh.R.-S 33). He blames this disorganized state of sexuality on the institution of bourgeois marriage, whose basis in economics and the ideology of possession leads to dissipation and sexual fever.

Unlike the more conventional advocates of a new socialist sexuality, Tret'iakov imagines a future social order in which reproduction is no longer organized according to patriarchal marriage structures, and children become collective social objects rather than private fetishes. The whole enterprise of reproduction must shed its structures of possession and become more collective:

> Only where the former form of marriage is smashed and great responsibility is assumed by the individual, the former "small proprietor," the present "co-worker," before his or her comrades in life and before future generations, will it be possible to return to conception the purity, all the clarity and social responsibility, that it lost choking in orgasms and gonococci. (Kh.R.-S 33–34)

In his emphasis on the sexual partner as a "comrade in life" and his critique of the former status of the lover as a "proprietor" of another, Tret'iakov echoes the Bolshevik feminist Aleksandra Kollontai, who argued in her famous 1923 essay "Make Way for Winged Eros! A Letter to Working Youth" that a woman could only become an equal in a romantic relationship if it were freed of the physical and psychological effects of the property relation, which made women the possessions as well as dependents of men.[33] Rather than taking her ideas seriously, the party had disparaged Kollontai for her feminist "subjectivism" and "deviationism," just as representatives of party organs in Glavrepertkom would censor Tret'iakov's play five years later for its "sexual anarchy," its "vulgarity" and "unhealthy interest."[34] In some respects Tret'iakov strays even further from tradition than Kollontai, because whereas her writings focus on the problem of love in the new collective, and betray a belief in natural gender difference and the emotional significance of maternity, the hard-nosed Tret'iakov imagines a future in which women can choose to have children independently of love for any one man, and in which men and women would not have to be organized within the strict gender categories of masculinity and femininity.[35]

Despite his fantastic rhetoric, fueled by paranoia about the dangers of modern Western sexuality, Tret'iakov offers an insightful critique of the sexist and commodified structures of bourgeois sexuality and marriage. This was a critique that he believed should be applied to the Soviet policies of the *novyi byt*. Only in the Soviet Union, his introduction continues, the "land of un-believable experiment," can there exist a "solicitous hand" that will lead "a humanity choking in its own filth onto new paths" (Kh.R.-S 34). The role of this solicitous hand is partly filled, he states, by Okhmatmlad (*Okhrana Mate-rinstva i Mladenchestva*, the State Department for the Protection of Maternity and Infancy). Not surprisingly, however, this Soviet institution advanced a fairly traditional rhetoric of morality and gender roles that was very much at odds with Tret'iakov's. Ironically, the Glavrepertkom member who voted to censor the play for its "sexual anarchy" was a representative of Okhmatmlad, Dr. Abraham Gens, signalling the gap between the nonpossessive and gender-egalitarian *novyi byt* of the future imagined by Tret'iakov and the more tradi-tional vision of the Soviet state.[36]

In other aspects, however, Tret'iakov's *novyi byt* could itself be described as traditional in comparison to that of the Soviet state. His concern with promoting rational production leads him to endorse a form of putatively so-cialist morality as limiting as the morality of the pope: he cites the "barren fox-trotters" of the West as examples of people who have "severed the moment of pleasure from the moment of production of their own" (Kh.R.-S 33). His quest for an act of conception characterized by "purity" and "clarity," and his de-mand that vision and transparency replace the swampy murk of the desiring body, "choking in orgasms and gonococci," leave no room for a differently desiring body. He cannot imagine an alternative sexual desire. In the end, he offers a critique of bourgeois forms of sexual desire, on the one hand, and the promise of collective state institutions that will ensure, not a different model of pleasure, but only a different model of reproduction without private property, alienation of labor, or gender oppression, on the other. His vision of the future is limited by his conviction that the industrial creativity of production will be adequate to providing a model for all forms of creativity and procreativity.

The Socialist Object as a Model for the New Soviet Subject

The Constructivists and *Lef* writers may not have advanced a new model of socialist sexual desire, but they did imagine new forms of object desire under socialism, through their theorization of the socialist object as a counter-part to the commodity fetish. In Tret'iakov's play it is not surprising, then, that the problem of how to reconcile old attachments to material objects with a *novyi byt* that will be without possessions continually stands in for the larger dilemma of reconciling old forms of sexual desire with new ones.

As if to demonstrate the tenacious power of material *byt*, Tret'iakov elab-orately stages an entire domestic and private object world to reveal the desires of his characters and to delineate their identities. In one scene, a group of women in the communal kitchen of Milda's building sit enveloped in steam that comes damping out from an enormous array of bubbling pots on the *primusy*, or primus stoves (single propane burners) surrounding them. Within the setting of this literal material density—the exclusive province of women in the new as in the old *byt*—they gossip about how Milda has been bringing a young worker to her room at night, and worry that she will steal their husbands and spread syphilis to their families. This communal but otherwise old-fashioned kitchen—inefficient, low-tech, and overcrowded, the antithesis of the gleaming collective dining rooms of propaganda posters—is the object-equivalent of the women's old-fashioned, if legitimate, female response to new-fangled, Bolshevik notions of "free love" in the context of their low-income lives. These neighbors' voices are also heard through the thin walls from the next room during the seduction scene; an older female voice laments that "the Bolsheviks are copulating" (Kh.R. 228), an unflattering if not inaccurate verb to describe the Bolshevik seduction devised by Tret'iakov. A material object has given Milda away: her squeaky bed. By making his depiction of *byt* so crowded and lively, Tret'iakov deliberately rejects the stark visual rhetoric of the propaganda posters for the *novyi byt*, such as an image from around 1924 with the slogan "Woman worker! Don't forget that public dining rooms emancipate you!" (fig. 7.3).[37] A woman worker is shown literally sweeping away all her domestic material objects—a primus stove, frying pans, a tea pot—the jumbled forms of which contrast with the clean lines of the modern, collective building at the top of the picture, labeled "Worker's Cafeteria." This cafeteria is part of the future world that Milda dreams of building, but Tret'iakov's agenda is to force her future visions into constant mediation with the imperfect present. The poster itself inadvertently pictures the intrusion of the oppressive present into the supposedly emancipated future, because the woman worker is still doing the sweeping.

A key scene revolving around material objects demonstrates that firmly rooted beliefs about possessions and their significance will always interrupt the futuristic visions of characters like Milda. The day following Milda's successful seduction of Iakov, he expresses his newfound feelings for her through an object: he comes uninvited to her room to hang a pair of curtains that he has just found at a good price at the Smolenskii market. Her room was "like a garage," he says, and addressing her with an affectionate diminutive, he asks "It's nice that I brought you some comfort, isn't it, comrade Milka?" (Kh.R. 228). He went to the market, the heart of the free NEP marketplace, to bring home a decorative domestic object that demonstrates his pleasure in the fact that they are building a family together. He has gravely misunderstood the situation, and his gesture is misbegotten, yet it illustrates the difficulty of any scheme that will attempt to do away with the objects of private *byt* and the proprietary emotions they embody.

A verbal battle of domestic objects and their personal associations breaks out later in the scene, when a crowd of snoopy neighbors spill into Milda's empty room, groping and fumbling at the objects they find there:

Christina Kiaer

Figure 7.3. Propaganda poster, "Woman worker! Don't forget that public dining rooms emancipate you!" circa 1924. Courtesy of the Russian State Library.

—A briefcase! Is she a Party member?
—Lenin's works.
—Eugen . . . eugenics.
—Salami. Now what do you say! Smoked.
—For entertaining a fancy gentleman.
—A revolver. Careful, a revolver.
—Probably without a permit.
—It squeaks. (*about the bed.*)
—The blanket is full of holes. The pillows are made from feathers.
—The sheets probably haven't been washed for a week.
—Maybe they were dirtied from what happened yesterday.
—And in the bag?
—Dirty underwear. Stop! A bra.

—Lookie here. Powder. A box of powder. With a powder-puff.
—And "Fialka" [violet] perfume. Heh-heh-heh.
—Say "Fialka" please. And lipstick.
—Soldiers' trousers. (Kh.R. 229)

The detail with which the neighbors ransack Milda's things testifies to their confidence that the individual objects in her room will add up to a coherent identity for Milda that will explain the strange goings-on there. But the objects do not add up to a coherent image—either of femininity (the bra, the "Fialka" perfume),[38] or of a Bolshevik, soldier-like anti-femininity (the revolver, the trousers); either of *meshchanstvo* (the nice salami, the feather pillows) or of Bolshevik asceticism (the blanket full of holes, Lenin's collected works). In contrast to this random list of objects, the Constructivists aimed to produce new everyday objects that would support socialist identities rather than the outmoded ones associated with capitalism. Yet while these Constructivist objects would be rational and expedient, they would still carry emotional significance. Tret'iakov's *Lef* colleague Boris Arvatov, a strong supporter of Constructivism and the concept of the socialist object, expressed this succinctly: "There exists the opinion . . . that the course toward expediency murders the so-called humanity of things, deprives things of 'emotionality' . . . such an opinion can only be maintained by those for whom the thing in and of itself, in its rational functioning, cannot be the embodiment of human thought."[39] The Constructivist difference would be that the "humanity" of things would now be one that had shed the negative qualities of human beings under capitalism but maintained the positive human qualities of reason and emotion in socialist form.

The ultimate socialist object in Tret'iakov's play, characterized by both rationality and "emotionality," is the eugenic baby. Genetically purged of the capitalist traits of the past, a literal embodiment of the creativity of production, the eugenic child will be an object of properly socialist desire and emotional affect, existing in public nurseries and kindergartens rather than in the materially and emotionally cluttered lap of the family. The final scene of the play, which takes place at a Healthy Baby contest set four years later in 1930, displays the eugenic baby as a perfected product of socialist reproduction. In this imagined future, the *stroika* has been completed. Banners proclaim "Healthy parents mean a healthy new generation"; "A public children's day care center means the liberation of the woman worker"; "Healthy conception —healthy pregnancy"; and the blunt "Give birth to children" (Kh.R. 235). Milda announces a public lecture in the club later that day for any young men who wish to become fathers and any young women who wish to become mothers, implying that perhaps more collective structures for organizing conception and parenting are already in place. The first prize for one-year-old babies in the contest is awarded jointly to a boy—the second son of Iakov and Milda—and a girl—the daughter of Iakov and his wife. This is the moment

Figure 7.4. Cover of *Hygiene and Health of the Worker and Peasant Family,* no. 4 (1927), announcing the prize winners in the first Soviet Healthy Baby Contest.

when Iakov gets his alienated product returned to him, for he is announced as the father of Milda's son, and therefore gets to beam with double pride at having sired not one but two first-prize children. Public display for the approval of the collective replaces the private, exclusive relation of possession fostered by traditional family structures. Milda's desire to have a perfected child for the Soviet collective replaces the traditional bourgeois desire for privatized parenthood and, by extension, the individual commodity desire of capitalism.

In his journalistic style, Tret'iakov seems to have gotten the idea for the ending of his play from the contemporary announcement of the first Soviet Healthy Baby contest (*Konkurs zdorovykh detei*), sponsored by the magazine *Hygiene and Health of the Worker and Peasant Family* and announced in September of 1926, as Tret'iakov was finishing his play.[40] The judging

Figure 7.5. Cover of *Hygiene and Health of the Worker and Peasant Family*, no. 5 (1927), announcing the results of the first Soviet Healthy Baby Contest.

of the contest would supposedly be based entirely on scientifically objective and measurable characteristics, such as weight and "skin tone." The magazine devoted two successive cover images in early 1927 to the young winners of the contest, producing a pair of somewhat inexpert photomontages of babies; most of them are plump, as desired, while the quality of their skin tone must be left to the imagination, as it is not revealed by the grainy newsprint of the cheap paper (figs. 7.4 and 7.5). The public and festive nature of the contest was meant to strengthen the magazine's propaganda for the hygiene and health components of the *novyi byt*, not to mention the effort to promote responsible sexual practices and committed parenthood. The ideology of the Soviet contest differed little from that of the same contests in England and the United States, where they originated. These contests placed full moral responsibility on the mother and celebrated the natural "psychological force" uniting mother and child.[41] The population had to be replenished in Europe after World War I just as it did in Russia after world war and civil war. In Europe and the U.S., these contests were always sponsored by department stores and mass magazines, and tapped into their culture of exhibition and display. In 1930s Russia, in Tret'iakov's vision, the contest became the opposite of commodity display, and instead became a collective, educational site of socialist festival.

Yet even in this triumphal ending for his eugenic theme, Tret'iakov inserts "discussion questions": is eugenics really necessary, when the regular love union of two healthy working people, Iakov and his wife, can result in as healthy a baby as the more rationally organized union of Iakov and Milda? Are the emotional losses entailed by the rationalization of reproduction justifiable? This question is posed by an exchange between Milda and Iakov before the result of the contest is announced. Milda tells him that she breast-fed the baby until it was time to send it away to the *detdom*. He asks if she did not find it difficult to tear herself away from the baby, and she responds, "It's always hard to tear yourself away. Do you think it was easy for me back then to let you go?" (Kh.R. 236). Even the rationalist Milda expresses regret at giving up her lover and her child, signaling the difficulty of relinquishing all the possessive desires of the past.[42] Tret'iakov may have hoped at one level for the implementation of Milda's rationalist, collective utopia—perhaps even replete with syringes and sperm banks—but his play leaves the impression that if the new Soviet subject is predicated on the destruction of the past, rather than on a redemption of its desires, it will not be a subjectivity that anyone will want to live.

A Theater without Properties:
Lissitzky's Transparent Stage Design

This essay has proposed that the text of *I Want a Child!* offers a complex depiction of the lived contradictions of the *novyi byt*. But its planned staging in the Meyerhold Theater seemed to downplay its material contradictions and to present, instead, a proto-totalitarian microcosm of Soviet citizens being relentlessly surveyed by an all-seeing and all-powerful state. Lissitzky's model set departs radically from the settings described in Tret'iakov's stage directions (see fig. 7.1). Instead of sets depicting the *stroika*, the workers' club, or the crowded communal building, Lissitzky's plan completely reconfigured the traditional theatrical space of audience and stage to emphasize total visual access and surveillance; only the red banners promoting healthy childbirth, taken from the stage directions for the final scene of the Healthy Baby contest, follow Tret'iakov's intent. Lissitzky's own words provide the most cogent description of his work:

> The stage is fully merged with the auditorium by the construction of an amphitheatre. For the play itself a new area in the theatre is created, a "ring"

that rises from the orchestra pit. The actors emerge from below, from the depth of the orchestra pit, from above, out of the balconies, and from the sides across bridges: they no longer have anything to do with the stage. Props roll down ropes from above and disappear into depth after every scene. Light sources move together with the actors, who perform on a transparent floor.[43]

The central ring of the stage was accessible by two ramps that extended to the sides of the theater, as well as by a bridge that connected one of the balconies with a spiral staircase leading down to, and piercing, the ring platform, which was raised above the ground on pillars. Far above the stage, Lissitzky constructed a set of pulleys and ropes with which to transport furniture and props from the upper balconies to the stage. In his model of the stage set, collapsible chairs are suspended above the stage, ready to be deposited on it by the pulley system. The production of the play would be as fully rationalized as industrial production, with the pulley system providing an assembly-line structure to minimize the labor of actors and stage hands.

Lissitzky's design provides a model for the most extreme vision of the materially denuded *novyi byt* imagined by propaganda posters. His literally transparent and open space responds ironically to the cluttered and claustrophobic spaces of the communal building in Tret'iakov's script. Rather than materially enacting these crowded spaces, the spare transparency of the set figures the total visibility and surveillance made possible by the material closeness and nosy neighbors of Soviet *byt*, as well as by the mechanisms of party control over peoples' personal lives, such as informants and the NKVD. The tissue of domestic objects that serves to complicate the rationalizing rhetoric of Tret'iakov's play is removed from the scene, to be replaced, conceptually at least, by the spectators on all sides who will participate in the discussion of the piece. There is good reason to believe that Lissitzky's design was produced in close accordance with the wishes of Meyerhold, who had hired Lissitzky to design the set specifically for the limited, experimental "discussion" format of the play that the censors had authorized to be produced by his theater alone.

The stage design of a luminous glass circle, lit from below, makes the actors available for visual investigation as if they were placed under a microscope. It may have been suggested to Lissitzky by Tret'iakov's film script, which opens with the image of the sperm and ovum observed through the round, illuminated lens of Milda's microscope. Lissitzky's design responds to this microscope image not only structurally, at the level of the glass eye of the microscope as an instrument of penetrating vision, but at the level of content. The wriggling sperm penetrating the glassy sphere of the ovum under the microscope take the visually appropriate form, in Lissitzky's model stage set, of the spiral staircase that penetrates the transparent glass circle of the stage in order to open it up and make it more efficient as a productive unit within the assembly line of the set. This reading, which emphasizes the totalitarian potential of Lissitzky's set, Tret'iakov's play and Meyerhold's proposed staging of it, supports Eric Naiman's conclusion that "if Boris Groys is correct and there is a direct line connecting the Russian avant-garde with Stalin's governance, that line surely runs through Meyerhold and *I Want a Child!*"[44] Naiman demonstrates that Meyerhold's plan for mounting the play as a "discussion piece" involved an Orwellian notion of "discussion": it would be carefully controlled and scripted in order to ensure that "all questions will be treated correctly."[45]

But the Russian avant-garde was not monolithic, and Lissitzky and Tret'iakov are not identical with Meyerhold. Lissitzky's open glass stage and spiral staircase might be read very differently, as responses to this description of the play given by Tret'iakov in a 1927 interview: "Not a play that closes in an aesthetic circle, but one that begins on the aesthetic trampoline of the stage and unfolds in a spiral, winding its way through the audience's arguments and through their extratheatrical experience."[46] Lissitzky's spiral staircase literally winds its way up from the stage, connecting with a bridge to the balcony with audience seating above. The spiral is a uniquely temporal graphic form, figuring always the movement from a point in the past toward an infinitely expanding future—in the case of many Russian Constructivist works, specifically the movement from the capitalist past toward the socialist future. Lissitzky's spiral staircase rising dramatically out of the flat stage stands as a graphic figure for a more voluntary and contested dissemination of Bolshevik visions of the future than the model of the penetrating eye of the microscope.

There is no evidence that Tret'iakov himself wanted to stage the play as a scripted discussion; his intention was for the audience member to experience a genuine challenge to his or her own subject position through the aesthetic form of a theater that rejected cathartic narrative and identification with heroes in the bourgeois tradition.[47] Lissitzky's bare stage could be read, then, as his interpretation of Tret'iakov's call for a stage as an "aesthetic trampoline"—a space cleared of the trappings of bourgeois culture, the better to facilitate the posing of new questions. It is a visual interpretation that partially contradicts Tret'iakov's textual emphasis on the emotional significance of the material objects remaining from the old *byt*, but it does not therefore necessarily dovetail with Meyerhold's desire to control audience participation.

These are the two sides of the *Lef* avant-garde coin: the dream of the transparent relay between human subject and socialist object that eliminates alienation but redeems the desires lodged in the past for the socialist future; and the nightmare transparency of the rationalized public sphere of total control and visibility. In conclusion, two images from *I Want a Child!* can stand for these two possibilities. The first is a photomontage by Lissitzky depicting his costume design for the character of Milda, made in 1929 (fig. 7.6). It maintains all the tensions and contradictions of Tret'iakov's text, at the level of form as well as content. It combines a delicate watercolor drawing of Milda's clothing, juxtaposed jarringly with a black and white photographic image to represent her face. This face is too small for the body, and it is decidedly masculine, as well as surprisingly Asian in its features when the play clearly

Figure 7.6. El Lissitzky, costume design for the character of
Milda in *I Want a Child!* Watercolor, pencil, and collage
on pasteboard, 1929. © 2004 Artists Rights Society (ARS),
New York / VG Bild-Kunst, Bonn.

specifies Milda's ethnicity as Latvian. Milda's watercolor feet float incongru-
ously above photographs of skinny schoolchildren and a single naked baby,
who resembles any one of the plump contestants from the first Soviet Healthy
Baby contest. Lissitzky's visual image parallels the montage-like form of
Tret'iakov's text, while its content similarly suggests that the futuristic, imagined character of Milda will have to be brought together in a "dialectical
image" with the conditions of present Soviet *byt*—signalled here through the
documentary photographs of Soviet children—in order for the "flash of recognition" for contemporary viewers to take place. The second image, also from
1929, is a photograph of Lissitzky leaning into the model of his stage set to
adjust the fragile railing around the glass circle (fig. 7.7). This photograph

Figure 7.7. El Lissitzky at work on the model of his stage design for *I Want a Child!* 1929. © 2004 Artists Rights Society (ARS), New York / VG Bild-Kunst, Bonn.

might be read as the literalization of the nightmare, in which the Constructivist has become pure Stalinist puppeteer, rearranging social space as if it were composed of cardboard human figures and toy objects. This image supports the notion of a direct line between the avant-garde and Stalin; but, as this essay has proposed, the Russian avant-garde contained many lines, the most promising of which could have led toward a very different kind of socialist culture and socialist subject.

NOTES

1. The play was not published in its entirety during Tret'iakov's lifetime. He published two scenes as "Khochu rebenka!" in *Novyi Lef* 3 (1927): 3–11, but the entire play (the first variant) was not published until 1988. See Tret'iakov, "Khochu rebenka," *Sovremennaia dramaturgiia* 2 (1988): 209–237. Future references to the play will be cited parenthetically in the text as "Kh.R.," with page numbers from this publication given. All translations from the Russian in this essay are my own, unless otherwise noted. An English translation of the play has appeared as Sergei Mikhailovich Tretyakov, *I Want a Baby*, trans. Stephen Holland, ed. Robert Leach, Studies in Drama and Dance (Birmingham: University of Birmingham, 1995).

2. S. M. Tret'iakov, "Chto pishut dramaturgi," *Rabis* 11 (1929): 11, cited in A. Fevral'skii, "S.M. Tret'iakov v teatre Meierkhol'da," in S. Tret'iakov, *Slyshish', Moskva?! —Protivogazy—Rychi, Kitai! (P'esy, stat'i, vospominaniia)* (Moscow: Iskusstvo, 1966), 204.

3. The script remains available only in a blurry carbon copy in the archives of Glaviskusstvo in the Russian State Archives of Literature and Art (RGALI). See RGALI,

f. 645, op. 1, ed. kh. 536, 28–55, which includes a two-page introduction to the script, written by Tret'iakov, and the handwritten comments of the Glavrepertkom censor. The narrative of the script is essentially identical to that of the play, though the play's extensive dialogue is replaced, in the silent film, by terse intertitles augmented by vivid images and montage sequences. Future references to the script will be cited parenthetically in the body of the text as "Kh.R.-S." The citation here is from p. 35.

4. Boris Groys, *The Total Art of Stalinism: Avant-garde, Aesthetic Dictatorship, and Beyond*, trans. Charles Rougle (Princeton: Princeton University Press, 1992).

5. *Vecherniaia Moskva*, 2 November 1926. A file of newspaper clippings concerning the play are held in the "Documents" section of the Bakhrushin Museum of Theater Arts in Moscow.

6. Announcements of the agreement between Tret'iakov and Meyerhold about the expected performance of the play were published in *Pravda, Novyi zritel', Vecherniaia Moskva, Zhizn' i iskusstvo, Vechernee radio*, and *Rabochaia pravda*, among others.

7. The circumstances of the play's fate are recounted in the commentary by Tret'iakov's daughter, T. S. Gomolitskaia-Tret'iakova, following the publication of the play in *Sovremennaia dramaturgiia* 2 (1988): 237, and in the accompanying reprinting of, and editorial comment on, the stenographic notes from the Glavrepertkom meetings, pp. 238–243. See also Eric Naiman's detailed account of these events in *Sex in Public: The Incarnation of Soviet Ideology* (Princeton: Princeton University Press, 1997), 109–114.

8. For the censor's comments on the film script, see RGALI, f. 645, op. 1, ed. kh. 536. Tret'iakov had planned the film to be directed by Abram Room, who had directed the highly successful film *Tret'ia Meshchanskaia* (known in English as *Bed and Sofa*) in 1927.

9. *Sovremennaia dramaturgiia*, 238.

10. *Sovremennaia dramaturgiia*, 238.

11. See Walter Benjamin, *The Arcades Project*, trans. Howard Eiland and Kevin McLaughlin (Cambridge, Mass., and London: The Belknap Press of Harvard University Press, 1999). Susan Buck-Morss writes that the project "put forth the notion that socialist culture would need to be constructed out of the embryonic, still-inadequate forms that preexisted in capitalism." See her synthesis and interpretation of the project in *The Dialectics of Seeing: Walter Benjamin and the Arcades Project* (Cambridge, Mass.: MIT Press, 1989); citation from p. 123.

12. On the socialist object, see Christina Kiaer, *Imagine No Possessions: The Socialist Objects of Russian Constructivism* (Cambridge, Mass: MIT Press, 2005).

13. Walter Benjamin, *The Arcades Project*, Section N "On the Theory of Knowledge," 462 [N2a,3].

14. L. Trotskii, *Voprosy byta* (Moscow: Krasnaia nov', 1923); translated as Leon Trotsky, *Problems of Everyday Life and Other Writings on Culture and Science* (New York: Monad Press, 1973).

15. These reasons for the upsurge in party interest in *byt* in 1923 are offered by Elizabeth A. Wood, in *The Baba and the Comrade: Gender and Politics in Revolutionary Russia* (Bloomington: Indiana University Press, 1997), 194–197. Wood proposes that the shift from the violence of the civil war to the attempt to introduce new ways of living can be understood as an instance of Michel Foucault's description, in *Discipline and Punish*, of a shift in strategies of power from a regime of punishment to one of discipline (p. 279, n. 16). On the extensive publications on the *novyi byt*, see also Eric Naiman,

Sex in Public, and Victor Buchli, *An Archaeology of Socialism* (Oxford and New York: Berg, 1999). Buchli argues that the actual implementation of ambitious *novyi byt* programs for public child care and so on—as opposed to discussions and propaganda—did not begin until around 1930.

16. The general history of Russian eugenics presented in this paragraph is drawn from Mark B. Adams, "Eugenics as Social Medicine in Revolutionary Russia," in *Health and Society in Revolutionary Russia,* ed. Susan Gross Solomon and John F. Hutchinson (Bloomington and Indianapolis: Indiana University Press, 1990), 200–223.

17. Adams, 213. Lunacharskii's script, entitled *Salamandr,* paid homage to the Viennese Lamarckian biologist Paul Kammerer, in whose voice these words were spoken.

18. An article in the magazine *Hygiene and Health of the Worker and Peasant Family* in 1927, for example, offered a balanced account that gave weight to all three models of practical eugenics, coming down against "negative" practices and in favor of education to promote the "positive" model, rather than coercive measures, and putting faith in the possibility of developing the Lamarckian model in the future. See Dr. L. Vasilevskii, "Chto takoe evgenika," *Gigiena i zdorov'e rabochei i krest'ianskoi sem'i* 4 (1927): 4–5.

19. Dr. Poltasenii, "Ne pozor, a neschast'e," *Zhurnal dlia zhenshchin* 7 (1924): 26.

20. "Krena" (pseud.), "Nash malen'kii fel'eton," *Zhurnal dlia zhenshchin* 7 (1925): 4.

21. Smur, V., "Mozhno li uluchshit' chelovecheskuiu porodu?" *Smena* 5 (1926): 20–21.

22. M. V. Volotskoi, *Podniatie zhiznennykh sil rasy (Odin iz prakticheskikh putei),* 2nd revised ed., Biologicheskaia Biblioteka (Moscow: Kooperativnoe izdatel'stvo "Zhizn' i znanie," 1926).

23. A. Serebrovskii, "Antropogenetika i evgenika v sotsialisticheskom obshche-stve," in *Trudy kabineta nasledstvennosti i konstitutsii cheloveka pri mediko-biologiche-skom institute,* vol. I, ed. S. G. Levit and A. S. Serebrovskii (Moscow, 1929), 3–19, translated and cited in Adams, 216.

24. Bernatskii, Dr., "Chto nuzhno znat', vybiraia muzha i zhenu," *Gigiena i zdorov'e rabochei i krest'ianskoi sem'i* 15 (1928): 2–3, and the conclusion in 16 (1928): 6.

25. Bernatskii, *Gigiena i zdorov'e rabochei i krest'ianskoi sem'i* 15 (1928): 2.

26. Bernatskii, *Gigiena i zdorov'e rabochei i krest'ianskoi sem'i* 16 (1928): 6. This conventional understanding of femininity was common in Russia in the 1920s; another example of it appears in a short book published by the Okhrana Materinstva i Mla-denchestva: Dr. El'be, *Krasota zhenshchiny i byt* (The Beauty of Woman and Everyday Life). Sem'ia i byt (Moscow: Okhrana Materinstva i Mladenchestva, 1927).

27. Eric Naiman has analyzed the extensive press accorded the Chubarov rape as an aspect of party efforts to exercise greater control over the private lives of youth; see *Sex in Public,* ch. 7.

28. This androgynous female figure quickly faded from view in the return to more "normalized" gender roles during NEP, only to reappear again briefly in the wave of industrial enthusiasm of the First Five-Year Plan. The paradigmatic example of the Bolshevik ideal of the unfeminine communist woman from the civil war years is the eponymous heroine of Aleksandra Kollontai's novella "Vasilisa Malygina" (1923), re-printed as *Svobodnaia Liubov'* (Riga: Stock, 1925). See Eric Naiman's reading of the novella in these terms in *Sex in Public,* ch. 6.

29. See Frances L. Bernstein, "Panic, Potency, and the Crisis of Nervousness in the 1920s," in this volume.

30. Tret'iakov's intervention in the Glavrepertkom meeting of 15 December 1928, cited in *Sovremennaia dramaturgiia*, 242.

31. Sergei Tret'iakov, "Otkuda i kuda?," *Lef* 1 (1923): 201.

32. "Otkuda i kuda?," p. 202.

33. Aleksandra Kollontai, "Dorogu Krylatomu Erosu! (Pis'mo k trudiashcheisia molodezhi)," *Molodaia gvardiia* 3 (1923): 111–124. She imagines that under communism, erotic love will be "winged" as opposed to "wingless," characterized by 1) emotional equality between men and women, 2) the end of the feeling of property between lovers, and 3) comradely sensitivity on the part of both men and women (p. 123).

34. See the minutes of the Glavrepertkom meeting in *Sovremennaia dramaturgiia*, 238–240.

35. Kollontai called the maternal instinct, and women's instinct to care for children, "natural-biological." See Aleksandra Kollontai, "Dorogu Krylatomu Erosu!" 119, n.1. Elizabeth Wood argues that Kollontai and others in the party's Women's Section (*Zhenotdel*) "perpetuated stereotypes of women" and concludes that "basic gender divisions remained unquestioned." See Wood, *The Baba and the Comrade*, 199–200 and 207, respectively.

36. *Sovremennaia dramaturgiia*, 238.

37. This poster is located in the Department of Graphics in the Russian State Library, Moscow, catalogued as number P2.XI.2; P2 signifies a poster (*plakat*) from period 2 (designating 1921–1925).

38. "Fialka" was a brand of perfume produced by the state trust Tezhe, literally the State Fats Trust. It produced all kinds of soaps and perfumes beginning in the 1920s and became the main source of such products in the more limited consumer marketplace of the first five-year plans. "Say Fialka please" seems to have been an advertising slogan, although I have not been able to find examples of it.

39. Boris Arvatov, "Segodniashnie zadachi iskusstva v promyshlennosti," *Sovetskoe iskusstvo* 1 (1926): 86.

40. In early September, an editorial article appeared about the popularity of such contests abroad, especially in England and America: "Konkursy grudnykh detei," *Gigiena i zdorov'e rabochei i krest'ianskoi sem'i* 17 (1926): 9. Two weeks later, the magazine's own contest was announced, and an entry blank was included in the magazine; see the first-page editorial "K konkursu zdorovykh detei," *Gigiena i zdorov'e rabochei i krest'ianskoi sem'i* 18 (1926): 1.

41. "Konkursy grudnykh detei," 9.

42. Another scene in the play strikes a similar note of loss and regret. Milda's friend Vopitkis asks her if she likes flowers, and she replies that she does not—they are merely the sex organs of plants. He calls her a terrible rationalist, and asks her how she gets along without "the gentle and the intimate in the human spirit." She replies, "Well, we don't live in easy times"(Kh.R. 213).

43. El Lissitzky, "Der Innen-Aufbau des Theaters Meyerhold-Moskau für Tretjakows 'Ich will ein Kind,'" *Das Neue Frankfurt* IV:10 (1930), 226, translated and cited in Peter Nisbet, ed. *El Lissitzky, 1890–1941: Catalogue for an Exhibition of Selected Works from North American Collections, the Sprengel Museum Hanover and the Staatliche Galerie Moritzburg Halle* (Cambridge, Mass.: Harvard University Art Museums, 1987), 40. Lissitzky signed a contract with Meyerhold's theater on 28 March 1929, to

complete the stage set for *Khochu rebenka!* by 10 April. The set formed part of a design for the total renovation of the theater into a more experimental theatrical space. On Lissitzky's contracts with the Meyerhold theater for the *Khochu rebenka!* set, see the Russian State Archive of Literature and Art (RGALI), f. 2361, ed. kh. 60, and Nisbet, 52, n. 102.

44. Naiman, *Sex in Public*, 114.

45. Naiman writes that "Meierkhol'd understood the theatrical, scripted character of the contemporary debate on sex, but he was disturbed by its (at least, apparent) lack of control from above"—hence his desire to mount the play as a controlled script that retained the appearance of an open discussion. See Naiman, *Sex in Public*, 112–114.

46. Quoted in Fevral'skii, "S.M. Tret'iakov v teatre Meierkhol'da," 204, translated in Naiman, *Sex in Public*, 110–111.

47. Walter Benjamin would associate Tret'iakov with this Brechtian notion of collaborative theater in his essay "The Author as Producer" of 1934. This involves a significantly different notion of the spectator as collaborator from Meyerhold's ruthless, cynical vision in the debates on *I Want a Child!*

eight
"The Withering of Private Life"

Walter Benjamin in Moscow

Evgenii Bershtein

Walter Benjamin stayed in Moscow in late 1926 and early 1927, recording his Soviet experience in his by now famous *Moscow Diary*. This German Jewish writer-philosopher's travel to Moscow can be (and has been) examined from many perspectives. From the point of view of his political biography, the Moscow sojourn was important as an unsuccessful attempt to enter into the reality of revolution-in-construction.[1] In terms of his creative biography, as Susan Buck-Morss proposes, Moscow was one of the sites in which Benjamin's unfinished but still formidable and influential "Arcades Project" had its origin.[2] Generically, as Jacques Derrida argues in his Moscow lectures, *Moscow Diary* can be read as constitutive of the genre of "a Western intellectual's travel to the Soviets."[3] A literary and cultural-historical reading such as Gerhard Richter's recent analysis discovers that, behind "all of its immediacy and narrative gestures of everydayness and clarity," *Moscow Diary* advances a particular philosophy that construes the body as subject of history.[4] An intellectual historian such as Howard Caygill interprets the work as illustrating the hope and eventual disillusionment with which Europe's left-wing intellectuals regarded Communist Russia.[5] In emphasizing certain specific aspects of Benjamin's experience in Moscow, each of these approaches is at once illuminating and limiting. My own reading of the Moscow episode in Benjamin's life will treat several seemingly divergent aspects of the trip as being closely interwoven. Specifically, I will provide new factual information about the circumstances and characters of Benjamin's journey and address the question of how these influenced Benjamin's conceptualization of early Soviet "private life." By so doing, I will argue that *Moscow Diary* documents the translation of Soviet cultural experience into the language of Western theoretical thought; the task of this essay is to illuminate the mechanism and the controlling factors of this translation.

Walter Benjamin spent almost two months—December 1926 and January 1927—in Moscow, brought there by a serious personal crisis. Since 1924 he had been deeply in love with the Latvian communist Asja Lacis, but the status of their relationship had remained unresolved. Benjamin had met Lacis in Capri in 1924, and though they later saw each other in Berlin and Riga, their romantic friendship somehow failed to develop into a steady relationship. In Moscow, Benjamin remained Asja's admirer rather than her lover. Her permanent companions during these years were the Latvian poet Linards Laicens and the Austrian-German theater critic and director Bernhard Reich.

Those who knew Asja Lacis noted that she never strove for strict monogamy in her liaisons.[6] She made no secret of her view that the traditional family was a relic of the bourgeois epoch. At the beginning of the Civil War, Lacis was married to her first husband, the Latvian journalist Julis Lacis, who was then working as a supply agent for the Red Army in Orel. Asja used her prerevolutionary training under Fedor Komissarzhevskii to run a theater studio for homeless children. After the birth of their daughter Dagmara (Daga) in 1919, relations between Asja and Julis began to deteriorate. According to Elvira Bromberg, an actress from Riga who had lived in Orel at the time, the reason for the change was Asja's unwillingness to spend her time looking after the child at the expense of her work. Bromberg recalled quarrels between Asja and Julis, during which Asja accused her husband of "limiting her freedom." Reportedly, Asja did not hide her extramarital affairs from her husband. The marriage soon fell apart, and she returned to Latvia.

In Riga, Lacis moved in the circles of leftist intellectuals. She directed a workers' theatrical studio that had a radical communist orientation. In 1922 she traveled to Berlin to study German proletarian theater, at which point she met Reich, who was working at the time with Max Reinhardt. In 1926 she followed Reich to Moscow, where Benjamin visited her.

According to Asja Lacis's daughter Dagmara Kimele, even decades later Asja often repeated her claim that when she met Benjamin in Capri it took her only a few weeks to convert him to Marxism. Behind this obvious exaggeration hides a grain of truth: Benjamin's letters to his friend Gershom Sholem testify to the fact that as Benjamin's infatuation with Lacis was turning into a passion, he not only began to study Marxist philosophy but also felt a growing sympathy for the "political practice of communism."[7]

During the years preceding his trip to Moscow, Benjamin became pro-foundly estranged from the institutions of cultural life in Weimar Germany. In 1925 his plan to secure a position at Frankfurt University fell through, and with it his hope of ending his total and humiliating dependence on his bourgeois family. The death of his father and a new strain in relations with his wife contributed to Benjamin's personal crisis of 1926. He sensed the need for a drastic change in his life and viewed the trip to the Soviet Union as a recon-naissance mission; he looked for the opportunity to establish radically new conditions of existence.

Alongside this general biographic outline of Benjamin's trip to the Soviet Union, it is useful to mention the trip's discursive background. One crucial element of this background is the genre of the "leftist intellectual's trip to Soviet Russia," so popular in the twenties and thirties. In Jacques Derrida's and Mikhail Ryklin's notes about this genre, Benjamin is assigned a deservedly central role, along with René Etiemble and André Gide.[8] I would argue that in Benjamin's trip the mix of the erotic and the political was not an accidental coincidence of biographical circumstances, but a reflection of a certain discur-sive tendency. As Michel Foucault has remarked, "the history of sexuality [. . .] must be written from the point of view of the history of discourses."[9] This suggestion also provides a productive approach to political history. Studying Western European memoirs, correspondences, and journals from the twenties and thirties, we see how widespread among European intellectuals was the conviction that a radical change in society's political structure would be imme-diately followed by a no less radical and liberating change in the structure of the sexual relations within society. Soviet Russia was looked upon as the center of this type of experimentation—and not only in the twenties, when there were serious foundations for such opinion, but also much later, when the forms of the bourgeois family (with the addition of total government control) were largely reestablished.

Among the first ranks of advocates for sexual reform were libertarians such as André Gide, who in 1931 remarked in his *Journals* that, to his mind, the most important aspect of "the Russian experiment" was the possibility of "a state without religion, a society without the family." "Religion and the family," continued Gide, "are the two worst enemies of progress."[10] Gide believed that the Soviet Union would become the center of sexual liberation. Subjectively important for Gide was his belief that homosexuals would enjoy full civil rights in communist society. A similar hope emerged among a group of English writers—among them W. H. Auden, Christopher Isherwood, and Stephen Spender—who settled in Berlin in the late 1920s and who kept a keen watch on events in the Soviet Union. To a significant extent the work of these writers determined the character of English literature as it developed in the 1930s, and their left-wing politics exerted a noticeable influence on their contempo-raries. The high proportion of homosexuals among the European activists involved in the Comintern (dubbed "Homintern" by an English writer) serves as anecdotal evidence of the same widespread eroticizing of the Soviet Union.[11]

A complex of political and erotic motives drove Benjamin's resolve to visit Communist Russia. He not only sought a personal "change of air," an escape from increasingly intolerable domestic tensions; he also had an acute interest in seeing at first hand the workings of Russian communism. In the diary he kept in Moscow, which will be my main source, his observations about private life are inseparable from those about political processes. A single thought runs like a *leitmotif* through his journal, the essay "Moscow," which he wrote upon his return to Berlin, and the letters he sent from Russia: "Bolshevism has abolished private life."[12] In Benjamin's opinion, Soviet society was extremely politicized, and as a result "the tensions of public life—which for the most part are actually of a theological sort—are so great that they block off private life to an unimaginable degree."[13] He drew his conclusions from the behavior of Lacis, Reich, and a few other Moscow acquaintances who spoke German (Benjamin did not know Russian).

During this time Lacis and Reich were making a great effort to gain a place in the newly forming cultural establishment of communist Moscow. On the political map of cultural life, they placed themselves left of center: while members of the VAPP (All-Russian Association of Proletarian Writers) and the Proletkul't were predominant among their professional and personal acquaintances, aesthetically they were drawn to the more avant-garde trends of Soviet culture, such as Meyerhold's theater and the LEF literary group. By 1927, however, the "left front" of Soviet art had already fallen out of favor with party leadership. An intuitive sense for the subtle nuances of the party general line was becoming increasingly crucial among those who sought if not a guarantee of survival, then at the very least some measure of success on the cultural front. Those of Benjamin's friends who had resolutely opted to build their lives in communist Russia understood this reality well.

Reich was devoting all of his time and energies to his theater and political work; Lacis was convalescing from a recent nervous breakdown in a sanatorium. Her illness had been triggered by an accident that had occurred in the orphanage where she worked: one of the children in her care had almost killed another. When he left his hotel, Benjamin was struck by a lack of private space and people's physical proximity in Moscow streets. Limited in his capacity to interact verbally with the world around him, Benjamin focused on studying the universe of objects, which he saw as iterating the end of private life. In physical space, he registered the bare walls and sparse furnishings of the communal apartments (Reich shared rooms in a dormitory, while Lacis resided in a sanatorium); in the space of sociality, he noted his friends' total absorption in political work. He observed the collapse of the institution of traditional marriage—neither Lacis nor her companion Reich associated their relationship with owning property, nor did they claim rights to each other. In Soviet art, particularly in cinema, Benjamin noticed a ban on the portrayal of sexual passion and unhappy love ("It would be considered counterrevolutionary propaganda to represent tragic love entanglements on film or stage").[14]

At this time, increasingly entrapped in the painful love triangle with his rival Reich and the unresponsive Lacis, Benjamin was himself experiencing an apogee of erotic passion and tragic love. The more unhappy he felt in this triangle, the more attentively he studied how Reich coped with Asja's "lovelessness" [Lieblosigkeit].[15] Benjamin's reflections on this matter constitute something like an ideological culmination to his journal, his journey, and his love. On 8 January 1927, he writes:

> It is becoming clearer and clearer to me that my work needs some sort of solid framework [Gerüst] for the immediate future. [. . .] Only purely external considerations hold me back from joining the German Communist Party. [. . .] At any rate, the period that lies ahead seems to me to distinguish itself from the previous one in that the erotic is becoming far less a determining factor. My observation of Reich's and Asja's relation has, to a certain extent, made me more conscious of this. I note that Reich manages to weather all of Asja's ups and downs and is, or seems to be, rarely ruffled by patterns of behavior that would make me sick. [. . .] It's because of the framework [Gerüst] he has found for his work here. In addition to the actual contacts with which his work provides him, there is also the fact that he is a member of the ruling class here. It is precisely this transformation of an entire power structure that makes life here so extraordinarily meaningful.[16]

Benjamin goes on to compare Moscow to the Klondike at the time of the Gold Rush: "The dig for power goes on from early morning to late at night." "Admittedly," he continues, "this can lead to a certain state of inebriation in which it becomes almost impossible to conceive of a life without meetings and committees, debates, resolutions, and ballotings (all of which are the wars or at least maneuvers of the will to power) [*und das alles sind Kriege oder zumindest Manöver des Machtwillens*]."

This journal entry is notable for the combination of philosophical discourses Benjamin uses to analyze Soviet daily life and the private lives of his friends. Key concepts from three philosophical systems are operative here. On the one hand, Benjamin thinks in Marxist terms: Reich became a member of *the ruling class*. On the other hand, to explain Reich's perplexing tranquility in the face of Lacis's nervous fits and probable unfaithfulness, he refers to the Freudian notion of the libido sublimated in social activities. For himself he considers a similar escape from the drama of his own private life through membership in the German Communist Party. Such membership would reduce the significance of *the erotic* in his life. (Curiously, he plans to attempt a *rationalized* sublimation, that is, a conscious effort to free oneself from sexual obsession). Finally, underlying all the routines of Soviet daily life, Benjamin discerns the workings of the Nietzschean *will to power* [*Machtwille*].

It would be easy to reproach Benjamin for philosophical eclecticism, as did his colleagues in the Frankfurt school of social research. Yet in the final analysis, Benjamin's *Moscow Diary* is not a philosophical tract and so is a priori not bound to honor ideological or conceptual consistency. Rather than testing the work against explicitly philosophical texts—and finding it wanting—it is more productive to compare the above passage from Benjamin's journal with a document from the same period that openly sets out to provide a philosophical foundation for the reform of everyday life.

The text in question was written by Lev Trotsky. Unlike Benjamin, who only considered himself a Marxist, Trotsky was arguably a leading theoretician of Russian Marxism. In his book *Literature and Revolution* (1923), Trotsky ventures far beyond a political analysis of contemporary literature. The famous finale of the first part of this work prophesies that the "*socialist man*" (*sotsialisticheskii chelovek*) will be transformed into "the higher sociobiological type, *superman*" (*sverkhchelovek*), and over the course of that transformation "he will begin to want to master *the subconscious and then unconscious* processes in his own organism" (*zakhochet ovladet' polubessoznatel'nymi, a zatem bessoznatel'nymi protsessami v svoem organizme*].[17] In Trotsky we see the combination of the same discursive elements we discovered in Benjamin's journal —Marxist, Nietzschean, and Freudian.

The question of whether or not Benjamin read Trotsky (he almost certainly did) is irrelevant for our analysis, because one cannot explain a discursive coincidence of this kind as direct influence or borrowing. We should rather assume that both Trotsky's and Benjamin's visions were based in a complex discourse that described the utopian project of communist construction. This discourse included the idea that rational regulation of sexuality accompanied the communization of life. This belief was prominent in Soviet literature and science in the twenties. In Osip Brik's story "Not a Fellow Traveler" (*Ne poputchitsa*, 1923) the protagonist's lovesickness leads to graft and expulsion from the party; in the end of his comedy *Bedbug* (1928), Mayakovsky demonstrates the eradication of uncontrollable sexual passion in the future communist society. Early Soviet psychology often combined Marx with Freud. Practically all its schools accepted the Freudian idea of sublimation, into which, however, they brought class content. Thus, according to Aron Zalkind, the leading figure in the new Soviet developmental science of pedology, membership in the "Soviet public" is the most important "sublimating factor" for a society building socialism.[18]

"The 'bagatellization' of love and sex life is part and parcel of the communist credo," Benjamin writes on 29 December 1926.[19] And it seems that the more tortuous his relationship with Asja Lacis became, the closer Benjamin came to embracing the idea of the abolition of private life in general. In Moscow, Benjamin came to seriously consider the possibility of attempting to start his life anew in communist Russia. On the one hand, he wanted to be closer to Lacis, but on the other, he was drawn to a society that made private life dissolve into the class power struggle without leaving anything behind.

The contradiction behind this duality can be explained in part by the position of Asja Lacis herself: even as she carried on an intense flirtation with Benjamin, she preached to him about the necessity of devoting one's life entirely to revolutionary work.

In support of this latter thesis she drew on the example of the LEF writer Sergei Tret'iakov, who developed the idea of "production art."[20] According to Tret'iakov, "the art worker" should become a "psycho-engineer, a psycho-constructor," working on "a reorganization of the human psyche with the goal of achieving the commune."[21] Art should actively participate in "life-building" (*zhiznestroenie*); this LEF term is reminiscent—not accidentally—of the Symbolists' "life-creation" (*zhiznetvorchestvo*).[22] While the Russian Symbolists embraced the idea of art that shapes life, Tret'iakov envisioned art that helped restructure life according to political and economical postulates. The reorganization of the psyche should be conducted in such a way that private interests (and thus private life) simply have no place in it.

Lacis and Reich knew Tret'iakov personally and talked to Benjamin about him. Indeed, one particular aspect of Tret'iakov's life would later make an enormous impression on Benjamin. The Soviet writer, as Asja Lacis recalled in a memoir fragment, used to visit a nascent collective farm, where he undertook frantic initiatives at reform:

> He patronized a collective farm, where he often went to introduce proper order: he organized a common dining-room for kolkhozniks; in order to free women of extra work, he organized day care for children; he was persuading the kolkhozniks to give up their private cow and demanding that milk be sold to kolkhozniks very cheaply. He managed to accomplish this. He even established literary evenings there and organized a library.[23]

It was to this aspect of Tret'iakov's "life-building" that Benjamin referred several years later in his programmatic lecture "The Author as Producer" (1934). Here he not only advocates the idea of "production art," but presents Tret'iakov and his kolkhoz project as an example of the "operating writer" in action, opposing him to the "informing writer." In his 1928 book *One-way Street*, dedicated to Lacis, Benjamin had already underscored the importance of propagandistic literature. By 1934 he had sharpened the formula for writing as political engineering and found examples. In Benjamin's opinion, art in the extremely politicized conditions of contemporary society must take on a new function: the writer should not mirror life but transform it. The implementation of this task would inevitably lead to the transformation of artistic form.

> His [Tret'iakov's] mission is not to report but to struggle; not to play the spectator but to intervene actively. He defines this mission in the account he gives of his own activity. When, in 1928, at the time of total collectivization of agriculture, the slogan "Writers to the *kolkhoz!*" was proclaimed, Tret'iakov went to the "Communist Lighthouse" commune and there, during two lengthy stays, set about the following tasks: calling mass meetings;

collecting funds to pay for tractors; persuading independent peasants to enter the *kolkhoz*; inspecting the reading rooms; creating wall newspapers and editing the *kolkhoz* newspaper; reporting for Moscow newspapers; introducing radio and mobile movie houses, etc. It is not surprising that the book *Commanders of the Field*, which Tret'iakov wrote following these stays, is said to have had considerable influence on the further development of collective agriculture.[24]

Tret'iakov's project of "production art" was connected more than just metaphorically to the idea of the rational regulation of sexuality. At the end of 1926 and beginning of 1927, Tret'iakov was working on the play "I Want a Child!" (*Khochu rebenka!*), which had been commissioned by the Meyerhold Theater.[25] The heroine of this propagandistic play, a Latvian communist named Milda Grignau, lives in Moscow. She resolutely resists the "sexual psychopathy" which penetrates every aspect of a still incompletely "Sovietized" daily life. Aiming to communize this daily life, she organizes a day care center, and in order to satisfy her own maternal instinct, she finds a physically healthy, non-drinking proletarian who agrees to conceive a child with her. She makes him consent to give up all rights of paternity. Milda's relationship to the sexual act oscillates between indifference and disgust. She categorically rejects the institution of family: "A husband is not important. What's important is a producer."[26]

Tret'iakov's theory urged art to reject its independence in order to become a part of communist *production*. Analogously, through Milda Grignau, Tret'iakov propagated a notion of sexual relations that would be limited to class *reproduction*. The dominance of production in all spheres of life excluded the possibility of nonpublic, private being.

It would be tempting to see Asja Lacis as a prototype of Milda Grignau. However, along with striking similarities, there are significant discrepancies between Tret'iakov's literary heroine and his real-life acquaintance. The main difference is that Milda is characterized in the play as a "soldat-baba" (unrefined soldier-woman), while Asja Lacis was an elegant and cultivated cosmopolitan woman.[27] Still, one could speculate that some of Asja's features were reflected, perhaps ironically, in this character.

In his *Moscow Diary*, Benjamin mentions Tret'iakov's work in a very telling psychological context. On 31 December Asja takes Benjamin to Meyerhold's theater where, among various models of stage sets for Meyerhold's productions, Benjamin spots the design for Tretiakov's "Roar, China!" (*Rychi, Kitai!*). However, the proximity of his beloved preoccupies and distracts Benjamin that night:

During the intermission [. . .] I was ahead of Asja on the stairs for a moment. Suddenly I felt her hand on my neck. My coat collar had gotten turned up and she was folding it back into place. At this contact I realized just how long it had been since any hand had touched me with gentleness [. . .]. I accompanied her home, saddened and silent. The snow that night had the sparkle of stars [. . .]. When we arrived in front of her house, I asked her, more out of defiance and more to test her than out of any real feeling, for one last kiss in the old year. She wouldn't give me one. I turned back, it was now almost New Year's, certainly alone but not at all that sad. After all, I knew that Asja, too, was alone.[28]

Situations such as this one represent the emotional background of Benjamin's stay in Moscow, a time during which he embraced the idea of the annihilation of private life and self-dissolution into the communist collectivity. As an example of the successful communist intellectual, Tret'iakov could appear to Benjamin to be everything that he was not: a writer who made his own life into an instrument for class warfare and who, as a side effect, freed himself from the irrational sufferings of jealousy and unrequited love.

Benjamin's Moscow experience did not result in a radical change in his life: he did not move to the USSR or join the German communist party. Nor did he resolve completely his relations with Asja Lacis. In late 1928, when Lacis went to Berlin to work at the Soviet Trade Bureau, their relationship flared up again, and she lived with Benjamin for about two months. He preserved his position of a "free-lance writer without party and profession,"[29] which he felt was socially unnecessary and at the same time the only one that was possible for him personally. It is hard to say what was behind his non-action: a conscious decision or the actual difficulty of switching to another register of existence.

The historian Martin Green has noted that in Germany in the first quarter of the twentieth century the practitioners of *Lebensreform* (a movement to reform everyday life) were in constant conflict with the philosophers who theorized the movement.[30] Benjamin's attempts to include himself in the propagandistic work of the German communists can serve as an example of such a lack of mutual understanding. Asja Lacis recalled one of these attempts: "When I told Becher about my children's theater for aesthetic education in Orel in 1918, he said 'We should organize a theater like that at the Liebknecht House. Write a program and give it to me and to Eisler.' Then I told Walter Benjamin about this. He said: 'It is impossible simply to compile a program. You must philosophically formulate it. I will write the program.' And he wrote a program a few pages long. I took it to Becher and Eisler. They read and started to laugh. 'Nothing is understandable here. Maybe the philosopher Walter Benjamin wrote it for you? (He wrote in very difficult German.) Give it back to him and tell him to write it in a normal human way.' "[31]

Paradoxically, in Communist Russia, all of Benjamin's acquaintances—mostly writers and men of theater—were finding non-marginal cultural roles for themselves in the service of the propaganda needs of the new power. Even Reich, whose Russian was far from perfect, held a membership in VAPP, published, and had hopes for "a high position." The age-old tradition of literature's participation in Russian social life determined the ease with which the Symbolists' *zhiznetvorchestvo* (life-creation) turned into the *zhiznestroenie* (life-building) of the communist avant-garde writers.[32] The latter did not feel alienated by the new society. Moreover, they considered themselves its creators. This situation contrasted sharply with the traditionally problematic relationship between philosophers and activists in Germany.

In Moscow, literary and political life was boiling over. Benjamin compared it to the Gold Rush, but he could only look at it from the sidelines. Without Asja and Reich he was helpless. On one frosty evening he came to a restaurant to have hot soup, spent a long time explaining his order to the waiter, and was finally served sliced cheese. His friends often forgot his presence and switched to Russian. Benjamin would take offense, get depressed almost to the point of crying, and suspect that he was a burden to his friends and acquaintances. One would expect alienation to be the main theme of his diary. However, immediately after his return to Berlin, he makes a striking entry:

> For someone who has arrived from Moscow, Berlin is a dead city. The people on the street seem desperately isolated, each one at a great distance from the next, all alone in the midst of the broad stretch of street. Furthermore: as I was traveling from the Zoo railway station toward the Grunewald, the neighborhood I had to cross struck me as scrubbed and polished, excessively clean, excessively comfortable. What is true of the image of the city and its inhabitants is also applicable to its mentality: the new perspective one gains on this is the most indisputable consequence of a stay in Russia.[33]

Hidden behind the Berlin pedestrians' excessive private physical space, Benjamin sees a pathological excess of private social space, which causes alienation and loneliness. Even without the reminder of the author, we would notice the connection between this remark and his Moscow reflections on the "withering of private life," whose practical and psychological advantages Benjamin by this time acknowledged.

Benjamin's awkward and painful romantic predicament in Moscow made him sympathetic to the utopian idea that promised to end all romance. The reform of the private sphere, which Benjamin observed in Moscow, did appear to him to be liberating, although not in the way of the unfettering of sexuality, which many Westerners expected to find in Soviet society. Benjamin conceptualized his friends' Moscow routines as reflections of private life in the process of its total annihilation. In his eyes, Soviet citizens were being liberated *from* sexuality. Benjamin's conclusion confirmed Westerners' widespread sense that a revolution was taking place in the sphere of private life and sexuality in Soviet Russia. Yet the direction of this transformation, as formulated by Benjamin, was dramatically different from the one predicted by Gide and many others in the West.

Postscript

In January 1938 Anna Lacis was arrested in Moscow by the state security police. Like many other Latvian émigrés in the Soviet Union, she was accused of spying for "a certain foreign country." After serving a ten-year sentence in a labor camp in the Soviet Far East, she returned to Soviet Latvia, where she later made a career for herself as a stage director. She was "rehabilitated" in 1954. The excerpts from her personal file in the Central State Special Archive (TsGOA) have been recently published.[34] These materials do not include a stack of Benjamin's letters that, according to her daughter, were confiscated at the time of Lacis's arrest. If preserved, these letters would be in Lacis's KGB file, among many other still classified documents. The released documents contain a synopsis of Lacis's file, compiled by a TsGOA investigator in 1954 when her case was reconsidered. The synopsis summarizes Lacis's 1934–1936 letters to Walter Benjamin, who then lived in exile in France.

The central theme of this correspondence is Benjamin's desire to move to the Soviet Union, which Asja Lacis supports. Discussing this plan, Lacis recommends that Benjamin ask André Gide for assistance. Gide, whom Benjamin interviewed in January 1928, was a prominent partisan of the Soviet Union in Western Europe. In 1936 he went to Moscow and was received with great pomp. However, after the release of Gide's travelogue *Retour de l'U.R.S.S.*, partly critical of the Soviet regime, the Soviet press labeled Gide a traitor and orchestrated a propagandistic outcry against him. In her letter to Benjamin, quoted in her dossier, Lacis duly notes:

> It's all over with Gide. I am not surprised that he wrote against the Soviets: the writing-desk aesthete will never understand the difficult methods of our construction work. The only thing I cannot understand is why he shed so many tears [here] and kissed [Nikolai] Ostrovsky.[35]

After Gide was discredited, Benjamin lost a connection who could help him secure political asylum in the Soviet Union (if he in fact had a serious intention to seek one). In another letter, Lacis suggested that the prominent Party journalist Mikhail Kol'tsov could also be approached for a reference. Kol'tsov, then in Spain, would soon return, only to be executed. On one occasion, Lacis mentioned responding to Tret'iakov's request for an article by Benjamin. The article in question was most likely "The Author as Producer" (1934), devoted to Tret'iakov's activities. Tret'iakov was arrested and shot in 1937.[36]

It is reasonable to assume that Lacis's KGB file featured her correspondence with Benjamin so prominently because of her suspected connection to Gide. In today's reader's perception, Benjamin's and Gide's Russian travelogues helped establish the genre of "a Western intellectual's journey to Soviet Russia." These two travels resulted in very different narratives, but they crossed at the life of Asja Lacis in a sad and ironic way.

NOTES

1. Bernd Witte's excellent biography remains a standard account of Benjamin's life. Bernd Witte, *Walter Benjamin: An Intellectual Biography*, trans. James Rolleston (Detroit: Wayne State University Press, 1991). For the Moscow travel, see 99–104. See

also Momme Brodersen, *Walter Benjamin: A Biography*, trans. Malcolm Green and Ingrida Ligers, ed. Martina Dervis (London and New York: Verso, 1996), 172–176; Gary Smith, "Afterword," in Walter Benjamin, *Moscow Diary*, ed. Gary Smith, trans. Richard Sieburth (Cambridge, Mass.: Harvard University Press, 1986), 137–146; the unsigned "Chronology, 1927–1934," in Walter Benjamin, *Selected Writings*, vol. 2 (1927–1934), trans. Rodney Livingstone and others, ed. Michael W. Jennings, Howard Eiland, and Gary Smith (Cambridge, Mass.: Belknap Press, 1999), 823–827.

2. Susan Buck-Morss, *The Dialectics of Seeing: Walter Benjamin and the Arcades Project* (Cambridge, Mass., and London: MIT Press, 1991), 11–22, 27–32. See also Graeme Gilloch, *Myth and Metropolis: Walter Benjamin and the City* (Cambridge: Polity Press, 1996), 21–55.

3. *Zhak Derrida v Moskve. Dekonstruktsiia poezdki* (Moscow: RIK Kul'tura, 1993).

4. Gerhard Richter, *Walter Benjamin and the Corpus of Autobiography* (Detroit: Wayne State University Press, 2000), 159.

5. In his *Walter Benjamin: The Colour of Experience* (London and New York: Routledge, 1998), Howard Caygill sees in Benjamin's depiction of Moscow the intimation of "the Soviet state . . . converting itself into a criminal organization" (p. 127). The author ignores completely the great attraction that the Soviet regime had for Benjamin.

6. My main source of biographical information on Asja Lacis is an interview that I conducted in August 1993 with her daughter Dagmara Kimele. I thank both her and Yuri Tsivian, who helped me arrange the meeting. See also the two published autobiographies of Asja Lacis, which unfortunately do not furnish reliable historical data: Asja Lacis, *Revolutionär im Beruf* (München: Rogner und Bernhard, 1971); Anna Latsis, *Krasnaia gvozdika: vospominaniia* (Riga: Liesma, 1984).

7. Gershom Sholem, *Walter Benjamin: The Story of a Friendship*, trans. Harry Zohn (Philadelphia: The Jewish Publication Society of America, 1981), 122.

8. *Zhak Derrida v Moskve*.

9. Michel Foucault, *The History of Sexuality, Volume 1: An Introduction*, trans. Robert Hurley (New York: Vintage Books, 1990), 69.

10. *The Journals of André Gide*, vol. 3, trans. and annotated by Justin O'Brian (New York: Alfred A. Knopf, 1949), 180.

11. Ian Hamilton, "Spender's Lives," *New Yorker*, February 28, 1994.

12. Walter Benjamin, "Moscow," in *Reflections: Essays, Aphorisms, Autobiographical Writings*, ed. P. Demetz, trans. E. Jephcott (New York: Schocken Books, 1978), 108.

13. Walter Benjamin, *Moscow Diary*, trans. Gary Smith, Richard Sieburth (Cambridge, Mass.: Harvard University Press, 1986), 127.

14. *Moscow Diary*, 55.

15. Walter Benjamin, *Moskauer Tagebuch*, Aus der Handschrift herausgegeben mit Anmerkungen von Gary Smith (Frankfurt am Main: Suhrkamp, 1980), 52.

16. *Moscow Diary*, 72; *Moskauer Tagebuch*, 106–107.

17. Lev Trotskii, *Literatura i revoliutsiia* (Moscow, 1923), 184–188, emphasis added.

18. Cited in Aleksei Markov, "Seksual'nost' i vlast': seksual'nye diskursy 1920-kh–nachala 1930-kh godov. Ot konkurentsii k ierarkhii" (manuscript in Russian). I am grateful to the late Dr. Markov for the permission to cite the manuscript of his work, presented at the conference "Russian Daily Life, 1921–1941: New Approaches" (St. Petersburg, August 1994). On Zalkind and *pedologiia* also see Aleksander Etkind, *Eros of the Impossible: The History of Psychoanalysis in Russia*, trans. Noah and Maria Rubins (Boulder: Westview Press, 1997), 259–285.

19. *Moscow Diary*, 55.

20. Sergei Mikhailovich Tret'iakov (1892–1937), a noted Soviet playwright, poet, and critic, belonged to the group LEF and collaborated with Meyerhold and Eisenstein.

21. Sergei Tret'iakov, "Otkuda i kuda?," *LEF* 1 (1923): 197, 198, 202.

22. Irina Gutkin, "The Legacy of the Symbolist Aesthetic Utopia: From Futurism to Socialist Realism," in *Creating Life: The Aesthetic Utopia of Russian Modernism*, ed. Irina Paperno and Joan Delaney Grossman (Stanford: Stanford University Press, 1994).

23. Anna Lacis, "Tret'iakov" (manuscript in Russian), the Rainis Literary Museum Archive (Riga, Latvia), fond of Anna Lacis, 25–26, no. 400.254.

24. Walter Benjamin, "The Author as Producer," in *Reflections*, 223.

25. The play was first published in *Sovremennaia dramaturgiia* 2 (1988): 206–243.

26. Ibid., 232.

27. Ibid., 224.

28. *Moscow Diary*, 57–58.

29. Ibid., 60.

30. Martin Green, *The Mountain of Truth: Counterculture Begins—Ascona, 1900–1920* (Hanover, N.H., and London: University Press of New England, 1986), 2.

31. Anna Lacis, "Becher" (manuscript in Russian), the Rainis Literary Museum Archive, Riga, fond of Anna Lacis, 25–26, no. 400.254.

32. Irina Gutkin, "The Legacy of the Symbolist Aesthetic Utopia."

33. *Moscow Diary*, 114.

34. V. F. Koliazin and V. A. Goncharov, eds., *"Vernite mne svobodu!" Deiateli literatury i iskusstva Rossii i Germanii—zhertvy stalinskogo terrora. Memorial'nyi sbornik dokumentov iz arkhivov byvshego KGB* (Moscow: Medium, 1997), 138–161.

35. Ibid., 154. Nikolai Ostrovskii (1904–1936), the disabled Soviet writer who, after publishing the novel *How the Steel Was Tempered* (1932–1934), was made into an object of an official cult, as a hero of communist construction.

36. See the materials of his KGB file in *"Vernite mne svobodu!"* 46–69.

nine

When Private Home Meets Public Workplace

Service, Space, and the Urban Domestic in 1920s Russia

Rebecca Spagnolo

Our position is worse than that of street urchins. We are herded along like cattle, nowhere do we matter. Who are we—housemaids or workers?[1]

[*Nashe polozhenie khuzhe besprizornykh. My valiaemsia kak skoty, s nami nigde ne schitaiutsia. Kto my—sluzhanki ili rabochie?*]

In the years following 1917, the Bolsheviks attempted, with varying degrees of success, to revolutionize almost all aspects of domestic life. However, even at its most utopian, Bolshevik zeal to reconstitute hearth and home never extended as far as the elimination of domestic service[2]—despite the fact that, prior to 1917, reformers and revolutionaries alike had decried service as being a thinly veiled form of slavery.[3] Instead, not only did service continue as an occupation after the revolution, but the number of domestics grew steadily throughout the 1920s, beginning with the end of the Civil War.[4] By 1926 it had risen to 460,687, and by 1929 it peaked at approximately 527,000 women in live-in or, much less frequently, in day service.[5] Even though the postrevolutionary figures still paled by comparison to the prerevolutionary number of well over a million domestics, by 1929 service comprised 15.95 percent of the total number of employed women and was second only in size to industry.[6]

The persistence of domestic service, as well as its growing numbers in the

1920s, can be attributed to three main factors. First was the steady influx of unskilled women from the countryside seeking an entrée into an otherwise unwelcoming urban labor market. Their availability helped depress wages, making domestic labor more affordable.[7] Second was the failure of Bolshevik policies aimed at transforming the position of women and severing their ties to housework.[8] In the years immediately following 1917, women were called upon to move "Away from pots and saucepans!" and to progress "From the kitchen to the factory bench!" Promises of collective childrearing, public day cares, central laundries and even special clothes-mending shops were used to lure women into the productive labor of the workplace. Yet throughout the 1920s these transformative promises remained largely unfulfilled, and women were left with nothing to replace their labor in the home. This situation was only exacerbated by those Bolshevik feminists who, in upholding their principled opposition to anything that smacked of domesticity, elected to deny women access to much-needed labor-saving devices such as "mops, irons, and frying pans," on the grounds that their availability would keep housework tied to the home and, by extension, to the women who lived there.[9] The emerging tension between an ideologically driven new everyday life (*novyi byt*), with all its broken promises, and an ingrained dependence on domestic labor is central both to the continued need for servants and the unenviable position in which these employees often found themselves.

A third factor contributing to the persistence of domestic service was the emergence toward the end of the decade of a new cadre of employers. Slowly but surely members of a newly forming Soviet elite replaced the vilified Nepmen of the mid 1920s. Members of this new elite favored the employment of experienced and skilled domestics, capable of meeting their increasingly demanding lifestyles and elevated notions of social comportment.[10]

Domestic service was a defining experience for hundreds of thousands of women over the course of the 1920s. Yet the record of this experience is conspicuously absent from the scholarly annals of Russian history, partly because, with the home as workplace, it was often unattended by an accessible paper trail.[11] Fortunately for the historian, three successive unions were actively involved with urban domestic servants during the period from 1917 to 1930. Their archives contain material documenting, in some depth, a broad range of the characteristics of this occupation, including its size and composition, the wages and benefits provided to the domestic, the conditions in which she was expected to live and work, the people who employed her, and the kinds of grievances her working conditions generated, as well as efforts to organize, regulate, educate, enlighten, and transform her.[12] By drawing on this material, by sampling the prescriptive literature written for domestics during the 1920s, and by analyzing the rich quantitative data contained in the 1926 census, it is possible to open a discussion of some of the many challenges confronting the urban domestic as she attempted to both work and live in her employer's home. The study of domestic service in Russia in the 1920s offers insights into the lives and experiences of a significant segment of the female labor force that has previously gone unexamined, as well as a new vantage point from which to observe the impact both of Bolshevik policies towards women during the 1920s and of efforts to introduce a new everyday life (*novyi byt*).

The decade following 1917 witnessed a series of unprecedented advances for domestics, at least on paper. A young woman entering into service, often without skills or training, was quickly meant to come under the protection of a series of labor regulations that governed every aspect of her existence, from hiring, length of workday, wages, work clothes, and responsibilities, through holiday time, maternity leave and sick leave, to firing or resignation. There also existed a union structure that sought to organize and protect her in the workplace. However, such accomplishments must be weighed against the fact that, whether inside or outside the union, domestics remained in an essentially servile occupation performing labor once described by Lenin as "the most unproductive, the most savage, the most arduous work a woman can do"[13]— valueless by definition in a revolutionary society that exalted the productive. Restricted employment opportunities for women outside of household service during the 1920s combined with an urban housing crisis to limit the domestic's ability to turn her live-in position into one of a day laborer or more traditional worker or employee. Instead, without space of her own, she was unable to exercise any sort of autonomy and was powerless to compel her employer to comply with any of the new measures put in place to protect her— that is, without risking her own dismissal and likely eviction.

Initially, in the spring of 1917, the momentum for change seemed to be promising. Building on prerevolutionary foundations, activists once again brought together all categories of household servants to form the Professional Union of Domestic Servants (*Professional'nyi soiuz domashnei prislugi*).[14] With incredible speed, domestics in urban centers such as Kharkov, Minsk, Kiev, Petrograd, and Moscow joined in common purpose.[15] Over the course of the next decade, however, domestic servants were shunted from union to union—each shift resulting in a further dilution of their numbers. Where initially they were at the core of their first union, they subsequently became a somewhat smaller part of the larger Professional Union of Home Employees (*Professional'nyi soiuz domovykh sluzhashchikh*).[16] By May 1920 they had become a less than welcome part of the Professional Union of People's Food Service and Dormitory Workers (Narpit) (*Professional'nyi soiuz rabotnikov narodnogo pitaniia i obshchezhitii*). Ultimately, according to the 18 September 1930 resolution of the All-Russian Central Council of Trade Unions (VTsSPS), domestics were tucked away in the Professional Union of Municipal and Domestic Workers (*Professional'nyi soiuz rabochikh gorodskikh predpriiatii i domashnikh rabotnikov*).

Calls by servants in the 1920s for better working conditions, higher wages, guaranteed benefits, increased respect in the workplace, and improved living conditions had changed little from those first put forth decades earlier by their prerevolutionary counterparts, and they were comparable to those being made by their contemporaries in Western Europe and particularly in America.[17] Moreover, their demands were very much in keeping with the demands of other working class groups in Russia during the decade following 1917. The primary difference was that domestics placed an even greater emphasis on the need for privacy and improved living conditions so that their demands proved even more difficult to fulfill than those of other workers. This was due in no small part to both the nature of service, with its conflation of work and home, and its ties to everyday life. Though the revolution appeared to have little impact on the specific nature of the demands levied by servants, it did provide them with both an opportunity to organize and a union structure that was unparalleled anywhere else in the world. However, at the same time as the revolution added strength to the domestic's voice, its ideals threatened to undermine the legitimacy of her work within the home and thus the position from which she could seek to improve her lot in life.

One of the first demands made by servants concerned the length of their workday. Tired of working from before dawn until long after nightfall, domestics called for the introduction of the eight-hour day with one day off per week, time off for all statutory holidays, and a one-month paid holiday each year. Domestics wanted improved benefits such as unemployment insurance, adequate medical assistance, and maternity leave. In terms of financial compensation, domestics sought the introduction of a national wage scale that would mandate a higher level of wages with a regulated minimum amount that employers had to pay in cash, as opposed to simply in room and board.[18] In addition they sought protection in the workplace, with the introduction of a mechanism to resolve workplace conflicts along with uniform standards governing a servant's employment and dismissal or resignation.

Domestics were also adamant about the need to safeguard their privacy, to establish their personal space, and to improve their quality of life. They were concerned with improvements in the moral climate of the workplace and were no longer prepared to suffer the unwanted attentions of male employers or their relatives and guests. As Lisa Granik has discussed, unwelcome sexual advances were a feature of many a woman's workplace at this time.[19] However, the problem was especially demoralizing for the domestic, who lived and worked in her employer's home, with nowhere to escape to at the end of the day. At a minimum, domestics sought to gain for themselves some semblance of respect by insisting on being addressed at all times in the polite form *vy* as opposed to the more familiar *ty* form.[20]

The documentary evidence shows that domestics were equally vocal on the subject of the room and board provided to them as a condition of their employment. They were tired of living underfoot in corridors, in the corners of kitchens, or in damp, dark, disease-ridden basements with little in the way of comforts, an inadequate diet, and absolutely no privacy.[21] Somewhat unrealistically they called for employers to provide a minimum standard of accommodation that was, in most cases, better than the employers enjoyed themselves.[22] If domestics had to live in, they ideally wished to be given a separate space of their own within the home, one that was both warm and bright. However, with or without their own private space, domestics expected to be regarded as equal members of the household and as such to be free to entertain friends and relatives when off duty.[23] Outside their workday, or on their days off, domestics felt they should be able to spend their leisure time in the home if they wished, without being conscripted to work simply because they were physically present.[24]

In the push for better working conditions for the domestic, first the Professional Union of Domestic Servants and then its successors devoted varying degrees of attention to the establishment of norms regulating the domestic's labor.[25] The unions pushed for the introduction of special labor inspectorates, which were believed at the time to be "one of the best ways of combating the many evils that befall those who work in the home."[26] The Professional Union of Home Employees also worked to protect domestics by calling for the formation of *domovye komitety* in every building in which its members worked. Once established, these committees had the responsibility of ensuring that each one of the home employees residing in their buildings joined the union. More importantly, however, they had the right, if called upon, to adjudicate all conflicts occurring between domestics and their employers.[27]

In response to concerns over compensation, the Professional Union of Home Employees introduced a national wage scale that was designed to replace the rather haphazard system that had existed previously.[28] Effective 1 September 1919, the *Tarif Vserossiiskogo-Professional'nogo soiuza domovykh rabochikh* determined the salaries of all occupations included in the union according to clearly defined criteria: the minimum living wage required, the specific nature of the work, the level of difficulty, the provision of any non-cash benefits, as well as the geographic region in which the position was located.[29] No longer were domestic servants left to face employers in salary negotiations with nothing to support even their minimum demands.

Despite its considerable efforts and not insignificant achievements, the Professional Union of Home Employees survived only two years. At the Third All-Russian Meeting of Professional Unions in 1920 it was announced that this union would be dismantled. According to terms laid out by the All-Russian Central Council of Trade Unions (VTsSPS), the membership of domestics, doormen, yardkeepers, laundresses, footmen, nannies, cooks, cafeteria workers, waiters, and dishwashers was to be divided between a number of existing organizations: the Union of Municipal Workers (*Soiuz rabotnikov kommunal'nogo khoziaistva*), the Professional Union of People's Food Service and Dormitory Workers (Narpit),[30] the Union of People's Education (*Soiuz narodnogo obrazovaniia*), the Union of Transport Workers (*Soiuz transportnykh rabochikh*), and the Garment Industry Union (*Soiuz shveinoi promyshlen-nosti*).[31]

The decision to dissolve the Professional Union of Home Employees was as unpopular with its members as it was unwelcome to some of its heirs, even if they stood to benefit from the influx of new members and their dues.[32] Narpit, the intended home of all domestics, was especially vocal in its opposition. It viewed these women as a backward prerevolutionary legacy that would dilute its own rather tenuous, but nonetheless jealously guarded, proletarian status.[33] Despite its initial reluctance, Narpit nonetheless continued the work of its predecessors. During the first half of the 1920s extremely elaborate rules were drafted to improve workplace conditions through, among other things, the introduction of something approaching an eight-hour work day with guaranteed time off and prescribed holiday breaks.[34] In addition more equitable and transparent hiring and firing practices were carefully crafted, and employers were even required to provide all domestics annually with work clothes commensurate to their rank.[35] Narpit also worked to ensure the implementation of the guidelines outlined above, realizing that they would remain empty promises unless both domestic and employer were aware of their existence and agreed to adhere to them. To ensure the employer's compliance and to protect the domestic from her own vulnerability, local Narpit representatives campaigned vigorously to bind the parties to formal employment contracts signed in the presence of a union official, who would act as guardian of the domestic's interests. In the event of a contentious problem, the employment contract would offer to both parties a framework for recourse that was much more effective than a simple wage book.[36]

By 1924 Narpit embarked on an ambitious project to redefine the domestic. In response to persistent charges of "backwardness" leveled against the rapidly growing number of women who were once again flocking into service, Narpit set out to reforge[37] the domestic servant (*domashniaia prisluga*) into the domestic worker (*domashniaia rabotnitsa*). In her revolutionary incarnation, the domestic worker would be raised to a higher level of Soviet legitimacy as a member of the newly formed domestic proletariat (*domovye proletariata*).

The simplest and most striking testament to the drive to transform the domestic servant lay in the changing use of language. By 1923–1924 she was referred to as a domestic worker in all official discourse.[38] For approximately one year after its introduction, the words domestic servant in brackets almost always accompanied the term domestic worker—as if by way of explanation.[39] By mid-1924 the phrase domestic servant began to be used officially in an exclusively pejorative context, whereas the term domestic worker stood for someone who was no longer downtrodden and oppressed, no longer backward, and no longer illiterate. Instead, a domestic worker was expected to be active in her union, even seeking an elected position of some sort so that she could proceed to work tirelessly to locate and recruit other domestics as members. Once enrolled in Rabfak, she would dream of joining the Komsomol or one day even the party. In addition to all her newfound public responsibilities, the archetypal domestic worker also managed to meet her obligations to her employer. She was neither helpless nor easily exploited and was quick to seek assistance in the event of a conflict. She was also not afraid to stand up to her employer and quite possibly risk being fired because of her participation in union activities.

This image of the domestic worker, along with the less flattering portrayal of the domestic servant, was prominent in a collection of prescriptive materials specially constructed during the mid-1920s. These materials consisted of short stories, chastushki, poems, cartoons, and even plays, and they could be found in pamphlets, the pages of journals, or in local wall newspapers.[40] They were designed to target young single women who had recently arrived from the countryside and who were only slightly literate at best. In most cases they had obtained their positions as domestics through informal channels, and consequently they were considered to be tremendously vulnerable to exploitation and abuse by their employers.

The prescriptive stories tended to follow a consistent plot. They usually told the tale of a young peasant girl who had either willingly succumbed to, or been forcibly subjected to, the advances of a young man from her village community. Her reputation now in tatters, she fled to the city and contacted either a relative or a *zemliak* who agreed to house her temporarily while she sought employment. Not possessing any skills, she was forced to take up a position as a domestic servant working for her new employer and his family, all of whom were portrayed in the most disparaging of terms.[41]

In these stories the domestic servant, upon entering into service, was inevitably provided with a threadbare blanket on which to sleep and a corner in which to do so. She was forced to work her fingers to the bone from early morning hours until very late at night, with no time off, always at the beck and call of her master and mistress. The servant was barely provided with enough to eat and was paid a mere pittance, if at all. To cap it all she was subjected to constant verbal and even occasional physical abuse.

It was usually at this point in the stories that our poor downtrodden heroine accidentally, though most fortuitously for her, stumbled across the local Narpit delegate. Frequently this chance meeting took place while she was attempting to hang out to dry very heavy amounts of wet laundry and was both exhausted from her bone-wearying work and conveniently out of the earshot of her ever-vigilant mistress.[42] The delegate, herself a domestic worker, seized the opportunity to explain how the servant's plight could be lessened by joining Narpit. Explaining the role of the union and the many services it would provide, the delegate invited her to attend a meeting. Invariably the domestic in the story was immediately convinced of the need to sign up. Upon joining Narpit she learned that she had friends who supported her and a union that would protect her from her employer. She now had the resources necessary to improve her position at home in the workplace. She learned of her rights: of the eight-hour day, of the time off to which she was entitled, of the need to possess a wage book, and of the importance of concluding an employment contract with her employer in the presence of a local union representative, as well as the many other gains made to safeguard her interests.

Ultimately, as the story unfolded, the domestic became both literate and active in her local committee (*mestkom*), regularly attended meetings and was elected as a delegate, charged with the task of helping other young women from the area in which she worked and lived. In many cases the stories ended at this point. However, others ran full circle and ended with her triumphant return to the village she had previously left in shame. Or they ended with her having a chance encounter in the city with a friend or close relative from that same village during which she extolled the virtues of her new life. Not surprisingly this storyline served not simply as a staple in the prescriptive literature of the 1920s but also as a model for many domestic worker autobiographies compiled during this decade.[43]

The process of reforging the domestic servant into the domestic worker, however, consisted of more than simple changes in the use of language and the creation and distribution of prescriptive literature. It also involved the domestic's education, her enlightenment, and the creation of a socialist identity—one that emphasized the need for public work and volunteerism. In response both to unceasing calls for action and to sustained pressure from the Central Committee of Narpit, VTsSPS, and the People's Commissariat of Labor (Narkomtrud), local union officials, together with elected delegates and others, worked directly with domestics in an attempt to achieve these goals.[44]

In practical terms this involved a number of different elements, one of the most important of which was the establishment of literacy programs to combat the tremendously high level of illiteracy, believed to affect between 70 and 80 percent of all domestics.[45] Classes were offered throughout urban centers catering both to those who were completely illiterate and to those who had some small level of literacy. In terms of the transformation of the domestic servant into the domestic worker, literacy was the cornerstone upon which all other efforts at education and enlightenment rested. It was also an area in which local union efforts secured a noticeable level of improvement, despite being hamstrung both by the continuous influx into service of new women from the countryside and by a persistent inability to coordinate efforts with other similarly motivated groups, such as the *Zhenotdel*. In addition to becoming literate, domestic workers were also expected to participate in a wide variety of activities sponsored by Narpit. These included clubs, political circles, reading circles, lectures, and even field trips. A domestic worker was also to develop a sense of activism and be willing to assume additional responsibilities outside the workplace. For example, she was constantly urged to become a delegate and to go door to door in her neighborhood to help other domestics in need of assistance or representation.[46]

By the mid-1920s it seemed, at least on the surface, that urban domestic servants had obtained virtually all that they had been seeking since the early days of the St. Petersburg Artel of Male Domestic Servants in the 1880s—one of the first organized groups of domestics.[47] Their occupation was no longer unregulated, nor was their position in the workplace unprotected. There were even those who, in their own words or at least in the words attributed to them in letters, articles, and autobiographies, claimed to have successfully bridged the divide between domestic servant and domestic worker.[48] Yet for many of the women, an account of whose experiences are contained in the pages of the union archives, it seems these achievements—groundbreaking though they were—remained honored more in theory than in practice.

As early as September 1918, some within the Professional Union of Home Employees recognized that the success of any proposed measures to improve the position of the domestic required a move away from the model of the live-in domestic towards that of one who lived out.[49] As long as the domestic's workplace remained a fusion of the homes of employer and employee, her position would continue to be untenable—regardless of the many guidelines put in place to protect her. This refrain, though largely muted during the Civil War period, resurfaced by the mid-1920s and grew louder as reports of the mistreatment of domestics persisted. For example, in 1924 an article in Narpit's journal, *Rabotnik Narodnogo Pitaniia*, argued that in order to improve the domestic's life it was necessary to free her from the *"khoziaiskaia kabal'"* to which she was currently condemned.[50] In addition to limiting the potential for employer abuse, a move to live-out status would also provide the domestic with more free time to spend on self-improvement, education, and organization. If nothing else, at the end of her shift she would be able to escape her employer and return to a private space, simply by changing out of her work clothes and leaving for the day.[51] As a result, by the mid 1920s, measures were slowly introduced that distinguished between the relative rights and responsibilities of those domestics who lived in versus those who did not. Probably the most significant of the many little steps taken in this direction was the formalization of a differential wage scale that paid live-out domestics between 25 percent and 100 percent more in cash compensation.[52] Nevertheless, with the high cost of food and lodging in the prevailing economic climate, debate persisted as to the adequacy of such a token measure.

Not surprisingly, the very real urban housing crisis of the 1920s further undercut any such efforts.[53] As some of the worst paid of the working classes, domestics were particularly hard hit by the tremendous shortage of affordable and habitable accommodation, to the point where it was unrealistic for them to even consider moving out of their employer's home.[54] Despite recognition within both Narkomtrud and Narpit of the need to separate the domestic's workplace from her home, neither organization offered her any material help in securing alternate accommodation.[55] Instead their attention and resources were committed to combating an even more pressing problem—the growing rate of homelessness among unemployed domestics, a condition that was thought to contribute to the noticeable increase in prostitution.[56] Their efforts to create additional temporary housing were insufficient to meet the rapidly growing demands of unemployed domestics, let alone of those who simply wished to live out.[57]

The anecdotal evidence suggests that the urban housing shortage in cities such as Leningrad and Moscow not only contributed to the inability of the domestic to move out; it also ensured that the quality of the accommodation provided by her employer, and the degree of privacy it offered, remained well below the levels originally sought by domestics and their union supporters. In letters written to local branches of Narpit, domestics repeatedly complained of having to sleep on flattened boxes in the corners of kitchens, or on the floor in darkened corridors—with neither time nor space to themselves.[58] The situation was scarcely better for the domestic who graduated from the corridor floor to a room shared with her employers. Subordinate by definition, she was forced to live according to the timetables of her employer-roommates, while still being at their continual beck and call.[59] Worse yet, if she attempted to complain, or insisted upon her own space, she ran the risk of being disciplined by her employer, and even summarily dismissed.

An example of this latter point can be found in the unfair dismissal proceedings instigated in Leningrad in the summer of 1925 by the domestic Kropacheva against her employer, Berim, and adjudicated by executive members of a local Narpit committee. In this case, Berim, who had hired Kropacheva only a few months earlier, shared a two-room apartment with his wife and family. In his statement, he openly admitted that he had only fired Kropacheva because she demanded to live in a separate room. He considered this to be a completely unmanageable arrangement given his own family circumstances. Ultimately, the matter was decided in favor of Kropacheva. She was to be financially compensated for unpaid salary, severance, and unused holiday time, as well as a prorated work clothing allowance. However, as was all too often the case in such proceedings, despite a favorable ruling and an award of compensation, the local Narpit committee did not award Kropacheva the opportunity to return either to her former position, or her former lodgings— such as they were.[60]

A sampling of letters and statements from live-in domestics paints a vivid picture of their general living conditions during the 1920s—a picture borne out by the available quantitative data. For example, in 1926 the Moscow branch of Narpit surveyed some 512 domestic workers. They were interviewed about all aspects of their employment experiences including length of workday, overtime, time off, compensation, work clothes, and of course living conditions. In answer to questions on living conditions, the primary problem identified was the lack of any sort of private space. Out of the 512 polled, only 10 percent had managed to effect the transition from a live-in domestic to one who lived out. Among the remaining 90 percent, only 16.7 percent had their own separate living space within the home. For the others, their accommodation ranged from the less desirable through the uninhabitable to the nonexistent—one lone domestic claimed to have no designated living area whatsoever.

The findings of this rather small sample of Moscow domestic workers are further supported in the much more comprehensive data contained in the 1926 census in which a total of 42,417 Moscow domestics were questioned about their living arrangements. Out of the total number surveyed only 4,184, slightly less than 10 percent, lived with one or more members of their own families; the remaining 38,233, or 90 percent, lived alone, most likely with their employers. Among this latter, more populous group, the overwhelming majority, fully 73.6 percent, lived in just a part of a room, and a further 20 percent beyond that lived in either a kitchen or some other form of space that was categorized as uninhabitable in the census.[61] These figures stand in stark contrast to those obtained for a total of 47,216 unskilled workers surveyed in Moscow, of whom 41,157, or 87 percent, lived with one or more members of their own families, while only 6,069, or 13 percent, lived alone. Out of this latter group, 22 percent had their own room, as opposed to only 5.4 percent of domestics. Only 4.2 percent of unskilled workers lived either in kitchens or other areas that the census deemed uninhabitable, as opposed to 20 percent of domestics.[62]

If we are to believe the large number of grievances and complaints lodged with Narpit during the second half of the 1920s, many live-in urban domestic servants continued to be disgruntled with the accommodation provided by their employers, and frustrated by the lack of alternative, affordable housing options. At the same time, however, they were also aware of the rising unemployment rate during NEP,[63] the difficulty in finding work outside of service,[64] and the prospect of homelessness that faced those domestics who were unfortunate enough to lose their position. The reality of any one of these three dangers often overshadowed the domestic's exasperation with her lot and left her trapped in a vicious cycle. The continued conflation of workplace and home left her vulnerable to employers, who, as a succession of cases show, used every means at their disposal to keep her ignorant of her rights, isolated from her peers, and unable to organize and establish a life outside the home.

The domestic servant experience in 1920s Russia was defined in no small part by the relationships that existed between servant and employer, and yet these employers of urban domestic labor remain largely one-dimensional characters, with little said about who they may have been and how they were represented. Unfortunately, in the absence of meaningful quantitative material, we must extrapolate evidence from available documentary and anecdotal accounts—though the last often tell us more about the employers' treatment of domestics than about the employers themselves. Nevertheless, we know that the urban employer was to be found, albeit in varying proportions, among most social categories and occupational groups, even among workers.

For administrative purposes, six general categories of employers were formally identified during the 1920s, including professionals, those engaged in trade, and even members of the working classes. These categories functioned as a coefficient in a formula that was used to either increase or decrease the domestic's wage according to a differential scale, first introduced in 1923, that linked her salary to a number of factors, not the least of which was the occupation of her employer. The resulting disparity between the salary of a domestic in the employ of a worker versus that of one in the employ of a Nepman could be as much as 250 percent.[65] The rather surprising affordability of domestics for some workers was as much a function of this prevailing wage differential as it was the result of an influx of low-cost domestic labor from the countryside. It was also due in part to the existence of communal apartments. As with the artels in the prerevolutionary period, it was not unheard of for workers and their families living in a communal apartment to band together to hire a domestic. In fact, such collective behavior within the communal apartment was officially encouraged. However, if the practice had the advantage of creating employment opportunities for the domestic, it also confronted her with new and difficult challenges in the form of her hydra-like employer, from whom she had to try to pry portions of her salary according to an informal piece rate that depended upon what tasks were performed for whom each month.[66]

While employers of domestic labor were undoubtedly a heterogeneous group, they were nonetheless collectively depicted throughout most of the 1920s in a negative light in newspapers, pamphlets, journal articles, prescriptive literature, and even poetry.[67] Biting caricatures were most in evidence.[68] If a man, the employer or "*barin*" was consistently presented as a rotund, balding, and sweaty Nepman, with beady eyes and a lascivious expression on his face. If a woman, the employer or "*barynia*" was depicted in an equally unflattering light, as a lazy, morally suspect, overly made-up, and demanding shrew of a housewife, whose abusive punishments included pinching her domestic and throwing things.[69] It was only toward the end of the decade, with the emergence of a new revolutionary elite, that employers began to receive more sympathetic treatment.

Although exaggerated, the negative image of the employer as Nepman was not entirely undeserved. There is ample evidence to show that, despite the considerable efforts at regulation and organization, many live-in domestics continued to suffer. The transgressions of the Nepman and his wife were certainly numerous and well advertised; however, they were no more egregious than those committed by the Nepman's worker or professional counterparts. A 1926 investigation into relations between domestics and their employers noted numerous instances of abuse and somewhat shamefacedly acknowledged that in at least half of the examined cases, the offending employers were either workers or white-collar employees—all union members themselves who could be expected to be more enlightened in their behavior.[70]

Some indignant domestics even reported in their grievances that their offending employers were no less than party members.[71] Ultimately, those employers who persisted in denying their domestics the same rights and privileges they themselves enjoyed rendered meaningless the hard-won battles over pivotal workplace issues.

Many employers undermined workplace reforms from the outset by ignoring requests that they hire all domestic help only through the official Labor Bureaus, which kept registers of all those who passed through their doors.[72] Instead, in order to secure a cheap, pliant, and less traceable workforce, many employers turned to a plentiful underground labor market. Recruiting among "quiet" and inexperienced girls recently arrived from the countryside was sardonically described as "strengthening the ties with the countryside."[73] It ensured that these girls, desperate for somewhere to live and work, remained isolated, dependent upon their employers and tied to their homes.

Narpit's grassroots efforts to acquaint domestics with their rights remained a challenge throughout the 1920s, as many domestic workers proved to be extremely difficult to locate. Their elusiveness was as much a function of their rapidly growing numbers and high rate of job turnover as it was a function of their obstructive employers. Determined to avoid costly wage books, employment contracts, quotas for work clothes, fixed wage scales, mandatory time off, and paid holidays, many employers contrived to keep their domestics out of Narpit's reach. Local-level union organizers tried to counter with measures designed to identify and enroll domestics. Cities and towns were divided into microregions, and Narpit delegates, working alongside representatives of the Zhenotdel and other organizations, were sent door to door to compile an inventory of all domestic labor.[74] Yardkeepers, traditionally considered to be an invaluable source of information about building residents, were encouraged to report all suspected domestic workers to their respective housing committees, which in turn were expected to complete questionnaires prepared by union organizers.[75]

Nevertheless, the lengths to which employers would go to stop their domestics from falling into the union's clutches were staggering.[76] The employer's most benign tactic was simply to ignore the new protective regulations in the hope that the domestic would remain blissfully unaware. If, however, a domestic expressed an interest in joining the union or in acquainting herself with its protective measures, an employer might initially try to appear deceptively supportive by offering to apply for union membership on the domestic's behalf. Needless to say, the applications were either conveniently lost or said to have been rejected. In fact prescriptive literature warned domestics against falling for this basic ruse. Worse yet, an employer might keep his/her domestic so busy as to ensure that she never had the time to attend union meetings, speak with delegates, or learn about her rights.[77] If such tactics were unsuccessful, the employer might try to feed the domestic misleading information about the consequences of asserting her rights in the workplace. If all else failed, the employer could resort to threats of summary dismissal and even violence.[78]

An all too typical example of this sort of escalation can be found in the case of Alexandra Kopskaia. In 1925, this barely literate young woman had been employed as a domestic in Leningrad for approximately one and a half years when she first sought to protect herself by joining Narpit. At first her employers had tried to claim that she wasn't eligible for union membership, and then they had attempted to argue that Narpit had nothing to offer her by way of protection in the workplace. However, when this failed, her employers simply locked her in their apartment. Finally, after injuring Kopskaia during an argument by shattering a glass against the wall beside her head, the mistress of the house fired her outright, put her out on the street, and immediately hired a replacement. Kopskaia retaliated by writing a complaint to the local group committee of Narpit outlining the details of her situation and charging that she was unfairly dismissed as a direct result of her stated desire to join the union and protect herself in the workplace.[79] When confronted formally, Kopskaia's employers claimed that they had dismissed her simply because of a change in their material circumstances and that at no time did they hire someone in her place. In the end, Narpit's local conflict commission determined that Kopskaia had in fact been wrongfully dismissed. Her former employers were told to compensate her with two weeks of severance pay, and if, within two months of that date, they resolved to hire another domestic worker, they were required to offer Kopskaia the right of first refusal.[80] Ultimately, however, though Kopskaia won her case against her former employers, they remained just that—her former employers. Like hundreds of domestic workers who came before her and many hundreds who were to follow her, Kopskaia was left without a position or a place to live—all because she had simply wanted to join the union and avail herself of the rights that had been won on her behalf.

Employers were also notorious for trying to avoid concluding formal employment contracts that might threaten their control of the conflated domestic spaces. Efforts by employers to maintain a much less formal relationship were given a boost on 8 February 1926, when the All-Russian Central Executive Committee (VTsIK) promulgated a law that, among other things, repealed the once-mandatory employment contract and put in its place the much less intrusive wage book.[81] What was more, even if an employer voluntarily agreed to sign the employment contract with the domestic, it was no longer necessary that this be done in the presence of a union representative and/or on union premises. These measures undermined the union's ability to protect the domestic by removing it from the negotiation process. Without anyone to represent their interests in negotiations, domestics continued to fall victim to unscrupulous employers who misrepresented what was being written in the wage book, or who failed to provide a wage book at all.[82] Moreover, even if an employer respected the new law and faithfully completed the wage book, the domestic was still potentially at a disadvantage, as the standard template of the once-compulsory employment contract contained provisions that almost always exceeded the minimal requirements of Narkomtrud at that time.[83]

This law also undermined the reasonable definition of an eight-hour workday by stating that, while a domestic must still work no more than a total of eight hours a day, those eight hours need not be continuous. Instead, they could be broken up at the employer's convenience. The specific length of any breaks was left to the discretion of the employer (if nominally in consultation with the domestic).[84] Yet again the domestic's workday could extend from dawn to dusk, providing it did not exceed a total of eight hours of actual work.[85]

While these changes seriously weakened the legal pillars buttressing the position of domestics in the workplace, mistreated domestic workers were not left entirely without recourse.[86] Many continued to pursue complaints through official channels. Disputes were often adjudicated by local-level Narpit committees and, in almost all of the cases heard, decisions favored the domestic. At first glance this high success rate appears to be an impressive vindication of the domestic and recognition of her mistreatment at the hands of her employer. More often than not, however, these were pyrrhic victories, offering only financial compensation for unpaid salaries or for benefits withheld. Even in cases of unfair dismissal, the wronged domestic remained unemployed and homeless despite being victorious. Beyond exacting a modest fine, no real effort was made to reform the employer's errant ways.

Repeated grievances, along with a succession of court cases, eventually focused attention on certain important issues, such as the degree to which domestics were wholly dependent on their employers, not just for their livelihoods but also for their homes. As a result, at least on paper, domestics were granted a significant concession in the event that they lost or left their positions for whatever reason. In 1927 the Supreme Court ruled that domestics who were members of the housing associations where they had lived for at least three years, retained the right to continue to reside in the premises of their former employers at least until such time as each housing association was able to offer independent square footage in the same building.[87] By 1928 the minimum residence requirement was reduced from three years to two years, after which the domestic was, in principle, entitled to accommodation within the building—sometimes even within her former employer's own apartment.[88]

The archival sources do not contain sufficient information to evaluate the extent to which urban domestics exercised their new right by the end of the 1920s. It is clear, however, that this was not an ideal solution. The case of the domestic worker, Sopkova, and her employer, Agreeva, provides an interesting example of the complicating tensions that accompanied this novel way of allocating space. By 1927 Sopkova had lived and worked as a domestic for more than three years in a two-room Moscow apartment. Originally, she had served the family of a former factory owner whose apartment it had been. After it was expropriated and reallocated to Agreeva and her husband, Sopkova remained there in their employ. However, when a representative of the building's residents association inspected the apartment and discovered that one of the rooms was empty, and was only being used for storage, Agreeva, fearing a subdivision of the apartment, justified the need for the room by assigning it to Sopkova for her living space. After some months, though, for reasons that are not made clear in the historical record, Sopkova's employment contract was terminated. In an effort to reclaim the second room, Agreeva moved in her mother and promptly went to court to have Sopkova evicted. However, on 23 May 1928, after the court found that Agreeva's mother was in fact a registered occupant of her daughter and son-in-law's square footage, it ruled that the second room be given back to Sopkova for her personal use.[89]

Sopkova's success only further underlined the persisting ambiguities in the situation of Russian urban domestics by the end of the 1920s. On the one hand, her success was a significant indication of a potentially reduced dependency by some domestics on their employers for housing. On the other hand, it pitted employer against domestic in an even bitterer struggle for space. The enduring hardship lay in the fact that if the domestic were successful, she faced the prospect of cohabiting with her former employer as even more of an outsider in what the evidence describes as being a hostile and unwelcoming environment.

Over time domestic service has been a reality for millions of women worldwide, and yet, with few exceptions, the significance of domestic service to a broader rethinking of the dichotomy of public and private space has not been acknowledged. In fact, it is only relatively recently, primarily among anthropologists, that the literature on domestic service has begun to crystallize the notion of workplace as home and home as workplace.[90] Thus far the research indicates that, in most cases, live-in service is a study in the isolation of the domestic punctuated by an intensely personalized relationship with her employer who, by virtue of proximity and a distinct power imbalance, occupied an almost larger-than-life position in her rather proscribed world. Her everyday existence in her employer's home was organized along both geographic and chronological lines, where not only was her physical access to private space limited, but so too was the timeframe in which she could use it. Moreover, her ability to participate in extra-workplace activities was constrained by the continued live-in nature of her position and an interminable workday that defied equitable regulation.

This paradigm is only strengthened when tested against the experiences of many urban domestics in 1920s Russia. The effectiveness of the unprecedented efforts to regulate, reform and organize service was all too frequently undermined by the conflation of workplace and home. Moreover, the extent to which the suffocating relationship of service could be administratively tempered was limited both by the prevailing socioeconomic difficulties and by the persistent inability of developing Soviet society to reconcile its revolutionary ideals with the continued existence of such an ideologically anachronistic occupation.

NOTES

1. This comment has been attributed to a domestic upon attending a local meeting of her union, the Professional Union of Food Service and Dormitory Workers (*Professional'nyi soiuz rabotnikov narodnogo pitaniia i obshchezhitii* [Narpit]) in 1927. Gosudarstvennyi arkhiv Rossiiskoi Federatsii (GARF), f. 5452, op. 11, d. 85, ll. 8–9 (*Vnutrenniaia svodka—Obzor uslovii truda domrabotnits, profobsluzhivanie i ikh uchastie v profrabote po soiuzu Narpita, 1927 g.*).

2. I have come across only one reference to the desirability of completely eliminating private domestic service: a union representative stated at a regional meeting of the Professional Union of Home Employees (*Professional'nyi soiuz domovykh sluzhashchikh*) in 1920 that in a communist republic there should be no such thing as private service. GARF, f. 5554, op. 1, d. 10, ll. 1–3 (*Protokol 2-go Soveshchaniia predstavitelei gubernskikh otdelov vseprofsoiuza domovykh rabochikh—11* April 1920). Even Alexandra Kollontai, known for declaring both the family and the home to be outmoded, implicitly acknowledged a continued need for domestics, albeit of a possibly revolutionary kind, when she envisaged a future in which "the working woman will sooner or later need to take care of her own dwelling no longer," as "this work will be carried on by a special category of working women who will do nothing else." Alexandra Kollontai, *Communism and the Family* (London: Pluto Press, 1971), 13.

3. The image of the domestic as slave is a recurring one in both the prerevolutionary and postrevolutionary periods in Russia. It is also found in the literature on domestics in other countries, particularly Great Britain, where it was linked to a late nineteenth-century concern about the increased threat of white slave traffic among domestics. The report on this subject that came out of an international congress sponsored by the National Vigilance Association held in London in 1899 was translated soon after and published in a pamphlet in St. Petersburg. Rossiiskii gosudarstvennyi istoricheskii arkhiv (RGIA), f. 1335, op. 1, d. 2, ll. 5–62. For contemporary references to domestics as slaves see Evgeniia De-Turzhe-Turzhanskaia, *Belye Nevol'niki (Domashniaia prisluga v Rossii)* (Smolensk, 1906); I. A. Flerov, *Belye raby v Rossii: polozhenie prislugi* (Moskva, 1907); and N. B. Nordman-Severova, *Sleduet raskrepostit' prislugu* (Sankt-Peterburg, 1911).

4. Diane Koenker, "Urbanization and Deurbanization in the Russian Revolution and Civil War," in *Party, State, and Society in the Russian Civil War*, ed. Diane P. Koenker, William G. Rosenberg, and Ronald Grigor Suny (Bloomington: Indiana University Press, 1989), 92.

5. *Vsesoiuznaia perepis' naseleniia 1926 goda*, t. XXXIV [*Soiuz sovetskikh sotsialisticheskikh respublik—Zaniatiia*] (Moskva, 1930), 74–75.

6. Wendy Z. Goldman, *Women at the Gates: Gender and Industry in Stalin's Russia* (Cambridge: Cambridge University Press, 2002), 90–91. During the third quarter of the nineteenth century domestic service had been almost entirely "feminized." By the first decade of the twentieth century only a small, though not insignificant, percentage of males remained in service, and this number proceeded to decrease annually. For example, in 1882 less than 70 percent of Moscow domestics were women, but by 1912 their percentage had increased to 93 percent. A similar change took place in St. Petersburg, where the composition of service went from 50 percent female in 1864 to

91 percent in 1900. By 1926 far less than 1 percent of all domestics were male, and they appeared to be located almost exclusively in Central Asia. *Perepis' Moskvy, 1882 g.*, II, pt. 2 (Moscow, 1885), 101–340, and *Statisticheskii ezhegodnik Moskvy i Moskovskoi gubernii* (Moscow, 1927), 68–73, as cited in Joseph Bradley, *Muzhik and Muscovite* (Berkeley: University of California Press, 1985), table 5, 146–147. *Statisticheskii ezhegodnik S.-Peterburga za 1892* (St. Peterburg, 1894), 83, and *S.-Peterburg po perepisi 15 dekabria 1900 goda*, vyp. 2, 87–105.

7. During the 1920s and early 1930s domestic service was recognized as a stepping-stone in the journey of tens of thousands of women from field to factory. GARF, f. 5515, op. 13, d. 5, ll. 33–34 (*Postanovlenie Soveta Narodnykh Komissarov R.S.F.S.R. 1930 g.—"O piatiletnem plane zhenskogo truda"*). This pattern of female rural–urban migration combined with employment in domestic service can also be observed during the latter part of the nineteenth century and the first decade of the twentieth century in Western Europe, particularly Britain and France, as well as in North America. For comparative information see Theresa McBride, *The Domestic Revolution: The Modernization of Household Service in England and France, 1820–1920* (London: Croom Helm, 1976), and Donna L. VanRaaphorst, *Union Maids Not Wanted: Organizing Domestic Workers, 1870–1940* (New York: Praeger Publishers, 1988).

8. "V-I Vserossiiskii S"ezd Soiuza, Otchet o S"ezde (22–26 ianvaria 1923 g.)," *Rabotnik narodnogo pitaniia* 2 (February 1923): 14–18.

9. For example, A. V. Artiukhina, head of the Zhenotdel from 1925–1930, felt that access to such items would simply serve to reinforce traditional ideas of a woman's relationship to housework and as such should be opposed. "Za sotsialisticheskuiu peredelku byta," *Rabotnitsa* 4 (1930): 3. By the second half of the 1920s there was a growing recognition that domestics were not always luxury items, and that in many instances the employer's decision to hire a domestic grew out of a genuine need. "Otvet tovarishchu profrabotniku," *Rabotnik narodnogo pitaniia* 1 (January 1927): 9.

10. "Domrabotnitsam nuzhna pomoshch'," *Rabotnik narodnogo pitaniia* 2 (February 1927): 5–6.

11. For the most part, the history of domestic service has been relegated to the occasional mention or passing footnote. This situation, however, has improved of late with reference to the prerevolutionary period, about which more has been written. However, for the postrevolutionary period, mention in secondary works is minimal. On the earlier period, see Barbara Alpern Engel, *Between the Fields and The City: Women, Work and Family in Russia, 1861 1914* (Cambridge: Cambridge University Press, 1994); Catriona Kelly, " 'Who'll Clean the Boots Now?': Servants and Social Anxieties in Late Imperial St. Petersburg," *Europa Orientalis* 16 (1997:2): 9–34, and Angela Rustemeyer, *Dientsboten in Petersburg und Moskau, 1861–1917: Hintergrund, Alltag, soziale Rolle* (Stuttgart, f. Steiner, 1996).

12. The picture these union archives paint, although undeniably compelling, may not be as representative as one would wish. Only a minority of the total estimated number of women working in domestic service in the 1920s came into direct contact with any of the succession of unions designed to accommodate them. Moreover, among those who did there were inevitably a disproportionate number who were dissatisfied with their lot and who sought some sort of redress.

13. V. I. Lenin, *The Emancipation of Women* (New York, 1934), 63.

14. Prior to 1917 there had been a succession of makeshift efforts to organize domestics—first into artels in the 1880s and 1890s, and then subsequently into unions

during both the Revolution of 1905 and the years immediately prior to World War I. Though noteworthy in the context of a history of domestic service, these early efforts were easily eclipsed in scale, organization, militancy, and longevity by the activities of artisans in workshops and of skilled and unskilled workers in factories and mills.

15. GARF, f. 6861, op. 1, d. 99, ll. 4–11, 13, 17–18, 21–22, 24 (selection of articles from newspapers *Nash golos*, *Moskovskie Izvestiia*, *Utro Rossii*, *Russkoe slovo*, *Vpered*, *Sotsial-Demokrat*, *Professional'naia zhizn'*, *Professional'noe dvizhenie*, and *Trud*, all collected by the *Komissiia po izucheniiu istorii professional'nogo dvizheniia pri Tsentral'nom Komitete professional'nogo soiuza rabotnikov narodnogo pitaniia*).

16. Without the relevant records, the organizers of the Professional Union of Domestic Servants must remain the unsung protagonists of their cause. Though the existing materials include union communiqués, protocols, reports, and organizational plans generated at the local and regional level, along with surveys compiled by the Petrograd Committee of Professional Unions (*Petrogradskii sovet professional'nykh soiuzov*), as well as a collection of articles published in a variety of newspapers ranging from the conservative *Utro Rossii* through the liberal *Russkoe slovo* to the socialist publications *Sotsial-Demokrat*, *Moskovskie Izvestie*, *Vlast' Naroda*, and *Trud*, it has been virtually impossible to obtain any real information about the individuals directly involved. Information is equally scarce in the case of the Professional Union of Home Employees. Much more information, however, is available regarding the organizers at all levels of Narpit.

17. VanRaaphorst, *Union Maids Not Wanted*, 187–190.

18. GARF, f. 6861, op. 1, d. 99, ll. 1, 21–2, 29–31, 42–3, 45, 99, 104, 126–128 (selected articles from *Moskovskie Izvestiia*, *Vpered*, *Sotsial-Demokrat*, *Trud*).

19. Lisa Granik, "The Trials of the *Proletarka*: Sexual Harassment Claims in the 1920s," in *Reforming Justice in Russia, 1864–1996: Power, Culture, and the Limits of Legal Order*, ed. Peter H. Solomon, Jr. (Armonk, N.Y.: M. E. Sharpe, 1997).

20. Domestics were particularly insistent about the use of "polite address" by their employers. This echoes demands made by domestics in the prerevolutionary period, along with workers in other areas of the economy. Reginald E. Zelnik, "Russian Bebels," *Russian Review* 35 (July 1976): 265, 272–277; Victoria E. Bonnell, *Roots of Rebellion: Workers' Politics and Organizations in St. Petersburg and Moscow, 1900–1914* (Berkeley: University of California Press, 1983), 43–72, 90, 102, 170–171, 183–184, 191, 264, 449, 452; and Mark D. Steinberg, *Moral Communities: The Culture of Class Relations in the Russian Printing Industry, 1867–1907* (Berkeley: University of California Press, 1992), 235–236, 242–245.

21. Tsentral'nyi gosudarstvennyi arkhiv g. Sankt-Peterburga (TsGA SPb), f. 6276, op. 3, d. 74, l. 29 (Communiqué from Tsentral'noe Biuro Professional'nyi soiuz domashnikh sluzhashchikh to petrogradskii sovet professional'nykh soiuzov—17 June 1918). This particular communiqué dealt specifically with the high incidence of cholera among domestics who were forced to live in basement living quarters.

22. GARF, f. 6861, op. 1, d. 99, l. 1 ("K domashnei prisluge," *Moskovskie Izvestiia sov. rab. dep.* 6 [8 March 1917]: 1).

23. Ibid., l. 45 ("Professional'noe dvizhenie soiuz domashnei prislugi," *Vpered* 53 [10 May 1917], 5).

24. Numerous domestics reported that as long as they were in the home, their employers wanted them to be available to work. Even on their days off it was expected that the domestic would work until at least 2:00 P.M. to ensure that both breakfast and

lunch were made. GARF, f. 6861, op. 1, d. 99, l. 127 ("Soiuz domashnei prislugi," *Vpered* 235 [December 17, 1917]: 3); TsGA SPb, f. 6276, op. 43, d. 44, l. 16 (*Protokol No. 14—Zasedaniia chlenov Pravleniia Petrogubotdela Soiuza Rabochikh Narpitaniia i Obshchezhitii—19 November 1923*) and GARF, f. 5452, op. 11. d. 85, l. 7 (*Vnutrenniaia svodka—Obzor uslovii truda domrabotnits, profobsluzhivanie i ikh uchastie v profrabote po soiuzu Narpita*).

25. GARF, f. 5452, op. 1, d. 2, l. 2 (*Arkhiv Kantseliarii Prezidiuma Leningradskogo Gubprofsoveta—Skhema organizatsii professional'nogo soiuza domashnei prislugi g. Petrograda—za 1917 g.*); GARF, f. 6861, op. 1, d. 99. l. 84 ("Rabochaia zhizn'—Professional'nye soiuzy," *Vlast' naroda* 67 [15 July 1917], 4]; TsGA SPb, f. 6276, op. 3, d. 74, l. 27 (*Polozhenie ob usloviiakh i normakh zarabotnoi platy domovykh sluzhashchikh goroda Petrograda i ego okrestnostei, 1918 g.*); "Tarifnyi otdel," *Domovyi rabochii* 1 (January–February 1920), and P. Sudakov, "O Pervom Vserossiiskom S"ezde Domovykh Rabochikh," *Domovyi rabochii* 1 (January–February 1920): 3.

26. GARF, f. 5554, op. 1, d. 2, l. 10 (*Protokol No. 7—Chastnogo soveshaniia delegatov 2-go Vserossiiskogo s"ezda Professional'nykh soiuzov domovykh sluzhashchikh —5 July 1919*).

27. In the event of a particularly difficult conflict, the matter was to be referred to the union's central conflict commission (*Tsentral'naia konfliktnaia komissiia soiuza*). GARF, f. 5554, op. 1, d. 1, l. 172 (*1-i Vserossiiskii s"ezd domovykh sluzhashchikh, 20 September 1918, v Moskve—Rukovodstvo po organizatsii komitetov soiuza domovykh sluzhashchikh*) and GARF, f. 5554, op. 1, d. 2, ll. 207–209 (*Protokol—Soveshaniia delegatov na Vseukrainskii s"ezd professional'nykh soiuzov ot soiuzov dvornikov, kur'erov i domashnikh sluzhashchikh, 26 April 1919, g. Khar'kov*).

28. "Ob ustave Vserossiiskogo professional'nogo soiuza domovykh rabochikh," *Domovyi rabochii* 1 (January–February 1920): 3.

29. "Tarifnyi otdel," *Domovyi rabochii* 1 (January–February 1920): 5–7 and "Tarifnye poiasa R.S.F.S.R. s 1-go sentiabria 1919 g.," *Domovyi rabochii* 1 (January–February 1920): 9–10. The salaries for the city of Moscow and neighborhoods in a thirty-verst radius were set at 100 percent of the wage scale. For the remaining regions of Russia, wages were set at a percentage established by the People's Commissariat of Labor and calculated in relation to the city of Moscow. For example, Petrograd was included in the first zone, where all union employees residing in the city were entitled to receive 150 percent of the salary stated on the wage scale. However, the Petrogradskaia province was in the second zone, with an entitlement factor of 120 percent. Those working in the Tul'skaia province were entitled to receive only 60 percent of the scale.

30. I would like to thank Elena Osokina for her assistance in helping me translate *Professional'nyi soiuz rabochikh narodnogo pitaniia i obshchezhitii.* It was particularly problematic as, even in Russian, the name of the union is far narrower than the list of the occupations it included.

31. "Plan sliianiia s soiuzom domovykh rabochikh," *Rabotnik narodnogo pitaniia* 1–4 (January–April 1920); 39, and GARF, f. 5452, op. 4, d. 13, ll. 1–2 (*Tsirkuliarno—Vsem otdelam, deleniiam i komitetam soiuzov domovykh rabochikh, narodnogo pitaniia i obshchezhitii i rabotnikam kommunal'nogo khoziaistva, a takzhe gubernskim sovetam i biuro profsoiuzov*).

32. Rather than distributing members among a total of five other unions, the majority of the Central Committee of the Professional Union of Home Employees

supported a plan to divide the union membership simply between two organizations—Narpit and the Union of Municipal Workers. This preference, however, was overruled by VTsSPS in accordance with its larger effort to organize all trade unions along productive lines. GARF, f. 5554, op. 1, d. 9, l. 5 (*Protokol No. 30—Zasedaniia TsK Vserossiiskogo profsoiuza domovykh rabochikh ot 21-go fevralia 1920 g.*) and GARF, f. 5554, op. 1, d. 10, ll. 1–3 (*Protokol 2-go Soveshaniia predstavitelei gubernskikh otdelov vseprofsoiuza domovykh rabochikh—11 aprelia 1920 g.*). For additional discussion of the Professional Union of Home Employees' reaction to its dissolution see Elizabeth Wood, "Gender and Politics in Soviet Russia: Working Women under the New Economic Policy, 1918–1928" (Ph.D. dissertation, Ann Arbor, University of Michigan, 1991), 596.

33. GARF, f. 5452, op. 3, d. 11, ll. 9–10 (*Zapiski* written by Vserossiiskii professional'nyi soiuz rabotnikov narodnogo pitaniia to Vserossiiskii tsentral'nyi sovet professional'nykh soiuzov, July 1919).

34. The workday for domestics was to remain an extremely contentious subject throughout this period. Officially it was eight hours with a maximum of two hours in allowable breaks. However, the reality was quite different, and by 1923 it was increasingly acknowledged to be an unenforceable measure. "Kto zabyt—O vykhodnom dne dlia domashnei prislugi," *Rabotnik narodnogo pitaniia* 8–12 (August–December 1923): 8, and GARF, f. 5452, op. 8, d. 8, ll. 4–6 (*Tezisy—TsK Vserossiiskogo profsoiuza rabochikh narodnogo pitaniia i obshchezhitii po rabote sredi rabotnits domashnego truda, 1924 g.*). On 16 February 1926 *Trud* published the Mossovet decree "O revoliutsionnykh prazdnikakh i osobykh dniakh otdykha 1926 goda."

35. On 25 September 1925 the Central Executive Committee (VTsIK), along with the Soviet of People's Commissars of the Soviet Union (Sovnarkom), laid out specific guidelines for those people employed in the domestic economy. See "O sotsial'nom strakhovanii lits, zaniatykh po naimu v domashnem khozaistve," *Sobr. Zak. SSSR, 1925 g.*, no. 66, p. 491; Erokhin, *O Pravakh domashnikh rabotnits*, Giz, 1926, 8–10; Z. A. Bogomazova, *Domashniaia rabotnitsa* (Moscow, 1928), 39; GARF, f. 5452, op. 10, d. 48, ll. 16–18 (*K proektu dekreta VTsIK ob usloviiakh truda dlia domrabotnits, 1926 g.*) and GARF, f. 5452, op. 11, d. 86, ll. 21–22 (*Postanovlenie tsentral'nogo ispolnitel'nogo komiteta sovetov i soveta narodnykh komissarov—16 August 1927*).

36. GARF, f. 5452, op. 10, d. 48, l. 24 (*Protokol—Soveshchaniia po okhrane truda Profsoiuza Rabochikh Narpita i Obshchezhitii—11 September 1926*).

37. The idea of "reforging" (*perekovka*) has been used as a metaphor for the process of reeducation through labor, specifically within the context of the GULAG; see Thomas Lahusen, *How Life Writes the Book: Real Socialism and Socialist Realism in Stalin's Russia* (Ithaca: Cornell University Press, 1997), 46. This term has come to represent the process by which an individual is transformed from one who is socially unacceptable, or undesirable, to one no longer tainted by a social stigma. Although normally applied to the reclamation of criminals and class aliens, this term could also be used to describe the process by which the domestic is transformed from the position of a bourgeois servant into a domestic worker.

38. It took a considerably longer period of time for domestics themselves to stop using the term servant as a means of self-identification. In some cases, though, particularly in the context of grievances—it is quite possible that a domestic's decision to refer to herself as a servant was designed intentionally to underscore her beleaguered

position. TsGA SPb, f. 4487, op. 8, d. 223, l. 46 (*V Gubkom Tsentral'nogo raiona Soiuza Narpit* from G. Makarova—Written from Orenburgskaia ulitsa d. 7, kv. 3—1925).

39. "Bakhmut—Prosnis' ot spiachki domashniaia rabotnitsa," *Rabotnik narodnogo pitaniia* 3 (March 1923): 19.

40. For example, in one cartoon, first published in the pages of *Krokodil* and then reprinted in *Rabotnik narodnogo pitaniia*, a women was depicted busy cooking cutlets with one hand, cleaning the floor with the other, and feeding a child from her breast; she was described as a domestic worker, with that term crossed out and the word servant appearing in brackets beside this. The caption below the cariacture reads: "A hundred part-time jobs and not one is paid" ("Sto sovmestitel'stv i ni odno ne oplachivaetsia"), *Rabotnik narodnogo pitaniia* 3 (March 1923): 19. Other cartoons include "Podpol'nye domashnie rabotnitsy," *Rabotnik narodnogo pitaniia* 12 (December 1925): 33; "Domashniaia rabotnitsa v 'zubakh' zubnogo vracha," *Rabotnik narodnogo pitaniia* 5 (May 1926): 5; and "Za takoe obrashchenie soiuz naidet vozmeshchenie," *Rabotnik narodnogo pitaniia* 12 (December 1926): 13. Various chastushki on the subject of domestic workers can be found in Bogomazova, *Domashniaia rabotnitsa*, 79. One example of a very short prescriptive play was "Prislugi—P'esa v 4 aktakh." It was written by a member of a local branch of Narpit in Khar'kov. GARF, f. 6861, op. 1, d. 17, ll. 1–9.

41. Some examples of prescriptive stories include N. Stepnoi, *Ternistyi put'*, Giz, 1925; *K novoi zhizni—sbornik*, VTsSPS, 1926; and T. Shchepkina-Kupernik, *Krasnye platochki*, Molodaia Gvardia, 1926.

42. Laundry and the tremendous burden it placed on domestic servants was a recurring image throughout the 1920s and a constant source of complaint.

43. The pages of Narpit's journal are full of testimonials by domestic workers such as Domrabotnitsa M. Mandrygina, who was orphaned at the age of three and then lived with her grandmother in the countryside until the age of ten. By sixteen she had moved to the city, where she worked without an employment contract for a merchant and his family. Eventually she began working for a party member who encouraged her to join Narpit and attend its meetings. Ultimately she ended up joining the Komsomol, and she began to help other young domestics, in addition to performing her regular duties for her employer. "Partiitsy pomogli domrabotnitse," *Rabotnik narodnogo pitaniia* 10 (October 1925): 11. Other such examples can be found in "Ot mraka k svetu," in the section "O chem pishut rabochie i rabotnits," *Rabotnik narodnogo pitaniia* 1 (January 1925): 13–17; "Shkola otkryla mne glaza," ibid. 7 (July 1925): 9; and "Soiuz, pomogi aktivnoi domrabotnitse," ibid. 9 (September 1925): 20.

44. TsGA SPb, f. 6276, op. 12, d. 74 (*Protokol No. 13—Zasedaniia Prezidiuma TsK Professional'nogo soiuza rabochikh narodnogo pitaniia i obshchezhitii SSSR—1927 g.*).

45. According to figures released at the Third Plenum of Narpit's Central Committee, held from 10–14 January in 1924, illiteracy was placed at 18.2 percent of its entire membership. However, it was believed that between 70 and 80 percent of domestics in Narpit were illiterate. The rate of literacy depended upon which type of domestic worker was surveyed—approximately 60 percent of urban domestics were illiterate, but approximately 90 percent of domestics coming straight from the countryside were considered to be illiterate. However, various figures were bandied about with no clear explanation as to how they were constructed. This large group of individuals who could not read was referred to as the "third front." TsGA SPb, f. 6276, op. 44, d. 33, ll. 9–10 (*Stenograficheskii otchet shestoi gubernskoi konferentsii vserossiiskogo profsoiuza*

rabotnikov narodnogo pitaniia i obshchezhitiia—utrennee zasedanie 10-go oktiabria 1924 g.).

46. TsGA SPb, f. 4487, op. 8, d. 5, l. 6 (*Plan rabot 13'go gruppkoma na 2 kvartal—aprel', mai, iiun' 1925 g.*) and TsGA SPb, f. 4487, op. 15, d. 512, l. 1 (*Instruktsiia perevybornoi kampanii delegatskogo instituta domrabotnits—1926 g.*).

47. *Peterburgskaia artel' muzhskoi domashnei prislugi: Ustav* (St. Petersburg, 1887).

48. Some examples include A. F. Popova, who worked as a domestic for a number of years and went on to become the chairwoman of Narpit's first group committee in Moscow along with a member of one of the union's central standing committees; or Ol'ga Bekker, a domestic worker since the age of twelve, who joined Narpit against the express wishes of her employer and eventually became an active member of the Komsomol and then the party. Probably the most prominent of all the domestic workers, however, was M. K. Borisova. Borisova worked as a domestic for some seventeen years and ultimately became a model to other domestics through her example. She eventually became not simply a member of the party but also a full member of the Central Committee of Narpit, where, ironically, she was to play a leading role in the restoration, by 1926, of traditional attitudes towards domestic servants. Bogomazova, *Domashniaia rabotnitsa*, 92–97.

49. GARF, f. 5554, op. 1, d. 1, l. 158 (*Zadachi professional'nykh soiuzov—Tezisy Tov. Bakhutova*).

50. "Domashniaia prisluga," *Rabotnik narodnogo pitaniia* 3–10 (March–October 1924): 26.

51. GARF, f. 5452, op. 11, d. 85, ll. 6–7 (*Vnutrenniaia svodka—Obzor uslovii truda domrabotnits, profobsluzhivanie i ikh uchastie v profrabote po soiuzu Narpita*), and Bogomazova, *Domashniaia rabotnitsa*, 60.

52. Domestics who lived out but who still ate all their meals at work were paid a minimum of 25 percent more in cash compensation. However, those domestics who lived out and provided for all of their own meals were paid up to 100 percent more in wages. GARF, f. 5452, op. 10, d. 48, ll. 1–4 (*Instruktsiia—Po regulirovaniiu uslovii truda domashnikh rabotnikov i rabotnits*).

53. "O domashnie rabotnitsy—O zhilishchnom nuzhde," *Rabotnik Narodnogo Pitaniia* 8 (August 1926): 14

54. Despite efforts to the contrary, a domestic's salary remained extremely low throughout the 1920s. This was due in no small part to the fact, alluded to earlier in this chapter, that there was a steady stream of young women migrating from the countryside who agreed to work for little or no money, merely room and board, just in the hope that they would ultimately be able to find something better for themselves. GARF, f. 5452, op. 11, d. 85, ll. 6–7 (*Vnutrenniaia svodka—Obzor uslovii truda domrabotnits, profobsluzhivanie i ikh uchastie v profrabote po soiuzu Narpita*).

55. Bogomazova, *Domashniaia rabotnitsa*, 60.

56. GARF, f. 5452, op. 10, d. 48, ll. 8–15 (*Sovet po bor'be s prostitutsiei—Tsentral'nyi sovet po bor'be s prostitutsiei—Otchet o deiatel'nosti*); Bogomazova, *Domashniaia rabotnitsa*, 28, and "Soiuz Narpita v Zashchitu Prislugi," *Delegatka* 7 (September 1923): 7.

57. "Voprosy soiuznoi raboty—Zhilishchnye usloviia domashnikh rabotnits," *Rabotnik narodnogo pitaniia* 5 (May 1925): 3, and "Rabochaia i soiuznaia zhizn'—Obshchezhitie dlia domashnikh rabotnits," *Rabotnik narodnogo pitaniia* 5 (May 1926): 17.

58. GARF, f. 5452, op. 12, d. 159, ll. 33–34 (*Obsledovanie truda i byta dom-rabotnits*).

59. TsGA SPb, f. 4487, op. 8, d. 223, l. 22 (*Protokol No. 15—Zasedaniia R.K.K. pri 2-m gruppkome soiuza Narpita*).

60. TsGA SPb, f. 4487, op. 8, d. 223, ll. 43–45 (*Protokol No. 7—Zasedaniia R.K.K. pri 2-m gruppkome soiuza Narpita*).

61. *Vsesoiuznaia perepis' naseleniia 1926 goda*, t. LIV (*Soiuz sovetskikh sotsialisti-cheskikh respublik—Zhilishchnye usloviia gorodskogo naseleniia*) (Moskva, 1932), 12–13.

62. Ibid.

63. TsGA SPb, f. 6276, op. 45, d. 42, ll. 138–139 (*Tekstovyi otchet tarifno-ekonomi-cheskogo otdela Leningradskogo gubotdela profsoiuza rabochikh narpitaniia i obshche-zhitii SSSR*) and "O bezrabotnitse," *Rabotnik narodnogo pitaniia* 1 (January 1928): 20.

64. The level of industrial development during most of the 1920s was simply not adequate to support an influx of women seeking employment outside of service. More-over, there was also considerable resentment and active resistance among other work-ing class groups, even within Narpit, towards those domestics who sought to better themselves by changing jobs. For example, at the insistence of public dining workers, Narpit introduced restrictive measures that would strip a domestic of her union mem-bership and associated benefits if she attempted to transfer from service to another occupation within the union.

65. "V-I Vserossiiskii S"ezd Soiuza. Otchet o S"ezde (22–26 ianvaria 1923 g.)," *Rabotnik narodnogo pitaniia* 2 (February 1923): 14–18, and "Nasha tarifnaia Rabota," *Rabotnik narodnogo pitaniia* 7 (July 1925): 22.

66. Bogomazova, *Domashniaia rabotnitsa*, 61–62, and TsGA SPb, f. 4487, op. 8, d. 223, ll. 49–51 (*Protokol No. 4 i zaiavlenie—Zasedaniia R.K.K. pri 2-m gruppkome Soiuza Narpita—22 May 1925*).

67. "Dobraia barynia," *Rabotnik narodnogo pitaniia* 8 (August 1925): 13.

68. "Podpol'nye domashnie rabotnitsy," *Rabotnik narodnogo pitaniia* 12 (Decem-ber 1925): 33; "Domashniaia rabotnitsa v 'zubakh' zubnogo vracha," *Rabotnik narod-nogo pitaniia* 5 (May 1926): 13; "Trebuetsia speshno uchitelia profgramota," *Rabotnik narodnogo pitaniia* 9 (September 1926): 13; "Na chernuiu dosku," *Rabotnik narodnogo pitaniia* 5 (May 1927): 21; and "Sudom—po nosu," *Rabotnik narodnogo pitaniia* 7 (July 1927): 3.

69. "Za takoe obrushchenie soiuz naidet vozmeshenie," *Rabotnik narodnogo pitaniia* 12 (December 1926): 15.

70. GARF, f. 5452, op. 10, d. 48, ll. 16–18 (*K proektu dekreta VtsIK ob usloviiakh truda dlia domrabotnits*).

71. TsGA SPb, f. 4487, op. 8, d. 223, l. 54 (*Zaiavlenie v 2 gruppkom*).

72. GARF, f. 5452, op. 8, d. 8, ll. 1–3 (*Tezisy—TsK Vserossiiskogo profsoiuza rabochikh narodnogo pitaniia i obshchezhitii po rabote sredi rabotnits domashnego truda k Vserossiisk. Soveshchaniiu o rabote sredi zhenshchin, 1924*); TsGA SPb, f. 6276, op. 44, d. 32, l. 3 (*V prezidium soiuza Narpitaniia—Plan raboty*); and TsGA SPb, f. 4487, op. 7, d. 45, l. 8 (Poster—"*Vozzvanie ko vsem rabotnitsam domashnego truda*"). Inter-estingly enough, there was a running battle throughout the 1920s between those in Narpit who wanted to make it mandatory for all employers to hire domestic workers through Labor Bureaus and those in Narkomtrud who repeatedly refused to do so despite the obvious potential benefits to domestic workers. Instead, Narkomtrud sought

to isolate domestics from more traditional worker groups by proposing the creation of special intermediary bureaus solely for domestic labor. The Narpit membership remained very skeptical of such a proposal. TsGA SPb, f. 6276, op. 44, d. 33, l. 23 (*Stenographicheskii otchet shestoi gubernskoi konferentsii vserossiiskogo profsoiuza rabotnikov narodnogo pitaniia i obshchezhitiia—utrennee zasedanie 10-go oktiabria 1924 g.*).

73. "Bytovye Kartinki—O baryniakh i prislugakh, soznatel'nykh chlenakh soiuza, smychke goroda s derevnei i tikhikh derevenskikh devushkakh," *Rabotnik narodnogo pitaniia* 8 (August 1925): 16.

74. "Vsem Gubotdelam nashego soiuza—Tsirkuliarnoe pis'mo," *Rabotnik narodnogo pitaniia* 4–5 (April–May 1923): 28–29, and "Viatka," *Rabotnik narodnogo pitaniia* 4–5 (April–May 1923): 19–20.

75. GARF, f. 5452, op. 8, d. 8, ll. 1–3 (*Tezisy—TsK Vserossiiskogo profsoiuza rabochikh narodnogo pitaniia i obshchezhitii po rabote sredi rabotnits domashnego truda k Vserossiisk. Soveshchaniiu o rabote sredi zhenshchin, 1924*).

76. Dozens of examples and references to this problem are available. For further information on this problem, see "Domashnie rabotnitsy, borites' za svoiu soznatel'nost'," *Rabotnik narodnogo pitaniia* 6 (June 1925): 21.

77. It can be argued that in some instances, they even went so far as to create an "arrhythmia of unpunctuated and irregular now-frenetic, now-idle work," which was unpredictable and deprived the domestic of the ability to control her own time and thus her own activities. Katherine Verdery, *What Was Socialism and What Comes Next?* (Princeton: Princeton University Press, 1996), 57. I would like to thank Ben Eklof for introducing me to the work of Katherine Verdery. She developed her ideas on the "seizure of time" in an attempt to demonstrate the way in which the Romanian government expropriated the time of its citizenry. Unlike E. P. Thompson's description of the linear use of time as a medium for producing profits during early capitalism, Verdery argues that in the case of Ceausescu's Romania time "stood still" and was purposefully wasted so as to ensure subjection. While Verdery developed this idea in an attempt to explain the actions of a socialist government, it is also applicable to the actions of private employers in Soviet Russia during the 1920s as reflected in some of the complaints of domestics. They seem to be deliberately deprived of time to participate in union events. See E. P. Thompson, "Time, Work Discipline, and Industrial Capitalism," *Past and Present* 38 (1967): 56–97.

78. It is not possible to cite all the cases of domestics whose employers either threatened to or did fire them simply for joining Narpit, or for attempting to conclude an employment contract, or for merely asking for a wage book. TsGA SPb, f. 4487, op. 74, d. 118, ll. 1–2 (*Protokol No. 1—Sobraniia domrabotnits 14-go gruppkoma—25 avgusta 1926 g.*); "Minsk," *Rabotnik narodnogo pitaniia* 1 (January 1923): 21–22; "Domashniaia Prisluga v Baku," *Rabotnik narodnogo pitaniia* 3–10 (March–October 1924): 26; and "Soiuz Pomogi!" *Rabotnik narodnogo pitaniia* 5 (May 1925): 22.

79. TsGA SPb, f. 4487, op. 8, d. 223, ll. 2 (*Zaiavlenie Aleksandry Kopskoi*).

80. Ibid., l. 3 (*Protokol—Zasedaniia R.K.K. pri 2-m gruppkome Soiuza Narpita—25 oktiabria 1925 g.*).

81. This law was titled "About the working conditions of hired workers, performing work in the home of the employer (domestic workers) in the personal service of the employer and his family." ("*Ob usloviiakh truda rabotnikov po naimu, vypolniaiu-*

shchikh na domu u nanimatelia [domashnie rabotniki] raboty po lichnomu obsluzhi-vaniiu nanimatelia i ego sem'i.")

82. "Domashniaia rabotnitsa i soiuz—Pis'mo nizovogo rabotnika," *Rabotnik narodnogo pitaniia* 1 (January 1927): 8, and GARF, f. 5452, op. 1, d. 85, l. 7 (*Vnutrenniaia svodka—Obzor uslovii truda domrabotnits, profobsluzhivanie i ikh uchastie v profrabote po soiuzu Narpita*).

83. GARF, f. 5452, op. 1, d. 86, ll. 3–4 (*V Prezidium VTsSPS—O dogovornoi rabote Soiuza Narpita sredi domashnikh rabotnits—Dokladnaia zapiska—1927 g.*)

84. Erokhin, *O pravakh domashnikh rabotnits,* 14–16.

85. The definition of a domestic's workday has always been difficult. Abuse of the eight-hour day was already commonplace; however, this provision opened the door to potentially exploitative employers. According to a 1927 study done of 497 domestic workers, it was found that 457, or 92 percent worked more than 8 hours per day. Of these, 81 percent worked approximately 12.5 hours per day and some 10 percent worked unlimited lengths—until all their work was done. This was made all the more possible by keeping domestics "on call" for an indefinite period during the day, though theoretically only working them for the maximum eight hours. GARF, f. 5452, op. 11, d. 85, l. 7. (*Vnutrenniaia svodka—Obzor uslovii truda domrabotnits, profobsluzhivanie i ikh uchastie v profrabote po soiuzu Narpita, 1927 g.*)

86. "Novyi zakon o domashnikh rabotnitsakh," *Rabotnik narodnogo pitaniia* 3 (March 1926): 7–8.

87. "Trud i sud—Domrabotnitsa imeet pravo na zhilploshchad'," *Rabotnik narodnogo pitaniia* 7 (July 1928): 21.

88. Bogomazova, *Domashnaiaia rabotnitsa,* 47.

89. "Trud i sud—del rabotnitsy t. Sopkovoi," *Rabotnik narodnogo pitaniia* 9 (August 1928): 19.

90. Roger Sanjek and Shellee Colen, eds., *At Work in Homes: Household Workers in World Perspective* (Washington, D.C.: American Anthropological Association, 1990); Kathleen M. Adams and Sara Dickey, eds., *Home and Hegemony: Domestic Service and Identity Politics in South and Southeast Asia* (Ann Arbor: University of Michigan Press, 2000); and Lesley Gill, *Precarious Dependencies: Gender, Class and Domestic Service in Bolivia* (New York: Columbia University Press, 1994).

ten
Shaping the "Future Race"

*Regulating the Daily Life of Children
in Early Soviet Russia*

Catriona Kelly

The Bolsheviks' determination to efface all traces of the past and to construct a radically different new society meant that, from the first, young people and children were pushed to the forefront of ideological discussion. "A revolution does not deserve its name if it does not take the greatest care possible of the children—the future race for whose benefit the revolution has been made," Lev Trotsky proclaimed in May 1923.[1] Two months later, in July 1923, Trotsky listed the "social education" (*vospitanie*) of children alongside "the emancipation of women from household slavery" and "the emancipation of marriage from all economic compulsion" as three major elements in "the complete transformation of morals" that would eventually take place under Soviet power.[2] Other revolutionary leaders in whose statements and work children were given a particular prominence include Feliks Dzerzhinskii, the founder not only of the Soviet secret police but also of the "children's commission," set up in 1921 in order to help combat the problem of child abandonment, which had reached epidemic proportions during the revolution and civil war.[3]

From the mid-1930s, the concern of the top-level administration with child welfare crystallized into a propaganda trope, expressed particularly in the icon of some member of the leadership (most often Stalin) in the company of an adoring junior.[4] At this point also, a reconceptualization of young people's role took place: they were now supposed to inherit a world made by their elders and to preserve it in the form in which it had reached them. In the words of a poem of 1950:

> My vyrastem skoro, okonchitsia detstvo,
> I iunost' svoiu my ukrasim trudom,
> My mir neob"iatnyi poluchim v nasledstvo,
> I delo otsov do kontsa dovedem.[5]

> [Fast we will grow, and our childhood will end,
> And we'll deck our young years with hard work.
> Our fathers will leave us the world when they're dead,
> To finish their job we won't shirk.]

But in the 1920s, politicians and other adults were supposed to take their lead from children, and Pioneers (members of the children's communist association, set up in 1922) could confidently write to prominent Bolsheviks, reminding them of their needs and of their claims to supremacy once they reached a mature age. The following letter was sent by a troop of Pioneers from Mozyr to "the ideological leader Com. Stalin" in February 1925:

> You stood proudly at your post and your still standing at it. We the young
> Pioneers are goin to replace the Komsomol and then go from their
> into the Party and in the future we'll replace you.[6]

At this stage too, "children's rights," in the sense of their entitlement to adequate living conditions and a reasonably full education,[7] were not just the concern of high-level politicians. A broadly based campaign to transform housing standards and domestic practices, "the drive to revolutionize daily life" (*bor'ba za novyi byt*), began gathering speed in 1924 and reached its height during the Cultural Revolution of 1928–1932. This included campaigns to transform "children's daily life" (*byt*), which were in turn reflected in propaganda aimed at a juvenile readership, in the agitational work of the Pioneer movement, and in reportage for adult audiences.

Children themselves were used as instruments of indoctrination, disseminating hygiene information and haranguing adults, particularly their parents, about the advantages of modern ways. At the First All-Russian Congress on Nursery Education in April–May 1919, a resolution was passed stating that "public nursery education which is imbued with the spirit of collectivism, and which brings into the child's life the inspirational principles of free, creative labor, is sure to be a powerful factor not only in the transformation of children, *but of the milieu in which they live.*"[8] Propaganda aimed at older children contained instructions about exactly what should be done in order to achieve this "transformation." For instance, a 1925 article for *Pionerskaia pravda* suggested that Pioneers should not only help their mothers with the housework, but also set up a "Pioneer corner" displaying hygiene propaganda in their home.[9] And a to-do list published at the beginning of 1931, this time in *Pioner* journal, specified that children should, among other things, help with the labor turnover problem by trying to argue their male relations into job loyalty, and carry out antireligious agitation:

> *What You Must Do*
>
> Agitate with your father, brothers, relations and friends and urge them to stick with their job to the end of the five-year plan.
>
> Fight for cultured daily life, for hygiene (air rooms, take care to keep things clean, etc.).
>
> Stamp out the drug of religion, expose priests' fairy tales for what they are.
>
> Explain the decisive significance of the third year of the Five-Year Plan to your relations.
>
> Make contracts of [socialist] competition with your father or with any of your brothers who is in employment.[10]

But in sum the "campaign to revolutionize daily life" was about control of children as much as it as was about training up juvenile activists. The ostensible materialism of Bolshevik ideology notwithstanding, this in fact privileged the intellectual sphere over the physical sphere: like other categories of persons who were assumed to be closely connected with the physical sphere (women,[11] members of "backward" social categories such as peasants and unskilled workers), children could be admitted to the Bolshevik heaven only if they were purified and inculcated in reasonable modes of thought and in ascetic, self-denying modes of behavior. The drive to propagandize hygiene to children and child-carers had practical roots—the eradication of infant mortality above all—but it was also a form of externally imposed discipline, a means of control over a population whose lack of ability to regulate its own physical needs was sensed as potentially troublesome.

Children of preschool age, in particular, were maintained under close surveillance to establish the extent to which their intellectual, moral, and ideological development measured up to the assumed norms for a given age. At nursery and primary schools in the Moscow area operating under the aegis of the First Experimental Station of Narkompros, an academic institute devoted to research on progressive teaching methods, teachers recorded a massive amount of information about their charges. Records about three- to six-year-old preschoolers that were kept in Velkino, Dobroe, and Krivskoe villages during 1928–1929 give some idea of the scope. Teachers noted such details as whether a child knew its age, name, and sex, whether it could find its way to the nursery from home and back, its grasp of the purpose of different village buildings (barns, stables, etc.) and of dimensions and colors, whether it knew the difference between the teaching and technical staff of the nursery, and its command of "the rules of social life and the habits of politeness" (*pravila obshchezhitiia i navyki vezhlivosti*). The questionnaires indicate that children's behavior was carefully regulated: at three, they were expected to be able to sit on a pot by themselves and to avoid wetting the bed, to queue up, at least for a short time, to wash their hands before meals, and to avoid eating off other children's plates or getting up before the meal was finished.[12]

Surveillance was not the only method of inculcating physical discipline. The decoration and furnishings of children's institutions themselves, streamlined, rational, and hygienic, were also crucial. "Everything should be simple, beautiful, comfortable [. . .] There should be nothing pretentious, fussily elegant, or luxurious on view at the kindergarten."[13] Crucial, too, was the strict regulation of the child's day. Manuals for nursery teachers tirelessly emphasized the importance of establishing a fixed daily routine (*rezhim*) and provided authoritative models in order to show how it should operate. In early manuals, such models were usually skeletal: a health inspection on arrival, five meals a day, alternation of play with more obviously didactic activities.[14] By the mid-1920s, however, the stipulations were considerably more precise and more exacting. A methodological brochure of 1926 laid out a day divided into strictly defined segments:

> 6:00–7:30 arrival
> 7:30–8:00 washing and teeth-cleaning
> 8:00–8:30 preparations for tea-drinking
> 9:00–10:00 tidying up
> 10:00–11:30 free play and excursions
> 11:30–12:00 bathing, sun baths
> 12:00–12:30 preparations for dinner
> 12:30–13:00 dinner
> 13:30–15:00 rest
> 15:00–17:00 free activities, excursions, outings
> 17:00–17:30 preparation for supper
> 17:30–18:00 supper
> 18:00–19:00 free activities, story-telling
> 19:00 departure for home.[15]

Advocates of "modern" child-care practices resolutely set their faces against the laissez-faire that they believed to obtain in traditional peasant and worker families: here, disapprovingly stated one writer in 1919, the attitude was, "Who cares what the child does provided it keeps quiet?" (*Chem by ditia ne teshilos', lish' by ne plakalo*).[16] The Soviet nursery school, on the other hand, was meant to offer upbringing of the most active kind: an introduction to rational modern living.

Early Soviet socialization of small children was in many respects a continuation of the Enlightenment tradition of rational upbringing initiated by John Locke, whose aim was to correct children's inclination to childish silliness as quickly as possible.[17] It had contemporary Western parallels too, in, for example, the baby-care books of Truby King, which also underlined that the imposition of a regime from the earliest days was essential.[18] But such ideas seemed more curious and pernicious according to the traditions of "free education" that had dominated some intelligentsia circles, particularly in St. Petersburg, in the 1910s. Here, the suspicion of over-regimented intellectual education set out in the writings of Lev Tolstoy was fused with emphasis on "learning through play" derived from the writings of Western pedagogues such as Froebel and Montessori. Indeed, one influential St. Petersburg activist for nursery education, Elizaveta Tikheeva, was to criticize Montessori's work as excessively rigid and stereotypical.[19] After the revolution, Tikheeva at first continued voicing her warm advocacy of noninterference by carers. "Neither drawing nor modeling should be taught in the kindergarten. Children draw and model according to the uncurbable needs of their own soul," Tikheeva insisted. The essential task of the nursery school was to "encourage a *joyful mood*" in its charges. Rather than a "regime" as such, Tikheeva advocated what she called "a program of analysis of the soul," involving regular visits to museums and exhibitions, and divided into broad areas of activity: 1. excursions and discussion of what had been seen; 2. modeling; 3 reading; 4. linguistic work with material covered in the reading; 5. sensory development; 6. puzzles, riddles, and proverbs; 7. games; 8. songs.[20]

Even in the early 1920s, however, numerous voices were raised against this enthusiastic and fluid interpretation of the purpose of education. A commentator at the 1921 First All-Russian Congress of Nursery Education condemned the expression "harmonious personality" as "formulaic" (*formal'noe*) and meaningless, and pointed towards Marx as the ultimate authority for nursery teachers (albeit alongside Pestalozzi, Froebel, and Montessori).[21] And by the mid-1920s, the trend had moved definitively toward regimentation and centralization, as manifested not only in the appearance of recommended, and later mandatory, curricula for schools, but also in the universal dissemination to institutions (orphanages, sanatoria, and Pioneer camps as well as educational establishments) of hygienic regimes. The most prescriptive regulation was evident in Pioneer camps, which in the early Soviet era were primarily understood as places for political consciousness-raising and dissemination of hygienic values, rather than as leisure facilities, as they came to be seen in the post-war and especially the post-Stalin era. A program of 1937, for example, laid out the Pioneers' daily routine thus:

> Reveille 7:00 A.M.
>> Exercises, tidying of beds, morning toilette 7:00–7:45 A.M.
>> Assembly (*lineika*), raising of the flag 7:45–8:00 A.M.
>> Breakfast 8:00–8:30 A.M.
>> Work in "links" (*zven'ia*), activity groups (*kruzhki*), organized occupations according to the children's own desires and interests, excursions, visits to the woods and gardens, fishing 8:30–11:00 A.M.
>> Preparation for and enactment of hygienic procedures (sun baths, air baths, bathing, cold rubs, showers) 11:00 a.m.–12.30 P.M.
>> Free time 12:30–1:00 P.M.
>> Lunch 1:00–1:30 P.M.

Rest 1:30–3:00 P.M.
Free time and preparations for tea 3:00–3:30 P.M.
Evening tea 3:30–4:00 P.M.
Free time 4:00–7:00 P.M.
Bathing 7:00–7:30 P.M.
Supper 7:30–8:00 P.M.
Sitting round the bonfire and [political] discussions, amateur performances by the children, film shows, etc. 8:00–9:00 P.M.
Assembly and lowering of the flag 9:00–9:15 P.M.
Preparations for bed (doing teeth, washing bodies and feet) 9:15–10:00 P.M.
Bed 10:00 P.M.[22]

At the bottom of the hierarchy, in terms of the weight given in them to physiological regimentation, came schools, where intellectual subjects were definitely supposed to take priority. Yet, despite the commitment to academic values that made itself felt from the mid-1930s, hygienic regulation had some currency in the program. *The Primary School*, a luxuriously presented compendium of information published in 1950, for example, included not only sections on how to teach the different subjects on the program, and on child psychology and moral education, but also on hygiene: the "Regime for Schoolchildren" appearing here included regular meals and sufficient quantities of sleep, alongside fresh air and light, as primary essentials of health and well-being.[23]

The imposition of the *rezhim* on children had, one may suppose, two effects. The first was, obviously, policing of the body and the regularization of physical functions. While Soviet guides were generally quite coy about areas such as the regimentation of defecation (for instance, methodological guides for nursery teachers were inexplicit about the age at which potty training was supposed to occur and how it was supposed to be carried out), the ordering of the model day strongly suggested that visiting the lavatory was meant to occur at certain well-ordered times—when washing and "hygienic procedures" were down on the timetable.[24] At this level, the character of the *rezhim* accorded with a broader tendency directed at monitoring and regulating children's physical life, such as was also evident in attempts to prevent masturbation through the assignation of night clothing that restricted movement, for example.[25]

The second function of the *rezhim*, though (which I will dwell on at greater length here, as I have already discussed the physical monitoring of children in another article),[26] was the inculcation in the young of a sense of exact time and of punctuality. Children were at the interface of the modernizing drive to spread "rational" and "modern" concepts of time usage; and primary school timetables closely resembled the "Gastev chart" and other schemas that were meant to regulate the working adult's every minute, from sleep to work tasks to time spent in the lavatory. Such schemas aimed to substitute for the elastic, cyclic comprehension of time supposedly characterizing agricultural societies a grasp of time as relentlessly linear and rigid, and thus to effect a transformation in attitudes that historians such as E. P. Thompson have seen as essential to the development of industrial society.[27] But if "capitalist" attitudes to time were endorsed in early Soviet society, the political and social context for the operation of such attitudes was slightly different. The efficient disposal of time on a personal level was seen less as a prerequisite of success in the workplace than as a contribution to the well-being of the collective more generally: the disciplined worker was the primary unit in the planned economy. The completion of a visit to the lavatory in two minutes and fifty seconds was a metonym for the efficient execution of all domestic and work tasks. Among children, too, the link between personal endeavor and collective success was brought out. From the first, the activities of the Pioneer movement stressed the importance not only of using time rationally, but also of forward planning: Pioneers were made subject to the same regime of composing "plans" (*plany pionerskoi raboty*) in advance, and "reviews" (*otchety*) in retrospect, that was used in the Komsomol and the party.[28] The school day, divided into equal periods by bells, or at the very least the teacher's watch, was an equally effective way of learning industrial time.

On the other hand, the performance of activities offset against the operation of the clock (or in the case of Pioneer work, against the calendar) was not the only way in which children were taught about time. They were also given a practical grounding in how to name and measure the phenomenon. Children at the nursery schools in rural areas of Moscow Province run by the First Experimental Station of Narkompros during the 1920s were tested on elementary temporal distinctions, such as whether they knew the difference between "yesterday" and "today" and were able to give their own age.[29] While the first test reinforced a distinction that is crucial in most, if not all, human cultures, the second required information that was not necessarily current in a society without written records, and where time reckoning was usually related to seasonal festivals (Easter, Shrove, Epiphany, St. John's Day) rather than by days and months.

The primary school syllabus also required reinforcement of time-related concepts. The 1932 program for the entry level (class one, or "group one" as it was then termed, the word "class" being regarded as politically incorrect) specified "the clarification of spatial and temporal concepts" as part of the work in mathematics. In their first term children learned the words "six-day week" (*shestidnevka*) and "seven-day week" (*semidnevka*) alongside basic geometrical figures; in the second term they were taught about half- and quarter-hours as well as about weights and measures; and in the third term they began learning how to tell the hours of the day, an exercise that continued in the second year, when the concept of minutes was introduced.[30] In mathematics problems also, calculation of "time spent" was a standard technique required, whether this was "time spent doing homework," or hours passed working on the school allotment, or then again, decorating the school for a festival (such as

1 May or 7 November).[31] At later stages of Soviet history, learning how to name and to budget time was also part of the primary school program. Though tuition was given slightly later and was not so extensive, this did not signify a decrease in the significance of the subject. Rather, it pointed to a rise in the number of children who could be expected to remain in school until the higher years, and to the fact that children were now expected to have a stronger sense of time divisions before they arrived in school (which, given the spread of the kindergarten network and of radio coverage, may have been a reasonable assumption).[32]

Learning how to read clocks, in cultures where clocks exist, is one of the most important rites of passage for small children, comparable with learning how to read letters or make calculations according to the conventional Western systems (metrical measurements, etc.). Yet historians of modern education have hitherto neglected this central civilizing function of the school. For example, Ben Eklof's excellent and wide-ranging study of rural schools in late Imperial Russia includes nothing on "time literacy" alongside its material on literacy and numeracy, nor is timekeeping mentioned in the section on education in Eugen Weber's very influential study *Peasants into Frenchmen*.[33] To be fair, there in fact does seem to have been less emphasis on time in the nineteenth-century school than in the twentieth: as late as 1900, an article on teaching children about number and dimension included nothing on time as such, though the use of a clock was recommended as a way of teaching children to count.[34] But given the importance of teaching about time in the school programs, the absence of the topic from standard histories of Soviet education can only be explained by the engrained custom of neglecting day-to-day life in the school in favor of top-down educational policy and of the ideological content of the syllabus.

Significant as the dissemination of new ideas about time undoubtedly was to the history of modernization in Russia, however, excess historical specificity about the role played by the school here (and, by extension, in other "capitalist" or "state capitalist" societies) would be out of place. As Keith Thomas has pointed out, schools were equally obsessed with timekeeping in preindustrial England: "A factory-like routine, in an age before the factory, was enforced by a heavy emphasis on punctuality and the punishment of latecomers. More than any other contemporary institution, the school was dominated by the hourglass, the clock and the bell."[35] The school, then, was something of an exceptional institution, and the strict regulation of the day owed as much to the traditions of the Benedictine monastery, with its ordered routine of prayers, work, and contemplation, with a minimal concession to bodily needs, as it did to the demand for punctual factory workers. Once the latter demand emerged, however, institutions that had been manifesting commitment to regimentation for hundreds of years were ready to rationalize their teaching in a new way.

If teaching about timekeeping in the schoolroom was nothing new, it is also important to bear in mind that reckoning of time intervals and time efficiency is not a matter of complete indifference in "preindustrial" societies generally, even if calculations are not made as rigidly or as minutely as they are in the schoolroom. Traditional Russian culture recognized a distinction between ritual time (capable of infinite extension or compression) and ordinary time.[36] And in the everyday of Russian villages, adults spent a good deal of effort on nagging children about the need not to waste time and on attempting to ensure they spent their days in useful activities, such as helping around the farm. Children themselves learned to absorb these attitudes and to feel contempt for those who spent time in wasteful ways.[37] The syllabi of Russian primary schools, with their terminology of minutes, hours, and days, represented no more than a codification of a conflict between adults' attempts to make children's lives purposive, and the desire of many younger children to resist this, that seems to be a transcultural universal. In his recent memoirs, the British writer Martin Amis has felicitously explained children's constant and repetitive questioning, of the kind that drives adults nearly insane, by reference to the different pace of life in each generation: "Children need a beat of time, to secure attention before the thought is framed."[38] Conversely, adults, it would seem, associate effective thought above all with economy of duration.

This age-old struggle between adults and children also made itself felt in Soviet children's reactions to indoctrination about temporal compartmentalization. There is abundant evidence from school compositions that modern perceptions of time in the sense of utopian fantasies about better worlds set far in the future had considerable appeal to Soviet children. In a school essay penned in the late 1920s, one child imagined the world fifty years later, after the Soviet Union had taken over the world. His particular utopia was a fifty-five-story school in London, where there were not only "wonderful playgrounds" but also a daily routine of a thoroughly orthodox kind, beginning with cold-water bathing and physical culture, after which "everyone goes instantly, calmly and in a friendly manner to the spotless dining-rooms" for a breakfast of fruit, sandwiches, and sweets.[39] In 1932, a drawing by a seven-and-a-half-year-old boy published in *Murzilka*, a magazine for seven- to ten-year-olds, showed a crystal-palace–like Palace of Culture under a bright sun, next to a wonky-looking, collapsing church. It was captioned "The palace of culture has been built for the workers and now the trap set by the priests will melt away. Signed TOLIA KOLOMOITSEV aged seven and a half, ROSTOV."[40] Similar representations from a later era can be found also in *LISTEN, EVERYONE!* a collection of short essays by 517 Pioneers from the mining town of Gorlovka, in the Donbass. The participants in the anthology expressed fizzing enthusiasm about Soviet achievements to date, about the children's own Pioneer activities, and about their hopes for the future. The coming of Communism would make everyone honest and intellectually developed; it would make it easier to fly to the moon; wishes for the future included hopes that the children's school would produce only good marks from now on and that the Pioneer druzhina would win the "Friend of the Seven-Year Plan" prize.[41]

But if children's and adults' fantasies marched in step when it came to imagining the future, this was partly because such fantasies lay beyond chronology. Where time in the sense of diurnal rhythm, or enactment of efficiency, was concerned, adult and child desires were more inclined to come into conflict. Early twentieth-century children's feeling for time could be described as "preindustrial" in the sense that hurry and deadlines were meaningless to them. Nabokov has captured, in characteristically inimitable style, the elastic endlessness of the child's contemplative world:

> As a small child, however, I was assigned a more modest arrangement [than the "sumptuous but gloomy" toilet he used later on], rather casually situated in a narrow recess between a wicker hamper and the door leading to the nursery bathroom. This door I liked to keep ajar; through it I drowsily looked at the shimmer of steam above the mahogany bath, at the fantastic flotilla of swans and skiffs, at myself with a harp in one of the boats, at a furry moth pinging against the reflector of the kerosene lamp, at the stained-glass window beyond, at its two halbardiers consisting of colored rectangles. Bending from my warm seat, I liked to press the middle of my brow, its ophryon to be precise, against the smooth comfortable edge of the door and then roll my head a little, so that the door would move to and fro while its edge remained all the time in soothing contact with my forehead. A dreamy rhythm would permeate my being. The recent "Step, step, step," would be taken up by a dripping faucet. And, fruitfully combining rhythmic pattern with rhythmic sound, I would unravel the labyrinthian frets on the linoleum, and find faces where a crack or shadow afforded a *point de repère* for the eye. I appeal to parents: never, never say, "Hurry up," to a child.[42]

The relationship with time that Nabokov sketches here has a defensive note: time seems particularly precious when someone *has* said "Hurry up" to a child. The emphasis on efficiency and achievement could work as much to reinforce indolence as to combat it. When some Moscow pupils were asked, in the early 1930s, to write an essay about how they would like to spend a free day, one of them responded: "I would like to sit by the window and be bored." There were stages when the relentless round of activities simply got to be too much.[43] An informant of mine, recalling her detestation of Pioneer camp in the late 1930s, elaborated similar views: "I hated any kind of order, that social stuff, that compulsion."[44]

Most poignantly, Gidon Kremer has recalled his rebellion, in the late 1950s, against the rigorous regime of practice imposed on him by his parents and his high-powered music school in Riga: "Getting put to bed was something I had to be forced into, just like practising was later. The submission to the rhythm of time seemed an act of cruelty."[45] The extracts from the diary Kremer kept as an eleven- and twelve-year-old show him chafing, almost unawares to himself, against the discipline of temporal rhythm: "How time flies! A month has gone by and I've got lots to write in this diary, but I don't get the chance" (16 November 1960).[46] "I keep quarrelling with Papa. He thinks I wasted (!) too much time on learning *Carmen*" (14 December 1960).[47] To underline all this, Kremer published in his autobiography a page from the formidable practice chart kept during his childhood. On days when he was ill or had a concert, Kremer could get away with an hour or so of practice; but otherwise, he put in at least four hours every day of the month, on top of his schoolwork.[48] Occasionally, conflict led to attempted rebellion: among the materials preserved in Kremer's archive is a pathetic letter in which the boy confesses to an assault on his enemy, the clock, in order to escape from being tied to its motions:

> Dear Papa,
> *Please forgive me.* But I didn't touch the clock *at the back* but two weeks ago and then again yesterday I *moved the hands.* I'm *sorry I promise you 1000 times I won't wind the clock I won't touch it again.* And *I'll never lie.* Sorry. And I'll be nice to mama so she'll always be my friend too but tomorrow I'd like to *stay at home please I've done my homework and I'd like to do some practice* [. . .] 11 February 1957[49]

Despite this evidence of the violence done to some children's feelings by inflexible regimes, however, it is important to avoid being too categorical about the effects of these in a broad sense. To begin with, dissatisfaction with temporal compartmentalization was not ubiquitous in children.[50] Secondly, dissatisfaction tended to occur among those who were marginal to the school system in any case, among whom it became one of a series of behavior traits signifying espousal of an annoying (in pedagogical terms) but finally containable subculture. In the words of Paul Willis: "The subversion of ordered and sequential time implicit in the rhythm of the counter-school culture, whilst potentially radical in its implications, and whilst avoiding the tyranny of the 'narrative which follows,' is delivered into inertia and domination by being profoundly naturalised."[51] Memoirs would suggest that this analysis of the 1970s British schoolroom fits the schoolroom of the early Soviet period too.[52]

Whichever way, adults readily subscribed to new ideas about saving time because time-saving was universally seen as a virtue already (at any rate, in secular Russian society). Quite logically, *rezhim* seems to have been one of the less controversial areas of the school program: there was general consensus that teaching about hygiene and time were good things. An area that was subject to more dispute, on the other hand, was the regulation of nonwork time: leisure, or to use the term more often employed in a child-centered context, play (*igra*). For supporters of "free education," the sacrosanct character of play—which was seen by them primarily as a mode of developing the child's personality and creative faculties—was self-evident.[53] Especially in the nursery school, "learning through play" was a central tenet in methodology;

syllabi for small children published in the 1910s and 1920s not only made room for "free play" on the program, but also integrated games into the educative process more broadly.[54] Throughout the Soviet period, a residuum of such attitudes was preserved in preschool education: long after "academic values" had become dominant in school education proper, Soviet kindergartens continued giving a central place to "free play" and "active games."[55] At the same time, powerful voices were also raised in favor of the regulation of play and of the imaginative faculties with which it was customarily linked. The "Letters on Method" published by the People's Commissariat of Enlightenment from 1926 onwards distinguished carefully between acceptable and unacceptable forms of play. It was vital that such manifestations of backwardness as "fights, drinking, superstition, rudeness, slovenliness, mendacity, laziness, cowardice, deceit, and social isolationism" should not be reflected in children's leisure activities, the brochure proclaimed. It continued:

> It is absolutely not a matter of indifference to us which features and processes of domestic, production-related and social existence are of relevance to children's play and what sort of relationship to these children manifest in the course of their games. Children may play at christenings with all the associated religious ceremonies, or at October baby ceremonies [*oktiabriny*]; they may act out drunkenness and fighting or visits to the club and the theatre; they may manifest a positive attitude to the Pioneers, the Red Army, to the worker movement, or may manifest indifference or even hostility. All of this is extremely important from the point of view of the kindergarten supervisor.[56]

Thus did the "class war" ideologies of the day leak into the definition of appropriate conditioning for the Soviet Union's future generations. In a similar vein, a lengthy blacklist of "cruel," "silly," and "old-fashioned" games circulated by the Komsomol Central Committee in 1936 commanded that Pioneers and Octobrists were not to play, or be allowed to play, "cruel" games such as "Lame Vixen" (a Russian equivalent of the game "Grandmother's Footsteps" where the Vixen got revenge for the taunts lavished on her by pouncing on any children who were slow to run away), or games involving boyars and princesses (described as "old-fashioned").[57]

Early Soviet unease about "socially harmful" types of play ran parallel to anxiety about other types of leisure activity for children, particularly reading (famously, the late 1920s saw an all-out attack, headed by Nadezhda Krupskaia, upon the *skazka*, or fairy tale, as a primary genre for children, less because Krupskaia disapproved of the genre per se—though she had doubts about providing children with material of a fantastical kind—than because of her belief that the main literary practitioner of the fairy tale, Kornei Chukovskii, used it as a vehicle for views that were subversive in class terms).[58] Inevitably, the classification of play and games into "acceptable" and "unacceptable" also leaked over into classification of toys along the same lines. An article of

1926 by N. Bartram, for example, lambasted as frivolous and superficial French and Western toys (with the honorable exception of Meccano, a British construction game consisting of small brackets and gantries to be screwed together into the simulacra of cranes, oil rigs, etc.). Bartram emphasized the penchant of Russian peasant producers for political objects (such as a 1905 model tsar squatting on three policeman), and spoke with approval of simple wooden toys that could be used to make a variety of different scenes suitable for collective play, such as zoos, markets, villages, and cities.[59] The official Toy Museum, founded in 1918 as a department of Narkompros, was organized along similar lines, combining displays of outmoded "bourgeois" items with incentive displays of ideologically sound and educational items, such as bricks, models on various agitational subjects, and (once again), Meccano.[60]

As argued earlier, Soviet attitudes to the disciplining of children's bodies and perceptions of time were, in international context, broadly orthodox. The rational instrumentalism with which dominant voices spoke about play and leisure, on the other hand, was, in broader context, rather more unusual. Certainly, there had been doubts raised about the *skazka*, and "make-believe" more generally, well before Krupskaia and her colleagues attacked the genre. Catherine II, in her didactic writings of the 1780s, had voiced doubts about the efficacy of immersing children in folklore.[61] Valerii Briusov, brought up a century later, recollected that his mother—typically for a Russian radical—would not let him read fairy tales, *chertovshchina* (i.e., stories about demons, devils, and other spirits), or even, for that matter, specialized children's literature.[62]

Equally, educational toys were not an invention of the Soviet period, any more than regimented days were. Even middle-of-the-road child-care books published in the late nineteenth and early twentieth centuries mentioned them. A "home encyclopedia" published in the early 1900s, for instance, emphasized that the function of toys was primarily educative (toys aided the development of the perceptions), before going on to recommend, in the first instance, toys that would have a direct impact on the child's relationship with the real world and, particularly, knowledge of modern life. Among the items recommended were miniature gramophones, telephones, and phonographs. Dolls were said to be good because of their usefulness in imitative games. Model farms and factories could be purchased so that play with dolls became a way of learning about modern life, or the child could be given dolls outfitted as different types of professionals (milkmaid, fireman, sweep, sailor, maid, etc.), or as members of different nationalities (e.g., a Kalmyk woman, a Moldavian man), to provide a basis for sociological understanding.[63]

At the same time, many toys—including very popular ones—were not "educational" in this obvious sense. These included the small furry animals that were customarily given to children, such as the teddy bear (*mishka*)— which, as in the West, was a thoroughly unnaturalistic, cute object that resembled its real-life model very little. While childhood lasted, children should be childish, it was felt. Special toys, like special children's books, were regarded as essential. Where toys figure at all in recollections of the early Soviet era, it is usually traditional varieties, such as were supplied by the private vendors operating under NEP, rather than modern, educational items, that are mentioned. Lidiia Libedinskaia (b. 1921), for instance, remembered being presented in 1928 with a red flannel bear that she had coveted, and eventually with a dress and shoes for the toy ursine. She also remembered the sobering cost of the items: one ruble, or five per cent of her grandmother's pension, for the shoes (with the bear, the cost was less important than the fact that the only place where such a toy could be got was the special outlet for employees of the secret police).[64]

As the presence of "bourgeois" toys in "distribution centers" for the "soldiers of the revolution," the secret police, indicates, attempts to censor toy ownership stopped at the publication of disapproving articles. Dolls and bears might be condemned, but no attempt was made to force them out of circulation. And the half-hearted nature of attempts to regulate children's play in private (as opposed to activities on the street, which remained a focus of official concern up to the end of Soviet power)[65] was confirmed by the reversal of official policy towards appropriate items that came about in the mid-1930s. Concern with *rezhim* and with physical regulation endured till the end of Soviet power, but from late 1935 onwards, at least lip-service was paid to the importance of providing Soviet children with attractive toys, not necessarily (although this point was never made directly) of an educational kind. In 1936, *Pravda* exploded into a positive plethora of articles criticizing the poor quality of objects that were available, and the unimaginative choice of what to produce on the part of Soviet factories. The youngest children were fairly well served, but there was much less for older ones, and objects were often of poor quality. Smudgy and ungainly wooden figures passed for dolls, shaggy and savage-looking hairy lumps for toy animals; it was impossible to buy dolls' tea sets and other miniature furniture, and "a real teddy bear is becoming a deficit creature." There were no model metro trains or even model cars, even if it was now possible to buy a fairly adequate toy telephone. The Narkompros authorities spent more time engaging in idiotic efforts to censor perfectly innocent items than they did in encouraging factories to produce things that children might actually enjoy playing with. And there was still not a sniff of the "excellent Meccano."[66]

The last reference indicates that some obeisance to educational objectives was still made. Equally, in an uncompleted article about toys and children's books begun just before his death in June 1936, Maxim Gorky (a trusty barometer of government priorities) concentrated on objects of a strongly didactic kind (even the tinies were to have games such as a geography-quiz globe and a model block of flats).[67] Yet more striking in the newspaper coverage, broadly speaking, was the prevalence of items whose educational function was hard to grasp or even nonexistent. A return to the principle of "the pleasure of active fantasy" (in the words of Giovanni Colozza, quoted earlier) had come about.

Certainly, in practice most Soviet children of the late 1930s were lucky if they got even the lumpish bears about which *Pravda* complained. Shortages were endemic (for instance, teddy bears were made of a knitted fabric called *trikotin*, which was itself critically scarce).[68] Toys were often prohibitively expensive—for instance, a child's bicycle cost, in 1936, one-third of a Stakhanovite's 980-ruble bonus, which in turn was only slightly lower than the average monthly wage for industrial workers.[69] According to memoirs, many children, including those from the middle classes, were expected to make do with at most one or two purpose-manufactured toys—a few miniature cars, a horse on rockers, alphabet blocks.[70] In villages, home manufacture continued to be the sole method by which toys were acquired in most families: the only bicycle in Pavel Starzhinskii's village was cobbled together from odds and ends, including the remains of an old spinning wheel.[71] A fair number of individuals from less privileged circles who grew up at this time are certain that they never had any toys at all.[72] More opulent collections were the prerogative of children from the Soviet elite—such as the daughter of a successful actress whose "family" included a doll with eyes that actually shut, a celluloid baby doll, two teddy bears, a model tiger and a miniature bunny rabbit.[73]

The point was, though, that the celebration of quality toys, mendacious as it was in practical terms, was genuine in terms of its ideological resonance. It was a contribution to the reemergence of an important cliché of the late nineteenth and early twentieth centuries, the idea of the "children's world." An idyll originally of impeccably bourgeois provenance had been restored, but this time in different form: it was now all children, irrespective of their social background, who were supposed to inhabit a world of wonder and magic. The Pioneer Palace became an important instrument of this state-sponsored fantasy. Decorated with *skazka* themes to emphasize their status as special worlds of wonder and magic, such palaces invariably contained games rooms (*igroteki*) stocked with traditional "bourgeois" toys, but they were open to all. Propaganda obliquely recognized that working-class children might not have access to toys elsewhere, but put the main emphasis on the transforming, *skazka*-like world of the palace. An article about the Khar'kov Pioneer Palace published in 1936, soon after the palace first opened, contained a vignette of a boy who had not at first wanted to surrender the beautiful ball he had been given to play with. On successive visits, he had gradually been brought to realize that there were plenty of other ones, and that it was possible to play with other children without losing out. "The sense of plenty in the environment surrounding him overcame the 'greed out of deprivation' that he had felt before."[74] However, for the most part the word "deprivation," even in inverted commas, was avoided altogether; and the effect of the story just quoted was less to give the lie to the myth that Pioneer palaces represented some kind of paradise available to Soviet children than to insist that they did, that here all wants would be satisfied, and all social ills healed, and that the child would then be sent back, remade, into the world from which it had come.

From the mid-1930s, then, childhood had a paradoxical status in Soviet ideology. It was a phase to be lived through with constant mindfulness of its outer boundary, the progression into adulthood, yet at the same time it was seen as an imaginative space beyond time. It was at the center of politics, yet also beyond politics. In the adult world, the "hygiene and efficiency" ethos was beginning to be challenged by an ethos of "luxury for all"; the youngest denizens of the Soviet realm were still supposed to submit themselves to the physical and temporal discipline of the *rezhim*, but also to enter freely into a world of wonder and magic where real time counted for nothing.

At the level of lived reality, *rezhim* often impacted less than campaigners for *novyi byt* would have held desirable. A dire picture of day-to-day existence in a Soviet orphanage was sketched in 1928 by a contributor to a specialist journal for children's home workers:

> A cracked bell sounds. A tousled inmate leaps from his lopsided bed. His head aches from the stale air and he has cramp in the side because the bed is so uncomfortable. He's half asleep: last night he was kept awake late by the squeaking and slamming of the door, he couldn't drop off.
>
> He drags his fingers through his hair to tidy it, hauls his trousers out from under his pillow, pulls them on and struggles to the wash-basin. Where there's a queue. Foul language hangs in the air. What's this? The boy on duty hasn't brought any water—the bucket was swiped to use in the kitchen, and it got left there, and then someone took it to the canteen to use for doling out milk.
>
> About ten minutes later, however, the water appears. It's cold and damp in the corridor . . . Hurriedly rinsing out his nose and splashing his hands, the inmate gets his towel out from inside his pillow case, which he uses to store all kinds of interesting things, and gives himself a rub, which makes the towel even dirtier than it was to start with. He wants to style his hair, but he's got nothing to do it with. He did have a comb and a tooth-brush, but he lost the toothbrush when he went down to the river for a wash once, and the tooth-powder got squashed under the mattress, and the comb lost its teeth after he tried cleaning it with a nail. And in any case there's no time for any more—he has to go and find a broom so he can sweep out the dormitory, and clean the toilet.

The story was narrated as an illustration of how better supplies were no good on their own: what was needed was a change in attitudes. In other words, *rezhim* was supposed to be self-sufficient.[75] But in fact, the evidence presented cuts the other way too: without adequate equipment and services (comfortable beds and clean laundry) regimentation could scarcely be effective.

Not all orphanages were nightmarish establishments of the kind just depicted. The Second World War changed attitudes (albeit temporarily) to institutional care: it was universally understood that war orphans were deserving innocents uncompromised by contact with the street of the sort that had been endured by the stereotypical *besprizornyi* (waif) in the 1920s and 1930s. According to the memories of a former inmate of Children's Home no. 58 in Leningrad, staff displayed exemplary dedication; facilities were good (clean dormitories, plentiful food), and *rezhim* was suspended only in the most benevolent sense—children could ask for more food if they wanted it, and time was allowed for relaxed conversation in the canteen after the evening meal had been served, rather than the children being pressed to get on with something more worthwhile. Here, *rezhim* applied more than anything else to ensuring that a full program of activities was available all the time: board games, and in summer, exercises and sport, organized in the home itself, and visits to hobby circles in the local House of Pioneers.[76] In other words, whether neglected or treated flexibly, *rezhim* played only a limited role even in the orphanage, which was supposed to be the spearhead of collective, rational child care in the new Soviet Union.

Yet a drawing a hard-and-fast distinction between "theory" and "practice" would be oversimplifying. For one thing, the standard childhood *rezhim* itself allowed far more time to unshaped leisure (a full three hours free time in the 1937 Pioneer camp schedule, for example) than comparable behavior codes for adults. For another, oral history work indicates that *rezhim*, and the associated concept of discipline, impacted a good deal on the consciousness of those who grew up in the early Soviet period. Informants in an oral history study carried out in St. Petersburg during late 2002 and early 2003 were eager to assure the interviewer that their childhood had been quite different from that experienced "these days" (in the early twenty-first century): pupils at schools had been well disciplined, and children obedient. At the same time, the concrete details that they offered (for example, pupils who had arranged a boycott of a new math teacher to try to get her popular predecessor reinstated, or who had systematically disrupted classes in, of all subjects, civil defense) pointed in rather a different direction.[77] In other words, the two views of childhood (as disciplined and also as carefree) became entangled even among children themselves, who believed they were internalizing "discipline" even as they disrupted its rules. By extension, the painful process of learning "discipline" did not, one may suppose, become any easier if an alternative view of childhood identity suggested that escape to a different type of reality was both possible and permissible. What is astonishing in the context of Stalinist Russia is less that children rebelled during boring classes on civil defense than the fact that little decisive action was taken even when they deserted the school on the day that examinations in the subject were to take place: the school authorities called in their parents but settled for a fudge, according to which the pupils received a course credit even though they had not in the end taken a test.[78]

Adults, then, were not certain how to treat children, or at any rate younger ones (entry into the Komsomol marked a transition to a phase when a greater sense of responsibility was expected). On the one hand, it was argued that *rezhim* should be imposed as early as possible; on the other, it was tacitly assumed, if not necessarily openly argued, that children thought and behaved differently. It should be emphasized that some thoughtful adults were keenly aware of the tension between these two different points of view, a tension which could still be recorded in public during the 1920s. Particularly interesting in this regard are two early stories by Mikhail Zoshchenko. In "Happy Childhood" (1925), an adult encounters a schoolboy and hears with astonishment that the child is even more overburdened with political meetings and bureaucratic duties than he is himself; in "The Thief" (1922), a burglar becomes so preoccupied by the sight of children and their nurse playing with windup toys outside their dacha that he nearly betrays himself. Later, when he actually manages to enter the dacha, the man is mesmerized once more by a windup wolf and, when he eventually tears himself away, leaves his jacket behind him.[79]

A primary, and disturbing, motif in both these stories is adults' desire for children, which figures just as prominently as does adults' desire to be children. In "The Thief," the protagonist not only disappears into a timeless space, a sphere of fairy tale and myth of the kind that was often named with the cliché phrase "children's world,"[80] but loses part of his clothing, rendering himself farcically and dangerously exposed in the proximity of real children. In this grotesque reworking of "Red Riding Hood," it is not the wolf but the exploratory consciousness of the would-be child that presents a danger.

This quasi-erotic motif, subdued in "The Thief," comes closer to the surface in "Happy Childhood." Here, the encounter between narrator and small boy takes place in the Tavricheskii Gardens in St. Petersburg. It is initiated when the adult narrator, overcome by sentiment, invites the small boy to sit on his knee. The boy's reply, "*Nekogda, govorit, mne na tvoikh kolenkakh triastis'. Der'ma tozhe tvoi kolenki. Idiet takoi*" (I've got no time to screw round on your lap. Your lap is crap. You're just stupid, you are), is shocking in its "unchildish" harshness and crudity. It is more shocking when its broader context is explored. The Tavricheskii Garden had been well established for decades as the number one homosexual cruising spot in St. Petersburg, so that the boy's refusal to sit on anyone's knee was probably prudent, rather than gratuitously offensive (while the verb *triastis'* appears in the full force of its double meaning: "to mess around," but also "to screw" in the sexual sense). The fact that the adult narrator's lamentation over lost childhood happens in this particular spot gives it an ironic flavor: is this solitary man's desire to find a juvenile boon companion pathological, rather than (as he thinks) an expression of adherence to normal values?

Zoshchenko, then, was more self-conscious than most of his contemporaries in recognizing that adults who tried to police childhood innocence might also be giving voice to their own illicit desires.[81] He also foregrounded a central problem for the idyll of the "children's world": the issue of how to deal with burgeoning sexuality. Once children were beyond the stage where they could be laced into restrictive nightgowns and induced not to play with themselves, their physicality became seriously threatening. On the whole, preservation of the ideal of children's innocence accordingly required that adolescence be presented as a time of difficulty and conflict. In "Happy Childhood," the boy's behavior is so alienating that pedophile desire is baffled, but sympathy of a broader kind is also made impossible.

But these are underground motifs in the two stories, which at a more superficial level address the conflict between play and regimentation, the autonomy of action and *rezhim*. The adults in these tales are more childish than the children, who appear as mature and self-possessed; the children are empowered, the adults disenfranchised, but the children have also lost touch with something essentially human. Other early Soviet intellectuals who had an ambivalent (or hostile) relationship to Bolshevism, including Vera Inber and Evgeny Zamiatin, were to produce very similar quasi-documentary representations of encounters with emboldened and politicized children.[82] By extension, the effect of regimentation during childhood was often to reinforce resistance to regimentation in adulthood, rather than to disseminate respect for cleanliness, punctuality, and rigorous thought. Though a swathe of childhood memoirs emphasizing that prerevolutionary socialization had stunted development was published in the 1920s,[83] by the 1930s, overworked and harassed Soviet adults themselves came to value the view of childhood as wondrous, stable, and timeless; for them, it was an escape from the increasing professional and bureaucratic pressures of the day. In his private diary, Vladimir Stavskii, writer and functionary in the Writers' Union, was moved by an encounter with the natural world to retreat to his lost past: "And the moon the snow and the smoke the pale blue glow of the stars aroused an overwhelming feeling in me, my distant, irretrievable and eternally beloved childhood."[84]

Once happy childhood had become associated with the beneficence of the state, or, to be more specific, the leader himself (as in the slogan "Thank You Stalin for a Happy Childhood," which began to be systematically disseminated in 1936),[85] admission that one's childhood had been less than joyful (even if it had been experienced in the prerevolutionary past) became more problematic. The troubled history of Mikhail Zoshchenko's memoir *Before Sunrise*, which relentlessly pursues trauma earlier and earlier in the writer's existence, eventually laying bare a psychic wound inflicted in infancy, is partly related to the sensitivity of childhood, in the broadest sense, as a subject.

The post-Stalinist era saw oppositionist intellectuals becoming more ambivalent about childhood, with the authoritarian state increasingly figured as a controlling parent keeping its citizens in a perpetual state of infantile dependence. In the words of a 1987 sketch by the satirical comedian Mikhail Zhvanetskii: "This isn't a country, it's a kindergarten. Radio and television announcers talk to us all as though we were feebleminded, or children."[86] It was not so much the liberation of children themselves as the liberation of adults that was now at stake: rather than the transformation of family relations (dreamed of by utopians in the 1960s), childlessness by choice was the preferred method of protest against biographical linearity.[87] Escape from parenthood signified translation to a zone beyond time, to the joy of perpetual childhood: a perception which, of course, maintained the established assumption that children had a peculiar, atemporal relationship with the world. The combination of insistence on the need for rigid "regimes" and the understanding that somehow the reality of childhood lay elsewhere provoked a kind of principled and self-conscious commitment to the infantile: a determination not to be regimented, not to be defined, at some level not to exist. The state's obsession with *vospitanie* (character education) was to prove in some respects less influential than the myth of universal entitlement to childhood happiness. And in turn this myth was one factor (alongside resentment of foreign influence) that made the "internationalization" of childhood after 1991 (and especially, the acceleration of maturation times that seemed to go with this) especially painful for Russian observers, turning the "corruption of Russian childhood" into a standard theme in nationalist discourse during the late 1990s.[88]

NOTES

This essay presents preliminary findings from a large-scale history of childhood, *Children's World: Growing Up in Russia, 1890–1991*, to be published by Yale University Press in 2006. Research for the book has been supported by the Leverhulme Trust under grant no. F/08376/A, "Childhood in Russia 1880–1991: A Cultural and Social History"; by the British Academy through Small Research Grants for travel; and by the Ilchester Fund and the Faculty of Modern and Medieval Languages, University of Oxford. The interviews with informants cited as Oxf/Lev SPb-02 PF 1 (A) etc. are part of the work sponsored by the Leverhulme. The questionnaire was designed by Catriona Kelly in collaboration with Professor Albert Baiburin and Ms. Aleksandra Piir of the European University of St. Petersburg; the interviews were conducted by Aleksandra Piir beginning in November 2002. (The oral history project, running between late 2002 and late 2006, is to involve in total about 150 informants in St. Petersburg, Moscow, and a number of provincial cities, including Taganrog and Khabarovsk, and selected rural sites; see the project website, http://www.mod-langs.ox.ac.uk/russian/childhood. Interviews with the prefix "CKQ Ox-03 PF 1 (A)" etc. were carried out by Catriona Kelly using the same questionnaire with émigré informants domiciled in the UK in January–March 2003. Gratitude is expressed to the funding bodies concerned, and to Albert Baiburin and Aleksandra Piir, for their help.

1. Lev Trotsky, "The Struggle for Cultured Speech" (1923), in *Problems of Everyday Life*, trans. anon. (New York: Pathfinder, 1973), 53. Lenin is credited with similar views in the newspaper *Vechernie izvestiia Moskovskogo Soveta*'s record of a speech on Red Square, 1 May 1919: see *Sochineniia*, 4th ed., vol. 29 (Moscow: OGIZ, 1950), 303.

2. Trotsky, "Habit and Custom," in *Problems*, 29.

3. *Dekrety sovetskoi vlasti*, vol. 12, no. 102; see also Alan Ball, *And Now My Soul Is Hardened: Abandoned Children in Soviet Russia, 1918–1930* (Berkeley: University of California Press, 1994), 91. The literature on child homelessness is large. Sources in Western languages include, besides Ball's book, Jennie A. Stevens, "Children of the Revolution: Soviet Russia's Homeless Children (*Besprizorniki*) in the 1920s," *Russian History* 9:2–3 (1982), and Dorena Caroli, "L'assistance sociale à la déliquance juvénile dans la Russie soviétique des années 20," *Cahiers du monde russe* 40:3 (1999); material

is also to be found in Wendy Z. Goldman, *Women, the State and Revolution: Soviet Family Policy and Social Life, 1917–1936* (Cambridge and New York: Cambridge University Press, 1993).

4. See my articles, "Uncle Stalin and Grandpa Lenin: Leader Cults for Little Children," in *The Leader Cult in Communist Dictatorships*, ed. B. Apor, J. C. Behrends, P. Jones, and E. A. Rees (Basingstoke: Palgrave, 2004) 102–122; "Riding the Magic Carpet: Children and the Stalin Cult," *Slavic and East European Journal* 49:2 (2005).

5. Georgi Rublev, "Deti mira—za mir," *Pioner* 10 (1950): 14.

6. Tsentr Khraneniia dokumentov molodezhnykh organizatsii (henceforth TsKhDMO) f. 1 op. 23 d. 458 l. 15. My English spelling reproduces the haphazard Russian spelling in the original. In the context of the evolution of the Stalin cult, interesting as well is the abbreviation of the word "Comrade," which during the full flowering of the cult (1929–1953) was almost never allowed.

7. As defined also in the League of Nations Declaration of the Rights of the Child (1924), which specified that a child should be provided with the means requisite for its normal development, both material and spiritual, and provided with sufficient food, help appropriate to any specific needs such as illness, the means of earning a living, and protection against exploitation. For the text of this document, see Geraldine von Bueren, ed., *International Documents on Children* (The Hague: Kluwer Law International, 1998).

8. See *Pervyi Vserossiiskii S"ezd po doshkol'nomu vospitaniiu: Doklady, protokoly, rezoliutsii* (Moscow: Gosizdat, 1921), 195. Italics added.

9. "Kak rabotat' s sem'ei," *Pionerskaia pravda* (henceforth PP) 6 (1925): 1.

10. Frontispiece to *Pioner* 1 (1931).

11. See, e.g., Elizabeth Wood, *The Baba and the Comrade: Gender and Politics in Revolutionary Russia* (Bloomington: Indiana University Press, 1997).

12. See Rossiiskaia Akademiia Obrazovaniia, Nauchnyi Arkhiv (henceforth RAO NA) f. 1 op. 1 d. 294, l. 14 recto and verso, l. 15 recto and verso, l. 16 recto and verso, l. 37 recto and verso, l. 38 recto and verso. My thanks to Vitalii Bezrogov for arranging access to these materials.

13. *Spravochnik po doshkol'nomu vospitaniiu* (Moscow: Literaturno-izdatel'skii otdel Narodnogo Komissariata po Prosveshcheniiu, 1919), 50.

14. *Spravochnik*, 59–64.

15. *Metodicheskie pis'ma po doshkol'nomu vospitaniiu* 1 (*O doshkol'noi rabote v derevne*) (Moscow and Leningrad: Gosizdat, 1926), 19.

16. *Spravochnik*, 82.

17. Cf. the approving citation of a passage from Locke's *Some Thoughts on Education*, section 38, in a pedagogical manual of the 1940s: "If they [children] were never suffered to obtain their desire by the Impatience they expressed for it, they would no more cry for other Things, than they do for the Moon." E. P. Esipov and N. K. Goncharov, *I Want to Be Like Stalin: From the Russian Text on Pedagogy*, ed. G. Counts (London: Victor Gollancz, 1948), 133. The book is an abridged English translation of B. P. Esipov and N. K. Goncharov, *Pedagogika*, 3rd ed. (Moscow: Gosudarstvennoe uchebno-pedagogicheskoe izdatel'stvo, 1946), which remained a standard textbook well into the 1960s.

18. See, e.g., Mary Truby King, *Mothercraft* (London: Simpkin, Marshall, 1934), 4. On Truby King's biography, see ibid., pp. 1–4.

19. E. I. Tikheeva, *Dom rebenka Montessori v Rime: ikh teoriia i praktika. Po lichnym vpechatleniiam* (Petrograd: tip. A. Ia. Ganzburga, 1915), 41.

20. M. Ia. Morozova and E. I. Tikheeva, *Doshkol'noe vospitanie i detskie sady* (Kazan': Gosizdat, 1920); italics original. On the early history of the Soviet nursery school, see particularly Lisa Kirschenbaum, *Small Comrades: Revolutionizing Childhood in Soviet Russia, 1917–1932* (London: RoutledgeFalmer, 2001).

21. *Pervyi Vserossiiskii s"ezd*, 16 (the speaker was Comrade Sazonov).

22. *Pionerskii lager': Spravochnik dlia vozhatykh i rabotnikov pionerskikh lagerei* (Moscow and Leningrad: Molodaia gvardiia, 1937), 58. The term *"besedy za kostrom"* was used for political discussions led by the *vozhatyi*: specialist literature included guidance on how to lead such discussions. See, e.g., the section "Rasskazy u kostra" in *Pionerskii lager'*, 251–256.

23. *Nachal'naia shkola: Nastol'naia kniga dlia uchitelia* (Moscow: Akademiia pedagogicheskikh nauk/Gosudarstvennoe uchebno-pedagogicheskoe izdanie, 1950), 209–211.

24. That said, a very approbatory article about the regime at Bedales School also expressed some surprise that children at the school did not seem to mind being restricted about when they could use the lavatory (see M. Shteingauz, "Bidel'skaia shkola," *Prosveshchenie na transporte* 3 [1926], 87), so perhaps Soviet teachers were less repressive about this particular area of "lower body" activity than their British counterparts.

25. See *Odezhda rebenka-doshkol'nika: instruktivnoe pis'mo* (Moscow and Leningrad: Gosizdat, 1929), 19, 22.

26. See "'Khochu stat' traktoristkoi!' Gender i detstvo v dovoennoi sovetskoi Rossii," *Sotsial'naia istoriia* (2003).

27. E. P. Thompson, *Customs in Common* (London: The Merlin Press, 1991), ch. 6.

28. See, e.g., "Organizatsiia sel'sko-khoziaistvennykh rabot derevenskikh pionerotriadov Moskovskoi organizatsii na leto 1927 goda," TsKhDMO f. 1 op. 23 d. 789, l. 4.

29. For the test, see RAO NA f. 1 op. 1 d. 294, "Doshkol'naia rabota 1-i Opytnoi Stantsii Narkomprosa. Rabota po obsledovaniiu navykov i mirovozreniia detei. Belkino, 1929—Dobroe, 1929—Krivskoe, 1928," e.g., l. 14: interestingly, this particular five-year-old girl did know her own age, but not the difference between "today" and "yesterday."

30. *Programmy nachal'noi shkoly—gorodskoi i sel'skoi* (Moscow: Narkompros/ Uchpedgiz, 1932), 9.

31. *Nachal'naia shkola*, 46.

32. See *Programmy nachal'noi shkoly* (Moscow: Uchpedgiz, 1945), 31–32, and *Programmy nachal'noi shkoly na 1957–1958 g.* (Moscow: Uchpedgiz, 1957), 78–79. In both cases, time was taught as part of the math syllabus for years 2 and 3 of the primary school.

33. See Ben Eklof, *Russian Peasant Schools: Officialdom, Village Culture, and Popular Pedagogy, 1864–1914* (Berkeley: University of California Press, 1986); and Eugen Weber, *Peasants into Frenchmen: The Modernization of Rural France 1870–1914* (London: Chatto and Windus, 1977), ch. 18.

34. P. A. Litvinskii, *Izuchenie chisla i mery malymi det'mi*, in P. V. Kapterev, ed., *Entsiklopediia semeinogo vospitaniia i obucheniia*, 3 vols. (St. Petersburg: "Roditel'skii kruzhok" pri Pedagogicheskom muzee Vysshego Uchebnogo Zavedeniia v Sankt Peterburge, 1898–1902), vol. 2, issue 26.

35. Keith Thomas, *Rule and Misrule in the Schools of Early Modern England* (The Stenton Lecture 1975, University of Reading, 1976), 6.

36. See A. K. Baiburin, *Ritual v traditsionnoi kul'ture: strukturno-semanticheskii obzor vostochnoslavianskikh obriadov* (St. Petersburg: Nauka, 1993), 175. Interesting observations on the offsetting of notions of linear and cyclic time in traditional society, based on evidence from accounts of *obmiranie*, or near-death experience, are made in Faith Wigzell, "Concepts of Time in East Slavonic Popular Visions and Dreams about Visiting Heaven and Hell," *New Zealand Slavonic Studies* 36 (2002) (Festschrift in Honour of Arnold McMillin), 289–302.

37. See, e.g., the recollections of Anna Dubova (b. Smolensk Province, 1916): "[My cousin] and his family often sat round and gossiped. They had time for that. And this cousin was always in debt to us; he was forever coming over to borrow something. First, they didn't have enough bread; then it would be something else, and then something else, and all because they would just sit around for hours on end. But our family lived better than others, thanks to father. He was industrious himself and forced his whole family to be industrious, too, and not idle away the time." (B. Engel and A. Posadskaia-Vanderbeck, eds., *A Revolution of Their Own: Voices of Women in Soviet History* [Boulder, Colorado: Westview Press, 1998], 24.) Admittedly, Dubova's family was unusual in that they were Old Believers, but this indicates that even the most conservative groups were quite capable of attaching importance to concepts such as "industry" and "idleness."

38. Martin Amis, *Experience* (London: Vintage, 2001), 3.

39. V. Kozlov and E. Semenova, "Obydennyi NEP: sochineniia i pis'ma shkol'ni-kov 20-kh godov," *Neizvestnaia Rossiia: XX vek* 3 (1993) (full page spread 259–323), 297.

40. *Murzilka* 5 (1932): 7.

41. *SLUSHAITE VSE!* comp. Anatolii Markushka (Moscow: Detskaia literatura, 1962), 152–153, 12–13. *Druzhina* was a term used for Pioneer governing bodies in schools from the war years onward.

42. V. Nabokov, *Speak, Memory* (Harmondsworth: Penguin, 1969), 67–68. As Eric Naiman has pointed out to me, this passage has literary antecedents (in Proust's *A la recherche du temps perdu*, vol. 1). Nevertheless, whether based on Nabokov's actual experience or not, it is a witty and plausible evocation of a child's capacity to, in adult language, "fiddle" and "dawdle."

43. See Beatrice King, "Soviet Education: Its Phases and Purpose," *Slavonic and East European Review* 17:49 (1938–1939), 149.

44. CKQ Ox-O3 PF 6 (B), 11 March 2003, informant b. Leningrad 1931, inter-viewer C. Kelly, transcript p. 14. The Russian original is less coherent than the render-ing above: "strashno ne liubila nikakogo poriadka, tak skazat', nikakoi obshchestvennoi, nikakuiu obshchestvennost', i vsiu etu prinuditel'nost'."

45. G. Kremer, *Oskolki detstva* (Moscow, 1995), 19.

46. Kremer, *Oskolki detstva*, 144.

47. Kremer, *Oskolki detstva*, 146.

48. Kremer, *Oskolki detstva*, 136.

49. Kremer, *Oskolki detstva*, 134 (emphasis follows original).

50. For instance, Iakov Avidon, a schoolboy in the late 1930s, liked the daily rituals and the security of sameness that came with schooling at that point. See Leonard J. Kent, *A Survivor of A Labor Camp Remembers: Expendable Children of Mother Russia* (Lewiston, N.Y.: Edwin Mellen Press, 1997), 187–188.

51. P. Willis, *Learning to Labour: How Working-Class Kids Get Working-Class Jobs* (1973; reprint, Aldershot: Ashgate, 1993), 163.

52. See, for example, Andrei Sergeev, *Al'bom dlia marok*, in *Omnibus* (Moscow: Novoe literturnoe obozrenie, 1997).

53. See, e.g., Giovanni Colozza's description of play as "the free and essential expression of those interior things which need to be outwardly expressed," and as "the pleasure of active fantasy." Dzh. Kolozza (G. Colozza), *Detskie igry: ikh psikhologicheskoe i pedagogicheskoe znachenie*, trans. anon (Moscow: Mosk. knigoizdatel'stvo, 1909), 139, 237. On free time generally, see Stephen Lovell, "O pol'ze 'svobodnogo' vremeni," *Antropologicheskii forum* 2 (2004).

54. See, e.g., *Detskii sad i Elementarnaia shkola E. P. Zalesskoi (Motirovannye uchebnyi plan i primernye programmy detskogo uchilishcha E. P. Zalesskoi [. . .])* (Moscow: Tip. Pechatnoe delo, 1907), which includes "free games" and "active games," songs, and games accompanied by songs (pp. 19–20), and emphasizes in the general comments at the beginning that the purpose of early education is not to inculcate literacy, but to provide facilities for the development and supervision of play and the development of general qualities such as curiosity and patience.

55. See, e.g., *Metodicheskie pis'ma po doshkol'nomu vospitaniiu* 13: *Igra i trud doshkol'nika* (Moscow: Gosizdat, 1927).

56. *Metodicheskie pis'ma po doshkol'nomu vospitaniiu* 13: 11.

57. PPBTsK 1936–1942, l. 8. For a description of "Lame Vixen," see S. M. Loiter, *Russkii detskii fol'klor Karelii* (Petrozavodsk: Kareliia, 1991).

58. "I think that [Chukovskii's poem] *Crocodile* should not be given to children, not because it's a fairy tale, but because it's bourgeois drivel (*burzhuaznaia mut'*)," Krupskaia observed in an article for *Pravda* on 1 February 1928 (reprinted in *Pedagogicheskie sochineniia v 10 tomakh*, vol. 10 [Moscow, 1962], 256). Two years earlier, in 1926, she had condemned an earlier volume of Chukovskii's, *Murka's Book* (*Murkina kniga*), on the grounds that it had a quiescent attitude to the social divide (see ibid., 220–221).

59. N. Bartram, "Igrushka," *Pechat' i revoliutsiia* 5 (1926): 39–62.

60. N. Bartram, *Muzei igrushki* (Leningrad: Academia, 1928).

61. See, e.g., Catherine II, "Tsarevich Fevei," (*Sochineniia Imperatritsy Ekateriny Vtoroi: proizvedeniia literaturnye*, ed. A. I. Vvedenskii [St. Petersburg, 1893], 375), which emphasizes that the young prince was "not swaddled or wrapped up or sung lullabies to or rocked in any way or ever; he was fed correctly and regularly."

62. B. Brainina, E. Nikitina, A. Dmitrieva, eds., *Sovetskie pisateli: avtobiografii*, vol. 1 (Moscow: Khudozhestvennaia literatura, 1959–1988), 183. The young Briusov did manage to read some adventure stories, however.

63. P. A. Litvinskii, *Igrushki, ikh naznachenie i vybor*, in Kapterev (ed.), *Entsiklopediia domashnego vospitaniia i obucheniia* vol. 1, issue 13. Litvinskii states that the miniature gramophones, etc., were available at Doinikov's, Gostinyi dvor no. 73. At 9 rubles for the basic machine and 40 kopecks for replacement cylinders (the prices he cites), such items can only have been for a moneyed public.

64. See Libedinskaia in *In the Shadow of Revolution: Life Stories of Russian Women from 1917 to the Second World War*, ed. Sheila Fitzpatrick and Yuri Slezkine, trans. Yuri Slezkine (Princeton, N.J.: Princeton University Press, 2000), 289–290.

65. On which see Catriona Kelly, "*Byt* and Identity," in Simon Franklin and Emma Widdis, eds., *National Identity in Russian Culture* (Cambridge: Cambridge University Press, 2004).

66. *Pravda* (3 February 1936): 4, toys for youngest children, lack of toy cars and metro trains, lack of Meccano, toy censorship by Narkompros; (22 February 1936): 4 shortages of teddy bears, celluloid dolls, cookers, and harmonicas; (25 March 1936): 4, toy telephone; (5 April 1936): 4, shoddy dolls and bears; (22 September 1936): 4, lack of toys in the newly opened Leningrad Detskii mir, including dolls' china and children's furniture. An article in the edition of 25 April 1936, p. 6, reported a session of "self-criticism" from manufacturers in Zagorsk (formerly Sergiev-Posad), but noted that production plans had still not been drawn up.

67. M. Gorky, "Zametki o detskikh knigakh i igrakh," in M. Gor'kii, *Sobranie sochinenii v 30 tomakh*, vol. 27 (Moscow: Khudozhestvennaia literatura, 1949–1955), 518–520.

68. See *Pravda* (22 February 1936): 4.

69. On the bonus, see Vlasovskaia in Fitzpatrick and Slezkine, eds., *In the Shadow of Revolution*, 361. On wages generally, see Sarah Davies, *Popular Opinion in Stalin's Russia: Terror, Propaganda and Dissent, 1934–1941* (Cambridge: Cambridge University Press, 1997), 24.

70. Andrei Sergeev, *Al'bom dlia marok*, 23, the cars; M. L. Gasparov, "Moe detstvo," in his *Zapisi i vypiski* (Moscow: Novoe literaturnoe obozrenie, 2000), 75, the horse on rockers and alphabet blocks.

71. Pavel Starzhinskii, *Vzrosloe detstvo* (Moscow: Sovremennik, 1991), 120.

72. Based on personal information from two informants (one male, b. 1935 in a major city in northern Russia, the other female, b. 1929 in a northern Russian village).

73. See Anna Marr's autobiographical story "Raznotsvetnye cherepki," in *Raznotsvetnye cherepki* (Moscow: Molodaia gvardiia, 1970), and cf. CKQ Ox-03 PF 5 (A) (transcript p. 8: female informant b. 1931, daughter of a top-ranking army commander, recalling her possession of a beautiful doll with real human hair, a set of antique doll's furniture, and various furry toy animals).

74. Em. Mindlin, "Liudi semidesiatykh godov," 5.

75. B. Sokolov, "O material'noi kul'ture v detskom dome," *Detskii dom* 3 (1928): 59.

76. Oxf/Lev SPb-02 PF 1 (A)—PF 5 (A) (St. Petersburg, 14 November–5 December 2002). Female informant, b. Leningrad, 1937.

77. For the details of the project, see headnote above. The informants concerned are Oxf/Lev SPb-02 PF1 (A)-PF 5 (A) (St. Petersburg, 14 November–5 December 2002) (female informant, b. Leningrad, 1937); Oxf/Lev SPb-02 PF 6 (A)—PF 7 (B) (St. Petersburg, 17 November–15 December 2002), female informant, born 1931; and Oxf/Lev SPb-02 PF 7 (A)-PF 8 (B) (St. Petersburg, 10 December–24 December 2002), male informant, b. Leningrad, 1931. The details of school disruption come from Oxf/Lev SPb-02 PF 7 (A) (p. 49, p. 47 of transcript).

78. See Oxf/Lev SPb-02 PF 7 (A), p. 48 of transcript.

79. Zoshchenko, "Schastlivoe detstvo," *Begemot* 10 (1925): *Sobranie sochinenii v 3 tomakh* (Leningrad: Khudozhestvennaia literatura, 1986), vol. 1, 296–298; "Vor," ibid., vol. 1, 136–139.

80. This phrase was ubiquitous in early twentieth-century Russian culture: it was used for books, pictures, poems, and indeed for shops ('Children's World' in St. Petersburg was a well-supplied clothing and book store, for instance).

81. Thus anticipating the arguments of, e.g., James Kincaid, *Child-Loving: The Erotic Child and Victorian Culture* (London: Routledge, 1992).

82. V. Inber, "O moei docheri," in *Sobranie sochinenii v 4 tomakh*, vol. 2 (Moscow, 1965), 312–313; E. Zamiatin, "Sovetskie deti" (1932), in *Sochineniya*, vol. 4 (Munich: A. Neimanis, 1988), 565.

83. See, e.g., F. M. Orlov-Skomorovskii, *Gol'gofa rebenka* (Moscow: R. V. Ts., 1921).

84. See "The Diary of Vladimir Petrovich Stavsky," in V. Garros, N. Korenevskaya, and T. Lahusen, eds., *Intimacy and Terror: Soviet Diaries of the 1930s*, trans. C. A. Flath (New York: The New Press, 1995), 221. (Punctuation follows this translation.)

85. See, e.g., the front cover of *Kolkhoznye rebyata* 10 (1936), which shows a lorry driving through the countryside with the more restrained version of the slogan, "Spasibo tov. Stalinu za schastlivoe detstvo." A more fulsome version, "Spasibo rodnomu Stalinu za radostnoe, schastlivoe detstvo" is visible over the veranda of the Trekhgorka Factory's summer dacha in E. I. Papkovskaya (ed.), *Knizhka o malen'kikh trekhgortsakh* (Moscow: Gosudarstvennoe uchebno-pedagogicheskoe izdanie, 1948), 37. See also Jeffrey Brooks, *Thank You, Comrade Stalin! Soviet Public Culture from Revolution to Cold War* (Princeton: Princeton University Press, 2000), esp. ch. 5.

86. M. Zhvanetskii, "Detskii sad," in *God za godom* (Leningrad: Eks libris, 1991), 437.

87. See Boris Slutskii, "Real people have children. We only have cactuses / standing silent and frigid" (U liudei–deti. U nas–tol'ko kaktusy/stoiat, besmolvny i kholodny), *Stikhotvoreniia* (Moscow: Khudozhestvennaia literatura, 1989), 302.

88. See, e.g., I. Medvedeva and T. Shishova, " 'Novye modeli povedeniia'?" *Vospitanie shkol'nika* 5 (1998), 26–28, which gets particularly steamed up about school-children being taught, Western-style, about subjects like sexual compatibility in marriage; and the same authors "Novoe vremya—novye deti?" *Oktiabr'* 2 (1997), 122–148, which argues that Russian compassion for the "little man" and emphasis on the need to share is becoming lost as entrepreneurial values are propounded to children. Cf. the comments of a Petersburg interviewee (b. 1937): "At fifteen we were still simply children, and where babies came from, we weren't really interested in all that [. . .] [And now] all those media, it's just so, simply so, so completely open. . . I don't know. Of course, it's a rotten era. I don't know, but I just can't . . . I mean to say, I can't stand it." Oxf/Lev SPb-02 PF 5 (A) (21 December 2002), transcript 115–116.

eleven

The Diary as Initiation and Rebirth

Reading Everyday Documents of the Early Soviet Era

Natalia Kozlova

Case History: Notes by Soviet People

This work has arisen from my wish to read texts authored by ordinary people who lived during the Soviet period of Russian history. As a researcher I was interested in people who, when asked who they were, would reply "I am a Soviet citizen." I was interested in people who could be defined as bearers of Soviet identity.

With this in mind, I consulted the Department of Private Archives at the Documentation Center of the People's Archive.[1] This department contains numerous private documents, mostly dating from the Soviet period. As a rule, these documents reach the center through unsolicited donations. Some are thick volumes, carefully typeset and bound. Other files contain chaotic private and family archives: packs of private letters, old identity cards and certificates, mandates and diplomas, and a miscellany of theater tickets, invitation cards, photographs, diaries, and family budgets. I saw "a shock-worker certificate," I learned what a "draftee certificate" looked like, I held a school examination "ticket" from the 1930s in my hand. I touched the traces left by a withering society.

To many people, this archival collection might look like a garbage can. But this kind of garbage helps to reconstruct the cultural and cognitive map of Soviet civilization, to understand the specific relations between discourse and narrative, discourse and bodily practices. It is important to become aware of the Soviet period not only as an arena of political games but also as an arena of life and death.

I examined dozens of personal files that represented donors who thought of themselves as "Soviet citizens." This article draws on several of them. One file contains personal memoirs that were written in 1994–1995 as a commentary to a collection of photographs submitted to the archive (TsDNA, f. 330, V. I. Vasil'ev). Another file contains memoirs written in the 1970s and 1980s (f. 366, V. I. Edovin). Another enormous and variegated one contains official documents from the 1920s and 30s such as certificates, licenses, diplomas, and questionnaires, as well as notes taken from the classic works of Marxism-Leninism and diaries (f. 306, I. I. Belonosov). Notes made "for my own memory" date back to the postwar period, but the author often writes about the time "before the War." The archivists refer to this file as the "orthodox file," reflecting their impression of the donor's Soviet allegiance. Still another file contains a memoir written in substandard Russian by a woman who had finished only five grades in school (f. 115, E. G. Kiseleva). Finally, yet another file contains the diaries that Stepan F. Podlubnyi had been writing since the age of seventeen (1931). These diaries are supplemented by comments and reminiscences provided by the author at the archive's request.

In reading these many archival files, I found that the authors who unconditionally defined themselves as Soviet tended to be from peasant backgrounds. I attempted to reconstruct their personal histories on the basis of the documents in the archive. The writing of different people began to take shape for me as a single narrative—that of the transformation of a peasant into a non-peasant, a city dweller, and a Soviet person. People of one social anthropological category were turning into people belonging to another.

This narrative seems typical if one analyzes its demographic context. My protagonists were born between 1908 and 1921, but in essence they all belong to the same social generation.[2] My interest lies in what hovers behind the laconic statistical data. What happened to a person who ceased being a peasant? How did he or she become an agent of the system, that is, become someone whose activity was essential to the existence and development of the Soviet social system?

Memoirs: The Problem of Discourse and Narrative

This research is a reflection on written texts. My objects of analysis are writing practices themselves, rather than the things described in the documents—although these very things do give us a material sense of the symptoms of social mobility and of the course of everyday Soviet life. Some of the former peasants whose documents I examined were successful in inscribing themselves into the new society, and even in ascending the social hierarchy. These authors use a more or less correct version of standard written language. Those who were less successful often spoke in a language that was a far cry from the standard. A difference in language often represents a difference in social status. E. Kiseleva, for example, uses a "substandard" language, and her horizontal social mobility did not exceed fifteen kilometers; she moved from her native village to a nearby "workers' settlement" where she spent the rest of her life (f. 115). By 1933 she was no longer a peasant, but she spent her entire life at the lowest levels of the social hierarchy. Her last job was as a cleaner at a coal mine.

The socially successful donors not only mastered the standard written language; their writing is composed of citations from the ideological metanarrative. At first glance, they resemble string-puppets of ideological discourse. Irrespective of the genre of writing—from the minutes of Komsomol meetings to love letters—these people were fluent in the ideological clichés of the time. Their readiness to adhere to such clichés and to observe the rules of the social game—even in the most critical moments of their lives—is amazing.

A party functionary and former peasant who lived in Leningrad during the blockade wrote about how he could never be sure that each day was not going to be his last. Nevertheless, during those hard times he makes the following diary entry: "The other day I sent my wife many interesting newspaper clippings, for the most part about Leningrad and the Leningrad front. Not only will she be interested in reading them, she can also use them in her conversations with the little ones from the boarding school and with kolkhoz members. I cannot believe they have neither newspapers, nor radio, nor movies over there. As if they were not living in the Soviet Union. As if they did not have a local Party organization, a local executive committee or other bodies that are supposed to take care of the cultural services for working people."[3]

Diaries and memoirs sometimes manifest the use of two speech registers by one and the same writer. One is the register of official language and appears to be built into the body of the writer. It turns on automatically and works according to its program. This is the language of the newspaper—not that of *Pravda*, perhaps, but of the small, local periodicals to which one of my protagonists would write letters to the editor. The other register is for private consumption. It reveals doubts, timidity, and violations of standard usage. I. I. Belonosov's file (f. 306) is especially representative in this respect, as is that of V. I. Edovin (f. 366).

One way or another, the reading of such memoirs shows how readily a person can inscribe himself into the form of life determined by ideological discourse. In these writings, cries from the heart, poems, and love letters go side by side with quotations from Lenin. When I. I. Belonosov broke his right arm, he taught himself to write with his left, with which, struggling, he expounded on "the struggle for existence," "working class brigades," and "war in present-day conditions" and took notes on his reading of Lenin's work on union movements. His writing is extremely stereotyped. He borrows clichés from political brochures and *The Course on the History of the Communist*

Party. He continually takes notes, cramming his writing with quotations from the ideological metanarrative as he provides legitimacy for his own life. Citations grow into his flesh. In this way, he smuggles his private existence into the confines of ideological language. The violent passion of his unique and singular life experience is transformed in writing into something like: "The time of the first five-year plans was the greatest event in the life of the Soviet people. During a short span of time, the industrial base of the country was created, and mass collectivization of agriculture was carried out . . . The construction of socialism directed the economic development of the country along a new route . . . In 1929, mass collectivization in agriculture achieved its full force, which radically changed peasants' private life, including my own."[4] This extract is a diary entry for the writer's own exclusive reading. Even when his diary assumes a more traditionally personal tone, however, it does so with the worldview of a socialist realist novel: "And what blows life used to deal me, the 30s were the hardest time (the second half, yes!). But still, *I stood up to the hard fight with difficulties and found the right path.*"[5] The linguistic mask seems to have grown onto the face, and there is nothing behind the face. What is written in the diary functions as an illustration of the totalitarian concept of ideology: the language of ideology seems nothing but a tool of domination.

Reflecting on situations in their private lives, the diary writers make use of oppositions provided by ideological discourse, such as "revolutionary/reactionary," "backward/advanced," "cultured/primitive," "not one of us [*ne nash chelovek*] / a celebrated hero of labor," "inferior/superior." A "bad mood" is synonymous with a "decadent mood" (*upadochnoe nastroenie*). "A person who harbors doubts" easily begins to describe himself as a "reactionary renegade" (*otshchepenets*), a "degenerate" (*pererozhdenets*), a person still harboring the "surviving traits of origin and upbringing" (*perezhitki proiskhozhdeniia i vospitaniia*). The diary writers seem to command no other language for self-expression.

Belonosov moved to Moscow in 1936. Only after the war did he start writing his memoirs. His whole life, however, he collected the scraps of paper that envelop the life of a Soviet citizen: certificates, licenses, rough copies of official applications, and so on. Because his memoirs consist of citations from the metanarrative, only in encountering other documents from his life does one realize that he is, in fact, quite corporeal. A rough copy of an application submitted to the residence management office (*Domupravlenie*) in 1938 can serve as an illustration: "The tenants of apartment no. 13, which is populated by seven families (35 persons) have been living for two months without a lavatory."[6]

In short, if one wishes to reconstruct the everyday life of Belonosov, one has to restore the construction from its ruins, from its traces. The same applies to other writers' lives. It is difficult to understand how Belonosov, a peasant from the Urals, transformed himself into an urban resident and prominent archivist; why a child from a dekulakized family from the north of Vologda

Region developed into the party functionary V. I. Edovin; how it happened that V. I. Vasil'ev, who was not a party functionary, nevertheless managed to get a higher education at the department of physics of Moscow State University, but still could not evade the use of clichés and codes from official Soviet discourse even in his old age, when he finally realized that not everything written in *Pravda* was actually the truth (*pravda*).

In their childhood, adolescence, and early youth, all of my protagonists lived in traditional peasant environments, even though these environments were often in a state of decay. Had they remained in the countryside and survived collectivization, they would all have lived lives that differed far less from traditional peasant lifestyles than their lives in the cities. By the end of their lives all of them had become urban residents and had acquired good command of standard (literary) Russian language. The process of transformation, as seen from the memoirs, takes place behind a curtain that prevents the researcher from seeing behind the wings of the social theater. What are the conditions under which a peasant "tries on" a typical social construction that is represented by a language mask? How painful is the fitting?

Diary, or Initiation and Second Birth

The diary written by Stepan Filipovich Podlubnyi is the document that helped me, personally, to answer some of the questions concerning the role of discourse in the formation of narrative (and not only narrative) practices of the 1930s. This document is the product of a complicated social and historical process and can help us reconstruct the anthropological transformation undergone by a large segment of the Soviet population.[7]

Podlubnyi was born in 1914 and started keeping his diary in 1931. Anticipating repression as a member of a family with a dekulakized and exiled father, Podlubnyi moved to Moscow from Ukraine in the second half of 1930. After a winter of hardships, he tried to find a job through the employment center (*birzha truda*) for minors. His diary reproduces a mosaic of everyday life. The reader learns of damp basements, privileged residential buildings, movies, parties, and, often, hunger ("I drink tea in the morning and have soup in the evening and that's it for the whole day"—7 July 1932).[8] This mosaic allows the reader to feel the motivation, the life choices, the very method of acculturation to the ideological metanarrative. One can witness human transformation not only in terms of mentality, but also in terms of corporeality. The relation between discursive and bodily practices is a central theme in the diary.

Entries from Podlubnyi's diary for the years 1931 through 1938 provide us with striking glimpses into the process of the transformation of a peasant into an urban resident. On the opening pages one reads lyrics of songs, partly traditional folk songs, partly semi-urban folklore—all inscribed in the diary by Podlubnyi and testifying to the original, rural culture of the writer.[9] His coming into manhood coincides with his initiation into Soviet society. This son of a

Figure 11.1. Apprentices from the Pravda printing plant who had just been admitted to the Komsomol, 1931. Stepan Podlubnyi is second from left, back row. Photograph courtesy of Jochen Hellbeck.

peasant gradually acquires novel methods of social reproduction, the lifestyle of a "big" society. Accordingly, his manner of writing also changes. In 1931–1933 he is still writing in a language far from the standard norm, but entries made in 1938 already show that he has become fully initiated (*stal svoim*) in the world of writing. He has a fluent command of the standard idiom of Russian literary language.

Podlubnyi's desire to be accepted, to stop being an alien element, is intense, and in his efforts to penetrate the new society, he strives fervently to master and manipulate necessary forms of behavior. For his visit to the labor exchange, he chooses Easter: Moscow is celebrating, bells chime all around, and officials are not too diligent in their examination of documents on that day. He is seventeen years of age, but he draws on traditional peasant experience in evading rules that work to his disadvantage. In his archival file, in a notebook with notes on a synopsis of the first volume of *Capital*, I found a draft copy of an application that he submitted to the labor exchange. It is written in the genre of a classic peasant's petition:

> *Application*
> I hereby request the chief of the adolescent section to assign me to a job as I came from the town of Arkhangel'sk and having no relatives reside with my mother who is employed as a cleaning lady and having nothing for existence have to live on my mother's scanty earnings, i.e. 12 rubles and eking

out a semi-famished existence in order not to be thrown homeless out into the street I ask you to sympathize with me in my difficult situation and give me a job where I could earn at least a little to support myself for which I ask my request not be turned down.[10]

The young man cleverly conceals his nonproletarian origin. As early as the end of the same year he is elected a member of the bureau of the local Komsomol factory unit at the Pravda publishing house. Why did he join the Komsomol? Did he do so because he began "to be a believer in the idea"? Had he become a different person?

He had become a different person—he had transformed himself. By the end of the 1920s peasants were stigmatized as a "withering class." An efficient propaganda machine (a nomination machine) was at work to oedipalize young people like Podlubnyi. The writer never doubted that he belonged to a class that was withering. For him, the village was a place "where [his] backwardness flourished," where he spent his childhood without seeing a train until the age of fifteen. His origin never ceased to worry him. According to his diary, the young man wanted to write a novel that would describe "the life of a bygone class, its rebirth and adaptation to a new situation. I cannot get anybody's advice, and there is no one who could give it because if I ask for advice I reveal myself . . . This is quite a new theme, I think, and if a book were written about it now, the censor would not let it pass, of course" (25 September 1933).[11] He was sent to a kolkhoz and had to be careful not to reveal his secret: "No, I should not work in the field too fast during the first days . . . Or they might ask: how come you can work so well, you worked [in the field] before, didn't you? Suspicion. For they think I am a full-blooded worker . . . I'd better not speak on a/c [agricultural] subjects with them" (28 August 1933).[12] He attests to his experience as a peasant in the city: the experience of illegitimacy.

There is another significant factor in the transformation of peasants into Soviet subjects. Each of my protagonists had a traumatic experience accompanied by a feeling of imminent death. Podlubnyi experienced this fear when his father was dekulakized. Other writers invariably had similar experiences. The memory of hunger was often built into their bodies, incorporated. They "felt" that hunger could return if they did not live the lies of "normal" members of society. "The horror of hunger does not leave my head," Podlubnyi wrote on 7 February 1933.[13] The motif of the fear of poverty and of becoming a has-been runs throughout the professional and nonprofessional texts of the 1930s, as does the motif of "living on the edge," on the border between society and non-society. On 13 September Podlubnyi wrote: "Can it be that I look different from everybody else? When I ask this question, my hair stands on end and my body trembles."[14] For peasants like Podlubnyi, staying in the village seemed dangerous, or at least hopeless. They knew only too well the meaning of the word "ssylka" (exile). At best their fate would be a life of hard physical labor. Of course, peasants were accustomed to physical labor. Their essential life choices were not dictated by fear alone. In the 1930s they knew very well that one could enter a higher educational institution for workers (*rabfak*) or a technical school, that one could become a worker promoted to an administrative post (*vydvizhenets*), that one could become an urban resident—in short, they would know only too well that there existed life choices other than following in the footsteps of their fathers. Those who were most active and most vital would not suffer a victim's fate.

The road to self-transformation was extraordinarily onerous, requiring stratagems and maneuvers. A former peasant's certificate might identify him as a middle peasant (*seredniak*), but in a questionnaire to be filled out for staff management and control (*listok po uchetu kadrov*) he never hesitates to identify himself as a poor peasant (*bedniak*) and sometimes would even dare to claim full-blooded proletarian origin. Peasants would pass through multiple stages of initiation in the hope that each new "sieve" would be the last and the long-awaited reward would finally be received. Obviously, this was not necessarily the only scenario. Utterly frustrated by the ordeal of renewing their internal passport, by job cuts and endless purges, many would take their own lives by poisoning or shooting themselves or throwing themselves under trains. Each document I read contained many mentions of suicide among young people. Podlubnyi's diary is no exception. He saw his transformation and survival as a painful purifying process that he described using the metaphors of a "seed sorting machine" (*sortirovka dlia semian*) and "a man-peeling machine" (*liudechistka*). His passage through initiation caused him much pain, but it also gave him the joy of a second birth.

Volition / Coercion

The process of self-transformation was characterized by certain parameters of agreement between the dominating and the dominated, by an intimate connection between volition and coercion.[15] The society coerced young former peasants into transforming their personal lives. Yet at the same time, the peasants appreciated and welcomed the possibility of a radical change in their destiny. They studied the structures of transformative society and, playing a deadly serious game, adapted their behavior in a quite calculating manner. They ascertained risk and demonstrated a vital interest in the ideological stakes. Their ideological capital was invested in the language of ideology. This capital was forced upon them (there was no other) and they were responsible for its profitable investment, but the game was structured so that they wanted to play. Another capital investment was the cultural capital that the writers would refer to as *kul'turnost'* (culturedness).[16] *Kul'turnost'* is the key ideologeme of the 1930s; it implied personal hygiene, eating behaviors, habits of dress, and lifestyle in general. *Kul'turnost'* also implied a program of collective public conduct, a mode of signifying interpersonal relations through everyday consumption, a representation of the social position so acquired, and a self-image of a "decent person." *Kul'turnost'* also implied cultured language (*kul'turnyi iazyk*).

On People Who Did Not Play Word Games and Never Thought of *Kul'turnost'*

It is commonly believed that power structures and rules are the only subjects of transformation, elevated to the very heights, static and immune to any transformation of their own selves but only engaged in the transformation of others. From this point of view, the masses are nothing but an object of domination. This would only be the case, however, with regard to a type of transformation that relied entirely on external compulsion and violence. In fact, the ratio of external to internal compulsion varied in each individual case, even if those who kept diaries reflect a higher degree of self-transformative desire.

When we attempt to understand those urbanized peasants who did not desire self-transformation or consciously work toward it, we may find that we are stepping inside a world of silence, a world of inscription on the body. The written evidence of this type of transformation—when it exists—is often a scream signifying the onslaught of absence, the withering away of traditional values that were not, the writers thought, being replaced by anything of worth. Such people—those who were not motivated by ideological desire—were doomed to remain at the nethermost levels of the social hierarchy even though their horizontal mobility could be considerable.

Stepan Podlubnyi's diary contains a description of drinking parties attended by young former peasants whom "it was impossible to set on the right path, the path of a cultured person" (12 February 1933).[17] "The young people who get together for dancing and singing at the Rodins' [friends of Podlubnyi's] all come from the most backwards village milieus . . . Their relations with each other, their practical jokes, are just beastly . . . Dancing with skill to an accordion. Boys with drunken mugs. They paw the girls, push each other, and shout."[18]

These kinds of people took no part in discursive games. They were transformed but never transformed themselves. Those who "worked on themselves" differentiated themselves from those who did not. For peasants such as Podlubnyi, transformation resulted from the sort of self-restriction, self-control, and self-normalization on which Norbert Elias puts special emphasis in his works on civilization. Self-restriction can be useful as a source of power and an instrument of status. Many young former peasants sought transformation as they attempted to achieve at least a measure of favorable redistribution of power, to play along with power and simultaneously exploit power for their own personal ends.

Social Theater

The acquisition of a Soviet identity began with mimicry. Roles would be tried on and cast off like masks. The person looked into mirrors. "How am I to live? How am I to be? Where can I see a mirror of myself? How am I to behave . . . How? What do I look like [*vygliadu*, a substandard form for *vygliazhu*—N.K.]? Why isn't there a place to read about this?" (6 January 1933).[19] Other people (those whom one wanted to be like) acted as a mirror, providing "occasional snatches, fragments, partial information (like interesting phrases that one writes down after coming upon them in a book) about the vital manipulation of a machine with a complicated mechanism, the mastery of which requires close attention and thorough selection out of everything that I saw and that I did not see in a certain fragment of the time I have lived" (22 August 1932).[20]

An individual like Podlubnyi was looking for a new manner of conduct: "I have been observing people very much. Observing the conduct of guys who are my equals. How they behave in similar situations. Learning to imitate manners . . . All this is inhumanly difficult, killing my strength. At the same time, they make me more cautious professionally, more observant" (15 October 1934).[21] "Eh, how can I strike up more friendships with journalists, writers, students, and young people in general in my specialty? It is only from them that I can grab some experience. And soak up something useful" (13 August 1932).[22]

Given the universal craving for transformation, it is not surprising that the theater should have become a key factor in cultural transformation. Notes on theater proliferate in Podlubnyi's diary: "Today the three of us had a good and cultured evening at the theater. An exceptionally pleasant feeling of the soul. It resembles something grandiose, adult but at the same time new. This is not like going to the movies for a ruble. It's respectably cultured to go to the theater for five rubles. And the price you pay when you go places has enormous moral significance" (24 October 1933).[23] My protagonist felt ever so distinctly that a social abyss gaped between him and others, and he strove to leap over it. "Why do I like foreigners so much? Why do I respect them so? It seems I would pay a lot to spend time in their company, in their cultured atmosphere [*v ikh kul'turnosti*]. Every time I see a poet, a writer, or any other distinguished person, how intently I gaze at their foreheads, their heads; perhaps by chance my own forehead might happen to look like one of their foreheads. It's funny, but that's how it is. I am afraid of, I avoid meeting with a man whom I have not studied and consider above me. Members of Agitbrigades, for instance" (1 August 1932).[24] Former peasants were consumed with envy of students, whom they viewed as "experts in *kul'turnost'*." The opposition of the cultured and the uncultured, of acculturation and cultural backwardness, appears as a characteristic of the time.

Throughout the 1930s there are many diary entries in which the concepts of *kul'turnost'* and cultural privilege are central. "I dressed in a cultured manner, went to the movies, I wanted so much to go to the Park of Culture and Rest but was short of money" (18 June 1934).[25] "She was quite an advanced girl [*razvitoi divchinoi*, a Ukrainianism for young woman]. From a family of the Soviet aristocracy. Perhaps in our level of development we were equals, but we were far from equal in money and clothes . . . And it seems that the old proverb "Money can do anything" is still true in our new socialist conditions. Socialism or no socialism, money has to be given its due" (20 December 1937).[26] "Lately I have been feeling that I have started to grow culturewise; as compared to past years I have grown beyond recognition. This is also important because I live among guys who are cultured, too. How tremendously important in life are the environment you live in and the people you mingle with. I got hold of a good suit. A few days ago I bought a summer coat. I am dressed culturedly [*kul'turno*] and cleanly and am careful with respect to cleanliness. The material aspect is not bad. A colossal breakthrough in terms of the material aspect. This is a breakthrough in the right direction. Mobilize all strength, all energy until it is too late, because there is not so much time left" (18 June 1934).[27] "Moving among directors and, in general, among people who are materially prosperous, well-dressed, and always clean, I always tried to dress neatly, with a starched collar and an ironed suit. This has imbued me with outer culture" (1 January 1936).[28]

Podlubnyi sought—not always with success—to bring himself into harmony with the image projected onto him by the state: "I have become a good activist (maybe this excessive activism will ruin me), I have adopted a covert form of buttering up [*podkhalimstvo*] towards superiors. Mom is a good activist, a diligent pupil, a bonus-winner [*premirovannaia*]" (10 March 1933).[29]

Karl Marx: A Bet in a Social Game

Most of the diary writers had extremely limited financial means and social connections. Their youth and physical strength were their only assets, and they were eager to invest both in social or cultural capital. These young men believed that the right thing would be to stake their future on Marx, to invest in the study of texts produced by founders and leaders. Each of these ex-peasant youths would eventually have a "love affair" with the holy scriptures of their time.

Turning for a moment from Podlubnyi's diary to V. I. Vasil'ev's memoirs, written in 1994–1995, here is an extract that describes his studies at a regional party school in 1922–1923: "Leaving the classroom during the break, the teacher left the thick book lying on the table. Together with others, I came up and touched the book, on whose cover it was written: Karl Marx. [. . .] As far as I can remember, I never read *Capital*, either at that time or afterwards. Preserved in my memory is only Chapter 24, Initial Accumulation. Since the

Figure 11.2. Stepan Podlubnyi, 1936. Photograph courtesy of Jochen Hellbeck.

party school I have read and reread this chapter, more than once and not out of any necessity but out of sheer love for poetry."[30]

Podlubnyi also made an attempt to "get hold of the classics": "[I] was at the park . . . at a meeting. Took Karl M. along. When Sakun [a Komsomol leader] looked at what I was reading he roared with laughter and gave me the book back that very minute and went off laughing. True, he was somewhat abashed when he learned that I was already working through [the work of] Stalin. In haste. No spare time. Time to go to bed" (13 August 1932).[31] The writing of political leaders served as religious relics, but these relics were available for individual exploitation and for the fulfillment of individual desires. They were objects to be acquired, objects whose working through and possession provided pleasure and status just as did material possessions. I will quote from only two out of a vast number of cases in Podlubnyi's diary in which a diary entry combines "symbols of success" with information about attempts to read ideological texts.

"Bought me a mandolin. This is the second thing I have bought myself with my own hard-earned money. The first one was a watch that I bought in June 1932. I had a hell of a vacation with it [*Otpusk pogulial s nimi s forsom*]. To bed. Was absorbed in reading newspapers. Today there is a very interesting speech by Manuil'skii about the twelfth plenary meeting of the IKKI [Executive Committee of the Communist International]. Makes for easy and fascinating reading" (2 November 1932).[32] Another extract: "Yesterday, on the occasion of the fiftieth anniversary of Karl Marx's death there was a lecture sponsored by the Communist Academy in the Lenin Library about his activities. I attended. It was not the speech that was so remarkable but the room. Big, clean, comfortable, and cultured, in all respects" (15 March 1933).[33]

What is the writer more interested in and pleased by? Marx's jubilee or the possibility of spending time in the "cultured" atmosphere of a clean and comfortable room, a room that was so unlike his own dwellings? "Today I was in the park of the Timiriazev Academy. In the garden there were many students reading for their classes and sitting in cozy little groups. I wish I could make friends with some students and political workers, I wish I could ask them for help, support, and advice in my studies. It is pretty hard to study Marx on my own, and, who knows, maybe I'm aiming too high, maybe I should have preliminarily taken up something easier. Maybe I'm simply wasting time [*vremia tratiu*, illiterate form of the present tense] . . . Still, sooner or later, I have to handle [it]. How careless I am with punctuation" (3 August 1932).[34]

Podlubnyi and other former peasants used to carry Marx around, holding a volume under their arm, but they invariably had difficulty reading him. This difficulty reveals not only the diary writers' limited literacy but also their pragmatic attitudes towards the Name and the Book that contains "holy scriptures." Power resides, among other places, in the act of nomination. As they strove to become fluent in the ideological tongue, former peasants would engage themselves in a game of nomination. This was a significant part of their love affair with the ideological discourse; it was not only a pragmatic but also a pleasurable activity.

Young former peasants appealed to the discourse of ideology as a means of orientation. By speaking the language, they found self-determination and self-identity, their own place in Soviet reality. By the same token, they were seeking to introduce order into their lives and to reassemble a world that had gone to pieces. Today, one can hardly imagine the horror of "not knowing," their fear of getting implicated in events and circumstances for which they had no name. A person can hardly survive without a means of ordering events, without a basis for giving them names and including them into a corpus of community symbols. In ordering their worlds, these former peasants had to make use of the only ideological discourse available to them.

A historically innocent individual perceives a language cliché as a discovery. New words promise to fulfill desire. Words and names function not only pragmatically but as a form of magic. Rhetorical figures of ideological language act as figures of masked desire. Thus, those who sought a "cultured life" were engaged in a game of words, and their public works [*obshchestvennaia rabota*] were also closely connected with such games since it was required that their achievements be fixed in writing. In Podlubnyi's diary, I came across a highly symptomatic statement: "Lately, I have looked at public work not as careerism but as a system, a part of my body, my existence, as the bread that is necessary for living" (1 June 1933).[35] The metaphors of bread and body are symptomatic. In order to keep up their physical existence, my protagonists sought communion with public activities.

They attempted to "fit in," but the new language was difficult to master. They resorted to various epistemological shortcuts. One was graphology, an important detail in the Soviet cultural landscape.[36] In the years before the Second World War, graphology was considered by many to be a science. Addressing a graphologist, many ex-peasants believed that they were being provided with objective and scientifically grounded data about themselves and their place in the world. Sometimes they would spend their last money to pay for a graphological consultation. "And today I gave away my last kopek, not a single one left for lunch," Podlubnyi wrote on 16 March 1933.[37] It is important to note that graphologists frequently spoke the ideological language as they decoded it; they did not provide an alternative discourse. "I got a reply from Zuev-Insarov [the most famous graphologist of the time]. Don't know why, but it looks as if I believed everything that he wrote down. For instance, there is an interesting phrase from which an experienced person can guess my past. He says that 'ideologically I gave up my family's influence early in life,' and he is right . . . Also he says that my worldview is materialist . . . that I can establish my own authority and 'any form of public activity agrees with my character'" (1 April 1933).[38] Our protagonists consulted graphologists more than once. On 11 April 1935 Podlubnyi wrote in his diary: "Today I got a reply from a graphologist . . . During the course of two years there have been significant changes. And what is saddest of all is that he identifies egoism in me."[39]

How can I account for the ambiguous impression I derive from reading the documents of this epoch in which sacred names and writings not only generated awe but were put to the service of pragmatism and pleasure? On the one hand, each of the writers, by virtue of the very act of writing, inscribed himself into the existing symbolic order, into the hierarchy, as if participating in a roll call to confirm his own presence. In so doing, each one demonstrated his ultimate dependence on power. A person writing within a sociopolitical discourse can be likened to a person walking on an errand of his own along a street laid by someone else. Initially, it would appear as though these writers were only playing other people's game of power.

On the other hand, however, there is something special in their manner of playing. This can be seen from the very nonnormativity, nonstandardness of their language. A writer can affect the outcome of the game; he or she can acquire an alien tongue and invest it as he or she sees fit. The result never coincides with the expectation of power. Resistance surfaces and can be read between the lines in the very fact of individually induced distortion.

One should not underestimate the role of such language games. It goes without saying that symbolic verbal games helped implement the discourse of power. By speaking the discourse, former peasants helped to enshrine it. Soviet society had no alternative codified language. A special social (sociohistorical) code was created as a system of norms of enunciation about society and one-self, a system of nomination, a common ground for understanding among otherwise isolated individuals. This language was used by everyone, even by those who did not agree. A system of mutual understanding was thus instituted, which by no means implies that ideological dogmas were adopted by all. Soviet society is often referred to as a society of ideas, but it is, rather, a society of words and word games.

When scholars address narrative documents of the Soviet period, they can no longer afford to treat Soviet society as "a kingdom of Death," "a domain of Non-Life." It is a society heavily charged with potency, pleasure and over-powering vitality. People who belong to the social generation I have studied are still living among us. Their children and grandchildren are not like them. They are urban residents with new desires, and they implement these desires using new strategies. But as they seek to fulfill their desires, these new people will have to confront the consequences of their ancestors' investments.

NOTES

1. The Tsentr dokumentatsii "Narodnyi arkhiv" (TsDNA) was a child of Per-estroika and represents an innovative effort to establish Russia's first nongovernmental archival depository. The initial purpose of this Moscow-based archive was to collect materials from rank-and-file sources, testimony left by citizens who were not in any respect prominent. The archive differed from state-run depositories in that it accepted whatever documents donors wanted to give; no materials were rejected.

2. Statistics provide us with an impressive picture. In 1926 the USSR's urban population was 18 percent—the same level registered for the period before World War I. It was only in the early 1960s that the country's urban population share (66 percent) was comparable with that in most so-called developed countries. The new urban popula-tion was recruited from former peasants who largely belonged to the generation that is the subject of this research. See Z. A. Zaionchkovskaia, *Demograficheskaia situatsiia i rasselenie* (Moscow: Nauka, 1991), 20; L. L. Rybakovskii, *Demograficheskoe razvitie SSSR za 70 let* (Moscow, 1988); A. G. Vishnevskii, "Na polputi k gorodskomu obsh-chestvu," *Chelovek* (1922): 1.

3. "Ribkovskii's Diary," September 27, 1942. Ribkovskii's diary is contained in the file of I. I. Belonosov, TsDNA, f. 306.

4. Belonosov, TsDNA, f. 306.

5. Ibid. Emphasis added.

6. Ibid.

7. Editors' note: Natalia Kozlova wrote this essay before the diary of Stepan Podlubnyi became well known through the scholarship of Jochen Hellbeck; see his "Fashioning the Stalinist Soul: The Diary of Stepan Podlubnyi, 1931–9," in *Stalinism: New Directions*, ed. Sheila Fitzpatrick (London and New York: Routledge, 2000), 77–116, and his translation of an edited volume of the diary into German, *Tagebuch aus Moskau 1931–1939* (Munich: Deutscher Taschenbuch Verlag, 1996). Sadly, Dr. Kozlova has died since she wrote this essay, so it could not be revised to respond to the insights offered by Hellbeck in the spirit of scholarly dialogue. We believe, however, that her approach differs significantly from that of Hellbeck and therefore remains a valuable contribution to the project of "reading" Soviet identity.

8. TsDNA, f. 30, d.11, l. 35

9. Ibid., ll. 2–6.

10. Ibid., d.33.

11. Ibid., d.13, ll. 48–49.

12. Ibid., d.12, l. 71.

13. Ibid., d.12, l. 32.

14. Ibid., d.11, l. 63.

15. The interaction of these two concepts has been the subject of the work of Norbert Elias and Pierre Bourdieu. See Elias, *The Civilizing Process*, 2 vols. (Oxford: Blackwell, 1978 and 1982); Elias, *What Is Sociology?* (New York: Columbia University Press, 1978); Bourdieu, *The Logic of Practice* (Stanford: Stanford University Press, 1990), 52–65.

16. The importance of this ideologeme is underlined by Vera Dunham. See her book *In Stalin's Time: Middleclass Values in Soviet Fiction* (Cambridge: Cambridge University Press, 1977), 20 and 27 ff. [Editor's note: a key discussion of *kul'turnost'*, published since Kozlova's death, is Vadim Volkov, "The Concept of *Kul'turnost'*: Notes on the Stalinist Civilizing Process," in *Stalinism: New Directions*, ed. Sheila Fitzpatrick (London and New York: Routledge, 2000), 210–230.]

17. TsDNA, f. 30, d.12, l. 33.

18. Ibid., d.12, l. 33.

19. Ibid., d.12, l. 17.

20. Ibid., d.11, l. 52.

21. Ibid., d.13, l. 51.

22. Ibid., d.11, l. 49.

23. Ibid., d.12, l. 85.

24. Ibid., d.11, ll. 43–44.

25. Ibid., d.13, l. 24.

26. Ibid., d.16, l. 35, 36.

27. Ibid., d.13, l. 27.

28. Ibid., d.15, l. 84.

29. Ibid., d.12, l. 38.

30. TsDNA, f. 330.

31. TsDNA, f. 30, d.11, l. 50.

32. Ibid., d.12, l. 1.

33. Ibid., d.12, l. 44.

34. Ibid., d.11, l. 45.

35. Ibid., d.12, l. 54.

36. The second edition of the *Bol'shaia Sovetskaia Entsiklopediia* defines graphol-

ogy as a "pseudoscience." The entry is very short (12:472). The entry in the first edition (1930), however, defines graphology as "the study of handwriting for the purposes of determining the natural abilities, character, temper and other properties of the person who wrote [the text]." Applications were foreseen in psychiatry and jurisprudence. See A. Leont'ev and A. Surkov, "Grafologiia," *Bol'shaia Sovetskaia Entsiklopediia* (Moscow: Sovetskaia entsiklopedia, 1930), 18: 851–855.

37. TsDNA, f. 30, d.12, l. 45.

38. Ibid., d.12, l. 47.

39. Ibid., d.15, l. 30.

Contributors

Frances L. Bernstein is Assistant Professor of History at Drew University. She is author of the forthcoming *The Dictatorship of Sex: Gender, Health, and Enlightenment in Revolutionary Russia, 1918–1931* and of numerous articles on sexuality in the early Soviet period.

Evgenii Bershtein is Associate Professor of Russian at Reed College. His recent publications include the articles "*Psychopathia Sexualis* in Russia in the Early Twentieth Century: Politics and Genre," "The Russian Myth of Oscar Wilde," and "The Tragedy of Sex: Two Brief Essays on the Russian Cult of Otto Weininger." He is completing a book entitled *Sexuality in Russian Symbolism* and co-editing, with Harriet Murav, a collection of articles on Vasilii Rozanov.

Randi Cox is Associate Professor of History at Stephen F. Austin State University in Nacogdoches, Texas, where she teaches courses on Russian history and the history of consumer culture. She is currently working on a monograph on Soviet advertising, tentatively titled *Engines of Trade: Advertising, Consumption and Soviet Citizenship in the 1920s*.

Sheila Fitzpatrick is the Bernadotte E. Schmitt Distinguished Service Professor in Modern Russian History at the University of Chicago and an editor of *The Journal of Modern History*. Her most recent book is *Tear off the Masks! Identity and Imposture in Twentieth-Century Russia*.

Cynthia Hooper is Assistant Professor of History at the College of the Holy Cross. She received her doctorate from Princeton University. Her dissertation, "Terror From Within: Participation and Coercion in Soviet Power, 1924–1964," won the international Fraenkel Prize in Contemporary History in 2003.

Lilya Kaganovsky is Assistant Professor of Slavic, Comparative Literature, and Cinema Studies at the University of Illinois, Urbana-Champaign. Her publications include: "How the Soviet Man Was (Un)Made," *Slavic Review* (Fall 2004); "Forging Soviet Masculinity in Nikolai Ekk's *The Road to Life*," in the forthcoming volume, *Engendering the Nation*, ed. Andrea Lanoux and Helena Goscilo; and an essay on Sergei Livnev's 1994 *Hammer & Sickle* in the forthcoming special issue of *SEEJ* on post-Soviet film. She is currently finishing her manuscript on cultural fantasy and the articulation of male subjectivity in film and literature of the Stalin period.

Catriona Kelly is Professor of Russian at the University of Oxford. She has published many books and articles on Russian literature and cultural history, most recently *Refining Russia: Advice Literature, Polite Culture and Gender from Catherine to Yeltsin*, and *Comrade Pavlik: The Rise and Fall of a Soviet Boy Hero*, a study of the myth of Pavlik Morozov. She is now finishing work on *Children's World: Growing Up in Russia, 1890–1991*.

Christina Kiaer is Associate Professor in the Department of Art History and Archaeology at Columbia University. She is author of *Imagine No Possessions: The Socialist Objects of Russian Constructivism* and is currently working on a book about the painter Aleksandr Deineka and Socialist Realism.

Natalia Nikitichna Kozlova (1946–2002) was a pioneer in the study of everyday life in the Soviet Union. She taught in the Institute of Philosophy of the Academy of Sciences and at the Russian State University for the Humanities (RGGU). She was author of numerous scholarly and pedagogic publications, including *Everyday Horizons of the Soviet Epoch: Voices from the Chorus* (*Gorizonty povsednevnosti sovetskoi epokhi*) and co-author and co-editor of *That's What I Want To Call the Movie: Naïve Writing: An Experiment in Linguistic-Sociological Reading* ("*Ia tak khochu nazvat' kino*"—"*Naivnoe pis'mo*": *opyt lingvo—sotsiologicheskogo chteniia*).

Eric Naiman is Associate Professor of Comparative Literature and Slavic Languages and Literatures at the University of California, Berkeley. He is author of *Sex in Public: The Incarnation of Early Soviet Ideology* and the co-editor of *The Landscape of Stalinism: The Art and Ideology of Soviet Space*.

Rebecca Spagnolo is a doctoral candidate in the Department of History at the University of Toronto. She is currently completing a dissertation entitled *The Other Women: Urban Domestic Servants and Soviet Society, 1917–1928*.

Boris Wolfson is Assistant Professor of Slavic Languages and Literatures and Comparative Literature at the University of Southern California. He is working on a study of literature, theater, and modes of self-understanding in the Soviet 1930s.

Index

Index

Index

Index

Index